LOCAL ADMINISTRATION AND POLITICS IN MODERNISING SOCIETIES BANGLADESH AND PAKISTAN

LOCAL ADMINISTRATION AND POLITICS IN MODERNISING SOCIETIES BANGLADESH AND PAKISTAN

NAJMUL ABEDIN

Dacca
National Institute of Public Administration
Distributor
Oxford University Press

First Published in 1973

Published by
The National Institute of Public Administration (NIPA), Dacca, Bangladesh.

Production Supervision by
Sheikh Sirajuddin, Publication Officer, The National Institute of Public Administration, Dacca, Bangladesh.

Distributed by
Oxford University Press, Bangladesh.

Cover Design by
Bazla Moula, The National Institute of Public Administration, Dacca.

Printed by
Md. Hossain, The Star Press, 21/1, Sheikh Saheb Bazar Road, Dacca-1, Bangladesh.

To
Professor W. H. Morris-Jones

PREFACE

This book makes a study of the changing pattern of local administration and politics in Bangladesh and Pakistan during the period between mid-1947 to mid-1973. It also includes a brief account of the changing pattern in British India.

In preparing this book I have acquired many debts of gratitude and it is my pleasant duty to acknowledge my debts to all those who have helped me directly or indirectly. I am most grateful to Professor W. H. Morris-Jones who as the supervisor of my doctoral thesis, from which this book has emanated,[1] expended many hours in discussing various points in every chapter and showed me many things which I would have missed otherwise. His enormous patience, sympathy and scholarly and inspiring guidance contributed enormously to the completion of the thesis.[2] I am also very grateful to Mr. G. C. Atkinson, University of Durham, to Miss Margaret Beard, Institute of Commonwealth Studies, University of London, to Dr. Zillur R. Khan, University of Wisconsin, to Professor A. H. Somjee, Simon Fraser University and to Professor C. H. Dodd, University of Hull for going through various chapters, for making useful suggestions and for their encouragement and good wishes. I am indebted to Sir Percival Griffiths, ICS, to Mr. W. J. H. Christie, ICS and especially to Mr. J. L. Lyewellyn,

[1] The title of the thesis was "The Working of District Administration in Pakistan : 1947-1964" (Durham, February 1969) which was approved by the University of Durham for the degree of Doctor of Philosophy. Before publishing this book all the chapters of the thesis have been revised in the light of the recent changes and developments to make it uptodate. Information and data available upto mid-1973 have been added. Moreover, keeping the title of the book in view, new research materials have also been included.

[2] In 1965 when Professor Morris-Jones left Durham for London I was allowed by the University of Durham to reside in London so that I could do research under his direct supervision.

ICS[1] for enlightening me on various aspects of administration and politics in British India. I wish to thank the library staff of the following institutions: Institute of Commonwealth Studies (London), School of Oriental and African Studies (London), London School of Economics and Political Science, University of Durham, India House (especially Miss Thorne), India Office at the Commonwealth Office (especially Mrs. Weston) and the British Museum.

I am also indebted to a number of people in this part of the world. I express my profound gratitude to Professor R. I. Choudhury, Head of the Department of Political Science, University of Chittagong, and to Mr. L. R. Khan,* the Director of the National Institute of Public Administration (NIPA), Dacca for their advice and encouraging me to publish the book at an early date. I am also very grateful to Dr. M. A. Sattar,* a Secretary to the Government of Bangladesh, who helped me in collecting research materials and enlightened me on various aspects of administration. I am particularly grateful to some of my friends for their help in collecting research materials and for their advice and encouragement. I would like to mention the names of the following: Mr. Humayun Abdul Haye, Chairman, Department of Foreign Languages, University of Dacca, Mr. Bashirullah Majumder, Cost Accountant, Mr. Tufailur Rahman, Bar-at-Law, Mr. Khalid Shams,* General Manager, Agricultural Purchage, Bangladesh Agricultural Development Corporation, Dr. (Mrs.) Najma Chowdhury, Associate Professor of Political Science, University of Dacca, Mr. Jainul Abedin, Instructor, NIPA, Dacca, Mr. Munzur-i-Mowla,* Senior Instructor, NIPA, Dacca, Mr. M. Haq, former Librarian, O & M Division, Dacca, and Mr. Safiur Rahman, Instructor, NIPA, Dacca. So far as the technical aspect of the publication of the book is concerned, Mr. Sheikh Sirajuddin, Publication

[1] Mr. Llewellyn was the Secretary to the famous Rowlands Committee (1944-1945), the enormous importance of which in the administrative development of the country is discussed below, p. 117, fn. 1.

* Formerly CSP officer.

Officer, NIPA, Dacca gave invaluable and unstinted advice, read proofs, and personally looked after the production side. I remain ever grateful to him. My thanks are also due to Mr. Manzurul Islam, Manager, Oxford University Press, Bangladesh, to Mr. Sk. Md. Ismail, Publication Assistant, NIPA, Dacca and to Mr. Bazla Moula, NIPA, Dacca. Finally, I should express my profound gratitude to my wife Shireen for her constant encouragement at all stages, for going through proofs, for preparing the index and, above all, for her tolerant acceptance of all those quirks and vagaries of temperament which authorship engenders.

In spite of my best efforts, some typographical errors have crept in for which I crave the indulgence of the readers.

NAJMUL ABEDIN

NIPA'S NOTE

The need for adopting our administrative structure, procedures and practices to the increasing demands for national reconstruction has assumed a special dimension after independence. Though this country inherited a traditional system of administration which underwent adaptations during British days to suit changing standards of values, little attention was paid since 1947 to the problems of administrative growth and its relationship to socio-economic development. Unless administrative growth is properly balanced with reference to the needs of an egalitarian society, expected levels of political and economic growth will be hard to achieve.

Like the stages of economic growth, administrative process and growth of local governments are also subjected to stages of development towards maturity. Dr. Abedin has made an excellent systematic study of the changing pattern of local administration and political system during the authoritarian regime of the then Pakistan Besides being well-documented, a mass of difficult problems have been handled with rare skill. The book presents an account of the changes in administrative concepts that have occured in the past. Though a large part of it was retrograde in nature, not quite related to the present needs of socio-political development and was dictated under some necessity for political management, the analysis highlights how the value judgments were lost under an authoritarian rule. We need conceptual frame-work for administrative growth and development which will enable us to have an objective look on the needs for future administrative reform and change in accelerating the pace of economic and social development. Dr. Abedin had made valuable contribution to our understanding of this aspect of administration and politics. This book should be of considerable value to students engaged in serious research on comparative politics, administration and political developments in the new states of Asia and Africa.

One of the objectives of National Institute of Public Administration is dissemination of knowledge and information pertaining to research and investigation in the fields of public administration and related disciplines. Keeping this objective in view, we take the privilege of bringing out Dr. Nazmul Abedin's book with definite expectation of not only filling the gap which exists but also creating potentialities for future stimulation and development in this field.

L. R. KHAN
Director

CONTENTS

LIST OF TABLES

LIST OF CHARTS

ABBREVIATIONS AND MISCELLANEOUS NOTES

Abbreviations

BARD	Bangladesh Academy for Rural Development
CSP	Civil Service of Pakistan
C.A.B. Deb.	Constituent Assembly of Bangladesh Debates
C.A.P. Deb.	Constituent Assembly of Pakistan Debates
D.C.	Deputy Commissioner
D.M.	District Magistrate
D.O.	District Officer
E.P.A. Deb.	East Pakistan Assembly Proceedings [Debates]
E.P.C.S.	East Pakistan Civil Service
FCR	Frontier Crimes Regulation
ICS	Indian Civil Service
N.A.P. Deb.	National Assembly of Pakistan Debates
NIPA	National Institute of Public Administration
N.W.F.P.	North West Frontier Province
PARD	Pakistan Academy for Rural Development
PCS	Provincial Civil Service
S.D.O.	Sub-divisional Officer
S.P.	Superintendent of Police
V. AID	Village Agricultural and Industrial Development

Miscellaneous Notes

The terms in each following group have been used as interchangeable terms :

(a) Collector, D. C., D. M., and D. O. (Also see below, pp. 114.)

(b) Ministry and Secretariat Department. (Also see below, pp. 101.)

(c) Local Administration and District Administration. (Also see below, pp. xxii-xxiii.)

It may be noted that the spelling of the following word is not same in Bangladesh and Pakistan : *Tahsilder* (Bangladesh)/*Tehsilder* (Pakistan). (For example, see below, pp. 255-268.)

INTRODUCTORY NOTE

In Bangladesh and Pakistan the formal structure of local administration has changed very little from pre-partition days but it has operated in a considerably changed and still changing political, administrative and social environment. Of course, environmental changes originated long before partition, as a result of gradual social changes and political and constitutional reforms, but since partition they have been accelerated by the aftermath of World War II[1] and the transfer of power, later by the emergence of the concept of community development, the aftermath of the army *coup d'etat* of 1958 and the post-Martial Law administration and finally by the disintegration of Pakistan and the emergence of Bangladesh as a separate independent nation state. As a result, the last two and a half decades have witnessed some very important developments in local areas : Firstly, one of the major developments has been the emergence of a powerful class of politically oriented local leaders. These leaders are very eager to increase their influence on the members of the local bureaucracy, who are officially and hierarchically responsible to the government at the central[2]/provincial[3] level. Secondly, the local officials and the members of the local bodies have been required to undertake responsibility for planning and implementing the fast expanding community development programmes. Thirdly, with the expansion of, and the increase in the importance of the nation building departments, the officers of these departments have strengthened their position vis-a-vis the general administrative officers. Fourthly, the introduction of the four-tier system of local bodies cum electoral college[4] (called "Basic Democracies")

[1] Of course, the sub-continent began to feel the impact of the aftermath of the war sometime before partition.

[2] In Bangladesh. [3] In Pakistan.

[4] For electing the President of the country, and the Members of the National and the Provincial Assemblies (see chap. iii).

by the first Martial Law regime in former Pakistan institutionalised the relationship between local politics and provincial and central politics[1], accelerated the process of politicisation of the local leadership and changed the nature of the relationship between the local bureaucracy and the non-official members of the local bodies during the period between 1958 and 1969. Fifthly, social transformation has resulted in social tension which has considerable impact on the behavioural aspect of local administration and politics.[2]

All these developments pose certain questions for the student of politics and administration : what is the impact of these developments on local administration? Has the style of local administration undergone considerable transformation? To what extent and by what means do local leaders seek to exert influence or pressure on local administration? Has the bureaucracy become responsive to the demands of these leaders? Are the officials required to further the personal, factional and party interests of leading and powerful politicians and their close associates by means of their official influence and position? What is the nature of intra-bureaucratic tension and what are the causes? In what ways, to what degree and with what consequences has the emergence of the concept of community development minimised the importance of the traditional functions (i.e. law and order, and revenue functions) of local administration and added to the importance of its development function? What roles do the officials and the members of the local bodies play in the field of community development? What were the differences between the pre and the post-1958 systems of local bodies? Had the local bodies of the pre-1958 period improved or degenerated since 1947? Was the post-1958 system of local bodies a forward or backward step in the history of local bodies? As the electoral college what impact did the system of "Basic Democracies" have on local administra-

[1] For illustration of this comment, see chapter vii.

[2] Later in the text, we shall see that there have been many other less important developments.

tion? As the electoral college, did it impede or hamper its own working as the system of local bodies? In what ways and with what consequences did the post-first Martial Law political system affect local administration? In what ways and with what consequences does the politico-social environment affect local administration? What is the nature of bureaucratic behaviour and attitudes? Are there differences between the style and the structure of local administration in Bangladesh and those in Pakistan? If so, what are the factors that are responsible for these differences? Has the volume of work increased? If so, what impact does this have on the structure and the roles of local administration? To what extent did the changes and developments that characterise local administration in Bangladesh and Pakistan begin before partition? Obviously all these questions and the answers to them lead to many other minor questions. In the book the present writer endeavours to suggest answers to all these questions and to discuss some other general points relevant to the working of local administration in Bangladesh and Pakistan. He has also given a brief account of the evolution of local administration in British India without which the extent of recent developments and changes pertinent to local administration in Bangladesh and Pakistan would remain somewhat obscure. Such a study of the present system would not be "adequate in depth".[1] He has also briefly discussed the politico-social environment in Bangladesh and Pakistan. No doubt, the working of administration is not directly influenced by the politico-social environment, but certainly the latter has considerable indirect impact on the former, especially on its style because this is the context within which administration operates. Moreover, some of the questions that the present writer has raised cannot be adequately answered without showing the nature of the environmental impact on administration.

[1] The last part of Professor Braibanti's comment, quoted below (pp. xx, fn. 2), is indirectly pertinent to this comment.

Source Materials

The book is primarily based on an examination of both published and unpublished reports and documents of the government, published and unpublished survey reports and other papers of various academies and institutes,[1] and on field interviews. They have also been supplemented by a study of existing periodical literature and other secondary works.

The nature of the problems or difficulties that the students of social sciences encounter in doing research in Bangladesh and Pakistan may be briefly mentioned: The first problem is the dearth of informative and original as well as secondary materials. "The tradition of systematic publication of government documents was a legacy of British rule" but the post-partition period has not witnessed the "continuance of this tradition"[2]. The second problem, which is vexatious, rather irritating, is that it is extremely difficult to trace and obtain existing important materials. These materials are not properly and systematically preserved with the result that "much information" necessary to any study "is not accessible in convenient form in government sources".[3] This

[1] For example, the Bangladesh Academy for Rural Development, the Pakistan Academy for Rural Development, the National Institute of Public Administration (Dacca, Lahore and Karachi), Bureau of Economic Research of the University of Dacca, the Administrative Staff College, Lahore, the Social Science Research Centre of the University of Punjab, etc.

[2] Ralph Braibanti, *Research on the Bureaucracy of Pakistan* (Durham, April 1966) (Hereafter cited as Braibanti, *Research*), see jacket, first flap. "The purpose" of Professor Ralph Braibanti's book "is to identify, classify and evaluate source materials for the study of bureaucracy in [former] Pakistan". The "primary object" of the book is "that of ordering the public record issuance of [former] Pakistan during the period from 1947-1965". (*Ibid.*, p. vii, preface.) This problem is solved to a limited extent by making use of the "pre-partition documents of Imperial India [which] are of value as much because of their pertinence to contemporary problems as because of historical interest...[Of course,] This does not mean that the contemporary scene can be effectively studied through exclusive reliance on documentary sources of the past, but it does suggest that no analysis of bureaucracy in [former] Pakistan will be adequate in depth and in historical perspective without some immersion in sources antidating independence." (*Ibid.*, p. 3.)

[3] *Ibid.*, see jacket, first flap. For further comments on this problem, see

problem has become further aggravated by the fact that many reports including those of many important commissions and committees have been classified as restricted materials for official use only with the result that they are not on sale. It is very difficult to get hold of these documents. Professor Braibanti observed in his book, cited above, that "some of the simplest and most elementary kinds of information included in this book had to be searched for, sometimes over a period of several years."[1] Here it may be mentioned that Professor Braibanti not only visited former Pakistan several times from 1957 to 1965 in connection with his research but for two years (1960-62) he was the Chief Advisor to the Civil Service Academy, Lahore, where the members of the top administrative cadre (i.e. the CSP, the successor to the ICS) receive their training. It is quite certain that in that capacity he not only had easy access to many valuable documents but also came into close contact with both senior and junior officers. Yet, even he had to face great difficulties. A researcher like me is much less favourably placed. Nevertheless, I was able while doing research for this work to locate and consult a considerable number of very rare and valuable documents (printed, cyclostyled and typed).

Another problem is that a researcher finds very little cooperation and sympathy from both officials and non-officials (e.g., politicians), with some notable exceptions of course. Moreover, while discussing various aspects and problems of administration with the officials, a researcher usually finds that many of them often take an evasive attitude or in other words are reluctant to give any idea about what may be called the "'inside story' of actual operations".[2] "By far the most serious deterrents to

---

Gerard M. Friters, "Introduction to Problems of Public Administration in Pakistan" in Aslam's *book* (for full bibliographical particulars, see below, chap. iii, p. 120, fn. 2), p. iii.

[1] Braibanti, *Research*, see jacket, first flap.

[2] I owe this expression to Professor Morris-Jones. See Morris-Jones, *India* (see below, chap. i, p. 59, fn. 4), p. 48. Also see Morris-Jones, "India's Political Idioms" in C.H. Philips (ed.), *Politics and Society in India*

efficient research" in Bangladesh and Pakistan have been "the low status of scholarship as a profession and widespread lack of comprehension of the role of intellectual activity as a prerequisite for a modernized social order".[1] These two reasons also make both officials and non-officials indifferent towards research and researchers.

Local/District Administration

While there is no province in Bangladesh,[2] Pakistan is divided into four provinces, namely Sind, Baluchistan, the North West Frontier Province (N. W. F. P.) and the Punjab. For administering local affairs and for implementing the policies of the central/provincial government in regard to local areas, Bangladesh and each province in Pakistan is divided into districts.[3] The district is the focal and the most important unit of administration. In most South Asian countries (i. e. mainly India, Bangladesh, Pakistan and Ceylon) the terms 'district' and 'district administration' are quite familiar to and their importance is appreciated by all types of people. Generally

---

(London, 1963), p. 133. The above mentioned attitude of most officials may be further illustrated by the following passage : The officer may 'answer his [the researcher's] more superficial questions. Most worthwhile research projects, however, must go far beyond this surface investigation to a consideration of details". As soon as this becomes apparent, the attitude of the officer becomes "abrupt and evasive and the student finds that the interview has come to an end with no promise of any further opportunity to pursue the subject". This is not merely the case with an overworked officer "not wishing to waste his time. Many research projects require very little of the officer's time. The student may wish to prepare a job analysis of a group of clerks or make a work simplification chart of some cumbersome procedure or prepare a clear organisation chart. He may be a well-trained individual whose final product could be useful to the government, but he cannot get the necessary cooperation." [Goodnow (see below, chap. ii, p. 58, fn. 1), p 208.]

1 Braibanti, *Research*, p. 14.

2 Before 1971 i.e. before its emergence as a sovereign independent state, it was one of the five provinces of Pakistan which was created in 1947.

3 For the purpose of supervision districts are again grouped into 'division'.

speaking, various aspects (e.g. meaning, connotation, importance etc.) of these terms are more or less uniform in these countries.[1] But they are not exactly same throughout the world.[2] They vary, sometimes to a limited degree and sometimes to a considerable degree, from one area of the world to another area. As the book is intended to serve more than one group of readers, both inside and outside South Asia, in the title of the book the present writer has used the term 'local administration', the meaning and connotation of which are, generally speaking, more or less universal and which immediately gives an 'outside' reader some general impression or idea about the subject matter of the book. So, though the title is inexact, it is convenient. But in the text of the book the terms 'district' and 'district administration', which are popular and official terms in the sub-continent, have been used. Of course, occasionally the term 'local administration' has also been mentioned. In fact, in this book 'local administration' and 'district administration' have been treated as interchangeable terms.

[1] In fact, in most former British colonies in Asia and Africa these terms have, in varying degrees, same meaning, connotation and importance.

[2] The following are some of the common meanings of the term 'district': "Territory marked off for special administrative purpose ;...division of parish with its own church or chapel & clergyman ;...urban or rural division of county with District council ; assigned sphere of operations; tract of country with common characteristics, region". [*The Concise Oxford Dictionary* (Oxford, 5th edn.), pp. 356-357.] "...part of a country: *a mountainous district*; *the English lake districts; purely agricultural districts*......part of a town or country marked out for a special purpose: *the London postal districts...rural and urban districts* (for the purpose of local government); *the District of Columbia* (Washington, the Federal government area of the U.S.A.)." [*The Advanced Learner's Dictionary of Current English* (Oxford University Press, 2nd edn.), p. 289.] We have noted that district also means urban or rural division of a county. But in South Asia, so far as importance is concerned, generally speaking, a district may be regarded as the counterpart of the county in Great Britain and the U.S.A. and that of the *Department* in France, though the pattern and structure of administration of a district are widely different from those of administration of a county or *Department*. Of course, there are some similarities between the roles of the District Officer in South Asia and the Prefect of a *Department* in France.

"We may say that district administration is the total functioning of government in a district; that total and complex organisation of the management of public affairs at work, dynamic and not static, in the territory of a...district."[1] It is, therefore, "the total action of government in an area specified as a district".[2] Generally speaking, administrative organisation or set-up in a district may be divided into two halves : (i) the bureaucracy appointed by and responsible to the central/provincial government and (ii) the local bodies. One of the responsibilities of the first halve has always been to exercise control and supervision, in varying degrees, on the second halve. In this book the term district or local administration is used in the broadest sense to include both the halves.[3]

The head of district administration in Bangladesh and Pakistan is called Deputy Commissioner.[4] But before 1960s the designation varied from region to region. He was called either Deputy Commissioner or Collector or District Magistrate and Collector or Political Agent. So, in order to avoid confusion and ambiguity, in most places he is referred to as District Officer.

Notes on Some Names

For the sake of clarity and in order to avoid ambiguity, in some places of the book the present writer has distinguished between Pakistan of the pre-1971 period and Pakistan of the post-1971 period by calling them former Pakistan and present Pakistan. On the other hand, in some other places where there

1 S.S. Khera, *District Administration in India* (London, 1964), p. 5. (See the comment of the present writer at the end of the next footnote.)

2 David C. Potter, *Government in Rural India : An Introduction to Contemporary District Administration* (London, 1964), p. 8. (Above two comments on Indian district administration are equally applicable and pertinent to district administration in Bangladesh and Pakistan.)

3 In this sub-continent by district administration one usually means the activities of the first halve only. The local bodies are usually referred to as local self government. But in this book no such distinction is followed.

4 Of course, in political agencies (i.e. districts is tribal areas) and three districts in Pakistan he is still called Political Agent.

is no scope for confusion or ambiguity he has mentioned Pakistan to mean either former or present Pakistan (e.g. see chapter vii, pp. 360-366). Of course, in the title and in most places of the book Pakistan means present Pakistan.

Former Pakistan was divided into two parts each separated from the other by more than one thousand miles without any physical link whatsoever. Eastern and western parts of former Pakistan were usually called East Bengal/East Pakistan and West Pakistan respectively.[1] So, while discussing any aspect of district administration which has relevance to the period between 1947 to 1971, the former and the latter have usually been referred to as East Bengal and West Pakistan respectively. The present writer prefers East Bengal to East Pakistan mainly because 'Bengal' is the English version of the Bengali word 'Bangla' which is one half of the present name: Bangladesh (literally means Bengali Nation State). Moreover, the name 'Bengal' has direct relevance to and reminds the reader of the ethnic, racial and linguistic background of the area. It should also be noted that the name 'East Bengal' was much older than 'East Pakistan' in view of the fact that in British India a considerable part of this area was unofficially referred to as 'East Bengal'.[2] While discussing any aspect of district administration since 1971, the present writer has always used the present name: Bangladesh.

Abstract

We have already noted that the present work makes a study of the changing pattern of district administration and its interaction with politics in Bangladesh and Pakistan. While making such

[1] While from 1947 to 1955 the official name of the eastern part was East Bengal, from 1955 to 1971 that of the eastern part was East Pakistan. Before 1955 West Pakistan was the unofficial name of the western part which consisted of four provinces, whereas from 1955 (when four provinces were unified into one province) to 1970 (when it was again divided into four provinces) West Pakistan was the official name of that part.

[2] In some official documents also the name 'East Bengal' or 'Eastern Bengal' was mentioned. For example, see below, pp. 144.

study attempts are also made to compare and contrast the changes and developments in the former with those of the latter. Chapter I briefly discusses the development of district administration in British India, the doctrinal conflict between the Cornwallis and the Munro Schools of district administration, the influence of Whig and Utilitarian philosophies on such conflict and the differences between the administrative traditions inherited by Bangladesh and Pakistan. Chapter II gives a brief account of the politico-social environment and its impact on bureaucratic behaviour and attitudes. Chapter III discusses the horizontal and the vertical structures of administration, the organisational and functional relationship between various component parts of these structures, and the structural changes that have been introduced since partition in 1947. In chapter IV the traditional functions (i.e. the law and order, the land revenue and the general administrative or miscellaneous functions) of district administration have been discussed in the light of changes and developments that have taken place in the course of last three decades or so. Chapter V gives a brief account of the gradual emergence of the concept of community development in this part of the world and the roles played by the bureaucracy and the members of the local bodies in the field of rural development. Chapter VI discusses the problems involved in the organisational and functional relationship between the District Officer and the heads of other government departments in the district, and their causes. Chapter VII examines the nature and the extent of political pressure on district administration and its impact on the style and the working of administration. Chapter VIII summarises some major points discussed in the preceding chapters and indicates the nature of the changing pattern of district administration and its interaction with politics.

Chapter I

THE EVOLUTION OF DISTRICT ADMINISTRATION

Introduction

In modern states political and administrative systems have their roots deep in the past. They have evolved through the process of changing conditions and ideas. The earlier years have thus played a considerable role in moulding or shaping these systems. District administration in Bangladesh and Pakistan is no exception. It can be fully understood only if it is studied in the light of the past.

The foundations of modern district administration in Bangladesh and Pakistan were laid during the first hundred years of British administration in South Asia though its origin may be traced much earlier. The Mughal emperor Akbar (1542-1605) developed a highly organised and efficient system of administration and bureaucracy. He divided the vast Mughal empire into *subas* (provinces) each of which was in turn split up into *sarkars* (districts).[1] The officials in charge of provinces and districts acted as the agents of the emperor.

> "The Mogul dominion...was a government of discretion...The safety of the people, the security of their property and the prosperity of the country depended upon the personal character of the monarch. By this standard his delegates regulated their own demeanour."[2]

After his death Akbar's system continued for a considerable period of time. But after the death of Aurangzeb (1707), the vast Mughal empire fell to pieces and began to degenerate very rapidly. Almost all traces of Akbar's elaborate administrative organisation rapidly disappeared.[3] "The British found the wreck

[1] Percival Spear, *India*: *A Modern History* (Michigan, 1961), p. 133. (Hereafter cited as Spear, *India*.)

[2] Shore's minutes, "The Fifth Report of the Select Committee on the Affairs of the East India Company", *Parliamentary Papers*, 1812, vol. vii, p.10. (Hereafter cited as *Fifth Report*.)

[3] Vincent A. Smith, *Akbar, The Great Mogul, 1542-1605* (Oxford, 1917), p.355.

of this system and admired it even in decay."[1] It served as the foundation upon which they later built an efficient administrative system.[2]

As the administrative system had almost completely broken down long before the British assumed the administration of India, the government had to pass through a long and weary process of repeated experiments in order to develop a sound administrative system. The process of these repeated experiments began in the mid-1760s. Towards the close of the 18th century some definite principles of the pattern of district administration in British India were formulated. But district administration was still in a fluid state and was undergoing further changes. During the first half of the 19th century the process of evolution became further complicated, as we shall see later, by the doctrinal conflict between two schools of thought—the Cornwallis and the Munro (paternal) schools. It was not until the very end of the 1850s that district administration in the sub-continent took final shape.

As South Asia was primarily an agricultural country, land revenue was the traditional mainstay of governmental finance.[3] From time immemorial the bulk of the income of the government and the people was derived from land. Thus the system of land holding and the collection of land revenue were of "fundamental importance both to the administration and to the people themselves".[4]

During the early part of the British administration in South Asia each stage of development both in the field of general administra-

[1] Spear, *India*, p.238.

[2] "...from the time of Warren Hastings in the last quarter of the eighteenth century, the newly constituted Anglo Indian Authorities began to grope their way back to the institutions of Akbar. They gradually adopted the principal features of this system... The structure of bureaucratic framework of government also still shows many traces of his handiwork. His institutions, therefore, are...in some degree the foundation of the system of administration now in operation." (Vincent A. Smith, *op. cit.*, p.355.)

[3] Percival Spear, *The Oxford History of Modern India, 1740-1947* (Oxford, 1965), p. 192. (Hereafter cited as Spear, *Oxford History.*) Also see Spear, *India*, p.238.

[4] Spear, *Oxford History*, p.90.

tion and in the field of revenue administration passed through the same process of evolution and the former can only be understood with reference to the latter. In the course of our discussion we shall find that district administration was developed from revenue administration.

The First Phase of Administrative Reforms

In 1765 the *Diwani* (revenue administration) of Bengal (including Bihar and Orissa) was assumed by the East India Company. The criminal administration remained mainly in the hands of the *Nawab* (local king). Although the Company assumed the *Diwani* it was felt that it would be difficult for the officials of the Company to undertake direct responsibility for collecting revenue because they did not have adequate knowledge of the civil and revenue institutions in South Asia, the interior state of the country and the local language.[1] Moreover, the bulk of such revenue records as existed were in the hands of local *Kanungoes* (hereditary registrars)[2] and it was also felt that for political reasons the sovereignty of the Company should be 'masked'. Taking all these factors into consideration, Clive decided that the administrative machinery of the *Nawab* should also continue along with that of the Company. This system is famous as Clive's 'dual system'.[3]

Two *Naib-Dewans* (deputies of the *Nawab* in the field of revenue administration) remained directly responsible for the collection of revenue[4] and under their control and supervision *Zamindars* collected land revenue from the *ryots* (cultivators).[5] Two officials

[1] *Fifth Report*, p.5.

[2] R. B. Ramsbotham, "The Revenue Administration of Bengal, 1765-86" in H. H. Dodwell (ed.), *The Cambridge History of India* (Cambridge, 1929), vol. v, p.410. (Hereafter cited as Ramsbotham, *Cambridge History*.)

[3] E. Thomson and G. T. Garratt, *Rise and Fulfilment of British Rule in India* (London, 1934), p.105.

[4] Percival Griffiths, *The British Impact on India* (London, 1952), p.159.

[5] Originally the *Zamindars* had been hereditary tax-collectors. In the 18th century when the Mughal empire had almost completely degenerated, the *Zamindars* had consolidated their position and strengthened their hold over the land, the revenue of which they collected. They had begun to dispense justice among the villagers and to maintain peace within their

of the Company were responsible for supervising the functions of two *Naib-Dewans*. But they failed to maintain an adequate control over revenue administration. Inadequate and imperfect control over the *Naib-Dewans* proved "disastrous both to the Company as well as to the people".[1] While the *Naib-Dewans* and the *Zamindars* amassed great wealth, the Company incurred great financial losses, and the cultivators suffered great hardship caused by "the exactions and harshness of the *Zamindars*".[2] Verelst, the Governor, and his committee felt that the Company's officials were kept in complete ignorance "of the real produce and capacity of the country by a set of men who first deceive us from interest and afterwards continue the deception from the necessary regard of their own safety".[3]

In 1769 Supervisors of collections were appointed. Though the Supervisors were supposed to be consulted in doubtful cases they were not directly connected with the collection of revenues. Their main mission was to make a comprehensive and systematic study of the revenue, the economic condition, the administration of justice, the produce and capacity of land, the causes of arbitrary taxes, the manner of collecting them, the background and the history of the society, its customs, usages, etc. "They were, in fact, to lay the foundations of knowledge upon which a satisfactory revenue system could be built."[4] But the Supervisors soon

jurisdiction. They had succeeded in reducing the cultivators to a position almost similar to that of tenants. By 1765 "they possessed many of the attributes of an established aristocracy". [Thomas R. Metcalf, *The Aftermath of Revolt*: *India, 1857-1870* (Princeton, 1964), p.37.] But "they were not landowners nor a landed aristocracy in the British sense....Their estates resembled those of British landlords in appearance, but were essentially different in texture". (Spear, *Oxford History*, p.90.) Their position as landholders "had never received the sanction of a legal title". (Thomas R. Metcalf, *op. cit.*, p.37.) Later we shall find that in 1793 they received the sanction of a legal title and became feudal landlords.

1 R.C. Majumder, H.C. Raychaudhury, and K. Datta, *The Advanced History of India* (London, 1950), p.790.

2 Ramsbotham, *Cambridge History*, p. 410.

3 Quoted in *ibid.*, p.411.

4 Griffiths, *op. cit.*, p.160.

encountered very strong and formidable passive opposition from the *Zamindars* and the *Kanungoes* who made a point of seeing that the Supervisors could not get access to correct information which would enable them to have real knowledge of the amount of revenue actually paid by the cultivators to the *Zamindars*. "Between them, the *Zamindars* and *Kanungoes,* held all the essential information, but the *Kanungoes* were the dominant figures."[1] Thus the Supervisors failed in their mission.

In 1772 the Court of Directors of the East India Company declared from London that it had decided "to stand forth as *Dewan* and by the agency of the Company's servants to take upon themselves the entire care and management of the revenue".[2] 1772 witnessed several important administrative changes and reorganisations: Warren Hastings was appointed Governor of the Bengal Presidency (Bengal, Bihar and Orissa).[3] The posts of the *Naib-Dewans* were abolished and the revenue administration was placed under the direct control of the Governor-in-Council. The Supervisors were appointed Collectors with local *Dewans* to assist them. Hastings found that the operation of the courts was confined to a very limited area around "the city of Murshidabad (the Mughal capital of Bengal) and that justice was beyond the reach of the majority of the people".[4] To remedy this, two courts, namely *Diwani Adawlat* (civil court) and *Fauzdari Adawlat* (criminal court), were established in each district. The Collector and a local Judge were placed in charge of the civil and

[1] Ramsbotham, *Cambridge History*, p.411.

It was during the reign of Akbar that the *Kanungoes* had come into prominence. Their main purpose had been to see that the monarch received his dues and that the cultivators were not oppressed by the tax-collectors. They had been required to record the usages of the area concerned, the rates and modes of assessment and all regulations relating thereto, etc. Thus in the course of centuries all necessary information with regard to land revenue came into the possession of this corrupt and hereditary revenue agency. (*Ibid.*, pp.412-413.)

[2] Quoted in *Fifth Report*, p.5.

[3] In 1773, the Governor of the Bengal Presidency was made the Governor-General with jurisdiction over the Madras Presidency.

[4] Griffiths, *op. cit.*, p.161.

the criminal courts respectively. The proceedings of the latter were conducted according to old customs and precedents. The Collector who had some control over it was required to attend its proceedings to see that all necessary witnesses were summoned and examined and that the decision of the court was fair and impartial.[1] Thus the Collector became the most powerful officer in the district and it may be said that the first foundation stone of modern district administration was laid in 1772.[2]

The land tenure system also underwent a change in 1772. Land was farmed out for a period of five years by public auction in order to discover the real value of it. The highest bidder became entitled to collect the revenue for five years and those hereditary *Zamindars* who failed to be the highest bidders lost their right to collect revenues. Later it was found that the five-year settlement of land and the system of public auction were unsatisfactory and disastrous "from every point of view".[3] Two factors were mainly responsible for this unsatisfactory situation. Firstly, several motives such as gambling instinct, desire for power, the opportunity of inflicting injury on enemies or humiliating a hereditary *Zamindar*, etc. had resulted in raising the "bidding beyond the value of the revenue".[4] Secondly, under the new system the *Zamindars* had no permanent interest in the land and therefore mercilessly oppressed the cultivators to exact as much as possible during the period of their tenure. The cultivators found real protection and assistance

[1] *Fifth Report*, p.6.

[2] Of course the office of the Collector had emerged long before the Company assumed the administration of Bengal. In 1698 the Company had obtained from the Mughal emperor, the *Zamindari* right over three villages, namely Sutanati, Calcutta and Govindpur which in due course were to grow into the city of Calcutta, and had become entitled not only to collect revenue but also to administer these villages. In 1700 the post of an additional member of the council had been created by the Company who had become responsible for the administration of these areas and his designation had been Collector. The first Collector had been Ralph Sheldon. Though the functions of the Collector had varied from time to time, for a period he had been also magistrate and the head of the police force. (Griffiths, *op. cit.*, p.159; also see p. 145.)

[3] Majumder *et al.*, *op. cit.*, p.792.

[4] Ramsbotham, *Cambridge History*, p.416.

in the *Diwani Adawlat* (civil court) presided over by the Collector.[1] It was the Collector who enabled the voice of the oppressed cultivators to reach the government.[2] But the government did not take any notice because they were of the opinion that these young officers, who had recently arrived from Great Britain, did not have real experience to make a correct judgement of the situation. Hastings had 'sneered' at these officers, when they had held the posts of Supervisors, as 'boys'.[3]

The posts of Collectors, whose services received scanty acknowledgement from the higher authorities, were abolished in 1773, that is only one year after their creation. Several administrative changes followed: The Bengal Presidency was divided into six zones each under a provincial council responsible for the supervision and management of revenue administration. The administration of civil justice was now transferred to local *Dewans* called *Aumils* (originally employees of the *Nawab*). The local *Fauzders* (originally employees of the *Nawab*) were entrusted with the task of supervising the police.[4] Thus the Company deprived itself of the source of its increasing knowledge about the administrative and the revenue systems. There was now no powerful functionary at the local level to whom the cultivators could look for protection from the oppression of the *Zamindars*. "The change was unfortunate and worked badly in both the executive and revenue spheres."[5]

The contracts under the five-year settlement of land expired in 1778 when the system of annual settlement by public auction replaced the former system of five-year settlement.[6] But it did not solve the problems which we have already noted while discussing the effects of the five-year settlement.[7]

In 1781 Hastings again reorganised the administrative system which "carried concentration still further".[8] The six provincial

[1] *Ibid.*, p.418.
[2] *Ibid.*, p.417.
[3] R.B. Ramsbotham, *Studies in the Land Revenue History of Bengal* (Calcutta, 1926), p.10. (Hereafter cited as Ramsbotham, *Revenue History.*)
[4] *Fifth Report*, p.7.
[5] Griffiths, *op. cit.*, p.161.
[6] Majumder *et al.*, *op. cit.*, p.792.
[7] See above, p.6.
[8] Ramsbotham, *Cambridge History*, p. 428.

councils of revenue and the posts of the *Fauzders* were abolished. A committee of revenue was set up at headquarters and a Collector was appointed in every district. "The reappointment of Collectors appears to suggest an idea of decentralisation. This, however, was not the case."[1] They were not given any significant power. They were "merely figureheads" and "were not trusted".[2] The "distrust which the council showed in their appointment could lead to nothing but discouragement".[3] They "exercised their doubtful authority over a series of fiscal divisions".[4] The nature of their inadequate and doubtful authority may be further illustrated by two passages quoted below: John David Patterson, the Collector of Rangpur (now in Bangladesh) wrote on April 3, 1783

> "There is nothing but confusion; there is no kanungo to be found, he is fled the country; the ryots wanting to withhold their payments; the Farmer [*Zamindar*] seizing everything he can lay his hands upon and swelling up his demands by every artifice....No pains shall be spared on my part to get at the truth altho' it is wading through a sea of chicanery on both sides..."[5]

William Rooke, the Collector of Purnia (now in India) wrote on March 13, 1783 that the *Zamindar*

> "has repeatedly flogged those who preferred any complaint to me.... In the course of the last ten days a numerous body of ryots from all quarters have beset me on every side, uncommonly clamorous for justice. Their complaints exhibit an almost universal disregard and setting aside of their pottahs, an enormous increase exacted from them, etc."[6]

The letter ended with a request to be informed of "the degree of interference which is expected of me".[7]

Hastings' administrative system of 1781 which, as we have just noted, was over-centralised and which "placed secretariat theories before district experience"[8] even encountered the criticism of

[1] E. D. Ascoli, *The Early Revenue History of Bengal* (Oxford, 1917), p. 35.
[2] *Ibid.*, p.35. [3] *Ibid.*, p.36. [4] *Ibid.*, p.39.
[5] Quoted in Ramsbotham, *Cambridge History*, p.428.
[6] Quoted in *ibid.*, p.428. [7] Quoted in *ibid.*, p.428.
[8] *Ibid.*, p.430.

most members of his council. Those members (Shore, Anderson, Charters) who had experience in local administration knew that "throughout Bengal there are some district usages which cannot be known at a distance".[1] Shore said in 1782

> "I venture to pronounce that the real state of the districts is now less known and the revenues less understood than in 1774....With respect to the Committee of revenue, it is morally impossible for them to execute the business they are entrusted with."[2]

In practice Hastings' administrative system "broke down at every point".[3] Hastings, who was not on good terms with the Court of Directors, resigned in February 1785 and delivered over the charge to Macpherson who became the officiating Governor-General. In April 1786 a new scheme, which spelt decentralisation, was published. Decentralisation was the backbone of the whole system of the reforms. Districts were reorganised into regular fiscal units and the Collector of each district was entrusted with the task of settling and collecting the revenues. The Committee of Revenue was reconstituted and was renamed the Board of Revenue. Its duties consisted of "controlling and advising the Collectors and sanctioning their settlement".[4] District administration began to take shape.

Cornwallis' Reforms

Cornwallis, the new Governor-General,[5] reached Calcutta in September 1786. During the tenure of his office he introduced

1 Quoted in *ibid.*, p.430.

2 Shore's minutes (1782) in Harrington, *Analysis of Bengal Regulations*, vol. ii (1805), pp.41-43, quoted in *ibid.*, p.429.

3 *Ibid.*, p.428.

4 Majumder *et. al.*, *op. cit.*, p.793.

The Governor-General in council had already written in 1786 to the Committee of Revenue that "from experience we think it past doubt that situated as you are at the Presidency, you cannot without a local agency secure the regular realisation of the revenues, still less preserve the ryots and other inferior tenants from oppressions". [J. E. Colebrooke, *Digest of the laws and regulations* (1807), pp. 243-4, quoted in Ramsbotham, *Cambridge History*, p.429.]

5 Cornwallis was the first Governor-General who did not climb to that exalted position from the ranks of the Company's service. Although

sweeping and far-reaching administrative reforms which became the basis for future reforms. He introduced "a new spirit into British Indian Affairs which was never again wholly lost".[1]

Early Administrative Reforms. In June 1787 the Collector also became the judge and the magistrate with full control over the police.[2] He was given authority to try civil (excluding revenue) and less important criminal cases. In 1790 a Revenue Court called *Mal Adawlat* was created in each district because the revenue cases, which had been formerly tried by the Board of Revenue, had consumed too much of its time. The Collector was empowered to preside over it. "This change marks the culmination of the collector's power."[3] The union of revenue, judicial and magisterial authorities in his person gave him "unprecedented power.... In the hierarchy of administration the Collector had become by 1790 the bottle-neck through which all lines of control must pass."[4] But such concentration of powers was intended only for a short period during which the necessary arrangements would be made for introducing important reforms of a permanent nature. Later we shall find that this system underwent a complete change in 1793.

Land Reforms. Cornwallis also introduced permanent land reforms. As a Whig aristocrat he became inclined to create a class of permanent landlords.[5] He wanted the *Zamindars* to be given the sanction of legal title to land.[6] Thus he decided that annual

---

appointed by the Court of Directors of the Company, he owed his nomination to the British Cabinet. He was "the personal friend of Pitt, the Prime Minister" and had "a distinguished military career" (Spear, *Oxford History*, p.86.) behind him. For these reasons he not only enjoyed enormous prestige and status but also was treated with respect by the Court of Directors. "His position was so strong that he could afford to act on his own initiative." [A. Aspinal, *Cornwallis in Bengal* (Manchester, 1931), p.94.] Thus he could put forward his views forcefully and could get something done by the Court of Directors even if they were reluctant to do that.

1 Spear, *Oxford History*, p.86.

2 L.M. Penson, "The Bengal Administrative System, 1786–1818" in Dodwell (ed.), *op. cit.*, vol. v, p. 443.

3 *Ibid.*, p.444.

4 *Ibid.*, p.452.

5 Thomas R. Metcalf, *op. cit.*, p.38.

6 We have already noted the position of the *Zamindars*. (See above, p.3, fn. 5.)

settlement of lands should be replaced by 'permanent settlement'.[1] A settlement for 10 years was made with the *Zamindars* in 1790 and it was announced that this settlement would be made perpetual if the Court of Directors agreed. On March 2, 1793 the settlement was declared permanent after having received the approval of the Directors. This reform is known as 'permanent settlement' under which the "*Zamindars* tax-collectors were recognised as *Zamindars* landlords in the English sense".[2]

Under the 'permanent settlement' while the rights of the *Zamindars* over the lands were perpetually established, those of the cultivators were ignored and they were "placed absolutely at the tender mercies of the Zamindars".[3] This settlement affected the social and economic conditions of rural Bengal to a considerable extent. Its administrative advantages were "considerable but socially the loss was substantial".[4] Moreover the amount of annual revenue payable to the government was "fixed once for all" with the consequence that the *Zamindars* were "free to retain the balance between their payments to governments and collection from their tenants".[5] As a result when the value of the land began to increase the government did not get a share of the increased value of the land. But the *Zamindars* continued to enjoy the benefit of such increases.

1 Cornwallis had the support of the British Parliament. The then British Parliament which "was an assembly of landlords...felt affinity with Zamindars" (Spear, *Oxford History*, p.91.) and considered "them to be the tropical replica of themselves". (*Ibid.*, p.91.) Thus Parliament also favoured the abandonment of the annual settlement and "the preparation of 'permanent rules' for revenue collection". (*Ibid.*, p.91.)

2 *Ibid.*, p. 192.

3 Majumder *et. al.*, *op. cit.*, p.794.

Cornwallis also thought about the possibilities of oppression. So he made provisions for some safeguards in the Regulations of 1793 and looked to the Collectors for the protection of the cultivators. Later from time to time the government passed different types of land laws in order to protect the cultivators from the oppression of the *Zamindars.* But on many occasions the *Zamindars* were able to find loopholes in the regulations and to escape the limits and control. (*Ibid.*, p.794.)

4 Spear, *Oxford History*, p.193.

5 *Ibid.*, p. 192.

Later Administrative Reforms. Immediately after the announcement of the permanent settlement, a new administrative system, the essence of which was "the separation of powers" and "innumerable checks and balances"[1] was introduced by an elaborate code namely the Bengal Regulations of 1793, known as the Cornwallis Code. The new system replaced the former interim system of administration, the basis of which, as we have already noted, had been the concentration of powers in the hands of the Collector. Cornwallis, who was under the profound influence of John Locke's Whig philosophy, had no faith in the concentration of powers. He believed that the oriental principles of government were fundamentally at fault and was of the opinion that the source of the administrative evils was "the Company's adoption of Asian despotism".[2] He firmly believed in "the Whig conviction that political power is essentially corrupting and inevitably abused; that power, to be exercised with safety, must be reduced to a minimum, and even then kept divided and counterbalanced".[3] He, therefore, "consciously broke with the personal, authoritarian tradition of Indian government and based his work explicitly on the principles of English political tradition".[4]

In 1793 the offices of Collector and Judge were separated. The new post of District Judge was created to preside over the *Diwani Adawlat* (Civil Court) which was renamed the *Zillah Adawlat* (District Court). The *Mal Adawlat* (Revenue Court) was abolished and the District Court was empowered to try revenue cases.[5] The Collector was also deprived of magisterial powers (including the power to supervise the police) which were vested in the hands of the District Judge. Thus the Collector became merely what his designation implied—a mere collector of fixed revenue.[6] These administrative reforms are criticised by modern critics because

[1] Griffiths, *op. cit.*, p.162.
[2] Eric Stokes, *The English Utilitarians and India* (Oxford, 1963 edn.), p.4.
[3] *Ibid.*, p.5. [4] *Ibid.*, p.4.
[5] L. M. Penson, *op. cit.*, p. 453.
[6] The Board of Revenue was also deprived of all judicial powers to hear appeals against the decisions of the *Mal Adawlat* (Revenue Court), and was made a purely revenue body.

"The only official of that time who had developed any real contact with the people was the Collector, and he was expressly debarred from dealing with those aspects of Government which affected them most, namely the magistracy and the police. The Cornwallis theory was that an independent judiciary would, by itself, guarantee justice. In reality the judicial machinery was uncomprehended and indeed unknown by the great majority of the people of Bengal; the law administered was foreign to their ideas, and indeed the whole organisation was, by Indian standards of the time, hopelessly impersonal. Lord Cornwallis succeeded, indeed, in establishing a high standard of integrity in administration, but he made the mistake of trying to interpret India in terms of British thought."[1]

The Philosophical Basis of Cornwallis' Reforms

Locke's Whig philosophy, as noted above, profoundly influenced Cornwallis. In the course of our discussion we shall find that his minutes, his correspondence and the preamble to his code (1793) echoed Locke's classic statement of Whig philosophy.[2] Professor Eric Stokes has commented that the permanent settlement of Bengal was "a frank attempt to apply the English Whig philosophy of government".[3] Cornwallis firmly believed that "everything hinged upon the recognition of the property rights of the *Zamindars*, the great landholders..."[4] To him landed property was the most valuable property.

His approach to reform was twofold. Firstly, he wanted to introduce permanently property right in land. Secondly, he wanted to guarantee security of property and person. He believed that security of property would enormously contribute to the prosperity of the country.[5] He thought that security of property could

[1] Griffiths, *op. cit.*, pp. 162-163.

[2] See below, p.13 (fn. 5.), p. 14 (fns. 1, 2, 3.), p. 15.

[3] Stokes, *op. cit.*, p.5. [4] *Ibid.*, p.5.

[5] He said "if we wish to render the country opulent and the people happy, our great aim must be to establish security of person and property". [Cornwallis' Minute, 11 Feb. 1793, *Parliamentary Papers*, vol. v, 1810, p. 107. (Later cited as *Cornwallis' Minute*, 11 Feb. 1793.)] In another place he held that the "certainty" which the people would "feel of being allowed to enjoy the fruits of his own labour, must operate uniformly as incitements to exertion and industry". [Cornwallis to the Court of Directors, 2 Aug. 1789, C. Ross (ed.), *Correspondence of Charles, First Marquis Cornwallis* (London, 1859), vol. i, pp. 545-546. Also see the last sentence of the passage quoted on page 15 (below).]

not be guaranteed if there was a concentration of powers in the hands of one man or in one body (i.e. the Board of Revenue)[1] and if the "assessment is liable to frequent variation".[2] He was of the opinion that under such circumstances the executive arm of the government will have the opportunity to abuse its power. Thus he believed that security of property and person could only be granted through a system conforming to the rule of law under which landholders would not be required to depend on the good-will of officials and to look beyond the law.[3] Cornwallis aptly

[1] He said that if all powers "remained so united we cannot expect that the laws which may be enacted for the protection of the rights and property of the landholders ... will ever be duly enforced". [Cornwallis' Minute, 3 Feb. 1790, *Parliamentary Papers*, vol. vii, 1812, p. 492. (Later cited as *Cornwallis' Minute*, 3 Feb. 1790.)] He also believed that under such circumstances "the people can never be satisfied that their property is secured". (*Cornwallis' Minute*, 11 Feb. 1793, p.116.) He argued that "there are certain powers and functions which can never be vested in the same officers without destroying all confidence in the protection of the laws. This remark is particularly applicable to the various functions vested in the present collectors". [Cornwallis to the Court of Directors, 6 March 1793, G. Forrest (ed.), *Selections from the State Papers of the Governors General of India: Lord Cornwallis*, vol. ii (Oxford, n.d., 1926 ?), p.123.] Thus it appears that he believed that such faith was also essential for the prosperity of the country because it would give the landholders a feeling of certainty which, as we have already noted, would result in "incitements to exertion and industry". (See above, p. 13, fn. 5.)

[2] *Cornwallis' Minute*, 3 Feb. 1790, p.492.

He held that "until the assessment on the land is fixed, the constitution of our internal government in this country will never take that form which alone can lead to the establishment of good laws and ensure a due administration of them". (*Ibid.*, p.492.) Thus it would be difficult "to prevent the landholders being plundered..." (*Ibid.*, p. 492.) In another place he said that the "value of landed property is regulated by the profit which the possessor is certain of deriving from it. If the people know that there is a possibility of any part of the profit arising from improvement of an estate being exacted from the proprietor by the officers of government the value of the possession must be considered as of a very precarious nature." (*Cornwallis' Minute*, 11 Feb. 1793, p. 112.)

[3] He argued that "we should endeavour to establish a constitution for the country that will protect private property, and with it the internal prosperity of the state....By lodging the entire judicial authority in courts ... no single Member of Government, nor any individual in power, nor their connections or dependants will be able to invade the rights or property of the people; the injured will fly to the courts of justice, which

summarised his views in the preamble to Regulation II of the Bengal Code of Regulations of 1793 which stated that

> "Government must divest itself of the power of infringing, in its executive capacity, the rights and privileges, which, as exercising the legislative authority, it has conferred on the landholders. The revenue officers must be deprived of their judicial powers. All financial claims of the public when disputed under the regulations, must be subjected to the cognisance of the courts of judicature, superintended by judges, who from their official situations, and the nature of their trusts, shall not only be wholly uninterested in the results of their decisions, but bound to decide impartially between the public and the proprietors of land.... The collectors of the revenue must not only be divested of the power of deciding upon their own acts, but rendered amenable for them to the courts of judicature; and collect the public dues, subject to a personal prosecution for every exaction exceeding the amount which they are authorised to demand on behalf of the public, and for every deviation from the regulations prescribed for the collection of it. No power will then exist in the country by which the rights vested in the landholders by the regulations can be infringed or the value of landed property affected. Land must in consequence become the most desirable of all property; and the industry of the people will be directed to these improvements in agriculture which are as essential to their own welfare as to the prosperity of the state."[1]

The Ideological Conflict Between the Cornwallis School and the Munro School

The Cornwallis system began to function in the vast area of North India under the Bengal Presidency. But when attempts were made to extend this system to the Madras Presidency and to other parts of India over which the jurisdiction of the British Indian empire later extended, it encountered strong opposition from the Munro or paternal school of thought. The principal exponents of this school were Thomas Munro, Mountstuart

---

will expose the oppression and punish the oppressor." (*Ibid.*, p. 108.) In another place he held that "we have long been of opinion that no system will ever be carried into effect so long as the personal qualities of the individuals that may be appointed to superintend it form the only security for the due execution of it. In this country, as in any other, security of property must be established by a system upheld by its inherent principles and not by men who are to have the occasional conduct of it." [Cornwallis to the Court of Directors, March 1793, Forrest (ed.), *Selection from the State Papers of Cornwallis*, vol. ii, p. 123.)]

[1] Quoted in Stokes, *op. cit.*, p. 6.

Elphinstone, John Malcolm and Charles Theophilus Metcalfe. While Cornwallis was influenced by Locke's Whig philosophy they were under the influence of the Utilitarian philosophers. In spite of the fact that there was a disparity of age and temperament among them, there was also a "unity of thought in this knot of men".[1] Thus they may be considered as the "founders of a political tradition".[2] Against the Cornwallis system, the essence of which, as we have already noted, was the rule of law, "four men spoke with one voice".[3] Their aim was to substitute the rule of personal discretion for the rule of law.[4] While the Cornwallis or Bengal school was not in favour of concentration of powers in the hands of one man, the Munro school strongly favoured the continuation of the Indian tradition of personal government characterised by the concentration of powers in the hands of one man, making him all-powerful ruler of the area concerned. They wanted to make the Collector the representative of the government and the all-powerful officer in the district.[5] Munro held that

[1] *Ibid.*, p. 9. [2] *Ibid.*, p. 9. [3] *Ibid.*, p. 20.
[4] *Ibid.*, pp. 140-141.
[5] Munro said "we must even sometime make a man a judge where he may be said to be in some degree a party...it is...indispensable to the protection of the people". [Munro's Minute, 31 Dec. 1824, G. R. Gleig, *Life of Sir Thomas Munro* (London, 1830), vol. iii, p. 379. (Hereafter cited as *Munro's Minute*, 31 Dec. 1824.)] Metcalfe held that one officer "should superintend each district exercising all the local powers of the judicature, police and revenue in all its branches". He further added that the "best form of government...I believe to be that which is most simple...most free from artificial institutions...most conducive to an union of powers, and most free from the elements of collision and counteraction". [Metcalfe's Minute (papers referred to in the letter from the Bengal govt., 10 Dec. 1828), *Parliamentary Papers*, 1831-32, vol. xii, p. 407. (Hereafter cited as *Metcalfe's Minute*, 10 Dec. 1828.)] In another place Metcalfe held that "Our present Bengal system should be knocked on the head...Revenue and judicial and where practicable military powers should be exercised by the same person; union, not division, should be the order of our rule." [Metcalfe's Paper, 29 June 1820, J. W. Kay (ed.), *Selections from the Papers of Lord Metcalfe* (London, 1855), p. 151.] Elphinstone declared that "I would vest the fullest power...in the Collector." [Elphinstone's Report on the Territories Conquered from the Peshwa, n.d., G. W. Forrest(ed.), *Selections from the Minutes and Other Official Writings of the Honourable*

> "We should form a very erroneous judgement of the important influence of the office of the Collector if we supposed that it was limited merely to revenue matters instead of extending to everything affecting the welfare of the people. In India whoever regulates the assessment of the land, really holds in his hand the mainspring of the country."[1]

Against the Cornwallis system the Munro school held that by taking away all judicial and police powers from the Collector the "one visible representative of government"[2] was made powerless to redress wrong and to punish criminals. They were also of the opinion that "the peasant was in effect deprived of justice" because the sole administration of justice was confined to "distant courts presided over by foreigners and employing a highly technical procedure".[3] They held that to the cultivators government should be represented by a single officer and not by a multiplicity of officers. This officer should have

> "powers to inquire, to judge, and to punish, without the delay and intricacies of the Western legal process. This officer was not to be a distant and awful figure, presiding in his cutcherry like a deity in his temple, but a familiar lord, visiting and speaking with them of their quarrels and their crops, and looked up to as *ma-bap*..."[4] (mother and father).

The administration should be conducted from "the tent and the saddle" rather than from "the office".[5] They were strongly in favour of "a personal human and tangible form of government".[6] They "revolted" against what they considered to be "the cold, lifeless, mechanical principles",[7] "the abstractions of the rule of law, and the blind automatic operation of an impersonal bureaucracy..."[8] They held that the administration in South Asia should be simple and that there should be few regulations.[9]

Mountstuart Elphinstone (London, 1884), p. 322.] Also see the discussion of the system of district administration introduced by them in Madras and other parts of British India (below).

1 Selections from Revenue Records, N. W. Provinces, vol. iii, p. 63, quoted in B.B. Misra, *The Central Administration of the East India Company from 1773-1834* (Manchester, 1959), p.159.

2 Stokes, *op. cit.*, p. 141. 3 *Ibid.*, p. 141. 4 *Ibid.*, p. 21.

5 *Ibid.*, p. 20. 6 *Ibid.*, p. 20. 7 *Ibid.*, p. 15. 8 *Ibid.*, p. 20.

9 Munro held that "It would have been better to have curtailed nine-tenths of the regulations." (Munro to Thakery, n.d., Gleig, *op. cit.*, vol. i.,

They believed that while introducing administrative reforms the Cornwallis school had not sufficiently taken into account the social and political condition of South Asia at that time, of which they had had an imperfect knowledge; thus they had failed to take the right approach to the problems of administrative reorganisation.[1] They said that the Cornwallis school had derived their ideas and inspirations from British political ideas and institutions which they, like the Utilitarian philosophers, thought were completely unsuitable for South Asian society and would not have the same beneficial effects in British India as in Great Britain because the social and political conditions of the former were completely different from those of the latter.[2] They held that the Cornwallis

p. 373.) Metcalfe observed that "At all events, Lord Cornwallis School must first wear out, who think that all perfection is in the regulations of 1793." (Metcalfe's paper, Oct. 14, 1819 in Kay (ed.), *op. cit.*, p. 150.)

1 Munro held that the administrative "innovation has been so little guided by a knowledge of the people, that though made after what was thought by us to be mature discussion, must appear to them as little better than the result of mere caprice". (*Munro's Minute*, 31 Dec. 1824, p. 381.) He also thought that "Our great error in this country, during long course of years, has been too much precipitation in attempting to better the condition of the people, without hardly any knowledge of the means by which it was to be accomplished.... It is a dangerous system of government in a country, of which our knowledge is very imperfect..." (*Ibid.*, p. 381.) (See also Malcolm's view—fn. 1, p. 19.)

2 Munro held that the Cornwallis school wanted "to make everything as English as possible in a country which resembles England in nothing". (*Ibid.*, p. 381.) He also held that "We suppose that our laws are founded on just principles, and that they must therefore have the same beneficial operation here as at home ; but we forget that one great first principle, the freedom of the people, from which they derive their influence, does not exist here. Our institutions here, not resting on the same foundation as those of a free country, cannot be made to act in the same way. We cannot make the inanimate corpse perform the functions of a living body ; we must, therefore, in making regulations here, think only of their probable effect in this country, not of what such regulations have or might have in England." (*Ibid.*, p. 379.)

It is interesting to note that Utilitarian philosophers such as Jeremy Bentham and James Mill also expressed almost similar views. Thus it appears that the Munro school owed a great deal to the Utilitarian

system would destroy South Asian tradition and institutions.[1] They believed that the continuation of the South Asian tradition of personal government and institutions would solve all problems

philosophers. A few passages quoted below will illustrate this point:

Bentham wrote in his essay namely "Of the Influence of Time and Place in Matters of Legislation" that "the best possible laws for England being established in England, required the variations which it would be necessary to make in those of any other given country, in order to render them the best laws possible with reference to that other country". [J. Bowring (ed.), *The Works of Jeremy Bentham* (Edinburgh, 1837), p. 171.] He further held that "To a law giver, who having been bred up with English notions, shall have learnt how to accommodate his laws to the circumstances of Bengal, no other part of the globe can present a difficulty." (*Ibid.*, p. 172.) He also added that there was a "difference between the laws that would be the best for England and the laws that would be best for Bengal". (*Ibid.*, p. 172.) He further held that "It seems to be a common notion that those laws, which are the best with reference to the circumstances of a civilised nation, would not have been so with reference to the circumstances of a rude and ignorant nation: on the contrary, that rude nation must have rude and simple, that is, imperfect laws: I mean, not only that in point of fact the laws of a rude nation will have been rude, but that in point of expediency it was proper they should be so." (*Ibid.*, p. 189.)

While discussing the result of Cornwallis' judicial reforms James Mill held that "If much of the difficulty has arisen from the dominion of English prejudices, and especially that deeprooted prejudice, that English law is the standard of perfection to which everything should be fitted, considerable progress towards improvement will be made, as soon as we have emancipated ourselves from those prejudices." [James Mill, *The History of British India*, vol. v (London, 1820), p. 425.]

As Assistant to the Examiner of India Correspondence (1819-30) and then as Examiner of India Correspondence (1830-36) James Mill was at the very centre of the power and was in an advantageous position to exert his influence over Indian administration and policies. John Stuart Mill was also in the Company's service for a considerable period of time. He held the post of Assistant to the Examiner from 1823 to 1856 and that of Examiner from 1856 to 1858.

[1] Malcolm held that the "men who with their new system...proceeding to the demolition of the most ancient, I might say almost sacred, institutions of India, were virtuous and able, but in acting without local and minute experience, in venturing to legislate for millions of human beings and countries with whom they were imperfectly acquainted, they showed both ignorance and presumption...they have precipitated us into a fine mess." [Malcolm to Molony, J. W. Kay, *Life and Correspondence of Sir John Malcolm* (London, 1856), p. 391.]

within a very short time.[1] Munro stated that "We should take every country as we find it..."[2] Of course, though the Munro school wanted to preserve and continue the South Asian tradition of personal government, they were not in fact completely hostile to reform. They were in favour of slow and gradual change.[3]

District Administration in Madras and Other Parts of British India

District administration in Madras began later than in Bengal. The Collectors were first appointed in 1794.[4] Different functions of the government were combined in the person of the Collector who enjoyed considerable powers. In 1798 Wellesley, the Governor General, directed the Madras government from Calcutta to introduce the Cornwallis system in Madras without delay.[5] At

[1] Munro held that the "natives of this country have enough of their own to answer every useful object of internal administration, and if we maintain and protect them our work will be easy. If not disturbed by innovation, the country will in a very few months settle itself." (Munro to Elphinstone, 12 May 1818, Gleig, *op. cit.*, vol. iii, p. 253.)

[2] *Munro's Minute*, 31 Dec. 1824, p. 383.

[3] Munro held that the "fault of our judicial code is that there is a great deal too much of it for a first essay". He further added that "Our laws expanded gradually during several centuries, along with the increasing knowledge and civilisation of people, so that they were always fitted in some measure to their faculties." (Munro to Thakery, n.d., Gleig, *op. cit.*, vol. i, p. 372.)

Malcolm held that the "most important of the lessons we can derive from our past experience is to be slow and cautious in every procedure which has a tendency to collusion with the habits and prejudices of our native subjects.... That time may gradually effect a change, there is no doubt; but the period is as yet distant when that can be expected; and come when it will, to be safe or beneficial, it must be...the work of society itself. All that the Government can do is, by maintaining the internal peace of the country, and by adapting its principles to the various feelings, habits, and character of its inhabitants, to give time for the slow and silent operation of the desired improvement, with a constant impression that every attempt to accelerate this end will be attended with the danger of its defeat. [Malcolm, *The Political History of India* (London, 1826), vol. ii, p. 183, quoted in Stokes, *op. cit.*, p. 23.]

[4] J. T. Gwynn, "The Madras District System and Land Revenue" in H.H. Dodwell (ed.), *op. cit.*, vol. v, p. 468.

[5] *Ibid.*, p. 472.

that time Munro did not enjoy great influence and was not a very prominent figure. So he was not in a position to prevent the introduction of the Bengal system in the Madras Presidency.

The *Zamindari* system was gradually introduced into certain areas of the Madras Presidency. Simultaneously with the introduction of the *Zamindari* system a new administrative system and a code of regulations both modelled on those of Bengal were introduced.[1]

By 1814 Munro had gained considerable influence and importance. He was appointed Special Commissioner and was entrusted with the task of preparing a plan for administrative reorganisation in Madras. He proposed that the office of the District Magistrate should be transferred from the District Judge to the Collector, that in his capacity as Magistrate he should be empowered to punish offenders by corporal punishment, by fines and by imprisonment with certain limitations, that the superintendence of the district police force should be entrusted to him, that he should be given the authority to try revenue cases such as rent cases, boundary cases, etc., and that he should be associated with the District Judge in the trial of offenders at quarterly sessions.[2] The Madras Regulations of 1816 indicate that Munro's recommendations were approved and incorporated in these regulations.[3]

Munro was not at all in favour of the *Zamindari* system. He gradually introduced what was called the *Ryotwari* system throughout the Presidency especially during his Governorship of the Madras Presidency from 1819 to 1827. Unlike the *Zamindari* system, under the *Ryotwari* system settlement was made not with the *Zamindar* or any other intermediary but directly with the *ryot* (cultivator) of the land who enjoyed all rights in the land

[1] *Ibid.*, p. 474.

[2] Munro in his letter (24 Dec. 1814) to D. Hill, the then Chief Secretary, gave a short outline of his observation and recommendations. (For the letter see Gleig, *op. cit.*, vol. i, pp. 417-423; for the above mentioned recommendations see p. 419.)

[3] Important provisions of the Madras Regulations of 1816 have been discussed in J.T. Gwynn, *op. cit.*, pp. 479-480.

subject to regular payment of land revenue to the government. The settlement was made for a specific period of time and could be renewed.[1] The greatest merit of the *Ryotwari* system was that it eschewed all intermediaries and thus saved the cultivators from oppression by these intermediaries. In Madras the "State consciously assumed an administrative responsibility for the mass of the people which it had just as consciously abdicated in Bengal".[2]

The union of powers in the person of the Collector and the absence of landlords heightened the importance of the office of the Collector in Madras to an extraordinary degree. The "personal semi-military organisation of the Madras district stood in contrast to the divided and impersonal administrative system of Bengal".[3] In Madras the Collector was a "local governor" who exercised considerable discretionary powers and wide ranging superintendence over his district and came to be regarded by the people as their "helper and ruler".[4] But in Bengal there was no such representative of the government who could occupy a "position of pre-eminence and primacy and watch over and promote the general welfare, from every point of view, of the people committed to his charge".[5]

During his governorship of the Bombay Presidency from 1819 to 1827 Elphinstone adopted Munro's administrative and *Ryotwari* land tenure systems for the newly acquired areas of western India. His successor Malcolm, who was Governor of Bombay from 1827 to 1830, maintained and strengthened these systems in the Bombay Presidency. Later when the British Indian empire extended over the north western part of the sub-continent, Charles Metcalfe, who threw all the weight of his influence against the extension of Cornwallis' Bengal system to these areas,[6] wanted to introduce a very extreme form of paternal system. In fact, there were some important differences between the paternal philosophy

[1] Majumder *et. al.*, *op. cit.*, pp. 801-803.

[2] Stokes, *op. cit.*, p. 22.

[3] *Ibid.*, p. 144.

[4] H.V. Lovett, "District Administration in Bengal, 1818-1858" in H.H. Dodwell (ed.), *op. cit.*, vol. vi, p. 28.

[5] *Ibid.*, p. 29.

[6] Stokes, *op. cit.*, p. 9.

of Metcalfe and that of other exponents of the Munro or paternal school. Although Munro, Elphinstone and Malcolm, as noted above, wanted the Collector to be given control over the police and empowered to try revenue and less important criminal cases, they did not oppose a separate judiciary under the District Judge mainly responsible for trying civil and more serious criminal cases. But Metcalfe was strongly in favour of a completely concentrated and unified system of administration under which there would be no separate judiciary at all. He introduced such a system in the Delhi territory.[1] His system considerably influenced many administrators (e. g. John Lawrence) who worked under him. After his departure from British India towards the end of the 1830s, they introduced such a system in most areas (e. g. the Punjab) which were annexed to the British Indian empire in the 1840s and the 1850s.[2]

The local circumstances of the north-western part of British India caused considerable changes in Munro's *ryotwari* system. In these areas settlement was not made with the individual cultivator but with the village community or with the separate estate called *Mahal.* Hence the system came to be known as the *Mahalwari* system. Under this system "At first the village elders apportioned the demand amongst their members, but later the demand, having been agreed as a whole with the elders, was divided among the cultivators according to the measurements of detailed survey."[3] Later the Punjab was settled broadly on the same lines.

Subsequent Changes in Cornwallis' Bengal System

For a long time the Court of Directors had been pressing the Bengal government to introduce those administrative changes

1 As the Resident of the Delhi territory he combined in his person the powers and functions of the Governor, the Chief Judge, the Chief Collector and the Commander in Chief of the Army. (*Ibid.*, p. 144.)

2 We shall have a better idea of Metcalfe's system of district administration when we later discuss the differences that existed between the pattern of administration in Regulation Provinces and that in Non-Regulation Provinces.

3 Spear, *Oxford History*, p. 195.

which had been introduced in Madras by the Madras Regulations of 1816. But the Bengal government was reluctant to take any step in that direction. The Collector was, however, given some judicial powers in the early 1820s. The Regulation of 1822 empowered him to inquire into some revenue cases and to take necessary steps on the basis of his findings.[1]

On his arrival in Calcutta in 1828 Bentinck, the Governor-General, who was strongly in favour of the Munro system, came to the conclusion that considerable changes in the Cornwallis' system should be introduced. In 1831 he held that the offices of Collector and District Magistrate should be united in the person of the Collector.[2]

The District Judge was required by the Regulation of 1831 to relinquish the office of District Magistrate to the Collector who was thus given authority to try less important criminal cases and to control the police force in his district. He was also given summary jurisdiction to try revenue cases such as rent cases, boundary cases etc.[3]

Bentinck was in close contact with and under the direct influence of the Utilitarian philosophers.[4] When he was preparing to launch his massive social and administrative reforms

[1] Misra, *op. cit.*, p. 160.

[2] Bentinck said that on the basis of "all my investigation, now pretty extensive and very earnestly made, into the system of our administration.... the recommendation that I would, in the conclusion, the most strongly urge upon the Honourable Court is, that they would confirm and preserve in the system long since recommended by them to the Madras Government, upon the authority of Sir Thomas Munro, of uniting the appointments of collector and magistrate, of destroying the independence of each other of every officer employed in the same district, of making the collector's a great office, consisting of deputy collectors and joint magistrates and assistants, subordinate to one head, and acting upon the same system." (*Bentinck's Minute*, Nov. 10, 1831, *Parliamentary Papers*, 1831-32, vol.ix, p. 749.)

[3] Lovett, *op. cit.*, p. 28.

[4] Before leaving for British India in December 1827, Bentinck was given a farewell dinner at Grote's house where he was feasted on "the pure milk of the Benthamite word". (Quoted in Stokes, *op. cit.*, p. 51.) Bentinck said

in British India "Bentham was overjoyed"[1] and it appeared to him "as if the golden age of British India was lying before me".[2]

With the departure of Bentinck, Malcolm, and Holt Mackenzie, the then Territorial Secretary, and with Metcalfe's lessening influence, the Munro school became weak during the second half of the 1830s.[3] The supporters of the Cornwallis school took hold in Calcutta. They wanted the offices of Collector and District Magistrate to be separated. But Auckland, the new Governor-General, was not in favour of introducing another important change in the administrative structure so soon. He asked the Court of Directors for discretionary power to separate these offices whenever the pressure of work made this necessary. By 1845 in only three districts of Orissa in the Bengal Presidency did the offices of Collector and District Magistrate remain united.[4] And in other districts of the Bengal Presidency there were now three separate heads—the Collector, the District Magistrate and the District Judge. Of course outside the Bengal Presidency the Munro system continued to function as before. Thus the success of the Cornwallis school, which encountered strong opposition from other provinces, remained localised only in the Bengal Presidency. But this success was also temporary because the Cornwallis or Bengal school again began to lose influence in the Governor-General's Council, the composition of which was "constantly altering".[5] Moreover the energy and progress displayed in the administration of the North Western Provinces, where Bird and Thompson proved very successful, outshone the progress

---

there "I am going to British India, but I shall not be Governor-General. It is you that will be Governor-General." (Bentham to Col. Young, Dec. 28, 1827, *Bentham's Works*, vol. x, pp. 576-8, quoted in *Ibid.*, p. 51.) It is not very clear to whom this statement was addressed. Professor Stokes holds that "it would appear to be James Mill". (*Ibid.*, p. 51.)

[1] *Ibid.*, p. 51.

[2] Bentham to Bentinck (draft letter, Nov. 18, 1829), Bentham MSS., box, x, ff. 179-82, quoted in *Ibid.*, p. 51.

[3] *Ibid.*, p. 234.

[4] Lovett, *op. cit.*, p. 24.

[5] Stokes, *op. cit.*, p. 238.

made in the Bengal Presidency. In 1854 Dalhousie, the Governor-General, attributed the causes of unsatisfactory administration in Bengal, the senior province, mainly to "the separation of the offices of collector and magistrate contrary to the system which had long prevailed in the Lieutenant-governorship of the North-Western Provinces".[1] This view was also strongly supported by Halliday, the first Lieutenant Governor of Bengal.[2] Canning, the new Governor-General, during whose administration these two offices were to be permanently united in 1859, held in February 1857, that "reason, no less than experience, pointed to the necessity of concentrating the whole executive power of the Government in each district of Bengal in the hands of one experienced man".[3] He said that the division of authority and powers should be "avoided rather than sought".[4] As regards the people, he believed that

> "the patriarchal form of Government was in their present condition most congenial to them and best understood by them; and as regards the governing power the concentration of all responsibility upon one officer cannot fail to keep attention alive, and to stimulate his energy in every department to the utmost, whilst it will preclude the growth of those obstructions to good government which are apt to spring up where two coordinate officers divide the authority".[5]

Finally the Mutiny of 1857 played the most decisive role. It "killed the 'filtration theory' of early English Liberals" and "had a more subtle effect upon district administration".[6] It went a long way in strengthening the position of the paternal school of district administration. "Even at the highest levels of Government the

[1] Dalhousie's minute in Chakrabatti, *Summary of the changes in the jurisdiction of districts in Bengal, 1757-1916* (Calcutta, 1918), quoted in Lovett, *op. cit.*, p. 28.

[2] *Ibid.*, p. 28.

[3] C.E. Buckland, *Bengal under the Lieutenant-Governors from 1854 to 1898* (Calcutta, 1901), p. 24.

[4] *Ibid.*, p. 24.

[5] *Ibid.*, pp. 24-25. After the Mutiny of1857 this decision of Canning was endorsed by the Secretary of State for India in April 1859.

[6] Thompson and Garratt, *op. cit.*, p. 476.

Mutiny brought into sharp relief the merits of paternal rule."[1] After the Mutiny the government came to the conclusion that a close relationship should be developed between the executive arm of the government and the people.[2] The government believed that such a close relationship would enable the executive arm to know and redress without much difficulty the grievances of the people on the one hand and let the people know about the policies and intentions of the government on the other. It was felt that such a close relationship could not be developed in British India if the government continued a system of impersonal administration characterised by a complicated procedure of rules and regulations. It was believed that a simple and expeditious system of personal administration and reliance on and faith in the ability and the integrity of the officials would solve many problems.[3]

In 1859 the offices of Collector and Magistrate were finally united in the person of the former.[4] And they have remained united in India, Bangladesh and Pakistan ever since. The union of these two offices was the final victory of the paternal school over the Cornwallis or Bengal school and completed the triumph of the former.

The dignity of the office of Magistrate, command over the police force, powers to try criminal (except serious criminal) cases and revenue cases enormously contributed to the prestige and status of the Collector and enabled him to occupy a position

[1] Thomas R. Metcalf, *op. cit.*, p. 251.

[2] Thompson and Garratt, *op. cit.*, p. 476.

[3] Arguments almost similar to those of the exponents of the Munro school were put forward. Bartle Frere held that "We have enveloped ourselves in rules and regulations till we have left ourselves no power of individual action. We have guarded ourselves against doing evil till we have left no power of doing good.... The remedy is very simple, though not easy, for it is opposed, not only to existing habits and prejudices, but to all our English ideas of government...let every official be a real ruler in all things to those below him and let him be really ruled by the functionary above him." [Frere to Goderich, 15 June 1858, Martineau, *Life and Correspondence of Sir Bartle Frere* (London, 1895), vol. i, p. 276, quoted in Thomas R. Metcalf, *op. cit.*, p. 251.]

[4] Lovett, *op. cit.*, p. 28.

of pre-eminence in the district. Without any ambiguity he became the administrative and the executive head of the district. Thus the district administration in the Bengal Presidency was placed almost on the same footing as that of the Madras and the Bombay Presidencies.

The Emergence of a Landed 'Aristocracy'

The Mutiny also resulted in establishing a class of landlords especially in the north western part of British India. It was believed that one of the causes of the Mutiny was the discontent of the deposed class of landed 'aristocrats'. After the Mutiny the government decided that a class of landlords should be created. So in many places a class of landed 'aristocrats', called *Jaigirdars*, *Talukdars*, *Pattidars*, *Zamindars* etc., many of ancient lineage, was established.[1]

Moreover the role of the moneylenders in society indirectly contributed to a considerable extent to the growth of a landlord class.[2] At times of famine, drought and bad harvest the cultivators were compelled by circumstances to borrow from professional moneylenders. Improvident and extravagant, they also used to borrow heavily for unproductive purposes such as marriage feasts, social and religious ceremonies, purchase of jewellery etc. In fact, they were encouraged by moneylenders to take loans. "Once in debt a peasant was usually unable to extricate himself."[3] As the

1 Thomas R. Metcalf, *op. cit.*, chap. iv (The Restoration of the Aristocracy), pp. 134-173.

2 Both before and after the mutiny the moneylenders were an "established figure on the rural scene". (*Ibid.*, *p.* 204.) But it was during the second half of the 19th century that their position became strong because during the first half of the century the authority of the village headman and that of the village community, from which the individual cultivators previously had received protection against the oppression and the exploitation of the moneylenders, had begun to decline to a considerable extent. "By mid-century the village community of the Northwest had ceased to exercise effective political power." (*Ibid.*, p. 205.) The role of the moneylender in contributing to the growth of the landed 'aristocracy' is discussed in detail in *ibid.*, chap. v (Landlord, Tenant, and Moneylenders), pp. 174-218.

3 *Ibid.*, p. 206.

interest ranged upwards from 25 per cent, even small debts mounted up to an enormous amount in no time. Moreover the moneylenders were notorious for fraudulent practices in keeping accounts. The moneylender

> "did not in any case want to be paid off. His aim was to make the peasant into a perpetual bond servant by a mortgage which gave him control of the crop, or by a forced sale in which he would take title to the land while retaining the former proprietor as his tenant. In either case the moneylender had the upper hand, and the courts—restrained by their belief in freedom of contact and laissez faire—were little more than instruments of his will."[1]

Moreover "the sustained policy of selling up holdings for arears of taxes" further helped the moneylenders. "The process went on everywhere ; its tendency was to swell at every time of difficulty the number of landless men on the one hand, and the indebtedness of the survivors on the other. Many preferred virtual serfdom to the moneylenders to the outright loss of their holdings."[2]

Regulation and Non-Regulation Provinces

In the 19th century the provinces were broadly divided into what were called Regulation and Non-Regulation Provinces i.e. advanced and backward provinces. As the written regulations were introduced into Bengal, Madras and Bombay Presidencies they were called Regulation Provinces. "The expansion of British power during the early nineteenth century led to the annexation of areas less amenable to rule by ledger and law book"[3] than these advanced provinces. So the rules and regulations of the advanced provinces were not introduced into the newly annexed provinces which were called Non-Regulation Provinces. The Non-

[1] *Ibid.*, p. 206.

[2] Spear, *Oxford History*, p. 196. In chapter ii we shall find that the landed 'aristocracy' has profound influence on local administration and Politics of Pakistan (i.e. what was formerly called West Pakistan).

[3] Hugh Tinker, "Structure of the British Imperial Heritage" in Ralph Braibanti (ed.), *Asian Bureaucratic Systems Emergent from the British Imperial Tradition* (Durham, 1966), p. 27. (Hereafter cited as Braibanti, *Asian Bureaucratic Systems.*)

Regulation system of administration was also applied in certain backward areas within the Regulation Provinces, for example the Chittagong Hill Tracts district in British Bengal (now in Bangladesh). While in Regulation Provinces the District Officer was either called the Collector (Madras and Bombay) or the District Magistrate and Collector (Bengal since 1859), in Non-Regulation Provinces he was called the Deputy Commissoner. Usually a considerable number of military officers were employed in the civil administration of the Non-Regulation Provinces.[1]

The pattern of district administration in a Non-Regulation Province was not always exactly the same as that of district administration in another Non-Regulation Province. It was determined according to the conditions and circumstances of the province concerned. The common feature was that in Non-Regulation Provinces the district administration was "characterised by simple and more direct methods of procedure and by the greater accessibility of the officials to the people ; but chiefly by the union of all powers".[2] There was no separate judiciary and no such officer as the District Judge. The Deputy Commissioner combined in his person the offices of the Collector, the District Magistrate and the District Judge. Thus there was a complete union of revenue, executive, magisterial and judicial powers in the hands of the Deputy Commissioner who used to try criminal, civil and revenue cases, collect revenue and carry out all administrative orders. Under "certain defined principles" he was left to "do justice according to circumstances".[3] There was a rough Criminal Code but they decided civil cases by a mixture of custom, commonsense and a reference to standing orders.[4] In Non-

[1] L.S.S. O'Malley, *The Indian Civil Service, 1601-1930* (London, 1965 edn.), pp. 52-53.

[2] Griffiths, *op. cit.*, p. 164. In fact the Mughal system of local administration was introduced to Non-Regulation Provinces without much modification and the Deputy Commissioner had much in common with the local officers of Mughal India. (Thompson and Garratt, *op. cit.*, p. 477.)

[3] Griffiths, *op. cit.*, p. 164.

[4] Thompson and Garratt, *op. cit.*, p. 477.

Regulation Provinces "though legal principles were by no means set aside" the district administration "largely depended for its success on the personal character, initiative, vigour and discretion of the local officers".[1]

While the District Officer in the Non-Regulation Provinces was all in all within his district and had no rival, the District Officer in the Regulation Provinces was required to work in his district along with another officer of the same status i.e. the District Judge who was his "jealous rival".[2] Of course the District Officer in the Non-Regulation Provinces "was more closely subject to the personal supervision of his superiors than was the case in those provinces where everything had been reduced to rules and regulations".[3] In all branches of work every action of the Deputy Commissioner was subject to the appellate and supervisional jurisdiction of the Divisional Commissioner who was also an administrative officer and not a judicial officer.[4] Thus in the Non-Regulation Provinces the executive authority was welded into a single chain of command stretching from the headquarters down to the district level.

In the Punjab the most rigid Non-Regulation system which was "military in form and spirit"[5] was applied. Under the then social condition of the Punjab such a rigid system was essential and proved to be very successful. In fact, the "Non-Regulation

[1] Griffiths, *op. cit.*, p. 164.

[2] Thompson and Garratt, *op. cit.*, p. 477.

[3] Griffiths, *op. cit.*, p. 164.

[4] In Regulation Provinces also there were Divisional Commissioners. They were mainly concerned with the revenue administration and did not exercise such a close supervision over every branch of administration as was exercised by their counterparts in the Non-Regulation Provinces. The importance of the Divisional Commissioners in the Regulation Provinces was much less than that of those in the Non-Regulation Provinces. Later we shall see that mainly for this reason the Divisional Commissioners in Pakistan, which has mainly inherited the tradition of Non-Regulation Provinces, enjoy greater authority and importance than their counterparts in Bangladesh, which has inherited the tradition of the Regulation province of British Bengal. (See below, chaps. iii and iv.)

[5] Stokes, *op. cit.*, p. 243.

system was at its best in the Punjab, where it threw up, in the mixed military and civil commission, some of the finest characters in Indian administration".[1] In comparison with other Non-Regulation Provinces the Non-Regulation system in the Punjab was much more direct and simpler. John Lawrence said of the Punjab system

> "We have a procedure without any pretention to exactitude; but a procedure which provides for the litigants and their witness being confronted in open court, for decision being arrived at immediately and for judgement being delivered to the parties then and there."[2]

Though the District Officer in the Regulation Provinces was a powerful administrative head of the district he "was far less of an autocrat than the Deputy Commissioner in the Punjab".[3] Charles Metcalfe, who left British India towards the end of the 1830s and who, as we have already noted, was one of the most prominent exponents of the Munro school, may be regarded as "one of the founding fathers of the Punjab system, having been its pioneer in the Delhi Territory where John Lawrence received his training".[4] John Lawrence was the architect of the Punjab system.

Among the Regulation Provinces a comparatively more complex and rigid legal system was applied in the Bengal Presidency where though the paternal school ultimately became victorious and the offices of Collector and Magistrate were permanently united, it was difficult to completely disown the influence of the Cornwallis tradition which had in fact become part and parcel of the Bengal administrative tradition. Moreover

1 Griffiths, *op. cit.*, p. 164.

2 Quoted in Thompson and Garratt, *op. cit.*, p. 477. The attempt to separate the judiciary from the executive encountered strongest opposition in the Punjab. John Lawrence held that "I want no such person as a session judge here....I have a great objection to the civil and revenue work being separated. A regular civil court plays the very devil. Its course of procedure is ruinous to the tenures of the country, for the agriculturists cannot fight cases in the court." (Bosworth Smith, *Life of Lord Lawrence*, vol. ii (London, 1885), p. 202, quoted in Stokes, *op. cit.*, p. 244.)

3 Thompson and Garratt, *op. cit.*, p. 477.

4 Stokes, *op. cit.*, p. 243. also See above, p. 23.

in Bengal the presence of the *Zamindars* minimised the scope of the activities of the District Officer. In revenue matters he used to deal through the *Zamindars* and "knew little of his district. The Bengal and Punjab systems thus represented the extremes of rule of law and the rule of man."[1]

From the foregoing discussion we see that there were considerable differences between the paternal system in the Regulation Provinces and that in the Non-Regulation Provinces. While the former was more or less similar to what was worked out by Thomas Munro, the latter was more or less similar to what was worked out by Charles Metcalfe.[2]

Towards the end of the last century the judiciary was gradually separated from the executive, the post of District Judge was created and elaborate written regulations were gradually applied in most Non-Regulation areas.[3] Thus steps were taken to place the administration of the Non-Regulation Provinces on the same footing as that of the Regulation Provinces. But in practice there were still some differences between the administration of these two types of provinces. In 1915 the Bengal District Administration Committee observed that

> "Those members of our Committee from other provinces who sat by the Magistrate in his court, or by the Collector at his desk, noticed especially how matters which in less advanced provinces are settled by the exchange of a word or two, or by a few strokes of the pen, in Bengal necessitate long agreement, careful reference to rules and detailed orders in writing."[4]

Such differences between these two types of provinces continued to persist in varying degrees and the District Officers of the Non-Regulation Provinces continued to enjoy more discretionary powers and authority.[5]

[1] Thompson and Garratt, *op. cit.*, p. 477.

[2] The difference between Munro's system and Metcalfe's system has been discussed above. (See p. 28.)

[3] Thomas R. Metcalf, *op. cit.*, p. 255.

[4] *Bengal District Administration Committee, 1913-14*: *Report* (*Levinge Report*) (Calcutta, 1915), p. 25.

[5] For example, the maximum punishments that the D.O. in Pakistan, which

Within some Non-Regulation Provinces (e.g. the N.W.F.P., Baluchistan etc.) there were some areas inhabited by wild and tribal peoples. These areas were classified as tribal areas, the pattern of administration of which was completely different from that of the regular administration in both Regulation and Non-Regulation Provinces. The administration of tribal areas was based on tribal customs and values.[1]

The princely states constituted a fairly considerable part of the sub-continent. The regular administrative system of British India did not extend over these areas. As a result the administration of these areas remained undeveloped. The local rulers of these states enjoyed considerable autonomy. Generally speaking, the administrative pattern of these states was not much different from the administrative pattern of the period which had immediately preceded the British period. Usually the administration of one state varied widely from that of another because immediately before the British assumed the administration of some parts of the sub-continent there had been considerable differences between the administration of one state or region and that of another state or region. Generally speaking the administration of most states was very backward, inefficient and authoritarian. Once Jawaharlal Nehru commented that

> "Most of the Indian states are well known for their backwardness and their semifeudal conditions. They are personal autocracies, devoid even of competence or benevolence. Many strange things occur there which never receive publicity. And yet their very inefficiency lessens the evil in some ways and lightens the burden on their unhappy people. For this is reflected in a weak executive, and it results in making even tyranny and injustice inefficient. That does not make tyranny more bearable, but it does make it less far-reaching and widespread."[2]

---

at the time of partition (1947) inherited the tradition of Non-Regulation provinces, and his counterpart in Bangladesh, which inherited that of Regulation provinces, can award are 7 years and 2 years rigorous imprisonments respectively. (See below, chap. iv.)

[1] The pattern of administration in tribal areas, which has remained almost completely unchanged, is discussed in detail in chapters iii and iv (below).

[2] Dorothy Norman (ed.), *Nehru: The First Sixty Years*, vol. i (London, 1965), p. 105.

He further added that the "arbitrary regimes" were "thriving in Indian India".[1]

Some Concluding Comments on the Office of the District Officer (D.O.)

In 1859 when the offices of Collector and Magistrate were united once and for all, the most important and eventful formative phase of district administration in the sub-continent and the controversies over such union came to an end. Of course, in the Non-Regulation provinces, as we have already noted, the district administration did not take final shape before the end of the last century when the office of the District Judge was separated from that of the D.O. But it was in 1859 that the basic principles of modern district administration were formulated once and for all.[2] The subsequent period did not witness any significant change in the legal position of the D.O. as the Collector-Magistrate or as the administrative and executive head of the district. Of course changes and developments in other fields considerably affected his position. For example, the gradual appointment of the officers of other specialised departments from the second half of the last century onwards resulted in the problem of coordination and that of the organisational and the functional relationship of the D.O. with other officers;[3] the increasing importance of rural development gradually began to add a new dimension to his role especially from the beginning of the 1920s;[4] and the constitutional and political reforms introduced by the 1919 and the 1935 Acts

[1] *Ibid.*, p. 106. Professor Wilcox has briefly discussed the administrative pattern of some of the princely states in pre-partition days which are now a part of Pakistan. [See W.A. Wilcox, *Pakistan: The Consolidation of a Nation* (London, 1963), chap. i.]

[2] We have already noted that the basic principles were that the Collector-Magistrate would be the administrative head of the district and would have judicial powers over revenue and less important criminal cases; that in advanced provinces the District Judge would try civil and serious criminal cases; and that with the advancement of backward provinces the post of the District Judge would be gradually created in these provinces.

[3] See below, chap. vi.

[4] See below, chap. v.

brought fairly considerable political pressure to bear upon him.[1] Thus though his legal position remained unchanged he was required from time to time to adjust his position in the changed environment.

The "concentration of powers in the hands of the district officer was so great and his sharing of these powers so rare and minimal that it was scarcely surprising that he should have been called the '*man-bap*' (mother and father) of his area".[2] The House of Commons was told that such "power as that which collectors of India have over the people in India is not found in any other part of the world possessed by any class of functionaries".[3]

[1] See below, chap. vii.

[2] W. H. Morris-Jones, *Parliament in India* (London, 1957), p. 36. (Hereafter cited as Morris-Jones, *Parliament*.)

[3] Macauley, *Parl. Deb.*, 3rd series, vol. cxviii, June 24, 1853, cols. 745-6, quoted in Ralph Braibanti, "The Civil Service of Pakistan: A Theoretical Analysis" in *South Atlantic Quarterly*, vol. LVIII, no. 2, 1959, p. 272. (Hereafter cited as Braibanti, *The Civil Service*.) (Though this comment was expressed in 1853, it remained valid for a considerable period of time.) Towards the end of the last century, Sir William Hunter observed that "His own special duties are so numerous and so various as to bewilder the outsider; and the work of his subordinates, European and Natives, largely depends upon the stimulus of his personal example. His position has been compared to that of the French prefect, but such a comparison is unjust in many ways to the Indian district officer. He is not a mere subordinate of a central bureau, who takes his colour from his chief and represents the political parties or the permanent officialism of the capital. The Indian Collector is a strongly individualised worker in every Department of rural well-being, with a large measure of local independence and of individual initiative...his title by no means exhausts his multifarious duties. He does in a smaller local sphere all that the Home Secretary superintends in England...Police, jails, education, municipalities, roads, sanitation, dispensaries, the local taxation, and the Imperial revenues of his District are to him matters of daily concern. He is expected to make himself acquainted with every phase of the social life of the natives, and with each natural aspect of the country. He should be a lawyer, an accountant, a financier, and a ready writer of State papers. He ought also to possess no mean knowledge of agriculture, political economy and engineering." [William Hunter, *The Indian Empire* (London, 1892), p. 513.] Of course, with the passage of time he was relieved of specialised functions which were then entrusted to other officers with specialised knowledge. They performed these functions under his general control and supervision. (See

The D.O. occupied a very important and prominent place in the administration of the sub-continent. "Upon his energy and personal character" wrote Sir William Hunter, "depends ultimately the efficiency of our Indian Government".[1] It was "no exaggeration to describe the District Officer as the focal point of the Indian administration".[2]

The D.O. was usually a member of the famous Indian Civil Service, the members of which were "chosen and trained on Plato's principles as Guardians".[3] The ideal that was set for the D.O. was the "Platonic ideal" of public service.[4] The nature of his functions was such that it was not unnatural for him to go beyond his legal responsibilities. Usually he looked after the people of his district, whose well being was his trust, with paternal care and sympathy. The happiness of rural life depended to a considerable extent on the interest that he took in different aspects of rural life. Macauley said in the House of Commons: "In all that district there is not a single village—there is not a single hut—in which the difference between a good and a bad collector may not make the difference between happiness and misery".[5] To rural people the

---

below, chap. vi.) The improvement of communication systems also put some restrictions on the local independence of the District Officer. "... steam, the electric telegraph, the canal, brought England nearer...As London tried to tighten control on India, so Simla tried to tighten on the provinces and the provinces on the district officer." [Philip Woodruff (Philip Mason), *The Men Who Ruled India: The Guardians* (London, 1963 edn.), p. 14. See also O'Malley, *op. cit.*, p. 110.]

1 Hunter, *op. cit.*, p. 513.

2 Griffiths, *op. cit.*, p. 164.

3 Woodruff, *op. cit.*, p. 15.

4 *Ibid.*, p. 360.

5 Macauley, *op. cit.*, cols. 745-6, quoted in Braibanti, *The Civil Service*, p. 272. The following few passages written by those who had practical experience in district administration will not only further illustrate the diverse and multifarious nature of the D.O.'s functions but also his close and intimate contact with different aspects of the rural life:

"He [the villager] clothes government in a man's shape—that of a collector sahib, who tried his family lawsuit last year, who only yesterday was discussing with him the conditions of his wheat field, and who this morning cursed him roundly because there was a cesspool outside his door." [Edward Blunt, *The I.C.S.* (London, 1937), p.119.]

"The District Officer was thinking, for instance, of the best way of dealing

government meant the D.O. from whom they expected justice, sympathy and protection. Many D.O.s were looked on with real affection by the people of their districts.[1] Usually D.O.s remained in close and intimate contact with the rural areas of their districts. They "generally developed a kind of local patriotism".[2] This often made them

---

with Brij Mohan, an inspector of land records, widely reputed to be corrupt but so far too clever to be caught; of how to raise the money for an extension of the hospital at headquarters; of whether a primary school at Gopalpur was really essential or whether it might not be better to concentrate the scanty funds on existing schools; of the state of the road to Ramnagar at the thirteenth milestone; of the murder case from Gwalabad and how the defence could be prevented from tampering with the evidence; of what should be done about the pipal trees on the *Moharram* rout at Pitampura." (Woodruff, *op. cit.*, p. 178.)

"He [the D.O.] rises at daybreak and goes straight from his bed to the saddle. Then he gallops off across fields bright with dew to visit the scene of the late dacoity robbery; or to see with his own eyes whether the crops of the *Zamindar* who is so unpunctual with his assessment have really failed; or to watch with fond paternal care the progress of his pet embankment." (Quoted in *ibid.*, p. 92.) Philip Mason says that G.O. Trevelyan's above mentioned "description of a district officer's day in the [18]'sixties did no t need much modification seventy or eighty years later". (*Ibid.*, p. 92.)

When a district officer was trying a case a villager entered the court carrying the mangled leg of his son. "What sort of ruler are you?" the villager cried, "what are you doing, sitting here arguing with lawyers when a tiger is eating my son?" It was a view of the Magistrate's duty with which the District Officer Mr. Simon agreed. He left the court and shot the tiger. (*Ibid.*, p. 178.)

The Socrates in an Indian Village (London, 1929), written by F.L. Brayne, who was the D.O. of Gurgaon district in the Punjab, illustrates very vividly the nature of the intimate contact that existed between him and the villagers and his interest in the personal wellbeing of the rural people. Mr. Brayne vigorously launched his rural uplift campaign to increase produce [F.L. Brayne, *Better Village* (Madras, 1937), p. 3.], to clean the villages, to teach the villagers sanitary habits (*Ibid.*, p. 11.), to make the houses light and airy (*Ibid.*, p. 12.), to teach the villagers the methods of taking precautions against epidemics (*Ibid.*, p. 13.), to stop waste (i.e. the villagers were persuaded to stop useless expenditures on ceremonies, litigations, ornaments etc.) (*Ibid.*, p. 17.), to make the home sweet and beautiful. (*Ibid.*, p. 19.)

1 Woodruff, *op. cit.*, p. 96.

2 Griffiths, *op. cit.*, p.165.

"fight for the interest of their own district against all comers. This often produced a certain narrowness and did not always fit the District Officer for the higher posts which he might have to assume later; it did, however, ensure that he regarded himself as the friend of the people and that they in their turn came, not only to trust him, but to regard him as the beginning and end of government".[1]

With the passage of time the position of the D.O. in relation to rural areas began to change. Especially during the second quarter of this century he became overburdened with the rapidly increasing load of work and some new administrative functionaries or layers emerged which occupied a mid-way position between him and the rural people. This affected his direct contact with the rural people. His contact with them gradually became faint. This process became further accelerated after partition (1947) especially from the 1950s.[2]

Local Bodies

The development of local bodies in the sub-continent varied widely from province to province. Usually the provincial Acts on local bodies used to lay down broad principles and give considerable discretionary powers to the respective provincial governments for setting up local bodies and for making decisions from time to time about the structure of these local bodies, the ratio between the official and the non-official members, the nature of the franchise etc., on the basis of these broad principles. The local bodies also underwent frequent changes especially with regard to their composition and structure. The century that preceded partition in 1947 (and also the years that have followed) witnessed a stream of amending Acts on local bodies. As a result of these factors the development of local bodies was not uniform throughout the sub-continent. In this part of the chapter an attempt will be made to discuss very briefly the common features and the important stages of this development in British India.

1 *Ibid.*, p. 165.

2 See below, chap. iii. Later we shall find that nowadays such close and intimate contact does not exist between the District Officer and the rural people. The contact is rather formal and occasional.

The Period Before the 1880s. Some important steps towards the establishment of local bodies were taken during the 1860s and the 1870s when a series of acts were passed in major provinces.[1] The local bodies were first established in urban areas and then in rural areas. In general most of these municipal bodies in most

1 For the development of local bodies before the 1880s,see Hugh Tinker, *The Foundations of Local Self-Government in India, Pakistan and Burma* (London, 1954), pp. 22-42 (Hereafter cited as Tinker, *Foundations*); C.F. Strickland, "Local Government and Social Administration" (hereafter cited as Strickland, *Local Govt.*) in Edward Blunt (ed.), *Social Service in India* (London, 1938), pp. 354-356 (Hereafter cited as Blunt, *Social Service*); Malik M. Siddiq, Local Government in Pakistan (Sargoda, n.d.) (cyclostyled), pp. 1-5,15; S.D. Khan, Local Government Administration Development in Pakistan with Particular Reference to East Pakistan (typed) (Dacca, n.d.), pp. 4, 7-10. Mr. Khan has discussed in some detail the development of local bodies (especially municipalities) in Bengal.

Of course long before the development of local bodies in the 19th century the municipalities had been first constituted in three presidency towns namely Madras (1688), Calcutta (1726), and Bombay (1726). [See Tinker, *Foundations*, pp. 25-26; Strickland, *Local Govt.*, p. 354; Siddiq, Local Govt., p. 2; S.D. Khan, Local Govt., p. 7.]

One author says that in British Bengal local taxation for making provision for and maintenance of town *Chowkidars* (watchmen) outside the presidency town was first introduced in Dacca, the present capital of Bangladesh, in 1813. The subsequent important municipal legislations were enacted in British Bengal in the following years: 1814, 1816, 1837, 1842, 1850 and 1856. (S.D. Khan, Local Govt., pp. 7-8.) The subsequent developments in British Bengal are discussed later.

The areas which now constitute Pakistan were annexed to the British Indian empire much later. So the development of local bodies in these areas began mainly in the 1860s. In the 1860s and 70s important Acts were passed in the following provinces and in the following years: Municipal Acts (1860s): Bengal and Oudh, 1864; Madras, 1865; Punjab, 1867; North-Western Provinces and Central Provinces, 1868. (Tinker, *Foundations*, p. 36.) Municipal Acts (1870s): Madras, 1871; Bombay, North-Western Provinces, Punjab and Central Provinces, 1873; Bengal, 1876. (*Ibid.*, p. 37.) District Committee Acts (i.e. rural local bodies Acts) (1860s and 1870s): Bombay, 1869; Madras, 1870; Bengal, North-Western Provinces and Punjab, 1871. (*Ibid.*, p. 39.)

The Acts that were passed in the 1860s and those passed in the 1870s were the result of Lawrence's Resolution of 1864 and Mayo's Resolution of 1870 respectively. The former Resolution declared that "The people of this country are perfectly capable of administering their

provinces were either wholly or partially nominated bodies consisting of both officials and non-officials. Usually the D.O. selected the non-official members from amongst "respectable" persons of the town concerned. "The official influence was almost overpowering."[1]

Towards the end of the 1860s and especially towards the beginning of the 1870s important steps were taken to set up local bodies for rural areas. Under the District Committee Acts passed in most provinces[2] the District Committee was established in many districts. The D.O. became the president of the District Committee. In some statutes there were provisions that a certain percentage of the members could be elected. But "no members were in fact elected".[3] The committee consisted of officials and non-officials mostly drawn from the landed "aristocracy". In addition to the District Committees some village committees were also set up at the village level. But these committees were not at all effective and "led only a formal existence".[4] Usually these committees were nominated bodies.[5]

"From 1870 onwards the progress of rural self-government followed much the same lines as municipal self-government".[6] Of course the municipal bodies made faster progress than the rural local bodies.

Ripon's Resolution of 1882 and Its Impact. The most vital step in the history of the local bodies of the sub-continent was taken by Lord Ripon, the then Viceroy. He, in fact, laid down the real

---

own local affairs. The municipal feeling is deeply rooted in them. The village communities....are the most abiding of Indian institutions." (*Gazette of India*, 14 Sept. 1864, quoted in *Ibid*, p. 36.) Mayo's Resolution emphasised "the need of arousing local interest in the management of funds devoted to local purposes." (Strickland, *Local Govt.*, p. 355.)

1 Tinker, *Foundations*, p. 37. 2 See above, p. 40, fn. 1 (cont. on this page).

3 Tinker, *Foundations*, p. 39. 4 *Ibid.*, p.40.

5 Elliot Tepper, *Changing Patterns of Administration in Rural East Pakistan* (Asian Studies Centre Occasional Paper No. 5, Michigan State University, Aug. 1966), p. 46. Malik, Local Govt., p. 15.

6 Strickland, *Local Govt.*, p. 356.

foundations of modern local bodies in India, Bangladesh and Pakistan. Ripon's Resolution of 1882 declared that

> "In advocating the extension of local self-government and the adoption of this principle in the management of many branches of local affairs, the Governor-General in Council does not suppose that the work will be in the first instance better done than if it remained in the sole hands of the Government District Officers. It is not primarily with a view to improvement in administration that this measure is put forward and supported. It is chiefly desirable as an instrument of political and popular education....
>
> "It is not uncommonly asserted that the people of this country are themselves indifferent to the principle of self-government; that they take but little interest in public matters; and that they prefer to have such affairs managed for them by Government Officers. The Governor-General in Council does not attach much value to this theory."[1]

The Resolution emphasised that all local bodies, both urban and rural, should have a two-thirds majority of non-officials and in no case ought the number of the official members to be more than half the total number. The non-official members should whenever practicable be elected. The Resolution also strongly emphasised that these bodies should be headed by non-official chairmen whenever possible.[2]

The Resolution was followed by a series of Local Self-Government Acts, both urban and rural,[3] which gradually introduced

[1] Quoted in the *Report of the Indian Statutory Commission, Volume 1, Survey* (*Simon Report*) (London, 1930), para. 366. For two reasons the Resolution also gained added importance. Firstly, Lord Ripon had the support and backing of Gladstone, the Prime Minister, who was also strongly in favour of introducing some representative institutions in British India so that the people could gradually begin to receive political training. Secondly, the Famine Commission of 1880 had strongly emphasised the need for the extension of local self-government as a means to facilitate relief work. (Tepper, *op. cit.*, p. 47.)

[2] The principles, laid down by the Resolution, about local bodies' structure, composition, jurisdiction, franchise etc., have been discussed in some greater detail in *ibid.* (pp. 47-48.)

[3] Municipal Acts: North-Western Provinces, 1883; Bengal, Madras, Bombay, Punjab, 1884. District Board Acts: North-Western Provinces, Punjab, Central Provinces, 1883; Madras, Bombay, 1884; Bengal, 1885. (Tinker, *Foundations*, p.46.)

a network of local bodies in the sub-continent. The provincial Acts differed widely mainly because though the Resolution insisted on a uniform pattern of local bodies throughout British India it also "pointedly referred to the advisability of a variety in form to suit divergent conditions".[1] Though from time to time these Acts underwent repeated amendments they remained the basis of local self-government in Bangladesh and Pakistan until 1959.

The district board Acts resulted in introducing District Boards in most districts of all the provinces except Assam where only sub-district boards called Local Boards with jurisdiction over a sub-division of the district were set up. In addition to District Board most provinces also created sub-district boards.[2]

The Chairmen of rural local bodies in all the provinces except the Central Provinces (excluding Berar) were officials. The District Board was presided over by the D.O.[3] He as "the unchallenged head of rural affairs"[4] "held undisputed sway"[5] over the local rural bodies.

The percentage of the non-official Chairmen of Municipal Boards in the sub-continent was larger than that of the non-official chairmen of rural local bodies. While in the Central Provinces the non-officials constituted "the great majority of chairmen of municipalities", in Bengal and Madras they were "a substantial and increasing minority".[6] In some other provinces (e.g. Punjab and North-Western Provinces) the Municipal Boards were allowed to elect their Chairmen but "the still unchallenged prestige" of the D.O. "reduced the election to a formal invitation to the Head of the district, or to one of his sub-divisional officers".[7]

1 *Simon Report*, vol. i, para. 337.

2 The sub-district boards were called Local Boards in Bengal, Central Provinces and Assam, *Tehsil* or *Taluka* Board in other provinces. (Tinker, *Foundations*, p. 53; Strickland, *Local Govt.*, p. 356; S. D. Khan, Local Govt., p. 4.) In Bengal and Madras some attempts were made to introduce village council (with jurisdiction over a few villages.) These bodies were in fact constituted only in a very limited number of villages. (Tinker, *Foundations*, p. 56.)

3 *Ibid.*, p. 47.
4 *Ibid.*, p. 47.
5 *Ibid.*, p. 79; also see p. 70.
6 *Ibid.*, p. 46.
7 *Ibid.*, p. 47.

Following the recommendation of Ripon's Resolution the required two-thirds majorities of non-official members, both for urban and rural local bodies, were created but "a large majority of these non-officials were still dependent upon the district magistrate's favour for nomination..... The extent to which election was introduced depended..... upon the attitudes of Heads of provinces".[1] In most provinces the sub-district boards were required to act as the electoral college for electing certain percentage (determined by the government) of the non-official members of the District Board. Some members of the sub-district board were nominated and some were elected upon a "very narrow and often arbitrary franchise".[2] Municipal elections were also held on a restricted franchise. In most provinces the municipal electorate comprised less than two per cent of the urban population except in Bengal where it was perhaps five per cent.[3] Thus both the rural and the urban electorate was minute.

Subsequent Development. The Royal Commission upon Decentralisation which was constituted in 1907 and which submitted its report in 1909 opposed the view, which had been recommended in Ripon's Resolution, that the D.O. should be relieved of the responsibility of the Chairmanship of the District Board.[4] It recommended that the D.O. should continue to act as

[1] *Ibid.*, p. 47. [2] *Ibid.*, p. 53; see also p. 77. [3] *Ibid.*, p. 50.

[4] "We are of opinion that, in present circumstances, the Collector should remain president of the district board. To remove him from this post would be to dissociate him from the general interest of the district in such matters as roads, education, sanitation, drainage and water supply, and to convert him into a mere tax-gatherer and repressor of crime. Such a change would, we think, be very undesirable, and would have the effect of divorcing the Collector from healthy contact with instructed non-official opinion." [*Report of the Royal Commission upon Decentralisation in India*, volume i (London, 1909), para. 795. (Hereafter cited as *Decentralisation Commission's Report.*)] It also held that "Collectors have, in some instances, been in the habit of ruling rather than guiding district boards, and in so far as this attitude exists, we consider it unfortunate. But it is equally unfortunate that the Collector should be looked upon, as is too often the case at present, in the light of an outside authority, instead of as a necessary complement to the non-official element on the board. At the same time the Collector-president

the head of the District Board. But it held that the Chairman of the Municipal Board "should be an elected non-official"[1] and that "a municipal council should ordinarily contain a substantial elective majority".[2] It added that the system of nomination should be retained but its purpose should be to provide for the due "representation of minorities and official experience".[3] The Report also strongly recommended the creation of *panchayats* (village councils) throughout British India.[4]

But no significant changes were introduced in the field of local self-government. Although the provincial governments, who were entrusted with the task of working out detailed plans for the implementation of the recommendations of the Decentralisation Commission, accepted the general principles of the Report, they felt that under the then conditions no changes should be made in haste. They were of the opinion that while making further progress in those directions cautious measures should be taken.[5]

should not arbitrarily override the opinions of others, but should be sympathetic chairman, and should bear in mind that not the least important of his functions is to assist in the political education of the members. Such relations often exist now, and there should be no difficulty in making them universal hereafter." (*Ibid.*, para. 796).

1 *Ibid.*, para. 852.

2 *Ibid.*, para. 849. It made such recommendations about the urban bodies because the "circumstances of municipalities differ from those of rural boards in that they are much less connected with the general district administration, that political education has reached a higher level, and that the jurisdictional area is much smaller and more compact. The arguments which led us to recommend official president for rural boards do not, therefore, apply here." (*Ibid.*, para. 852.)

3 *Ibid.*, para. 849.

4 *Ibid.*, paras. 699, 701; also see para. 702.

5 The following two views expressed by two very high ranking officials will further illustrate official attitude towards the approach of the Decentralisation Commission: The then Chief Secretary to the Government of the then West Bengal had already expressed his disapproval to the Commission. He had said "My feeling is that it is never sound in Indian administration to go too fast." [*Minutes of Evidence taken before the Royal Commission upon Decentralisation in Bengal* (Calcutta, 1908), p. 7, quoted in Tepper, *op. cit.*, p. 62.] On behalf of the Lieutenant-Governor the then Chief Secretary to the Government of East Bengal and Assam had written in 1908 to the Secretary, Government of British India that he

Thus the period between the implementation of Ripon's Resolution and that of the recommendations of the *Montagu-Chelmsford Report* (1918)[1] did not witness any significant developments in the field of local self-government. Of course during this period the percentage of the elected members and chairmen was slightly raised. By 1918 "rather more than half the members of municipal and rather less than half of those of rural boards, including in this term sub-district boards," were elected.[2] A little less than one-fourth of the Chairmen of the Municipal Boards were non-officials in 1908 and by 1917 over one-third of those of the Municipal Boards were non-officials. This development varied from province to province. In the Punjab "there was virtually no advance whatever".[3] In Bengal in 1917 five out of twenty-five District Boards were allowed for the first time to elect their own Chairmen.[4]

After the reforms that had been introduced by Lord Ripon in the 1880s the next wave of reforms came in the early 1920s. This was the result of the *Montagu-Chelmsford Report* which not only introduced political and administrative reforms of great importance which had a far-reaching impact in determining the

---

had "no wish to dabble in constitution-making experiments" and that he considered "that the necessity of very cautious measures, and of following approved and tried lines, is clearly indicated". [*Papers Relating to Constitutional Reform in India*, vol. iii (Calcutta, 1908), Ag. 1205, quoted in *ibid.*, p. 62.] These views had given "clear indication what would happen to reform measures...." (*Ibid.*, p. 62.) The provincial governments' "new measures were drafted strictly in accordance with the existing state of political life in village and market-town". (Tinker, *Foundations*, p. 92.)

1 Later we shall see that the *Montagu-Chelmsford Report* resulted in a series of reforms in the early 1920s.

2 *Report on Indian Constitutional Reforms* (*Montagu-Chelmsford Report*) (Calcutta, 1928 print), para. 194.

3 Tinker, *Foundations*, p. 92.

4 *Memorandum submitted by the Government of Bengal to the Indian Statutory Commission* (London, 1930), para. 75. (Hereafter cited as *Bengal Govt. Memorandum*.)

future course of the politics and administration of the sub-continent but also had a great impact on the development of local self-government. Edwin Montagu, the then Secretary of State for India, who was a known Radical, and Lord Chelmsford, the then Viceroy of India, strongly advocated the enlargement and development of self-governing institutions in India.[1] Moreover an alliance between the National Congress and Muslim League developed. The government was thus also "faced with a coalition of two aggressive nationalist organisations, demanding reform".[2]

The Montagu-Chelmsford Report recommended that the "proportion of nominated members should not exceed one-fourth" and that the election of Chairmen should be "the general rule in future".[3] It held that only under exceptional circumstances an official Chairman could be appointed. It also strongly emphasised the need for the "development of the *panchayat* system".[4] The Report strongly criticised the rigidity of restricted franchise and held that "the present electoral system has great defects".[5]

Different provincial governments were required to take the necessary steps for the implementation of the recommendations of the Report. The measures which they took were more or less similar to what had been suggested by the Report. The majority of the members of all local bodies, usually varying from three-fourths to two-thirds of the total membership, were elected. In 1925-26 only 68 Municipal Boards of backward areas had *ex officio*

[1] On August 20, 1917, Edwin Montagu declared in the House of Commons that "The policy of His Majesty's Government, with which the Government of India are in complete accord, is that of the increasing association of Indians in every branch of the administration and the gradual development of self-governing institutions with a view to the progressive realisation of responsible government in India as an integral part of the British Empire. They have decided that substantial steps in this direction should be taken as soon as possible". (Quoted in the *Montagu-Chelmsford Report*, para. 6.)

[2] Tepper, *op. cit.*, p. 63.

[3] *Montagu-Chelmsford Report*, para. 194.

[4] *Ibid.*, para. 196.

[5] *Ibid.*, para. 83.

or nominated Chairmen while 681 Municipal Boards elected their Chairmen.[1] With the exception of a few District Boards in backward areas all District Boards in all provinces except the Punjab had elected non-official chairmen. In the Punjab "although the option to ask for the privilege of election exists, only two Boards have exercised it— a result due in the main to a preference for the freedom from communal bias of the District Officer".[2] Usually the sub-district boards also had the majority of elected members and had elected Chairmen.[3] Both the urban and the rural franchise was extended in every province. About 14 per cent of the urban population enjoyed the municipal franchise as a result of the reform.[4] The rural franchise "though greatly extended since the advent of the reforms, even now gives the vote to little more than 3.2 per cent of the population".[5] The village councils called either *panchayat* or Union Board were set up in some places in most provinces. Of course the progress of the village councils was satisfactory in only three provinces, namely Bengal, Madras and United Provinces. In most provinces the Chairmen and the majority of the members of these bodies were elected.[6] The Divisional Commissioner, the D.O. and the S.D.O. enjoyed supervisory, controlling and veto powers over the local bodies.

So far as the structure and composition of the local bodies were concerned the later period did not witness any other significant changes[7] except that the sub-district boards, which did not

1 *Simon Report*, vol. i, para. 344. 2 *Ibid.*, para. 346.
3 *Ibid.*, para. 347. 4 *Ibid.*, 344. 5 *Ibid.*, para. 346.
6 *Ibid.*, para. 347.

7 There were some minor changes in some provinces. For example, in 1932 the Bengal Government decided that the three-fourths of the members of the mofussil Municipal Boards except those of Dacca and Chittagong would be elected. And in case of the Municipal Boards of Dacca and Chittagong, the percentage of the elected members would be four-fifths of the total number. (S.D. Khan, Local Govt., p. 12.) When the Montagu-Chelmsford reforms were introduced in the early 1920s the percentage of elected members of the Municipal Boards in Bengal had been raised to two-thirds of the total number.

There was no significant difference between the structure, composition and function of the local bodies in pre-partition period and those of

prove successful and the importance of which was minimised because of the existence of the District Board, were abolished in the 1930s in all the provinces except Assam where, as we have already noted, there were no District Boards.[1]

Under the elected Chairmen the general standard of administration of local bodies began to decline. As the imposition of new taxes was regarded as an unpopular measure, the elected members and the Chairmen usually did not levy new taxes. Even the existing taxes were not regularly collected. As a result, most District Boards were in great financial trouble and consequently their functions and development work suffered very badly. Moreover, the great depression further aggravated local council finance.[2] The local bodies also suffered serious set back from the nationalistic movement.[3] They were "utilised as hot bed for political agitation".[4]

Thus we find that, as Professor Morris-Jones commented,

> "The record of these local self-government bodies was not glorious. For one thing the role of adjunct to dominant district officer was not inspiring and could be tricky; yet the boards could not be given substantial responsibility without undermining in some measures the accustomed position of the key administrator. For another, almost by the time Western education in general and familiarity with public affairs in particular had become sufficiently widespread to furnish an adequate number of participants for these bodies, the nationalist movement was ready and able to persuade most likely members that this was an enterprise to be scorned. In the result, the boards contributed only a little to the satisfactory functioning of administration and the civic instruction of their members, while constituting not infrequently a source of tedium or irritation to the effectively responsible official. Nonetheless a mass of complex legislation regarding these bodies lay on the provincial statute books by 1947 and an inescapable part of the legacies of government was this somewhat inconclusive experience of arranging a marriage between local self-government and centralised bureaucracy."[5]

---

local bodies in post-partition period. These aspects of the local bodies in the post-partition period are discussed in detail in one of the sections of chapter iii (below).

[1] Malik, Local Govt., p. 24.

[2] Tinker, *Foundations*, pp. 162-164, 167. Also see Tepper, *op. cit.*, p. 98.

[3] Tinker, *Foundations*, chap. viii; also sec chap. vii.

[4] S.D. Khan, Local Govt., p. 12.

[5] W.H. Morris-Jones, *The Government and Politics of India* (London, 1964), p. 22. (Hereafter cited as Morris-Jones, *India*.)

Some Important Legacies

In August 1947 British India was partitioned and power was transferred to two independent dominions namely India and Pakistan. The then Pakistan was divided into two parts each separated from the other by over a thousand miles without any physical link. One part was called East Bengal/East Pakistan and the other part was called West Pakistan. In 1971 East Bengal bacame a separate and independent state. The name of the new state is Bangladesh.

Bangladesh comprises the following areas of British India: (i) the eastern part of the province of Bengal, (ii) Sylhet district of the province of Assam and (iii) the Chittagong Hill Tracts district.[1] Of course it was a part of the province of Bengal; but as it was in the tribal areas (adjoining India and Burma), there were some differences between the administration of this district and that of most districts in Bengal. So it was classified as 'Excluded Area'.

Pakistan comprises the following areas of British India: (i) three Governor's provinces (or part thereof): North West Frontier Province (N.W.F.P.), Sind, and the western part of the Punjab, (ii) Chief Commissioner's (now governor's) Province of Baluchistan, (iii) ten princely states, and (iv) tribal areas in Baluchistan and the N.W.F.P.[2]

Thus we find that the administrative traditions and the land tenure systems which Bangladesh and Pakistan inherited at the time of partition of British India were not the same. While Bangladesh inherited the 'permanent settlement' system i.e. the *Zamindari* system,[3] Pakistan inherited both *Ryotwari*[4] (in Sind) and

[1] *Report of the Provincial Administration Commission* (Lahore, Feb., 1960), p. 6. (Hereafter cited as *Pro. Adm. Com. Report.*) This is one of the best administrative reports in the post-partition period. This is the only report in the post-partition period which has discussed district administration in former Pakistan in some greater detail.

[2] *Ibid.*, pp. 6-7.

[3] For detailed discussion of the *Zamindari* system, see above, pp. 10-11. (In 1950 the *Zamindari* System, as we shall see below, was abolished in Bangladesh.)

[4] See above, pp. 21-22.

Mahalwari[1] (in rest of non-tribal areas of Pakistan) systems. The most important difference was that while Bangladesh mainly inherited the tradition of the Regulation Provinces, Pakistan mainly inherited the authoritarian tradition of Non-Regulation Provinces including that of tribal areas and princely states which were personal autocracies. Only two of the 17 (since 1969,19) districts in Bangladesh did not inherit the tradition of Regulation province of Bengal.[2] In Pakistan, Sind, of course, inherited the tradition of the Regulation Province of Bombay.[3] But during the second half of the last century a very rigid Non-Regulation system had been in operation in Sind.[4] So Sind also had some link with the Non-Regulation system.

1 See above, p. 23.

2 In terms of population these two districts (Chittagong Hill Tracts district and Sylhet district) are not very important. In terms of population Chittagong Hill Tracts is the smallest district in Bangladesh though in terms of area it is the second biggest district of the country. Of course the population of Sylhet district is fairly high. According to 1961 census Bangladesh had a population of nearly 51 millions of which less than 4 millions were the inhabitants of these two districts. The Non-Regulation system did not undergo (and has not undergone) any significant change in Chittagong Hill Tracts district. At the time of partition, there was no great difference between the pattern of administration in the Sylhet district and that in most other districts of Bengal.

3 Before the 1930s Sind had been a part of Bombay.

4 Sind had been annexed to the British Indian empire in 1843. The then social condition of Sind had caused and warranted the introduction of "an entirely despotic military type of rule" (Stokes, *op. cit.*, p. 243; also see O'Malley, *op. cit.*, p. 52.) in the Sind region of the Bombay Presidency. Charles Napier, the first Commissioner of Sind, had first laid down the foundations of the Sind administration. Bartle Frere, his successor, and John Jacob of Jacobabad, who had been the Deputy Commissioner of the frontier districts, had continued Charles Napier's system for a considerable period of time. (For Frere's and Jacob's administration see Woodruff, *op. cit.*, pp. 20-35.) Towards the end of the last century the administration of Sind had been gradually reorganised and placed almost on the same footing as that of other parts of Bombay. But as Sind was a backward and depressed area, its administration was not so developed as that of other parts of Bombay.

Thus we find that there are differences between the administrative legacies of Bangladesh and Pakistan. Later we shall find that there are also social and cultural differences between the two countries. All these differences partly account for the differences that, as we shall see later in other chapters, exist between district administration in Bangladesh and that in Pakistan.

Chapter II

BUREAUCRATIC BEHAVIOUR AND ATTITUDES AND THE POLITICO-SOCIAL ENVIRONMENT

Introduction

There are considerable differences between the bureaucratic behaviour and attitudes and the politico-social environment in Bangladesh on the one hand, and those in Pakistan on the other. But most of such differences are not of kind but of degree. So in the first half of the chapter a general account of bureaucratic behaviour and attitudes and the politico-social environment in both the countries is given without showing any difference between them. Then in the second half of the chapter, attempts are made to give a general picture of differences between them.

In Bangladesh and Pakistan it is generally felt that the majority of both high ranking and petty officials are authoritarian and paternal in their behaviour and attitudes. An officer usually "stands in a superior-inferior relationship to the people";[1] he thinks that he belongs to a privileged class and that if he meets ordinary people on equal terms it will lower his prestige. The following statement of a village leader, himself a retired gazetted officer, is pertinent: "Not many weeks ago we were sitting outside the District Board Hall waiting for the arrival of the Deputy Commissioner, who was to preside over a public function. Some officers were also sitting beside me. 'Shall we go in?' asked one. 'No, commoners are sitting there; we better stay here' replied the other officer."[2] The following example is also pertinent: The inhabitants of a village requested the authority for a bridge across

[1] Masihuzzaman, "Public Service Tradition in Pakistan: A Case for Revision" in the Report on the *Seminar on the Expanding Role of the Public Servant in Pakistan's Democratic Structure* (Lahore, 1964), p. 12. (Hereafter cited as *Seminar on Expanding Role.*)

[2] Quoted in Nasim Mahmud, "The Officer Today" in *ibid.*, p. 21.

the hill torrents which passed by the village. A high ranking officer went to the village to enquire into the request. On his arrival at the village he inspected the site and then left the place without talking to the villagers. Then a village leader said "We don't care if the bridge is built or not. Why did he not talk to us? After all we are human beings." When some officers were told about this incident, they said "You do not know the people; they take undue advantage if you mix with them."[1] This kind of attitude has created a situation which stands in the way of the development of a closer and more intimate relationship between the bureaucracy and the ordinary people. The situation has further deteriorated because of the fact that most officers visit rural areas only infrequently with the result that the rural population, who expect that they should be frequently visited by the officers,[2] have become somewhat apathetic towards the officers and doubtful about their sincerity.[3] These points may be further illustrated by the following two tables:

[1] Quoted in *ibid.*, p. 21.

[2] One villager said "Why don't the officers visit us? Why do they stick to their chairs in their office? Who invented all their files and what do they keep on writing in them?" (Quoted in *ibid.*, p.21.) In an interview, 45 out of 50 persons said that they felt happier if an officer visited their areas. [Aquila Kiani, "Rural People's Image of Bureaucracy" in Inayatullah (ed.), *Bureaucracy and Development in Pakistan* (PARD, Peshawar, 1963), p.390. This is a collection of articles read in the Seminar on Public Administration organised by the PARD (Peshawar) in March, 1962. Also see "Contacts Between Villagers and Public Officials in Three Villages of Layalpur Tehsil" (cyclostyled) (a case study report prepared by Zuhra Waheed) (Administrative Staff College, Lahore, 1964), p. 20. (Hereafter cited as Waheed Report.) Also see below, table II, p. 55.]

[3] A villager said "You officers want to change our ways, but what do you know of our difficulties? Do you know that in the past ten years the only departments whose staff have visited us are the Police and the Revenue? How do we know that the recommendations of these young officers who have recently begun to pay us attention are sound? They do not know us; we do not know them; who will be responsible if our crops fail? Only fools believe strangers readily." (Quoted in Nasim Mahmud, *op. cit.*, p.21.) Here the comment of a Member of a Provincial Assembly may be quoted. He was of the opinion that nowadays the officers were more bureaucratic and proud than the officers who had worked in pre-partition

TABLE I[1]

TIME ELAPSED SINCE LAST CONTACT WITH A GOVERNMENT DEPARTMENT

	No. of respondents							
	VILLAGE A		VILLAGE B		VILLAGE C		TOTAL	
	NO.	%	NO.	%	NO.	%	NO.	%
Total	50	100	50	100	50	100	150	100
Under 3 months	25	50	10	20	9	18	44	29
3 to 6 months	9	18	8	16	7	14	24	16
7 to 11 months	4	8	10	20	10	20	24	16
1 to 3 years	8	16	10	20	13	26	31	21
Over 3 years	3	6	11	22	11	22	25	17
Never	1	2	1	2	—	—	2	1

Village A is situated on a metalled road and villages B and C are at a distance of 1.5 and 6 miles respectively from metalled roads.[2]

TABLE II[3]

ATTITUDE OF RESPONDENTS TO VISITS BY OFFICERS

	No. of respondents							
	VILLAGE A		VILLAGE B		VILLAGE C		TOTAL	
	NO.	%	NO.	%	NO.	%	NO.	%
Total	50	100	50	100	50	100	150	100
Want more visits	43	86	50	100	35	70	128	85
Do not want more visits	7	14	—	—	15	30	22	15

Table I indicates that the physical situation of an area determines the degree of contact of the officer with the rural people. The least attention is received by the people of those areas which are far away from metalled roads. The officer pays more visits to

days and that the former had no sympathy. He said that when he had been a student of his village school, a high-ranking British officer had gone to the village after riding a distance of ten miles in order to settle a dispute concerning the management of the school. But "nowadays the officers can neither ride nor walk....I have no hatred against these officers. They are the boys of our own country. We thought that after independence the people of the country would get more sympathy from the officers and that they would run administration more efficiently. But we have been utterly disappointed....Of course there are a few good officers, but they are exceptions." (*East Pakistan Assembly Proceedings*, 1957, vol. xvi, no.3, pp.205-6.)

1 Waheed Report, p. 52. 2 *Ibid.*, pp. 11-12. 3 *Ibid.*, p. 59.

those villages which are located on the roadside. Even in these villages "his contacts are limited to a few influential persons whose hospitality he enjoys in return for the departmental advice or equipment he is able to place at their disposal. In this mutual benefit association the interests of the common man, who is most in need of advice, are utterly ignored."[1] It is also next to impossible for an ordinary man to meet an officer in his office, however important and urgent his purpose of meeting might be.[2]

In 1964 the Chief Secretary to a provincial Government said that one of the good practices which had been followed by the officers of the pre-partition days "was to go on extensive tours". He also pointed out that sometimes these officers had "remained on tour for months at a stretch without indulging in formalities".[3] He advised the officers to become more accessible to the people, to establish closer contact with people and to give up formalities when they were on tour.[4] No doubt there are a fairly considerable number of officers (especially young officers), who sincerely feel that they should identify themselves with the people, that the trust and confidence of the people should be gained and that the behaviour and attitude of the bureaucracy should undergo necessary transformation. But it is very difficult for them to translate their wishes into practice. An officer may be misunderstood if he tries to associate himself closely with the people. They (people) may like him and he may also gain their

[1] M.H. Sufi, "Coordinated Approach by Administrative Services for Rural Development" in *Proceedings of the Seminar on Welfare Administration* (20th Sept.—1st Oct., 1959) (Karachi, 1960), p.58.

[2] The Chairman of a Union Council said "I had to go and see some officers of Irrigation and Revenue Departments a number of times. I was always stopped at the door by the peon who said that no one is allowed to enter as the officer is extremely busy. Once I managed to get past the peon and entered the room, but I was asked to wait for hours and hours in the passage.... This is the state of affairs of a chairman. I leave you to visualise the plight of a poor illiterate and resourceless villager." (Quoted in Waheed Report, pp. 25-26.)

[3] M. Khurshid (Chief Secretary)'s speech in *Seminar on Expanding Role*, p. 41.

[4] *Ibid.*, p. 41.

confidence and trust. He may also be able to carry a good deal of influence with the people. "But he may lose influence with his colleagues and his superiors. Influence assumes shared values and attitudes."[1] He may fail to influence the decisions of his superiors and his colleagues because of his failure to share their values and attitudes. He may, therefore, fail to obtain necessary and adequate support for his schemes and programmes "from the quarters" from where "he badly needs it. This may lead to lack of effectiveness in the field. This is a crucial dilemma in any public service which has lost its contact with the people."[2]

Corruption and Unsympathetic Behaviour. Especially petty government officials behave towards ordinary people in a most unsympathetic and irresponsible manner. Usually they are very rude. Ordinary people express "highly uncomplimentary opinions about the low-level employees of almost all the departments"[3] but they are "especially dissatisfied"[4] with the attitudes and behaviour of those of the Police, Irrigation and Revenue Departments. Bribery has become almost universal among the petty officials. The Chairman of a Union Council said "However simple a task may be, it takes years for completion and then it is done by paying illegal remuneration or on somebody's recommendation."[5] If the ordinary people are asked about the extent of integrity of the officials, they "go on for hours recounting stories of malpractices and corruption by subordinates".[6]

1 Masihuzzaman, *Public Service Tradition*, p. 10. 2 *Ibid.*, p.11.
3 Waheed Report, p. 44. 4 *Ibid.*, p.43. 5 Quoted in *ibid.*, p. 26.
6 *Ibid.*, p. 44. The following examples will further illustrate the nature of corruption and malpractices by petty officials:

An application was submitted by the people of a rural area to the Irrigation Department for an extra supply of water for laying out a fruit garden. While other neighbouring areas got the supply, they did not get their supply because they refused to give a bribe. A villager said, "Most of our genuine cases remain pending in a like manner because of unsatisfactory behaviour of the canal department." (Quoted in *ibid.*, p.24.)

Once the tobacco growers were exempted from tax, which was made incumbent on the buyers. The tobacco tax realisation officer went to a village and ordered the simple villagers to pay the tax. But fortunately

Petty officers can resort to such malpractices mainly because the ordinary people, who are usually completely illiterate, are ignorant of the powers and authority of the officers with whom they come into contact and do not know what should be expected and demanded by them from these officers. The latter take advantage of the former's ignorance and exploit them and thereby create "fear and suspicion towards their very offices".[1] They submit to the authority of these officers, but they do not have faith and confidence in them. When a rural leader was told "Trust your officers; they are from among your own people", he replied "Will you please say what the officers have done so far to win this trust."[2] This comment may be partially wrong but it gives us some idea about the nature of the treatment that the ordinary people receive from the petty officials.

Scepticism about people's ability. It is generally believed by a fairly considerable number of bureaucrats that the ordinary

---

the timely intervention of an educated person saved the villagers. The same tax collector managed to realise more than 1000 rupees from the adjoining village. (*Ibid.*, p.26.)

An officer of the Animal Husbandry Department took some superior breed of chickens to a village in order to encourage poultry farming, but nobody showed any interest and he was told that whenever petty police officers had come to the village they had taken away the fattest hens from the village. So they argued that there was no use in breeding them. (*Ibid.*, p.38.)

A poor villager said "I am an old man and have a small piece of land adjacent to the canal bank. That is my misfortune because the biggest landlord of my village has access to the canal department authorities and so his animals freely graze on the canal bank. This causes breach in the bank. When the canal authorities come to know of this, they come and fine me because my fields are near the bank. The landlord goes scot free and I suffer because I have no approach to any officers. "(Quoted in *ibid.*,p.30.)

1 *A Study On Knowledge and Attitudes Towards Basic Democracies* (Social Science Research Centre, University of the Punjab, Lahore, 1964),p.13.

Another author held that "unfortunate experiences with petty government officials have engendered a deep-seated distrust and fear of government". [Henry Frank Goodnow, *The Civil Service of Pakistan* (New Haven, 1964), p.200.]

2 Quoted in Nasim Mahmud, *op. cit.*, p.25.

people are incapable of doing anything of their own accord, that they are unable to exercise initiative by themselves, and that thus, it should not be left with them; rather it should be wrested from them by the officers concerned. No doubt, it is true that, generally speaking, the people, as we shall see below, are apathetic and usually do not take initiative in public or community affairs. But many officers magnify this apathy and inactivity to an unjustifiable extent. They have little faith in the idea that the people can gradually be persuaded to shake off their apathy and that in order to get things (especially development work) done by the people they should not be forced or ordered; rather they should be approached and guided.[1] A very high-ranking local officer said "Our people are accustomed to do work only under the pressure of force. I tell you, the only practical course is to make laws for development and to enforce them rigidly."[2] When the Village Agricultural and Industrial development (V-AID) programme was introduced in the mid-1950s in order to encourage the people to undertake development work on self-help basis, it was argued that the result which was expected to be achieved through the V-AID programme could be easily and more speedily achieved with less trouble through "force and command".

> "'Why don't we put the police or the army and get quick results?' Some people are anxious to enumerate the good points they see in a Martial Law regime. 'After all everyone is on his best behaviour, streets are cleaned up, the venders have proper wire gauze to protect the eatables. People queue up outside the cinema hall and no one dares to be funny about the law.' It is true that the people revert to the old habit as soon as Martial Law is removed. It is argued that things would register a distinct improvement if Martial Law was prolonged. The assumption is falacious...fear blights imagination. Regimentation of thought and mechanized society inescapably follow."[3]

---

1 Of course, there are some officers who believe that "What really matters is the 'approach'.' Approach' is perhaps the keyword." (Nasim Mahmud, *op. cit.*, p.21.)

2 *Ibid.*, p.22.

3 Manzoor Ilahi, "Changing Concept of Administration" in *Village AID in West Pakistan* (Lahore, 1957) (A collection of reports and papers read in a number of seminars on Village-AID), p.22.

In the mid-1950s when the concept of community development began to gain importance and attention in the then Pakistan, it was strongly felt by the economic planners that "a reorientation of attitude [of the bureaucracy] is necessary"[1] and that such a situation should be created as to enable the people to "have a sense of participation"[2] in the process of planning and execution of the community development projects. Since then the government made fairly considerable efforts to reorientate the attitude of the bureaucracy.[3] As a result the attitude of the officials underwent some transformation.

Authoritarian Social Life

The psychology and the personality of an individual are shaped or moulded to a considerable extent by the social and family environment in which he grows up. "As interaction between the individual and his environment proceeds, increasingly clear and complex images of the factual nature of the relationship between himself and the world around him form in his mind."[4]

[1] *The First Five Year Plan, 1955-60* (Karachi, December 1957), p.91.

[2] *Ibid.*, p.103.

[3] Towards the end of the 1950s and the beginning of the 1960's, such institutions as the Rural Development Academy (Comilla and Peshawar), the National Institute of Public Administration (Dacca, Karachi and Lahore) and the Administrative Staff College (Lahore), were established and the curriculum of the Civil Service Academy (Lahore) was also modified. Reorientation of the bureaucratic attitude is one of the important objectives of these institutions which attach considerable importance to development administration and development economics. [See Refiq Inayat, "The Civil Service Academy" in Inayatullah (ed.), *Bureaucracy and Development*, pp. 399-415; Abdul Qayum, "The Administrative Staff College" in *ibid.*, pp. 416-424; Inayat Ullah, "National Institute of Public Administration, Lahore" in *ibid.*, pp. 425-432; Inayatullah, "Pakistan Academy for Village Development, Peshawar" in *ibid.*, pp. 433-453; *The Academy at Comilla: An Introduction* (Published by the Academy, Comilla, 1963).] From the mid-1950s quite a considerable number of seminars have been organised to discuss the importance of community development programmes and of the necessary reorientation of the bureaucratic attitude. Some of the papers presented at these seminars have already been cited and a few more are cited below.

[4] Everett E. Hagen, *On the Theory of Social Change* (Illinois, 1962), p.102.

Thus, the authoritarian and paternal social values and environment of the sub-continent, discussed below, perhaps partly account for the authoritarian and paternal behaviour and attitude of the bureaucracy and also for the fact that the ordinary people are submissive to and afraid of the bureaucratic authority.

It is not only the administrative tradition of the sub-continent that is authoritarian and paternal but her social tradition is also authoritarian and paternal. "Profound respect for authority has its grounds in several features of Indian life and history."[1] There "is a sharply defined hierarchy of sex, generation and age".[2]

Any discussion of the authoritarian pattern of social life in the sub-continent would have to take into account the nature of family life. In the family the children are not encouraged to exercise independent responsibility.[3] There is no equality between the members of a family. Almost each and every member of the family enjoys some status and authority which he exercises over other members who are younger than him or her. Thus in the family in turn one rules and is ruled. In fact "authority and status are keynotes of Indian family life".[4] This characteristic of family life affects the psychology of the family members or rather becomes a part of their subconscious minds. Outside the family life when they come in contact with others in a wider social environment (including the administrative and political environment), the psychology which has been developed in the family has a substantial influence on their behaviour and attitudes of mind. "The extraordinary central position of the family in Indian life makes it practically certain that the values it enshrines will overflow outside it to society at large."[5] Of course, the social and family environment, as we shall see below, is "slowly moving in an egalitarian direction".[6]

1 Morris-Jones, *Parliament*, p.34.

2 W.A. Robson, *The Governors and the Governed* (London, 1964), p.53. Professor Robson made this comment while discussing the social life in the sub-continent.

3 Morris-Jones, *Parliament*, p.37.

4 *Ibid.*, p.35.

5 *Ibid.*, p.35.

6 Robson, *op. cit.*, p.53.

It is generally believed that the caste system does not exist in Muslim society. This is a mistaken view. A substantial number of sociological and anthropological studies have shown that in one form or another the caste system exists in Muslim society, especially in rural areas,[1] although the caste divisions are not always very clear and well-defined. The low status castes in Muslim society are "as strictly endogamous as the low-caste Hindus".[2] The caste system is partially responsible for a sense of status and authority in society.

Moreover, in the past the people of low status were usually oppressed by the people of higher status. The former are still oppressed or dominated (especially in Pakistan[3]) in one way or another, although to a lessening and varying extent, by the latter. One of the functions of the bureaucracy was (and still is) to protect the former against this oppression and domination.[4] One author observes that

> "There was stratification even outside the pale of administration. Each layer of society tyrannised the one below. If the public servant became too soft there was a fear that the masses might suffer under the tyranny

---

1 John B. Edlefsen and Jamila Akhtar, "Caste Differential Among the Muslims of West Pakistan" (cyclostyled) (A paper read at the annual meeting of the Pacific Sociological Society, San Francisco, April, 1959), NIPA (Dacca) Reprint no.164, April, 1963. W.L. Slocum, Jamila Akhtar, Abrar Fatima Sahi, *Village Life in Lahore District : A Study of Selected Sociological Aspects* (Social Science Research Centre, University of the Punjab, Lahore, 1959), pp. 27-28. *Human and Social Impact of Technological Change in Pakistan* (*Husain Report*) (A report prepared by Professor A.F.M. Husain on a survey conducted by the University of Dacca and published with the assistance of the UNESCO) (Dacca, 1956), p.82. A.K.M. Nazmul Karim, *Changing Society in India and Pakistan* (Dacca, 1956), pp.120-136. A.K.M. Nazmul Karim, "Social Stratification Pattern Among the Muslims of Certain Districts in East Pakistan", in John E. Owen (ed.), *Sociology in East Pakistan* (Asiatic Society, Dacca, 1962), pp.135-149. Donald N. Wilbur, *Pakistan : Its People, Its Society, Its Culture* (New Haven, 1964), pp. 117-118.

2 *Husain Report*, p. 82.

3 For elaboration of this point see the second half of this chapter.

4 Of course all the officials have not always performed this function justly because sometimes they have allied themselves with the people of the higher status.

of the upper layers of society. The people actually expected the officer to behave as he did. They would have felt insecure and confused if he had behaved otherwise. Perhaps it requires emphasis that the relationship of the public servant to the public is a matter of mutual accommodation. Today society understands the public servant only if he assumes a position of command."[1]

Public Apathy

It is not always the bureaucracy that stands in the way of local initiative. On many occasions the people's own apathy constitutes a serious impediment to local initiative. In the sub-continent decisions have always been made for them by others. In the field of administration the decisions have been made by the officers, in the family by the father or mother or by some other senior member of the family and "even in the education where books and teachers were law....there was [and is] little, if any, class discussion".[2] Being unaccustomed to make their own decisions, the ordinary people find it very difficult to exercise the task of decision-making and thus they continue to look to the officials for decisions and for answers to their many problems. Their position may be compared with that of an over-protected child who develops an attitude of over-dependence. "They are now on the receiving end waiting to be told what to do and how, instead of taking the command of the situation and moulding their own life and that of the community."[3] The same problem also perplexed the British administration in the sub-continent.

"Many District Officers, particularly during the later days of British rule, fought hard against this undue dependence upon them, but it was inherent in the system. Indeed the better the District Officer, the worse the evil, for his benevolence and strength were the measure of the extent to which the local inhabitants could afford to remain inactive in public cause. To some extent this was in keeping with Indian tradition."[4]

---

1 Masihuzzaman, *Public Service Tradition*, p. 10.

2 Goodnow, *op. cit.*, p. 201.

3 Salma Omar, "Rural Communities, District Administration and Civil Service" in *Five Articles on Development Administration in Pakistan* (Asian Studies Center, Michigan State University, 1966), p. 50. (Hereafter cited as *Five Articles.*)

4 Griffiths, *op. cit.*, p. 230.

The common men believe that government is capable of doing everything under the sun and that the interest of the people will be looked after by it.

> "A school wall is cracking up in the rural area; well, the government will set it right. A small bund is needed to save the village from the seasonal floods; why not address a representation to the government, that will do the trick. The result was obvious. Such an attitude killed initiative and snapped the confidence of the people in their own capacities. They would just sit back, smoke *huqqas* and expect the government to solve their difficulties with a switch of the magic wand."[1]

One author writes that as the D.O. of three districts, he had one common experience: whenever he went into the interior of his district and enquired whether the villagers had any problem or trouble, they came forward with the following three stock requests: (a) the school building needs urgent repair, (b) the dispensary does not have medicine or a doctor, and (c) the feeder road is not in a good condition and needs repair or does not exist at all. The people insisted that the government should take care of all these things. When they were told that the District Board should attend to these things or the people themselves should undertake the responsibility of minor repairs on a self-help basis, they were not convinced. They "would insist that the real authority flows from the Government and the Deputy Commissioners, who were over-lords, could easily do a thing if they so willed".[2]

The Isolation of the Rural Population

The bulk of the population in Bangladesh and Pakistan is spread over tiny isolated remote villages.[3] The road, rail, air and water communication system is still much less developed though it has been expanding and developing.[4] Another important

1 Ilahi, *op. cit.*, p. 21. 2 *Ibid.*, p. 22.

3 The rural population in Bangladesh, as we shall see below, is relatively less isolated.

4 One author observes that "'Rudimentary' is the kindest word to describe the transportation network and facilities of the country." [Karl von Vorys, *Political Development in Pakistan* (Princeton, 1965), p. 16.] This is, perhaps, to some extent an exaggerated comment.

reason for the isolation of rural areas is the absence of mass media of communication in these areas. The newspapers, radio, television, political rallies all mainly serve the urban areas. Moreover, the rural areas, with the exception of a few, have no telephone.

Political parties are mainly urban based and have no strong roots in rural society. As they have limited recruitment from the rural areas, they fail to communicate effectively with the rural masses, with the result that while the latter have poor political information and politically are less conscious, the former know little about the latter.[1]

The absence of associational interest groups, one of the most important functions of which is to articulate the interests and demands of the society into polity,[2] is one of the characteristics of rural society in Bangladesh and Pakistan. There are a few associational interest groups mainly in urban and semi-urban areas. Usually they are weak and poorly organised and do not have the necessary degree of autonomy. Most of these organisations are either government sponsored or have flourished under the government's patronage.[3]

Later we shall see that the bureaucracy and local councils, which are institutional interest groups, are the only major channels of communication that exist between rural society and the outside world. But the members of these local bodies, who are

[1] *Basic Democracies, District Administration and Development* [It is a research report (no. 9) prepared by Inayatullah on the basis of a case study of two districts in Pakistan. (PARD, Peshawar, 1964)], pp. 11, 73, 88. [Hereafter cited as *PARD (Peshawar) Report No. 9*.]

[2] Associational interest groups include trade unions, organisations of businessmen, professional, civic, educational associations etc. For an elaborate discussion of various types of interest groups see G. A. Almond, "Introduction: A Functional Approach to Comparative Politics" in G. A. Almond and J. S. Coleman (eds.), *The Politics of the Developing Areas* (Princeton, 1960), pp. esp. 15-17, 31-35. Also see H. V. Wiseman, *Political Systems: Some Sociological Approaches* (London, 1966), pp. esp. 120-129, 134-140.

[3] Inayatullah, "Changing Character of District Administration in Pakistan" (Hereafter cited as Inayatullah, *Changing Character*) in *Five Articles*, p. 40.

not experienced and mature enough to perform their functions efficiently, usually act under the supervision and guidance of the bureaucracy.[1]

The Communication Gap Between the Rural People and the Modernised Urban Elite.

From our discussion in the preceding section, we find that the isolation of the rural areas has resulted in a communication gap between rural society and relatively modernised urban society.[2] This problem is compounded by the "emergence of a bifurcated culture" which holds "in its fold two extremely divergent components, namely a modernised elite, the urban intelligentsia", who have modern education, "and a tradition-oriented, illiterate, passive peasantry".[3] In Bangladesh and Pakistan, as in many other developing countries, there is a "wide divergence in the styles of life and the associational outlooks of those with a modern.... education and those without it".[4] While the inarticulate illiterate rural masses, who are under the strong influence of religion and traditional thoughts and practices and who are very conservative and orthodox, stand at one extreme, the modernised elite, who are relatively much more secular and progressive and who are familiar with Western ideas, stand at the other extreme. Because of their "direct exposures" to modern ideas and practices the modernised elite "have committed themselves to modernising and industrialising their societies".[5] But their ideas and views are often different from those of the

[1] See below, chaps. iii, v, vii.

[2] Also see *PARD* (*Peshawar*) *Report no. 9*, pp. 11,31.

[3] *Ibid.*, p. 281.

[4] Edward Shils, *Political Development in the New States* (Gravenhage, 1962), p. 17. (Hereafter cited as Shils, *Political Development.*) Many of the generalisations made by Professor Shils in this book apply to Bangladesh and Pakistan.

[5] L. W. Pye, "Community Development as a part of Political Development" in *Community Development Review*, March 1958, p.17. Many of the generalisations made by Professor Pye in this article also apply to Bangladesh and Pakistan.

rural population. They are "often possessed with a vision of the future which is strange to the unurbanised village masses".[1] This has further increased the distance between these two polarised classes. On the one hand the modernised elite fail to represent adequately the interests and views of the rural masses and to communicate properly their demands to the administration or the polity[2] and on the other hand they are practically unable to articulate new and modern ideas into rural society with the result that they find it extremely difficult "to motivate the rural masses to march with them in transforming the antiquated structure of the society".[3]

Of course the situation is gradually and slowly undergoing transformation. Later we shall see that a class of semi-modern and semi-educated people are emerging who can partially bridge this gap between the polarised classes (chapter vii). The nature of the future politico-social conditions or environment at the local level will "in large part be determined by the evolving pattern of relationships between an elite that is now oriented to change and a peasantry that is now still largely oriented to tradition".[4]

The Bifurcation of the Cultural Values of the Higher Bureaucracy and the General Masses

There is also a very wide bifurcation of the cultural values of the masses and the higher bureaucracy which is, relatively speaking, one of the most modernised elite classes in Bangladesh and

[1] *Ibid.*, p.17.

[2] Of course this is not wholly a new problem. As early as in 1917 the question of the "extent to which the Western educated classes represent the masses" was discussed. The *Islington Report* held that "How far the western educated class reflect the views or represent the interest of the many scores of millions in India who are untouched by western influences is a question upon which opinion differs." [*Report of the Royal Commission on the Public Services in India* (*Islington Commission*) (London, 1917), p.15.] The *Montagu-Chelmsford Report* pointed out that "the prospects of advance very greatly depend upon how far the educated Indian is in sympathy with and capable of fairly representing the illiterate masses." (para.140.)

[3] *PARD* (*Peshawar*) *Report no. 9*, p.31.

[4] Pye, *op. cit.*, p.18.

Pakistan society. At the *thana/tehsil* level such petty officers as the Circle Officer, the *Tehsilder* and other similar officers, who are culturally closer to the rural masses but also manage to partially share the attitudes of mind and the cultural values of the higher bureaucracy, serve as the "connecting link between the two traditions".[1]

As there is such a cultural bifurcation the ability of the modernised higher bureaucracy to represent or reflect adequately the interests and ideas of the tradition oriented backward rural masses and to transmit adequately to them (and also to translate into practice) the policies and programmes of the government, is questioned. No doubt, the cultural bifurcation minimises its effectiveness in these respects.[2] But in spite of this drawback or limitation it has so far played its role with relative effectiveness and success in both, to quote the terminologies of Professors Almond and Verba, the "input process" and the "output process".[3] The nature of the powers and functions of the higher bureaucracy and also that of the administrative and the bureaucratic frameworks are such as to make

1 Braibanti, *Civil Service in Pakistan*, p.298, fn. 109.

2 Moreover, the disinclination on the part of a considerable number of high-ranking and petty officials, as noted above, to associate themselves with the ordinary people further adds to this problem.

3 By "input process we refer to the flow of demands from the society into the polity and conversion of these demands into authoritative policies. Some structures that are predominantly involved in the input process are political parties, various interest groups and the media of communication." [But in Bangladesh and Pakistan, as stated in the text, it is the bureaucratic structure which is more predominantly involved in the input process than any other structure. For the predominant influence and importance of the higher bureaucracy's role in policy making matters and in the process of interest articulation, see Goodnow, *op. cit.*, pp.esp.78-79; Omar, *op. cit.*, p.51, Khalid B. Sayeed, *The Political System of Pakistan* (Boston, 1967), pp.195-201; Khalid B. Sayeed, "The Political Role of Pakistan's Civil Service" in *Pacific Affairs*, no.2, vol.31 (1958); Albert Gorvine, "The Civil Service under the Revolutionary Government in Pakistan" in *The Middle East Journal*, no.3, vol.19 (1965).] By the "output process we refer to that process by which authoritative policies are applied or enforced. Structures predominantly involved in this process would include bureaucracies and courts." [G.A. Almond

this possible. Moreover, absence or relative ineffectiveness of other institutions or organisations[1] which could play important role in these processes, has required the bureaucracy from the earliest period of the administrative history of the sub-continent to make special efforts in order to be effective in these processes.

Transitional Society and Social Tension[2]

South Asian Society was a traditional society in which life of the people was enormously and almost solely influenced by the old practices and values. It is, however, undergoing transformation[3] which began long before but is "yet far from completed".[4] Now it is a transitional society.

The "mixture of old and new practices of modern ideas superimposed upon traditional ones...[is] one of the distinguishing characteristics of a 'transitional' society".[5] The following passage will further illustrate the differences between these two types of societies:

> "People in traditional society...lack empathy, the ability to understand a wide variety of people and situations. Their horizon is narrow and they cannot conceive of moving outside it. If in the process of transformation there is some widening of horizons through some acquisition of certain technical skills (including literacy and access to mass media) without the development of appropriate motivational goals and associational sentiments, all one learns about others in this new wide world is that

---

and S. Verba, *The Civic Culture* (Princeton, 1963), p.15.] In playing its role in these processes, the higher bureaucracy has usually been assisted by the subordinate or lower bureaucracy. But the success or effectiveness has mainly depended on the ability of the higher bureaucracy.

[1] For example, Political parties, interest groups, development councils, cooperative societies etc.

[2] The impact of social tension on district administration is discussed in chapter vi (below).

[3] Morris-Jones, *Parliament*, p.35. Also see *PARD* (*Peshawar*) *Report no.9*, p.281.

[4] Morris-Jones, *Parliament*, p.35.

[5] Fred W. Riggs, *Administration in Developing Countries*: *The Theory of Prismatic Society* (Boston, 1964), p. 12.

they cannot be 'trusted'. This causes aggression and hostility which can no longer be restrained by traditional institutions."[1]

Lessening Respect for Old Social Values and Authority. In a period of transition "it is perhaps to be expected that there should be something of a revolt against old values".[2] Moreover, in a transitional socicty there "is also a more general reluctance to accept hitherto venerated authority. This attitude when it encounters the old deeper feelings, reacts with some violence. This accounts for some of the abuse",[3] not only in society but also in politics and administration.

In the family and in the society at large the younger generations in South Asian countries, who have now much less respect for old and orthodox social values and authority, are increasingly becoming impatient and eager to exercise more and more independent authority and responsibility and to make themselves as free as possible from the control and influence of older generations.[4] But on the other hand, the older generations are not

[1] Alfred Diamant, "Political Development: Approach to Theory and Strategy" in John D. Montgomery and William J. Siffin (eds.), *Approaches to Development: Politics, Administration and Change* (New York, 1966), p.46.

[2] Morris-Jones, *Parliament*, p.35. [3] *Ibid.*, p.35.

[4] But though the authoritarian patterns of social and family life are gradually being challenged by younger generations, it may not be correct to conclude that the younger generations have an egalitarian outlook or that they do not have an authoritarian bent of mind. As they have been brought up in an authoritarian family and social environment it is not possible for them to shake off this authoritarian influence completely. Thus the nature of control and influence that they exercise (or will exercise in the future) over those who are much younger than themselves, is also authoritarian although the extent of their authoritarianism is not as great as that of older generations. Thus the nature of social interactions is very complicated and presents itself in a puzzling paradox. Of course the younger generations' impatience for exercising more and more independent responsibility and authority may be regarded as a sign that society is slowly moving away from authoritarianism to egalitarianism. But society is yet far from egalitarianism. It is still an authoritarian society with some rebels within it. And these rebels themselves, as just mentioned, have not yet developed an egalitarian attitude.

psychologically prepared to part with some authority or influence hitherto exercised by them and to adjust their position in the changing social environment. They are in varying degrees determined to retain their authority and influence as before. This attitude of younger and older generations results in a sense of hostility. This is a situation which seriously undermines the respect for and the influence of authority and creates a sense of strong contempt for it.

The Lack of Social Homogeneity. "The unduly harsh and unsympathetic attitude towards authority also stems from the lack of social cohesion."[1] In Bangladesh and Pakistan, as in India, "social life is cut up into many enclosures, and thought reared on such foundations gets fractured into particularisms".[2] Society, in fact, is stratified both horizontally and vertically into a number of social classes on the basis of economic, professional, linguistic, regional, rural, urban, tribal, family (kinship), religious and other backgrounds.[3] The values and the folkways or mores of a social class are often different from those of many other social classes. Those of one social class can even be diametrically opposite to those of another social class. As a result, in South Asian society, which is thus a heterogeneous society, there is no universal standard of social values or outlook.[4] People,

[1] Morris-Jones, *Parliament*, pp. 35-36.

[2] Ashok Mehta, *Politics of Planned Economy*, p. 31, quoted in *ibid.*, p. 33.

[3] The above mentioned class divisions, with the exception of a few, are neither very rigid nor very clear and well defined. As a result they are not easily identifiable. But close observation reveals that such divisions determine to a considerable extent the pattern of social interactions.

[4] No doubt, an egalitarian and homogeneous society is also divided, in one way or another, into a number of social classes and there are differences between the social values of these classes. But the extent or degree of these differences is not, perhaps, so wide as is the case in authoritarian and heterogeneous South Asian society.

Here it may be mentioned that in comparison with Pakistani society, Bangladesh society, as we shall see below, is much more egalitarian and homogeneous. Of course, there is no doubt that within Bangladesh society there are also considerable differences and inequality but the extent of such differences and inequality is much less than the extent of those in Pakistani society.

therefore, become unduly conscious of the differences that exist between the social or cultural values of various classes. The members of the same class or somewhat similar classes dogmatically believe that their values are the right guides to correct practices and behaviour in society. Moreover, the lack of social mobility strenthens such dogmatic beliefs because it makes it difficult for members of one social class to understand or appreciate the values of other classes.[1] This is a situation which strongly encourages mutual feelings of hostility or contempt between classes. Thus the "absence of cultural homogeneity and the lack of social mobility...become sources of social tension".[2]

Moreover, in a transitional society "new social classes emerge which aspire to elite status and begin to compete vigorously and often successfully with the traditional elites".[3] Bangladesh and Pakistan have also witnessed a similar development which further adds to social tension. This situation becomes further aggravated by the attitudes of those who think or believe that the classes to which they belong are "superior" or "upper" classes. Such attitude remained unchallenged when the society was traditional in character. But during a period of diversified changes[4] it is inevitable that such attitudes should be resented with increasing bitterness. This resentment is, in turn, resented by the privileged classes who monopolise most benefits or advantages that society can offer.

All the factors that we have discussed in this sub section of the chapter stand in the way of the development of a sense of unity

[1] Of course, social mobility is gradually, but slowly, increasing.

[2] Mehta, *op. cit.*, p. 31, quoted in Morris-Jones, *Parliament*, p. 33.

[3] Milton J. Esman, "The Politics of Development Administration" in Montgomary and Siffin (eds.), *op. cit.*, p. 66. Some of the generalisations made in this article apply to Bangladesh and Pakistan.

[4] The socio-economic structure and the attitudes towards the old values are undergoing change, speed of industrialisation and urbanisation is increasing, the communication system is being improved and expanded, and the political consciousness of the people, the educational and professional facilities, and the contact between the urban and the rural areas are increasing in varying degrees. (We have already discussed some of these changes.)

among the component units of the society and make favouritism or nepotism rampant in politics and administration. The following generalisations will illustrate these points: "Parochialism or particularism, afflicting societies which inherit a powerful kinship system, caste and communal loyalties, linguistic diversities, religious heterogeneity, or ethnic dissimilarities resist...unity."[1] Such diversities "confine the loyalties, and the capacities for loyalty, to a narrow, loyally circumscribed range. They inhibit the flow of loyalty to the larger territory and to the population which inhabits it and potentially constitutes the nation....the particularistic spirit which is....maintained and reinforced, spreads throughout the society and hinders the formation of the vague, intermittent, and genuine unity of spirit which is necessary for a modern political society".[2] This is a situation which also creates "so many strongly competing loyalties. A man may be irresponsible in relation to the State or Central politics [or administration], simply because he has a high sense of responsibility to his caste or district....It is also a familiar point that nepotism often reflects a loyalty to family and clan in excess of loyalty to the state".[3] "Strong attachments to kinship, caste and local territorial groups mean that, in administration and adjudication, it is more difficult to obtain justice, since there will be a tendency for....[the] administrator to favour his known men, his caste-fellows and co-believers. It will also be reflected in favouritism in appointments to administrative office."[4]

Increasing feeling of frustration. In transitional societies "new technologies and new needs give rise to new and more specialised institutions, especially in the growing urban areas. New institutions generate new roles [and] opportunities...."[5] Similarly, in Bangladesh and Pakistan new institutions, new needs and demands in old institutions and in the society at large, and the vacuum created by the departure of the British and some other

[1] Shils, *Political Development in the New States*, p. 33.
[2] *Ibid.*, p. 13. [3] Morris-Jones, *Parliament*, p. 37.
[4] Shils, *Political Development in the New States*, p. 13.
[5] Esman, *op. cit.*, p. 66.

communities, have resulted, in the course of last twenty five years, in an enormous increase in the prospects in and the scope of almost all higher professions—government services, business, industries etc. The positions now held by most people in different professions are almost certainly higher, often indeed much higher, than the positions that they could have expected to hold twenty or twenty five years ago. But the paradox is that there is a growing feeling of frustration. Most people are not satisfied or content with the positions that they hold or with the prestige or influence that they enjoy or with their incomes. There is a peculiar feeling among most people, especially among the educated (both better and less educated) and moneyed people that they deserve more. They usually think that those who, relatively speaking, hold better positions or enjoy more prestige or influence or earn better incomes, are not more brilliant or more capable. Often the former even think that the latter are less brilliant or less capable.

It seems that the increase in the scope of and prospects in most professions itself is responsible for these feelings of frustration because it has inspired such unlimited hopes and ambitions that the frustration is, in fact, unavoidable. Moreover, it appears that frustration also results partly from the fact that in Bangladesh and Pakistan nepotism, money and contacts with the high-ups in political, administrative and social hierarchies play a vital role in furthering one's interest, and partly from imaginary grievances. The second cause (i.e. imaginary grievances) is mainly the result of the first one because the above mentioned malpractices are so widespread that it is not surprising that most people imagine that for these malpractices they have failed to get, for example, promotions or appointments or permits or licences, which, they think, they deserve. It seems that frustration breeds hatred and antagonism which, in turn, become added sources of social tension.

But while the scope of and the prospects in various higher professions have increased, the conditions, especially the economic conditions, of poor and landless peasants, who constitute the bulk of the population, seriously deteriorated in the 1950s and

60s.[1] Thus we find that the causes of frustration of educated and moneyed people and those of frustration of poor peasants are not the same. While in the case of the former increased prosperity is the cause of frustration, in the case of the latter increased poverty is the cause of frustration.

The Desire to Show Off. Most people are inclined to display as publicly as possible their power, wealth, etc. They like to make their position or authority felt by others. In society or in politics or in administration one usually likes to exercise or impose his authority assertively or rather demonstratively over those who are below him and to make them feel that he is their superior. This attitude or behaviour is, of course, nothing new because the society, as noted above, was (and still is) authoritarian. But nowadays it is common for individuals to continue to maintain such attitudes towards those below them while strongly resenting similar treatment from those above them. If possible, they flout or disregard them. It appears that if an individual can flout or in one way or another undermine the authority of someone above him, he gets some sort of satisfaction and feels proud. He thinks that he has been able to show or demonstrate his authority to others and to win recognition from them by being aggressive. Social tension itself is, perhaps, mainly responsible for this attitude. It seems that this situation has mainly resulted, as noted above, from the fact that the respect for authority and for old social values is lessening, that the positions which most people now hold are much higher than the positions they could have expected to hold in the past and that they doubt and question the ability of one another and, therefore, criticise and denounce one another.

Concluding Comments. In this section of the chapter we have noted the factors that cause or accentuate social tension in some South Asian countries. In total all these factors create a situation

[1] In the early 1960s Aktar Hameed Khan, the former Director of the Academy for Rural Development, Comilla observed that the "village is now full of frustration, bitterness and distrust". [Comilla-US AID conference Report (cyclostyled) (Comilla, June 1963), p. 13.]

which seriously undermines the respect for and the influence of authority and discipline and encourages irresponsibility. People often become contemptuous, abusive and parochial, lack tolerance, patience, mutual respect and understanding, show arrogance, and indulge in irresponsible utterances and criticisms. Such behaviour and attitudes have a considerable impact on administration and politics. They are reflected in the behaviour and attitude of the officials or politicians towards one another and towards the public and vice versa. Social tension, as we shall see in chapter vi, partially accounts for administrative or intra-bureaucratic tension in Bangladesh and Pakistan.

Here it may also be mentioned that in transitional societies

> "governments typically involve a mixture of the traditional and the modern, the village elder or traditional chief combined with the urban, sophisticated secretariat official. This mixture can take place along several dimensions—for example, the urban-rural dimension extending from Bombay—New Delhi—Calcutta [or Dinajpur—Dacca—Chittagong or Karachi—Lahore—Peshawar] to remote hill tribes, with 'village India' [or village Bangladesh or village Pakistan] lying stretched out in between; or the class and community dimension extending from the university graduate and administrative officer to the illiterate and mystic...such a broad mixture of attitudes, practices and situations [is] heterogeneous...[Thus] substantive administration in any transitional society is quite heterogenous".[1]

"The presence" in Bangladesh and Pakistani society as "in Indian society of so many kinds of diversity, each of great importance, produces in political [as well as administrative] life a maze of cross currents".[2]

The Landed "Aristocracy" in Pakistan

In Pakistan the *Zamindars*, who constitute a very insignificant proportion of the population, own a very considerable proportion of the land in the country. In 1949 a survey revealed the following facts: In the Punjab more than 60% of the land was owned by only one per cent of the land-owners. In the North West Frontier province the big *Zamindars* held more than 50% of the cultivated land. In Sind about 5% of the population owned all the land of

[1] Riggs, *op. cit.*, pp. 12-13. [2] Morris-Jones, *Parliament*, p. 33.

which only 20% of land was held by the peasant-proprietors.[1] From time to time minor land reforms were introduced in West Pakistan which had, in fact, very insignificant effects on the pattern of ownership.[2] In 1959 the then Martial Law regime introduced a land reform scheme which had only minor effects. It "cannot be said that the West Pakistan land reforms [introduced in 1959] achieved anything astronomical".[3] The "basic structure of...agrarian economy remained unaltered".[4]

In an agricultural country like Pakistan, in which most people are solely dependent on land for their livelihood, the large concentration of landownership in a few hands has a very adverse social, political, economic and administrative effects. A great majority of the people in Pakistan are "under the thumb of *Zamindars*"[5] because the latter by virtue of their control over lands are in a strong position to maintain a very firm control over the social, political and economic life of tenants and labourers who are completely dependent on their mercy. The miserable conditions of the tenant class may be illustrated by the following passages:

> "*Haris* of Sind...have only one interest in life—food...the *hari* who has cultivated a piece of land for several generations does not know how long he will be allowed to stay on it. Fear reigns supreme in the life of the *hari*...The *Zamindar* might at any time get annoyed with him and oust him—he might have to leave his crop half ripe, his cattle might also be snatched and he might be beaten out of his village."[6]

---

[1] M. Haris Jafri, Elizabeth K. Bauer, Nikki R. Keddie, *The Economy of Pakistan* (Human Relations Area Files, South Asia Project, University of California, Berkeley, New Haven, 1956), p. 26. Figures on land ownership in Baluchistan are not available, but it is well known that the tribal and the feudal chiefs have control over most parts of the region, which, in terms of population, constitutes a very insignificant portion of Pakistan.

[2] Talukder Maniruzzaman, "Group Interests in Pakistan Politics, 1947-58" in *Pacific Affairs*, 1966, vol. 39, nos. 1 and 2, pp. 86-87.

[3] Herbert Feldman, *Revolution in Pakistan* (London, 1967), p. 59.

[4] Pakistan Today (cyclostyled) (London, summer, 1960), p. 27.

[5] *Time* (Magazine, Asia edn.), Sept. 17, 1965, p. 22.

[6] M. Masud (ICS/CSP), Minute of Dissent, *Hari Inquiry Committee's Report* (Govt. of Sind, n. d. It was published towards the end of the 1940s or the beginning of the 1950s), p. 3, quoted in Goodnow, *op. cit.*, p. 80.

"The *Zamindar* might at any time send for the *hari* for *begar* (forced labour) for the construction of his house or sinking of a well, or some other minor work. The *hari* might be called to come with his plough and bullocks to cultivate the private fields of the *Zamindar* or to spend a few days on shoot with him; or to render some domestic service. He is thus always at the beck and call of the *Zamindar* and he dares not refuse as annoyance of the *Zamindar* would spell his doom."[1]

"[In Pakistan] socially the position of the tenant...is that of a serf. Practically he belongs body and soul to the landlord who being the most influential man in the area succeeds in closing all channels through which the oppressed cultivator could get his position redressed by resort to law."[2]

Under such circumstances the *Zamindars* are virtually the masters of their tenants. They are, in fact, the unchallenged hereditary leaders of rural society of Pakistan. This hereditary leadership has never been seriously challenged partly because of the absence of a strong middle class and the lack of strong associational interest groups[3], and mainly because of the fact that during elections the tenants have no other alternative but to support his *Zamindar* or his nominee. The *Zamindar* knows that "he could

[1] Masud's Minute of Dissent, quoted in *Constituent Assembly of Pakistan Debates,* Feb. 14, 1956, vol. 1, p. 3060. The member of the Constituent Assembly, who quoted the above passage and who was from East Bengal, further added that "Now Sir, that is the condition of the *haris* in Sind. I myself have toured Sind and have seen some places. I also went there for hunting purposes and I have seen the poor cultivators of Sind...Conditions of the *haris* are becoming worse and worse." (*Ibid.*, p. 3060.) The position of the tenants is worst in Sind. But that of those in other parts of Pakistan is also not much better. Next passage in the text will give us some idea of the position of the tenant in various parts of Pakistan including Sind.

[2] Jafri *et. al.*, *op. cit.*, p. 28.

[3] The *Zamindars* have always prevented the growth of various types of interest groups outside their own sphere of control and influence. Their particularistic and vested interests have always made it indispensable for them that all sources of power, position and status in rural society should be controlled by them. Control over land and relatively higher education and social status have not only strengthened or legitimatised their claim for "exclusive leadership in the eyes of the bureaucracy as well as illiterate rural masses" [*PARD* (*Peshawar*) *Report No. 9*, p. 50], but also made it easier for them to provide leadership to various institutions or organisations (e. g. cooperative sociaties, local councils, development councils,

count on their vote as a matter of obligation. Since an unco-operative cultivator could be cut off from his only source of income, it was not likely that there would be many such persons. In any case, these constituents would neither know how their 'representative' voted nor be informed enough to care."[1] Thus a *Zamindar* or his nominee can win an election easily and hold office "without being subject to pressures, advice or even correspondence from his constituent".[2] Therefore, the elected bodies in Pakistan which take on "some of the characteristics of a conservative club" can "hardly be described either as representative or responsible".[3]

The feudal character of the land tenure system in Pakistan has thus given many *Zamindar*-politicians and their family members "the advantage of 'protected' constituencies"[4], with the result that "many hereditary leaders....are active in political life" and the "politician's map of...West Pakistan is dotted with the signs of entrenched areas of personal power".[5] The

---

etc.) which have been formed by the government from time to time.

Moreover even when the division of property or land threatens their powers and position, the leadership is usually maintained through marriages and alliances between themselves. Their social position is further "fortified by the myth of belonging to 'respectable castes'". (*Ibid.*, p. 49.)

The social welfare or community development programmes, the execution of which needs the support of the *Zamindars*, further add to their social position. [Masihuzzaman, "Administrative Obstacles to Voluntary Organisations in Pakistan" in Inayatullah (ed.), *Bureaucracy and Development*, pp. 72-73.] They try to utilise these programmes for their own benefit and for enhancing their own authority and influence. Although sometimes they make some "purely superficial improvements" (Goodnow, *op. cit.*, p. 84.), they are not at all interested in radical and significant development of rural society which would improve the socio-economic conditions of the tenant. The superficial improvements that they make "rather increase his dependence on his 'benevolent' landlord". (*Ibid.*, p. 84.)

1 *Ibid.*, p. 81. 2 *Ibid.*, p. 81. 3 *Ibid.*, p. 82.

4 G. W. Choudhury, *Constitutional Development in Pakistan* (Dacca, 1959), p. 260. Also see G. W. Choudhury, *Democracy in Pakistan* (Dacca, 1963), p. 125.

5 Keith Callard, *Pakistan: A Political Study* (London, 1958), p. 50.

leading landed families, in fact, hold the key to politics.[1] Before and since partition of British India in 1947, a very considerable section of the members of the assemblies and of the local councils have always come from landed families, and often held key political offices[2] and have successfully prevented any attempt to bring about radical land reforms.

Of course very big *Zamindars* or the leading members of their families, do not directly participate in the affairs of the lower local councils (i.e. *Tehsil* and Union Councils). Usually petty *Zamindars* and medium and small landowners become the members of these lower local councils and often serve as the agents of the big *Zamindars*. The Chairmen of the Union Councils, who are also ex-officio non-official members of the next higher (i.e. *Tehsil*) council, are usually bigger landowners or lords than the members of the Union Councils.[3] It has been observed in a research report that the fact that "the Chairmen are relatively bigger landowners shows that the informal hierarchy of power existing in the rural society is being formalised by the institution of local

[1] W. H. Morris-Jones, "Experience of Independence—India and Pakistan" in *Political Quarterly*, vol. 29, no. 3, 1958, p. 235. (Hereafter cited as Morris-Jones, *Political Quarterly*.)

[2] Such as those of the President and the Prime Minister of (former and present) Pakistan, the Chief Ministers and the Governors of the provinces, the members of the central and provincial cabinets, etc.

[3] These points may be illustrated by the following tables :

TABLE A

COMPARATIVE DATA ABOUT SIZE OF LAND OWNED BY U. C. CHAIRMEN AND MEMBERS OF THE TWO DISTRICTS IN PAKISTAN AND THEIR COMPARATIVE LAND TENURE STATUS

Acres	Ch. %	Mem. %		Ch. %	Mem. %
1 to 5	14	38	Absentee landlord	22	15
16 to 50	22	32	Landlord cum cultivator	67	43
Above 50	64	30	Owner cultivator	11	39
			Tenants	0	3
	100	100		100	100

Source: *PARD (Peshawar) Report No. 9*, p. 65.

Footnote continued on page 81

government. Influence and power...are significantly associated with the size of land one owns."[1]

As the big *Zamindars* figure very prominently in the politics of Pakistan, they are in a most advantageous position, especially since 1947, to exert considerable pressure on and to interfere in the administration of the district. Of course it does not mean that a big *Zamindar* can always bully a very high-ranking official—especially the District Officer who, as noted above, is traditionally the most powerful officer in the district. He is

TABLE B

THE SIZE OF LAND OWNED BY U. C. MEMBERS OF THE RAWALPINDI DIVISION AND NOWSHERA TEHSIL IN PAKISTAN

Acres	Rawalpindi %	Nowshera %
0	3	7
1-20	46	56
21-40	19	15
41-60	12	6
61-80	4	4
81-100	5	4
Above 100	11	8

Source: *Selected Union Councils in Rawalpindi Division* (A case study report prepared by Inayatullah) (PARD, Peshawar, 1962), p. 3. (Hereafter cited as *Rawalpindi Study.*) *Study of Union Councils in Nowshera* (A case study report prepared by Inayatulah) (PARD, Peshawar, 1961), p. 7. (Hereafter cited as *Nowshera Study.*)

In the *Rawalpindi Study* it has been stated that the "geometric mean of land owned by the total group is 18.5 acres, while it is 100 acres for the chairmen's group which is significantly higher than the former". (p. 4.)

Here it may be mentioned that small landowners can also become the members of the Union Councils mainly because of the fact that one member represents roughly one thousand people but within the jurisdiction of a Union Council, which extends over a few villages, a large number of big or medium size landowners are not usually available. Small landowners, therefore, get an opportunity to become members. But in varying degrees, they usually remain under the influence of the, relatively speaking, big landowners.

[1] *PARD (Peshawar) Report No. 9*, p. 66. In Bangladesh where there are no feudal landlords, the chairmen are usually bigger farmers than the members. Some chairmen and members come from other occupational classes.

responsible for the maintenance of law and order, and the collection of land revenue and has a great deal of patronage in his hands.[1] A *Zamindar* is, therefore, dependent on him for various kinds of favours—both big and minor favours. The former may be in a position to exert pressure on the latter through some high-ups in the political hierarchy and get something done by the latter. But he cannot always exert pressure on the D.O., unless he himself is a very influential and dominant figure in the national and provincial politics or unless he has very close and intimate contact with party bosses or influential ministers.[2] Moreover, a *Zamindar* may not belong to the ruling party or parties and thus, at least temporarily, is incapable of exerting political pressure on the D.O. In short, we may say that in the event of a tug of war between a *Zamindar* and the D.O., whether the former or the latter would win, in fact, would depend on the time and circumstances and on the issues and personalities involved.

Thus in the normal course, the *Zamindars* (with the exception of politically influential *Zamindars*) usually make special efforts to maintain a good relationship with the D.O. In rural areas where most people are illiterate, their higher social status and education make it easier for them to have an easy access to the D.O. and other high-ranking officials. When these officers go to a rural area on tour, the *Zamindar* of the area usually becomes the host and extends all shorts of hospitality.[3] They also consider him as the only suitable person with whom various problems of the rural area can be "intelligently" discussed.[4] The

1 Here it may be mentioned that the law and order aspect of district administration is also a subject of great interest to *Zamindars* because they often indulge in some activities which amount to serious criminal offences.

2 In chapter vii we shall see that in the early 1950s, one Mr. Sayeed Qureshi, a very close relation of Mr. Daultana (the then Chief Minister of the Punjab and one of the biggest *Zamindars* in Pakistan), virtually became the 'overlord' of the Sargoda district and could get illegal things done by the D.O.

3 Inayatullah, *Changing Character*, p.41.

4 Goodnow, *op. cit.*, p.81.

Zamindar, in fact, plays the role of an intermediary between the rural people and the higher bureaucracy. Thus, unlike its counterpart in Bangladesh, the higher bureaucracy in Pakistan has much less direct contact with the rural population.

As the *Zamindar* is in a position to maintain a cordial and friendly relationship with the D.O. and other high-ranking officials, it is not difficult for him to exert enormous influence over the petty officials at the *tehsil* and other lower levels, who also feel obliged to the *Zamindar* for the sumptuous hospitality extended to them by the latter.[1] The petty officials also cannot afford to incur the displeasure of the *Zamindar* because of the latter's cordial relations with the D.O. and other high-ranking officials.

The interests of the *Zamindar* including those of his village receive maximum attention by the administration because the information and data on which district administration depends to a considerable extent in making its decisions concerning law and order, revenue and general administration, the allocation of finances for development works and the extension of new services to rural areas, are provided by the petty *tehsil* level officials, who, as noted above, are obliged to and are indirectly controlled by the *Zamindar* and also because of his close contact with the higher bureaucracy. As the interests of the *Zamindar* are not usually in harmony with those of ordinary rural people, their interests are not forcefully placed before the district bureaucracy.[2] Thus in Pakistan, unlike in Bangladesh, the information and data which are communicated by the higher bureaucracy to the government often reflect, wholly or partially, the interests of the *Zamindars*.

Although in Pakistan, the CSP and other high-ranking officials and the big and medium size *Zamindars* have much in common, and although a fairly considerable section of the former, as we shall see below, come from the landed "aristocracy", it would be wrong to conclude that the high-ranking officials

[1] Inayatullah, *Changing Character*, p.41.

[2] *PARD* (*Peshawar*) *Report no 9*, p. 285.

and the *Zamindars* are allies and that the former always support the latter even in actions that are completely unlawful or very irregular.[1] The training and the orientation that the high-ranking officials receive in the government service make their outlook and attitudes somewhat different from those of the *Zamindars* and also make them conscious, in varying degrees, of the fact that for the purpose of socio-political development and the improvement of agrarian economy, land reforms are essential though a considerable section of them may not wholeheartedly approve of radical or sweeping land reforms. It is probably this consciousness that has prevented a closer alliance between the higher bureaucracy and the *Zamindars*.[2] As a result, it is mainly from the D.O. and other high-ranking officials that the ordinary rural people receive some degree of protection against oppression by *Zamindars*.

The Landed "Aristocracy" in Bangladesh

So far as the position of the landed "aristocracy" is concerned, the situation is completely different in Bangladesh. A brief account of the position of the *Zamindars* vis-a-vis the tenants in the past will put our present discussion in better perspective.

The Bengal Tenancy Act of 1885 gave the tenants the occupancy and transferable rights of their land. Important amendments were made to the Act in 1928, 1938 and 1940 "mostly in favour of the tenants".[3] These amendments considerably strengthened the position of the tenants vis-a-vis the *Zamindars* and brought "a sense of security and confidence among tenants hitherto unknown in the history of the system of land tenure in the country".[4] The tenants "virtually became the masters of their own destiny" and by the end of the 1930s the extortionate methods of assessment

[1] Of course, sometimes the former may overlook or indirectly support such unlawful activities under political pressure. Sometimes nepotism and favouritism also account for this.

[2] Goodnow, *op. cit.*, p. 84.

[3] *Gazetteer of Dacca District* (Dacca, 1969), p. 367.

[4] *Ibid.*, p. 367.

and collection of rents by the *Zamindars* "came to an end".[1] With the dwindling of the *Zamindars*' power and influence, the rise in the prices of agricultural products, and the increasing political consciousness among the masses[2], "a new resurgence and aggressiveness among the tenants were distinctly visible".[3] Moreover, the government, public opinion and the press were all in favour of the tenants. "The pendulum had now swung so completely in the direction of the tenants that.... it became difficult for them [*Zamindars*] to realise even legal rents[[4]] in time and in due proportion".[5] So far as the position of the tenants vis-a-vis their landlords was concerned, the *Zamindari* system was almost a dead system and the government of British Bengal was seriously considering the question of its complete abolition. That final blow to the system, as we shall see below, came after partition of British India.

1 *Ibid.*, p. 367.

2 Here it may be mentioned that politically British Bengal was one of the most advanced provinces. "Rural public opinion was most articulate in Bengal; the rural *bhadrolok* [the members of the middle as well as 'upper' classes; literally means gentlemen] and great Zamindars were alike much more interested in political questions than the vast majority of rural India." (Tinker, *Foundations*, p. 78.) Even the "cultivator took an interest in politics, participating actively in the local election which determined the membership of his union board". (Goodnow, *op. cit.*, p. 78.) The local bodies in British Bengal were much more vigorous than the local bodies in those areas which now constitute Pakistan. Unlike their counterparts in those areas, the *Zamindars* in British Bengal did not have complete control over the local bodies. These bodies in parts of British Bengal rather lessened the influence of the *Zamindars* on rural society. Here it may also be mentioned that the press in British Bengal was very vigorous. From the very beginning of the second half of the last century, it had been critically examining the social, political and economic problems of the province and playing a very vital role in accelerating the process of political awakening in the province.

3 *Gazetteer of Dacca District*, p. 368.

4 Previously the *Zamindars* could even have forced their tenants to pay more than they had been legally supposed to pay. This illegal rent had been called *abwabs*. (*Ibid.*, p. 367.)

5 *Ibid.*, p. 367.

Unlike the *Zamindars* in those parts of British India which now constitute Pakistan, most *Zamindars* in British Bengal were Hindus.[1] After partition most of them left East Bengal for India with the result that the position of the *Zamindars* as a pressure group was further weakened.[2] When the government of East Bengal decided to abolish the *Zamindari* system it encountered no serious opposition because of "the fact that most of those who would lose land through nationalisation were Hindus".[3] Finally the *Zamindari* system was completely liquidated by the East Bengal Acquisition and Tenancy Act of 1950. But, in fact, it was the political and social consciousness of the Bengali people which in the course of this century gradually paved the way for its elimination. Professor Braibanti observed that "the spirit of Bengali independence compelled the development of vigorous local self-government and early demise of large land holdings, while in the Punjab feudal conditions of serfdom prevailed and the *Zamindari* were not challenged".[4]

In Bangladesh the influence of the landed "aristocracy" is now almost nil. In the absence of *Zamindars* the rural population may be classified into the following three categories: (a) surplus farmers, (b) middle farmers and (c) landless or near landless farmers.[5] The surplus farmers are those who have surplus land and/or money. They form a very small minority of the villagers. The middle farmers are those who have one to five acres of land. Table III will give us some idea of landholdings in the rural areas of Bangladesh.

The surplus farmer usually leases his land. Sometimes he also employs landless labourers to cultivate his land or part thereof. Many surplus farmers are rural traders and money

1 At the time of partition, of 2237 big *Zamindars* in British Bengal only 358 were Muslims. (Wilbur, *op. cit.*, p. 219.)

2 Myron Weiner, "The Politics of South Asia" in G.A. Almond and G.S. Coleman (eds.), *op. cit.*, p.209.

3 Wilbur, *op. cit.*, p. 219.

4 Braibanti, *Research*, p.47. Also see above, fn. 2, p. 85.

5 Comilla US AID Conference Report, p. 8.

TABLE III

AREA OF FARMS, CLASSIFIED BY SIZE[1]

SIZE OF FARMS (IN ACRES)		% OF FARMS
Under	0.5	13.0
0.5 to under	1.0	11.0
1.0 ,, ,,	2.0	27.0
2.0 ,, ,,	5.0	26.0
5.0 ,, ,,	7.0	12.0
7.0 ,, ,,	12.0	7.0
12.0 ,, ,,	25.0	3.0
25.0 and over		1.0

lenders.[2] They are, in fact, the well to do class and the vested interests in rural society of Bangladesh. In their capacity of land lessers and money lenders they are in a position to squeeze and to exercise some control and influence over the small middle farmers and the landless labourers or near-landless farmers. But there is a world of difference between the extent of the control and influence exercised by the surplus farmers and the extent of those exercised by the *Zamindars* in Pakistan who, as noted above, are virtually the masters of rural society.

Other Differences Between Bangladesh and Pakistan

The "language, climate, economic and social life and attitudes of mind" of Bangladesh are widely different from those of Pakistan.[3] Professor Braibanti observed that "Probably no region" in the sub-continent, "certainly none" in the north

> "could be more opposite to the Punjab in externals and in spirit than East Bengal....The Bengalis are by ethnic origin more closely related to Southeast Asia than to Persia and Afganistan, the twin fountainheads of Punjabi and Pathan culture[4]. More importantly, Bengalis have a

1 *1960 Pakistan Census of Agriculture*, vol. i (n. p., 1962), p. 29.

2 Comilla US AID Conference Report, pp. 9-10.

3 Morris-Jones, *Political Quarterly*, p. 235. Also see Naville Maxwell in *The Sunday Times*, Feb. 23, 1969. (Professor Morris-Jones and Mr. Maxwell discussed the differences between former East and West Pakistan.)

4 Similarly in 1959 another author commented that "West Pakistan looks out upon the Middle East, whereas East Pakistan looks to Southeast

remarkably homogeneous culture, rich in art, music, dance, language, poetry and philosophy, epitomized in Rabindranath Tagore[1]. A highly developed aesthetic sensitivity makes them more akin to the culture of Southeast Asia than to the practical earthiness of the Aryan Punjabi[2]. Their temperament moulded by riverine, tropical lands in which they live, combines a quick, volatile sensitive independence with a keen love of political activity[3] and of intellectual disputation...so pervasive is the quality of Bengali culture that it has developed a very strong corporate sense. Bengalis, more aware of their Bengali culture than are Punjabis of their own heritage, are more likely to cling together and support each other simply because they are Bengalis."[4]

Relatively faster political development in Bangladesh and its causes. British Bengal, which "was in many ways the most important province in India"[5], was politically much more advanced than the provinces which (or the part of which) now

---

Asia." (Charles Burton Marshall, Reflections on a Revolution in Pakistan" in *Foreign Affairs*, vol. 37, no. 2, 1959, p. 252.)

[1] Nobel Prize winner Rabindranath Tagore was the great Bengali poet, novelist and dramatist.

[2] Another writer observes that "They [Bengalis] are neither Aryans nor Arabs....Nature has given their mind and body a distinctive stamp." [S.A. Kalam, "Social Questions in Bengali Fictions" in S.S. Husain (ed.), *Dacca University Seminars on Contemporary Writing in East Pakistan* (Dacca, 1958), p. 60.]

[3] Another writer observed that "Bengalis...are apt in competitive politics." (Marshall, *op. cit.*, p. 253.)

[4] Braibanti, *Research*, pp. 46-47. Professor Braibanti made the comment while discussing the impact of cultural differences between former East and West Pakistan on their styles of administration.

Time magazine also observed that "the only bonds between the diverse and distant wings...were the Islamic faith and Pakistan International Airlines. Sharing neither borders nor cultures, separated by 1,100 miles of Indian territory....Pakistan is an improbable wedding of the Middle East and Southeast Asia. The tall, lightskinned, Pathans, Baluchis and Sindhis of West Pakistan are descendants of the Aryans who swept into the subcontinent in the second millennium B.C. East Pakistan's slight dark Bengalis are more closely related to the Dravidian people...The Westerners, who eat wheat and meat, speak Urdu, which is written in Arabic but is a synthesis of Persian and Hindi. The Easterners eat rice and fish, and speak Bengali, a...language of Indo-Aryan Origin." (*Time*, Aug. 2, 1971, p. 30.)

[5] Wilbur, *op. cit.*, p.219.

constitute Pakistan.[1] During the period between 1947 and 1971, a series of vigorous political movements, which resulted from the economic, political and administrative grievances of East Bengal, further added to a considerable extent to the political consciousness of the Bengalis.[2] But in West Pakistan, where the people

[1] Also see above, p. 85 (fn. 2), p. 86 (Professor Braibanti's comment). Sometimes it is argued that in British Bengal it was the Hindus who were politically conscious and advanced. No doubt, it is true that in British Bengal Muslims were less articulate and less advanced than the Hindus; but at the same time, the Muslims in this region were much more articulate and advanced than the Muslims in those parts of British India which now constitute Pakistan.

[2] The following brief account of the nature of economic, political and administrative grievances will illustrate the causes and the nature of political movements and developments in East Bengal:

During the first several years of the post-partition (1947) period, the central government (which in one way or another was always under the control of West Pakistani politicians) continuously rejected the demand of the people of East Bengal that the Bengali—the language of the majority of the people of former Pakistan—should be made one of the state languages of the country. As a result there was a serious political unrest throughout East Bengal. Later Bengali along with Urdu was made the state language of former Pakistan. But Urdu was given more prominence by and received greater attention from the central government (Karl von Vorys, *op. cit.*, pp. 76, 80, 90-91.)

There was wide economic disparity between East Bengal and West Pakistan which constituted the major source of increasing bitterness and resentment in East Bengal. In 1967 Professor Khalid bin Sayeed observed that "In terms of the contribution of manufacturing to gross domestic product, East and West Pakistan started from about the same level, but after independence, the rate of industrial growth in West Pakistan far outpaced that in East Pakistan." [Khalid B. Sayeed, *The Political System of Pakistan* (Boston, 1967), p.199.] Bengalis strongly felt that the factor responsible for the higher rate of economic growth in West Pakistan was that the "center has shown preferential treatment to West Pakistan industrialists by granting them foreign exchange, by issuing licences and permits for the establishment of new industries and by making bigger allocations, loans and grants, both from its own resources as well as from foreign aid". (*Ibid.*, p.201.) Though East Bengal earned more foreign exchange than West Pakistan, a much larger amount of foreign exchange was allocated to feed the needs of the latter. The following tables illustrate some of these points:

were less articulate and politically less conscious, the situation was different. West Pakistan seldom witnessed political

TABLE C

TOTAL EXPORTS AND IMPORTS : 1947-1962 (RUPEES IN BILLIONS)

	EXPORTS	IMPORTS
E. Beng.	13.8	7.9
W. Pak.	9.9	18.7

Sayeed, *Political*, p. 199.

TABLE D

ALLOCATIONS OF FOREIGN LOANS AND CREDITS : 1947-1961

	DOLLARS
E. Beng.	$ 127,876,526
W. Pak.	$ 519,886,426

Vorys, *op. cit.*, p. 98.

TABLE E

DOLLAR DEVELOPMENT LOAN FROM THE U.S.A. (1955-65)

E. Beng.—$ 100.3 million. W. Pak.—$ 282.8 million.
During the fiscal year of 1958, West Pakistan received a dollar development loan of $ 12.8 million whereas East Bengal received none. (Sayeed, *Political*, p. 201.)

Because of rapid economic growth in West Pakistan the per capita income in that region was much more than that in East Bengal. The disparity between the per capita incomes of the two regions increased from 88 rupees in 1959 to 150 rupees in 1967. [*The Times* (London), June 25, 1968.]

The Bengalis were also very conscious of the fact that they were very poorly represented in higher public services and in the armed, air and naval forces. (Sayeed, *Political*, pp. 194-195.) Of course, at the time of partition (1947) the number of Bengali Muslims, who were in those services and forces, had not been very large. But although this number increased during 1947 to 1970 as a result of the demand and pressure from the Bengalis, it was still much less (especially in the forces) than the number of West Pakistanis who were in those services and forces. Bengalis strongly felt that the central government made no sincere effort to substantially increase this number and that the Bengalis were not deliberately appointed to the key posts. All these disparities made the Bengalis highly sensitive. In 1965 Karl von Vorys observed that the "issue of parity between the [two] wings is no longer limited to public investment. It has become the acid test of legitimacy for *all* national endeavours. East Pakistani politicians, journalists, businessmen, teachers, workers and students are alert to the slightest deviation." (Karl von Vorys, *op. cit.*, p.102.) As a result of such disparities, Bengalis strongly felt that complete provincial autonomy and adequate control over the resources of the region were essential in order to safeguard their interests. Moreover, greater political consciousness led Bengalis to demand fully democratic government, complete freedom of the press and the release of political prisoners, and to strongly oppose the system of indirect election and restricted franchise. All these factors, as noted

movements solely caused by political or economic questions or issues.[1]

The fact that in Pakistan political orientation is more traditional than in Bangladesh[2] relatively slows down the process of political modernisation and development in the former. Moreover, in Pakistan the people are under the profound influence of religion with the result that literature and the political and social issues are often influenced by religious and sectarian issues.[3]

---

above, are responsible for frequent political movements in East Bengal. In the first general election (1970) of the country the Bengalis overwhelmingly voted in favour of complete autonomy for East Bengal. But the then martial law regime completely ignored the election result and tried to crush the Bengalis ruthlessly with the consequence that the political movement for complete provincial autonomy resulted in a war for complete independence. [See *The Sunday Times* (London), April 18, 1971; *Time* (Magazine), Aug. 2, 1971; *Newsweek* (Magazine), Aug. 2, 1971.] Finally in a few months time former East Pakistan emerged as sovereign independent state of Bangladesh.

1 Though the importance of political movements in the process of political awakening is not significant in a politically advanced and articulate society, their importance in a country like former Pakistan was considerable which may be illustrated below:

As the presidential and assembly elections were held on the basis of very narrowly restricted franchise, during these elections no efforts were made to address and to establish close contact with the people. Moreover, as noted above, political party organisations, interest groups, and the mass media of communications were either absent or ill organised and inefficient. As a result, people, especially in West Pakistan, had poor and inadequate political knowledge and their grievances and demands were not adequately voiced. But, as was the case in East Bengal, political movements could at least partially, make the people of West Pakistan aware of some important political and economic issues and voice some of their grievances. Of course in the late 1960s and early 1970s West Pakistan witnessed some political movements and demonstrations caused mainly by political issues. So it appeared that the political culture of West Pakistan was in the process of change.

2 *PARD (Peshawar) Report no. 9* observed that "in West Pakistan political orientation is more traditional than in East Pakistan". (p. 53.)

3 Mr. Justice Munir, the former Chief Justice of former Pakistan and the late Mr. Justice Kayani, the former Chief Justice of the Punjab High Court, gave a revealing account of the extent and nature of the impact

The so-called religious leaders, i.e. *Ulema* (usually addressed as *Maulana*), who are responsible for a "ceaseless clamour for an Islamic state"[1], who are extremely dogmatic and fanatical in their religious beliefs and outlook, who are bent on following and preserving centuries-old Islamic laws in toto and who want to establish a theocracy[2], command great respect among the ordinary people of Pakistan and exert enormous influence on

---

of religious and sectarian issues on the political issues and activities of West Pakistan in the *Report of the Court of Inquiry Constituted Under Punjab Act II* of *1954 to Enquire into the Punjab Disturbances of 1953* (*Munir-Kayani Report*) (Lahore, 1954).

[1] *Ibid.*, p. 231.

[2] The following brief discussion will illustrate these comments:

The *Ulema* strongly oppose the concept of secular and modern democratic national state which was advocated by Jinnah, who at the time of partition (1947) declared that "the new state would be a modern democratic state, with sovereignty resting in the people and the members of the new nation having equal rights of citizenship regardless of their religion, caste or creed". He also declared that "you are free to go to your temples, you are free to go to your mosques or to any other places of worship in this State of Pakistan...that has nothing to do with the business of the State...in course of time Hindus would cease to be Hindus and Muslims would cease to be Muslims, not in the religious sense because that is the personal faith of each individual, but in the political sense as citizens of the State." (Quoted in *ibid.*, pp. 201-202.) When Mr. Justice Munir and the late Mr. Justice Kayani asked the *Ulema* "whether this conception of a State was acceptable to them...everyone of them replied in an unhesitating negative". To them "a State based on this idea is the creature of the devil...None of the *Ulema* can tolerate [such] a state..." (*Ibid.*, p. 203.) According to the *Ulema*, in an Islamic state the non-Muslims "will have no voice in the making of laws, no right to administer the law and no right to hold public offices". (*Ibid.*, p.212.)

The *Ulema* hold that "Legislature in its present sense is unknown to the Islamic system." (*Ibid.*, p. 211.) They argue that the legislature, which consists of those persons who are not experts on Islam, cannot make laws for an Islamic state and that the Islamic laws can meet all the needs of the modern age. *Maulana* Abul Hasanat, President, Jamiat-ul-Ulema -i-Pakistan said "Our law [i.e. Islamic law] is complete and merely requires interpretation by those who are experts in it. According to my belief no question can arise, the law relating to which cannot be discovered from the Quran and the hadith." (Quoted in *ibid.*, p. 211.)

The Government set up a Commission on Marriage and Family Laws in the mid-1950s. *Maulana* Ihtisham-ul-Haq, a very prominent

them. The following passage from a letter written by a District Officer to the Divisional Commissioner will illustrate the extent of such influence:

"The Muslim Family Laws Ordinance, 1961, was not readily accepted by the people of this district on account of enormous opposition by the *Ulema*. The grip of *Ulema* is very strong...The Chairmen [of Union Councils] do not cooperate in implementing...[the] Ordinance. The instances of violation of the...Ordinance are not usually reported by the Chairmen.

"In the final review I may add that the Basic Democrats [members of the Union Councils] of this district do not cooperate in the implementation of the Ordinance, unless the *Ulema* approve of the provision."[1]

---

member of the *Ulema* class, was one of the 7 members of the Commission. Six members recommended that Islam should be reinterpreted according to the changed modern environment. *Maulana* Ihtisham-ul-Haq widely disagreed with their views and issued a separate statement. He held that the Mulims with modern education were unable to understand the inner meaning of Islam and this led them to believe that under the changed circumstances, Islam needed to be readjusted and reinterpreted. He argued that many Muslims under the modern influence wanted to alter, in the name of elasticity, all those values of Islam which were not in conformity with the modern way of life. (*Gazette of Pakistan, Extraordinary*, Aug. 30, 1956, p. 1572.)

In fact the "*Ulema* would like to adopt the institutions of the early caliphate; they want to reproduce a society which no longer exists and a polity which was suited to the early days of Islam, as if all that was done at that time was the final interpretation of Islam and as if it were not possible for the human intellect to deviate from it in any detail. In constructing an Islamic constitution, the *Ulema* feel Pakistan's task is to look back to the past history of Islam and reproduce once again the actual state of affairs that obtained in the seventh century...They...wish to adopt...every...institution which was set up in the seventh century." (G. W. Choudhury, *Constitutional Development*, p. 66.)

For a detailed account of *Ulema*'s attitudes towards religion, Islamic state, *Jihad* (Holy War), religious minorities, secular and modern democratic national state, etc., see *Munir-Kayani Report*, esp. part iv (pp. 187-236).

1 *Quoted in PARD* (*Peshawar*) *Report no. 9*, p. 167. Here it may be mentioned that the Muslim Family Laws of 1961, which modernised and rationalised the institution of marriage and divorce procedure, had the whole hearted support of the intelligentia. But these laws "invited the wrath of the *Mullahs*" (i.e. the so called religious leaders). [*The Guardian* (London), Nov. 14, 1968.]

The serious anti-*Ahmadi* (a sect within the Muslim community) riots, which broke out in 1953 in several places of the Punjab and which ultimately caused and warranted the imposition of Martial Law in the Lahore city, are also a glaring example of the enormous influence of the *Ulema* over the ordinary people of Pakistan. The "determination of certain politico-religious leaders [i.e. *Ulema*] to return to public importance"[1] and their propaganda against the *Ahmadis* were responsible for Anti-*Ahmadi* riots.[2]

But in comparison with Pakistan, in Bangladesh the influence of religion and of the *Ulema* on the general public is much less. In the latter there is also no such renowned and influential *Maulanas* as Moududi, Ihtisham-ul-Haq and others. Moreover, unlike most Urdu writers, the Bengali writers, with the exception of a few, are secular in their thoughts and ideas.[3] The modern Bengali literature which "represents a very notable creative achievement"[4] and which has been "influenced by British and European ideas of liberalism and humanitarianism"[5] has considerable influence on the way of life and the social and political attitudes of the people of Bangladesh. In this country, the political and social behaviour and attitudes are relatively less influenced by religion. In 1967 one author pointed out that "it is apparent that there is a difference between the political culture of the two provinces. East Pakistan's public opinion seems to get stirred up very easily on political and linguistic issues; whereas West

1 Morris-Jones, *Political Quarterly*, p. 235.

2 Also see below, chap. iv.

3 A Bengali writer, who was a central Minister in former Pakistan, writes that "Let him...in proper time in a proper mood, come to religion as a blissful retirement from the humdrums of active social life...Let religion begin where politics ends. The two must not meet." A.M. Ahmad, "Secularism Versus Religion in Politics" in *The Concept of Pakistan* (monthly Journal, Dacca, November, 1964), p. 42.

4 Edward Shils, *The Intellectual Between Tradition and Modernity: The Indian Situation* (Hague, 1961), p.71.

5 Sayeed, *Political*, p. 188.

Pakistanis seem to react strongly only when religious or ideological issues are raised".[1]

Another factor which has further contributed to the process of political awakening in Bangladesh is that, in comparison with Pakistan, the rural areas in the former are politically less isolated. The student community in Bangladesh, who come from almost all sections of society, who have always acted as the spearhead of all political movements and many of whom go back to their village homes during vacations, have become the "carriers of a new political consciousness to the village and a contact point between urban centered political parties and rural masses".[2] Moreover, relatively higher degree of literacy (see table iv), the high density of population and the small size of the country, have further facilitated the communication and the mobility of political ideas in Bangladesh.[3] The percentage of literates

TABLE IV

LITERACY PERCENTAGE OF THE PEOPLE AGED 5 YEARS AND OVER[4]

	BANGLADESH	PAKISTAN
All areas	21.54	16.3
Urban areas	47.71	33.0
Rural areas	20.16	10.9

in the rural areas of Bangladesh is double the percentage of those in the rural areas of Pakistan. Moreover in comparison with

1 *Ibid.*, p. 194.

2 *PARD (Peshawar) Report no. 9*, p. 11. This point was also emphasised by one of the participants during the discussion of the paper namely "Constitutional changes and the Dynamics of Political Development in Pakistan" (cyclostyled), presented by H.A. Alavi at the postgraduate seminar on Political Institutions held on November 15, 1967, at the Institute of Commonwealth Studies, University of London. The present author was a participant.

3 Pakistan is almost six times larger than Bangladesh but it has 7 million less population than Bangladesh. According to 1961 census, in the former the average density of population was only 138 per square mile, whereas in the latter it was 922 per square mile. (See below, chap. iii.)

4 *Census of Pakistan, 1961*, vol. 2 (Dacca, 1962), p. iv-2; *Ibid.*, vol. 3 (Karachi, 1962), p. iv-5.

Pakistan, "the population is more sophisticated"[1] in Bangladesh. It is, therefore, relatively much easier to articulate political ideas in rural society of the latter.

Although in terms of population officially classified tribal areas in Pakistan constitute an insignificant proportion of the country, most of the non-tribal areas have also some tribal or clannish affinities. Such affinities, the absence of a strong middle class, the domination of the *Zamindar* feudal class and the relative lack of political consciousness among the general masses, have enormously added to the servile attitude of the ordinary people and to the authoritarian attitude of the "upper"classes with the result that in comparison with Bangladesh most people in Pakistan are much more subservient to those above and much more dominant over those below. This is also one of the reasons which has made Pakistani society relatively less conducive to political awakening and to the development of democratic and egalitarian environment.

East Bengal was much less industrialised than West Pakistan. Most of the big industries and business concerns in the former were also owned and controlled by the industrial and business magnates of the latter.[2] As a result, in East Bengal there was no powerful commercial class. Moreover, recently most of the big industries and business concerns have been nationalised in Bangladesh. In this country, as noted above, the *Zamindar* feudal class also no longer exists. It is the middle class which is the most influential class in Bangladesh. But in Pakistan the middle class is very small and its influence and importance in society and in politics are much less. Thus while in Pakistan "Political power came to be concentrated in these two groups"[3] (i.e. the *Zamindar*

[1] L.F. Rushbrook Williams, "Basic Democracies as Institutions of Local Government in Pakistan" in the *Journal of Local Administration Overseas*, vol. i, no. 4, Oct. 1962, p. 255.

[2] One survey revealed that the Bengalis had control over only 4% of the big industrial and business enterprises in the whole of former Pakistan. (G.F. Papenek, "The Development of Entrepreneurship" in *The American Economic Review*, LII, 1962, p. 49, cited in Muniruzzaman, *op. cit.*, p. 88.)

[3] *Ibid.*, p.84.

and the commercial classes),[1] in Bangladesh it "came into the hands of the professional middle class".[2] In Pakistan the leadership of these two classes, who are in fact the vested interests in society, who have practically nothing in common with the general masses and who have not encouraged, or rather discouraged the active participation of the masses in the political process, has not made any significant contribution to the political development and to the change in the socio-economic structure of Pakistan; whereas in Bangladesh, the leadership of the middle class, the members of which come from and represent in varying degrees the values, attitudes and interests of various sections of society, has further contributed to and accelerated the process of politicization of Bangladesh society.

In conclusion we may say that due to all the factors discussed in the preceding pages of this section of the chapter, Bangladesh has far outpaced Pakistan in the process of political development. In 1967 it was aptly observed that "as East Pakistan is lagging behind West Pakistan in economic development, in terms of political development it is West Pakistan which is backward as compared to East Pakistan"[3] with the result that "political consciousness and communication are intense in East Pakistan".[4]

Administrative Traditions. As noted in chapter I, Pakistan inherited the tradition of Non-Regulation provinces in which D.O.s and other officers had enjoyed enormous discretionary powers and also that of political agencies and princely states which had been personal autocracies; whereas, Bangladesh inherited that of Regulation Provinces in which they had enjoyed relatively much less discretionary powers and had been required to perform their functions within a relatively more rigid framework of rules and regulations.[5]

[1] Here it may be mentioned that the *Zamindar* class is much more dominant and influential in the field of politics than the commercial class whose influence is mainly localised in the urban areas.

[2] Muniruzzaman, *op. cit.*, p.84.

[3] Sayeed, *Political*, p. 258.

[4] Marshall, *op. cit.*, p.253.

[5] See chapter i, p. 29-34 (especially see p. 33, fn. 5). Also see p. 51.

Socio-Political Backgrounds of Higher Bureaucracies. There are considerable differences between the socio-political backgrounds of the high-ranking officials in Bangladesh and those of the high-ranking officials in Pakistan. In the former, both petty and high-ranking officials (including former CSPs,[1] who, as we shall see in chap. iii, are the elite of the bureaucracy and hold most of the top administrative posts at district, and higher levels) come from different classes or sections of society, whereas in Pakistan, a considerable section of the high-ranking officials mainly come from the landed "aristocracy" and other "upper" class families.[2] The environment in the educational institutions of the two countries, which has an enormous impact on the attitudes of mind of the recruits to the higher public services, is not the same either.[3] We have already noted that in Bangladesh the student community always acted as the spearhead of all political movements, and fought for the interests of the area and against the economic and other disparities. In fact, they played a very important role in voicing the economic,

[1] The members of the Civil Service of Pakistan which is the successor to the famous Indian Civil Service (ICS).

[2] Mr. Burgess, a former ICS and a former Director of the Civil Service Academy, Lahore, in which the CSP probationers of former East and West Pakistan received their pre-service training, held that "East Pakistan is a nation of small cultivators—there are few big landlords, few rich men at all. But East Pakistan is entitled to its share of vacancies. So the social background of the service [i.e. ICS/CSP] has changed. It has become democratised in something of the way that Oxford and Cambridge have become democratised under the impact of post-war taxation and post-war awards. It no longer draws the majority of its recruits from the 'best' families or even from the upper class; consequently, it no longer draws its ideas from as narrow a sphere as formerly. Diversity everywhere—of race, of culture, of language, of social and economic background." (Georffrey Burgess, "The Pakistan Civil Service" in *The Listener*, vol. LVIII, Sept. 19, 1957, p. 420.)

[3] Here it may be mentioned that those persons who want to join the Civil or other higher public services sit for the Superior Service Examination almost immediately after having completed their college or university education or while studying at the postgraduate level, mainly because of the fact that at the time of recruitment to higher public services, one must be between the ages of 21 and 25 and a graduate,

political and other grievances of the Bengali population. Thus before entering the public services most Bengali members of these services usually remained associated with or at least intimately aware of the issues that were involved in these movements. Their behaviour and attitudes as government officials are, therefore, influenced in varying degrees by these issues and reminiscent of their student life.[1]

Because of the differences that exist between the socio-political backgrounds of the bureaucracies of Bangladesh and Pakistan and also between the environment in the educational

[1] The following example will further illustrate the point: We have already noted that the demand that Bengali—the language of the majority of the people of former Pakistan—should be made one of the state languages of the country led to a vigorous political movement throughout East Bengal. During that movement, on February 21, 1952 police opened fire on students demonstration in Dacca with the result that several persons died. Every year the people of Bangladesh observe the 21st of February as the *Shahid Dibosh* (Martyrs' Day) and pay their homage to those who died on that day as a result of the police firing. The day was the turning point in the history of Bengali nationalism. In 1966, the Bengali students of the Punjab University held a meeting on that day in order to discuss various aspects of the language movement. They invited the Bengali CSP probationers who were undergoing training at the Civil Service Academy, Lahore. The Director of the Academy, who was one of the senior most CSP officers (formerly an ICS officer) and held the rank of a Secretary to the central government, told the probationers through another high ranking officer that "they, being government officers, are not supposed to participate in a students' meeting". Almost all the Bengali CSP probationers did not follow that instruction and participated in the meeting and some of them also gave lectures. (The present writer came to know about this because he had happened to be the class-mate of some of these probationers and he went to Lahore in February 1966, in connection with his field work for his present study and also attended that meeting.)

Here it may be mentioned that in Bangladesh during the war for Independence (March–December, 1971) many district officers and other high ranking and petty civil, police and military officials organised resistence against Pakistan army and took part in and actively supported the liberation movement. During this period many Bengali officers of the Pakistan Foreign Service, who were stationed abroad, defected and played a very important role in mobilising world opinion in favour of Bangladesh movement.

institutions of the two countries, the attitudes of mind of the bureaucracies of one country are naturally different from those of the bureaucracies of the other country. Thus while performing their official functions, they behave and react differently under the same circumstances. The bureaucracies in Bangladesh are more sympathetic towards the general masses, more aware of their problems and difficulties, much more tolerant about political and students' activities and movements and deal with political or students' demonstrations with greater restraint and patience than their counterparts in Pakistan. Professor Braibanti aptly pointed out that "Bengali administration [has] a different quality from that of the Punjab. It is more egalitarian in demeanor, more democratic in outlook, more informal, closer to the people in mood and attitude, and less haughty".[1] In Bangladesh, "district administration is also strong, but its style is leavened by the more egalitarian social structure of Bengal".[2]

From the foregoing discussion in this section of the chapter we find that there are considerable differences between the social, political and administrative environment or conditions of the two countries. In Bangladesh the officials, as we have just noted, are relatively less authoritarian and paternal in their approach and outlook. And at the same time the people of this country, relatively speaking, are more conscious and more assertive and less apathetic and less afraid of bureaucratic authority.

[1] Braibanti, *Research*, p.47. [2] *Ibid.*, p.161.

CHAPTER III

THE ADMINISTRATIVE FRAMEWORK AND PATTERN OF ADMINISTRATION

Introduction

Before going into the details of district administration, a brief discussion of the structure of the government at the central and provincial levels[1] will enable us to have an idea of the place of district administration in the total administrative framework of Bangladesh/Pakistan and its position in relation to the administrative hierarchy stretching from the central level down to the grassroot level.

From 1947 to 1958 parliamentary form of government was in operation in former Pakistan. In October 1958 an army *coup d'etat* replaced the parliamentary system by an authoritarian presidential system. After the emergence of Bangladesh as a separate and independent state, parliamentary system has been again introduced in this country.[2] In Pakistan the presidential system is still continuing.

Secretariat. Below the Cabinet there is a Secretariat as well as Directorates. The Secretariat consists of all the Ministries/Secretariat Departments. Generally speaking, though Ministries and Secretariat Departments may be regarded as synonymous terms, there is a minor difference. While at the central level they are called Ministries, at the provincial level they are usually called Departments or Secretariat Departments. In this book both Ministries and Secretariat Departments are usually referred to as Secretariat Departments.

[1] In Bangladesh, as noted above, there is no provincial government.

[2] *Provisional Constitution of Bangladesh Order* (Dacca, 1972). For important provisions of the Order see *The Bangladesh Observer*, Dacca, January 12, 1972.

Each Secretariat Department is in charge of a member of the Cabinet. He is assisted by permanent government officials namely Secretary, Additional Secretary (only in very big departments), Joint Secretary (if the volume of work is very heavy), Deputy Secretaries, Section officers[1] and a huge clerical staff. Under the Minister, the Secretary is the head of the Secretariat Department. The position of the Secretary "is analogous in relation to the Minister to that of the permanent Under Secretary of a British Department."[2]

Directorates. Besides the Secretariat there are Directorates. They are also called 'Functional' or 'Operating' or 'Attached' Departments of the Secretariat Departments. Each Directorate is required to operate in close contact and under the general supervision of its counterpart in the Secretariat. For example, the Directorates of Education, Agriculture and Police mainly work in close collaboration with the following Secretariat Departments: Education, Agriculture and Home respectively.[3] There is no uniform designation for the Heads of the Directorates. For

[1] In British India and in the first decade of former Pakistan the designation of the Section Officer was Assistant Secretary.

[2] *Simon Report*, vol. i, para. 312. *Decentralisation Commission's Report* (1909) had also held that the position of the Secretary "corresponds very much to that of a permanent Under Secretary of State in the United Kingdom." (para. 20.) The position of the Secretary and the Secretariat has not changed in Bangladesh and Pakistan. Mr. Ashok Chanda also compares the position of the Indian Secretary with that of the permanent Under Secretary in the U.K. [Ashok Chanda, *Indian Administration* (London, 1958), p. 19.]

[3] Each Secretariat Department usually deals with several Directorates which perform more or less similar or inter-linked functions. For example, the Secretariat Department of Agriculture deals with the Directorate of Agriculture, the Directorate of Agricultural Marketing, the Directorate of Cooperation (Cooperative Societies), the Directorate of Fisheries, the Directorate of Forests etc. But in the normal course, usually a Directorate is not required to work with more than one Secretariat Department except under some special circumstances. The number of the Directorates is much more than that of the Secretariat Departments. In the *Report of the Provincial Re-Organisation Committee*, Part II (Dacca, 1962) there is a list of the Secretariat Departments and their respective Directorates. (pp. 154-156.)

example, the designations of the Heads of the Directorates of Education, 'Buildings and Roads' and Police are respectively Director of Public Instructions, Chief Engineer and Inspector General of Police.[1]

Differences Between the Secretariat and the Directorate. In short we may say that the Secretariat is "responsible for framing of governmental policies" and the Directorates are "responsible for carrying out these policies."[2] Sir Richard Tottenham in 1946 and the Provincial Administration Commission in 1960 aptly explained the differences between the Secretariat and the Directorates in the following passages :

> "At the risk of over simplification, I would say that the function of the Member [i.e. Cabinet Member] is to decide policy, of the Secretary to provide the material on which to reach such decisions, and of the Executive Head to carry the decisions into effect. On the analogy of the human machine, the Member would represent the Will, the Secretary the Brain and the Executive Head the Hands. I do not for a moment suggest that no Member or Executive Head should be expected to think and no Secretary to take a decision or see that it is followed up. All three parts of the machine must obviously work in the closest touch with each other. My point rather is that the duties of the Secretary should correspond broadly to those of the Staff in the Army Organisation and that just as the Staff Officer does not himself conduct operations in the field, so the Secretary should not ordinarily be charged with executive duties."[3]

> "It should be the duty of the Secretary to assist the Head of the Province in the formulation of policies and to direct and control their implementation by setting up a proper system of reporting, progressing and follow up actions. The Secretariat can and should lay down rules and principles within which executive functions should be performed. It is important however that it should not assume executive functions which it is neither intended nor qualified to perform. The Directorates have to implement the policies."[4]

---

[1] In the immediate post-71 period the chief of the police force of Bangladesh was called Director-General of Police.

[2] *Report of the Council for Administration of West Pakistan* (Lahore, Feb. 1955), p. 7. (Hereafter cited as *Council Report on West Pakistan.*)

[3] *Report on the Re-Organisation of the Central Government* : *1945-46* (*Tottenham Report*) (It was reprinted by the NIPA, Karachi, in July 1963. NIPA Reprint Series No. 1.), p. 12.

[4] *Pro. Adm. Com. Report*, p. 89.

In practice, however, the functions of the Directorates do not remain confined only to the execution of government policies. On the basis of their technical knowledge they are supposed to advise the Secretariat in framing policies.[1] The Directorates are responsible for the technical soundness or the specialised aspects of policies which are not "subjected to any technical examination by the Ministry concerned."[2] It is felt that "no realistic policies can be framed in the 'rarified mahogany-walled atmosphere of the top echelons' without lively appreciation of the conditions in the field and of experience gained in implementation."[3] Thus it is always emphasised that there should be "joint participation and two-way traffic between the policy making and the executive agencies."[4] But at the same time it is also pointed out that "though interlinked, they are nevertheless distinct and separate"[5] and that these two establishments should not be combined into one.[6] Of course, occasionally a few Heads of the Directorates have been appointed as ex officio Joint or Deputy Secretary thus blurring the line of division of responsibilities between the Secretariat and the Directorates. But such ex officio appointments are usually made on very rare occasions and temporarily.

In practice, however, the officers of the Directorates who are posted at the central, provincial and regional headquarters are

[1] *Pro. Adm. Com. Report*, p. 90.

[2] *Report of the Administrative Reorganisation Committee* (Efficiency and O. & M. Wing, Karachi, 1963), p. 271.

[3] *Pro. Adm. Com. Report*, p. 91. [4] *Ibid.*, p. 91. [5] *Ibid.*, p. 91.

[6] From time to time it has been suggested by some, especially by the staff of the Directorates that one person should hold both the posts of the Secretary and the Head of the Directorate, and that there should be one establishment instead of two i.e. Secretariat and Directorate. This view has not been accepted by all important Commissions and Committees which have studied this subject because it has been felt by them that for better and efficient administration they should be kept separated. (See *Tottenham Report*, p. 64 ; *Council Report on West Pakistan*, p. 7 ; *Pro. Adm. Com. Report*, pp. 91-92 ; *Report of the Administrative Reorganisation Committee*, p. 271.)

not first line executors of policies. Usually they do not participate directly in the process of execution. "As the executants of Government's policies the Directorates have to set up field units."[1] Unlike the Secretariat Departments, the entire staff of which are stationed at the central or provincial headquarters, the Directorates have a chain of officers stretching from the central/provincial headquarters down to various layers of district administration. The officers of Directorates posted at central, provincial and regional levels give necessary instructions to their respective field officers and frequently go on tour to supervise and direct the work of the latter.[2] Thus the role of the higher level officers of the Directorates in their capacity as the executants of government policies is mainly confined to supervision and guidance.

It is also generally felt that some of the local policies and programmes should be prepared locally because each local area has its own problems which are not always similar to those of other areas. Thus on the basis of the broad policies of the government and under the supervision of the central/provincial and regional officers of Directorates, the local officers as well as local councils formulate some policies and plans and execute them.[3]

Differences Between the Central and the Provincial Secretariats. The organisation and the structure of the central and the provincial Secretariats are more or less same. Of course, there is one major difference between them. At the head of the provincial Secretariat there is an officer called Chief Secretary. He is not directly responsible to any particular Minister but to the chief Minister/Governor[4] and to the cabinet as a whole. It is observed that in the province

1 *Pro. Adm. Com. Report*, p. 90.

2 Of course, in Pakistan where, unlike Bangladesh, there are provincial level officers, the central level officers seldom go on tours.

3 See below, chap. v.

4 In the provinces of former Pakistan the Chief Minister was the real executive in the pre-58 period, whereas the Governor was the real executive in the post-58 period. In present Pakistan also, the Governor is the real executive in his province.

> "The permanent head of the administration...is the Chief Secretary who is responsible for general administration and the proper functioning of the Secretariat and who handles many civil service matters, keeps Cabinet minutes and issues orders on behalf of the Cabinet. Much of his authority is derived from his responsibility for exercising administrative supervision over the division commissioners and district officers in the province."[1]

But at the central level there is no such officer as Chief Secretary. Of course in the post-partition (1947) period and in the immediate post-martial law (1958) period there was an officer called Secretary General. He was the head of the central Secretariat of former Pakistan. On both the occasions this post was filled for a very short time. This post has remained vacant for a long time in (former and present) Pakistan. In Bangladesh an officer was appointed as Secretary General in immediate post-71 period. Below the cabinet he was the head of the Bangladesh Secretariat. He held this post for a few months only. Then the same officer was appointed as the Principal Secretary to the Prime Minister. Since then no one has held the post of Secretary General.

In (former and present) Pakistan the relationship between the central Secretariat and the central Directorates is more or less same as that between the provincial Secretariat and the provincial Directorates. Of course, the number of central Directorates is much less than that of provincial Directorates mainly because the central government is primarily a policy making organisation and many of its policies are executed through the provincial governments.

We have already noted that in Bangladesh there is no province and consequently no provincial government.[2] Before 1971 i.e. before its emergence as a separate and independent state, it was one of the provinces in the then Pakistan and consequently there was a provincial government. The functions of that provincial government were similar to those of other provincial governments of (former and present) Pakistan. Now, in view of the fact that there is no provincial Secretariat in Bangladesh, the

[1] Wilbur, *op. cit.*, p. 261.

[2] See Introductory Note and Preface (above).

ecretariat at the national i.e. central level performs all the nctions of both provincial and central Secretariats. In addition the functions that are performed by their counter parts in the ntral Secretariat of (former and present) Pakistan, the Principal cretary to the Prime Minister, the Cabinet Secretary, the cretary, Establishment Division and some other Secretaries the Bangladesh Secretariat also perform those functions which ere previously performed by the Chief Secretary to the (pro-ncial) government of East Bengal.

In (former and present) Pakistan the administrative authorities the district perform their functions under the control and pervision of the provincial government. Usually they do not me into direct contact with the central government. Normally ey have no need for direct contact with the central government. ut if it becomes necessary under exceptional circumstances, ey are supposed to contact the central government through the ovincial government.

istricts : Area, Population and Density

For administrative purposes Bangladesh, which has an area 55,126 square miles, is divided into 19 (before 1969,17) districts; hereas Pakistan, which has an area of 310,403 square miles, is vided into 55 (before 1969,51) districts including 6 political encies in the tribal areas of the N.W.F.P. In 1961, while the rmer had a population of nearly 51 millions with an average nsity of 922 per square miles, the latter had a population of arly 43 millions with an average density of only 138 per square le.[1] At the present moment (1972) it is roughly estimated that ngladesh and Pakistan have more than 70 and 60 million

[1] For area, population and density see *Census of Pakistan, 1961*, vol. 2, pp. I—21-22, II—7; vol. 3, pp. I—34-35, II—12. In 1969 two new districts namely Patuakhali and Tangail were carved out of Barisal and Mymensingh districts respectively. According to the 1951 Census Report there were 40 districts (including 5 political agencies) in West Pakistan at the time of partition (1947). (*Census of Pakistani Population, 1951*, vol. I, p. 43.) In the 50s some districts (including one political agency namely Mohamand Agency) were created out of the former princely

TABLE V

DISTRICTS : AREA (SQUARE MILES)

	501-1000		1001-2000		2001-3000		3001-4000		4001-5000		5001-6000		6001-7000		7001-8000	
	No.	%	No.	%	No.	%	No.	%	No.	%	No.	%	No.	%	No.	%
Bangladesh	—	—	4	23·52	6	35·29	2	11·76	3	17·64	1	5·88	1	5·88	—	—
Pakistan	2	3·92	6	11·76	12	23·52	4	7·84	6	11·76	5	9·80	3	5·88	3	5·88

	8001-9000		9001-10000		10001-15000		15001-20000		20001-25000		25001-30000		Over 30000		Total	
	No.	%	No.	%	No.	%	No.	%	No.	%	No.	%	No.	%	No.	%
Bangladesh	—	—	—	—	—	—	—	—	—	—	—	—	—	—	17	100
Pakistan	—	—	2	3·92	4	7·84	2	3·92	1	1·96	—	—	1	1·96	51	100

Source : See below, p. 111.

TABLE VI

DISTRICTS : POPULATION (IN MILLIONS)

	$\frac{1}{4}$ or Less		Over $\frac{1}{4}$ to $\frac{1}{2}$		,, $\frac{1}{2}$,, $\frac{3}{4}$		,, $\frac{3}{4}$,, 1		,, 1 ,, 2		,, 2 ,, 3	
	No.	%	No.	%	No.	%	No.	%	No.	%	No.	%
Bangladesh	—	—	1	5·88	—	—	—	—	4	23·52	5	29·41
Pakistan	10	19·60	10	19·60	8	15·68	6	11·76	12	23·53	5	9·80

	,, 3 ,, 4		,, 4 ,, 5		,, 5 ,, 6		,, 6 ,, 7		Over 7		Total	
	No.	%	No.	%	No.	%	No.	%	No.	%	No.	%
Bangladesh	3	17·64	2	11·76	1	5·88	—	—	1	5·88	17	100
Pakistan	—	—	—	—	—	—	—	—	—	—	51	100

Source : See below, p. 111.

TABLE VII

DISTRICTS : DENSITY (PER SQUARE MILE)

	5 or Less		6—10		11—20		21—50		51—75		76—100	
	No.	%	No.	%	No.	%	No.	%	No.	%	No.	%
Bangladesh	—	—	—	—	—	—	—	—	1	5·88	—	—
Pakistan	2	3·92	2	3.92	4	7·84	1	1·96	3	5·88	6	11·76

	101—200		201—300		301—400		401—500		501—600		601—700	
	No.	%	No.	%	No.	%	No.	%	No.	%	No.	%
Bangladesh	—	—	—	—	—	—	—	—	1	5·88	1	5.88
Pakistan	9	17·64	8	15·68	4	7·84	2	3·92	4	7·84	1	1·96

Table continued on page 111.

TABLE VII (Continued)

DISTRICTS : DENSITY (PER SQUARE MILE)

	701—800		801—900		901—1000		1001—1100		1101—1200		1201—1300	
	No.	%	No.	%	No.	%	No.	%	No.	%	No.	%
Bangladesh	2	11·76	2	11·76	—	—	4	23·52	3	17·64	1	5·88
Pakistan	3	5·88	—	—	—	—	—	—	1	1·96	—	—

	1301—1400		1401—1500		1501—1600		1601—1700		Oxer 1700		Total	
	No.	%	No.	%	No.	%	No.	%	No.	%	No.	%
Bangladesh	—	—	—	—	—	—	1	5·88	1	5·88	17	100
Pakistan	—	—	—	—	1	1·96	—	—	—	—	51	100

Source : Tables V, VI, and VII have been prepared on the basis of the figures available in 1961 census. (See below, appendices A and B.) New districts which were created in 1969 and later have not been shown separately in these tables.

populations respectively.[1] Though in terms of area Pakistan is almost six times larger than Bangladesh, in terms of population it is smaller than Bangladesh. Tables v, vi, and vii enable us to make a comparative analysis of area, population and density of the districts in Bangladesh and Pakistan. They reveal that so far as area, population and density are concerned, the districts in Bangladesh and especially in Pakistan, lack uniformity. In comparison with Pakistani districts, there are less variations in area, population and density of Bangladesh districts. But most districts in Bangladesh vary widely from those in Pakistan.

While in Bangladesh none of the 17 (100%) districts has an area exceeding 7000 square miles, in Pakistan 13 (25.49%) out of 51 (100%) districts have an area ranging from 7000 to more than 30000 square miles. One (1.96%) of these districts, namely Kalat, which has an area of 30931 square miles,[2] is more than half the size of the whole of Bangladesh. On the other hand, the smallest districts (Mardan, Khyber Agency and Mohmand Agency), in terms of area,[3] are also in Pakistan.

In 1961 only one (5.88%) district in Bangladesh had a population of less than half a million, but 20 (39.21%) districts in Pakistan had less than half a million population. While in Pakistan no district had a population of over 3 millions, in Bangladesh 7 (41.18%) districts had more than 3 million population, one (Mymensingh) of which had a population exceeding 7 millions.[4] Of course in 1969 a new district namely Tangail was carved out of the Mymensingh district.

Bangladesh is one of the most densely populated areas in the world. The only exception is the Chittagong Hill Tracts district

---

states of Bahawalpur, Kairpur, Kalat, Mekran, Kharan and Lasbella. And a few districts were carved out of other districts by reorganising their boundaries. (*Census of Pakistan, 1961*, vol. 3, pp. I—44-53.) In 1969 former princely states namely Dir, Swat and Chitral were converted into districts. (See below, p. 123, fn.)

1 1971 census was delayed with the result that no census report or bulletin has yet been published.

2 See below, appendix B. 3 *Ibid.*, ap. B. 4 *Ibid.*, ap. A, B.

which has a very low density of population because a vast area of this district is covered with hills and jungles and not fit for human habitation. In Bangladesh 10 (58.86%) districts had a density of more than 1000 persons per square mile, of which 2 (11.76%) had well over 1500 persons per square mile. But only 2 (3.92%) districts in Pakistan had a density of more than 1000 persons per square mile and one of them, namely Karachi, had more than 1500 persons per square mile. But the density figure of Karachi district does not at all indicate the actual density of population of the district because there is a great variation between the percentage of urban population and that of rural population. Karachi, which was the central capital, is the biggest city in (former and present) Pakistan. In 1961 the percentages of urban and rural populations of Karachi district were 93·6 and 6·4 respectively.[1] In Bangladesh none of the districts except one (5.88%) had a density of population less than 500 per square mile. But in Pakistan 41 (80.39%) districts had a density of population less than 500 per square mile and 18 (35.29%) of them had less than 100 persons per square mile.

The size, both in population and area, of many districts in Bangladesh and Pakistan gives a general idea of the burden of work in these districts. It is felt by many that some of the districts are too big for effective administration. The load of work in many districts which have vast population, places an intolerable burden on persons entrusted with the task of running administration. Two important *Reports* (1915 and 1960) discussed the problem and recommended that some districts should be split up into two or more districts.[2] These recommendations were not implemented. Of course much later i.e. in 1969 two new districts were created in East Bengal. Recently (March 1972) the Government of Bangladesh has declared that it has drawn up a plan for converting all sub-divisions (i.e. sub-districts) into districts.[3] If this plan

[1] *Census of Pakistan, 1961*, vol. 3, p. II-25.

[2] *The Bengal District Administration Committee, 1913-1914*: *Report* (*Leving Report*) (Calcutta, 1915) (Reprinted by the NIPA, Dacca, 1966), chap. iii. *Pro. Adm. Com. Report*, chap. ii.

[3] See Prime Minister's speech on the Independence Day, *The Bangladesh Observer*, Dacca, March 27, 1972.

is translated into practice then there will be more than 50 districts in Bangladesh.

In the course of our discussion we shall find that the differences between the districts in Bangladesh and those in Pakistan, in respect of population, area and density, have resulted in some differences between district administration in the former and that in the latter.

District Officer (D.O.)

At the head of the district administration, which comprises the whole range of governmental functions operating within an area marked out as a district,[1] there is an officer who is appointed by the government. During the period between 1947 and 1960 he was variously known in different places as the District Magistrate and Collector, or Collector, or Deputy Commissioner or Political Agent.[2] Now his official designation is Deputy Commissioner in all the districts of Bangladesh and Pakistan except in 6 political agencies and 3 districts in the latter. In these districts and political agencies he is still called Political Agent.[3]

1 See Introductory Note (above) for further elaboration.

2 Before 1961 his official designation was the District Magistrate and Collector in all the districts of East Bengal except two—Sylhet and Chittagong Hill Tracts, in each of which he was called Deputy Commissioner.

Before the integration (1955) of all the provinces in West Pakistan into one province his official designation was Collector in Sind, Political Agent in Baluchistan and in 6 political agencies of the N.W.F.P., and Deputy Commissioner in other places, i.e. in the Punjab, and the non-tribal areas of the N.W.F.P. The *Council Report on West Pakistan* recommended the introduction of a uniform designation throughout West Pakistan except in tribal areas, (p. 15.) This recommendation was accepted and implemented in the post-integration period.

In the post-partition period the designation of the same officer had varied from one province to another province mainly because, as we have noted, former Pakistan had inherited both the administrative traditions of Regulation Provinces and Non-Regulation Provinces including tribal areas.

3 These three districts are Zhob, Lorali and Sibi (Braibanti, *Research*, pp. 159-160) which are located in the tribal areas of Baluchistan. We have

He is, in fact, a "miniature governor"[1] and acts as "the government's principal representative in his area".[2] The whole administration of the district revolves around him. He is frequently and variously called the 'pivot', the 'king pin', the 'keystone', the 'arch-stone', the 'backbone', the 'nerve centre' of district administration. He is, in fact, "responsible for the entire gamut of government activities in the district which means it can be anything. . . . which our life can conceive of".[3] He

> "comes into the picture in all matters that effect the people in his district vitally as individuals and more so as groups. If, for example, you are a person against whom a crime has been committed or is intended or suspected to be committed, the deputy commissioner is concerned, in some way. If you are again a person against whom an allegation is made that you have committed or are likely to commit a crime, the deputy commissioner is concerned in some manner. If you are a landlord or a tenant of any sort or description, the deputy commissioner has a finger in your pie. If you are an owner or a prospective owner of a cinema or any other business house in a district, you are bound to come across the deputy commissioner at some stage or the other. If you are an industrialist of any size or an intending industrialist wishing to set up a factory of some sort including such things as petrol pumps, you will have to deal with the deputy commissioner at some stage or the other. If you are a user of any of the municipal services, in a town and you are either aggrieved or want to see any of them improved, the deputy commissioner is involved in that too. If you are a resident of an area which has asked for a road, a canal, a hospital, a dispensary, a school or a fishing tank to be built near or through that area, the deputy commissioner is involved in it too. If you are a citizen of the thinking type wanting to discuss, criticise or amend any law or government policy, the deputy commissioner is the man to see and exchange views with. If you want to have a gun licence, a passport, a driving licence, a liquor permit or any such facility, the deputy commissioner is the person to be approached.

---

already noted that all (i.e. six) political agencies are located in the N.W. F.P. of Pakistan.

[1] A. M. A. Muhite, Analysis of the organisation of the D.C.'s Office (cyclostyled and in pamphlet form) (NIPA, Dacca, participation study no. 41, Aug. 1962.) (Hereafter cited as Muhite, D.C.'s Office), p. 30.

[2] *First Five Year Plan*, p. 101.

[3] G. U. Malik, "District Administration" (cyclostyled) (A talk delivered at the NIPA, Lahore on March 22, 1963, during the 5th advanced course in Development and Administration), p. 14.

In short unless you are a man who has no earthly needs or requirements and who lives fairly high above the earth not attached to land or subsisting in water on land, you cannot possibly ignore the existence of the deputy commissioner and refuse to reckon with his qualities, good, bad or indifferent."[1]

Thus in view of the magnitude of the diverse activities that he is required to perform it "must be appreciated that the deputy commissioner is not only a person but an institution".[2] Because of his vast powers, he enjoys enormous influence and prestige within his jurisdiction.

Classification of the D.O.'s Functions. In the course of the last two hundred years the nature and importance of the functions of the D.O. have undergone considerable changes. At the early stages of the British administration the basic assumption was that "a district officer must concentrate on the first essentials—public order, the swift administration of justice, the prompt payment of taxes moderately assessed, the maintenance of accurate and up-to-date land records which would prevent disputes. These had been the first four things. After them came minor matters."[3] All these functions were classified under three broad headings, namely (i) the maintenance of law and order, (ii) the collection of revenue, and (iii) general administration or miscellaneous functions.

But from the beginning of this century rural development began to become important and in the 1920s and especially in the 1930s it gained considerable importance and the attention of the government[4] with the result that the concept and philosophy of administration began to change fast and the government began to adopt a new outlook on administration and its functions. A Resolution of the Government of British Bengal which constituted the Rowlands Committee in December 1944 wanted it to make an assessment of the work to "be done by the Government of Bengal both now and in the foreseeable future in order to ensure the efficient government....on modern and

1 A. Qayyum, "The Role of the Deputy Commissioner in Basic Democracies" in M. Rafiq Inayat (ed.), *Perspective in Public Administration* (Lahore, 1962), pp. 135-136.

2 *Ibid.*, p. 132. 3 Woodruff, *op. cit.*, p. 303. 4 See below, chap. v.

progressive lines".[1] The *Rowlands Report* held that "the advances on the economic and social fronts....have increasingly become the major concerns of governments in progressive countries".[2] And with regard to the future role of the government it observed that "what is, however, clear is that the main emphasis in the activities of the government henceforth will be in the development field and directed to the full utilisation of the materials and resources".[3] It further declared that the primary objectives of the government should fall in future under the following four headings: (i) the provision of justice, (ii) the maintenance of public peace, (iii) the development of physical and human resources, and (iv) the financing of government activities, particularly development.[4] The *Report* observed that it "is the third objective which is becoming, and we hope and expect will increasingly become, the chief activity of government."[5]

[1] Quoted in the *Report of the Bengal Administrative Enquiry Committee* (*Rowlands Report*) (Calcutta, 1945), p. 1. The importance of the *Report* may be emphasised here because it proved to be a turning point in the history of the administrative changes especially at the district level. Though all of its recommendations could not be implemented immediately by the Government of former Pakistan because of the problems faced by it immediately after partition, these recommendations later became the guiding principles for, and the subject matters of, many reports in former Pakistan later resulting in administrative changes of considerable importance. These changes are discussed later in various chapters. Professor Braibanti commented in 1966 that the "Rowlands Report is the best empirical analysis of district administration in print, for it avoids the usual nostalgia and sentimentality of an approach which dwells on the district as a microcosmic empire ruled by a 'young Socrates'....A careful study of the Rowlands Report would do much to dispel the fantasy of the idyllic and would bring to the subject of district administrative reform the sense of reality and candor which is needed." (Braibanti, *Research*, pp. 109-110.)

This report tops the reprint list of the National Institute of Public Administration (NIPA), Dacca, which brought out the reprint of the report in 1962 and in the preface of the reprint, the then Director of the NIPA called it "a landmark in the history of commissions' reports on administration in undivided Bengal. We feel this report will be of immense value to those engaged in serious study in Public Administration in the country." (Reprint copy of the *Rowlands Report*, p. iii.)

[2] *Ibid.*, para. 18. [3] *Ibid.*, para. 12. [4] *Ibid.*, para. 22. [5] *Ibid.*, para. 24.

In the course of our discussion we shall find that this expectation of the *Rowlands Report* has materialised.

The change in the objectives of the government was bound to bring a change in the objectives of district administration because while "major questions of policy are settled at headquarters, the execution of that policy is carried out, for the most part, in the districts".[1] Thus the *Rowlands Report* reclassified the then functions of the D.O. under the following five headings:[2] (i) Maintenance of Law and Order, (ii) Collection of Revenues, (iii) Development, (iv) Civil Supplies (This was, of course, a temporary function warranted and caused by the Second World War), and (v) Services. (This group of functions was usually called general administrative or miscellaneous functions.)

Formerly 'Development' had been regarded as one of the miscellaneous functions of the D.O. But, as noted above, the *Rowlands Report* was the first important document to consider it one of the most important functions of the D.O. and to give it an independent status or position in the list of his functions. While discussing different problems that stood in the way of sound progress of development activities, the *Report* pointed out that "At the worst, the District Officer takes little or no interest in Development, regarding this as the function of 'Nation Building' Departments in his District...this adds up to a virtual negation of progress."[3] It was made clear by the *Report* that from now onwards development should increasingly become one of the principal concerns of the D.O. because no schemes would take roots unless they were pushed "vigorously, continuously and uninterruptedly"[4] by the D.O.

[1] *Ibid.*, para. 61. [2] *Ibid.*, para. 93. [3] *Ibid.*, para. 63.

[4] *Ibid.*, para. 63. The *Report* also pointed out that the change in the objectives of the government would result in the change of organisation and structure of the government because these were suitable only "when the functions of government were primarily quasi-judicial, regulatory, the keeping of law and order and raising the taxes." (*Ibid.*, para. 18.) In the course of our discussion we shall later find that the emergence of 'development' as one of the most important functions has changed to some extent the structure and organisation of district administration.

It appears from the comment of the *First Five Year Plan* (1955-1960) that by the mid-50s there was no change in the Rowland Committee's classification of the D.O.s functions and that the development or welfare function still continued to be preceded by the important traditional functions, i.e. the law and order and the revenue functions.[1] This classification remained valid till the very end of the 1950s. During the second half of the 1950s the development functions were intensified to a considerable extent and in 1960 the Provincial Administration Commission again reclassified the functions of the D.O. According to this new classification, now the development function tops the list of the functions of the D.O. and the law and order and the revenue functions respectively occupy the second and the third positions.[2]

Other Officers and their Relation with the D.O. Almost all the Directorates have their representative officers at the district headquarters. The following are the important district level officers: Superintendent of Police (S.P), District Education Officer, District Inspector of Schools, Civil Surgeon (Chief Medical Officer of the district), Executive Engineer (Roads), Executive Engineer (Buildings), Executive Engineer (Housing) (in a few districts only), Assistant Director of Industries, Assistant Director of Agriculture, District Controller of Food, Settlement Officer (in a few districts only), Assistant Registrar of Co-operative Societies, Assistant Director of Storage (in a few districts only), Assistant Labour Commissioner (in a few districts only), Superintendent of Jail, District Fishery Officer, District Fire Officer, District Organiser of Social Welfare, District Health Officer, Assistant Engineer (Public Health Engineering), District Animal Husbandry Officer.

1 "The district officer must continue to perform his important traditional functions, but he must also increasingly reflect the role of responsibility for the welfare of the people which the Government has assumed." (*First Five Year Plan*, p. 101.)

2 *Pro. Adm. Com. Report*, p. 183. This recommendation was accepted by the then central cabinet. [*Decisions of the Cabinet on the Report of the Provincial Administration Commission* (Karachi, 1962), p. 24. (Hereafter cited as *Cabinet Decisions*.)]

The D.O., whose official rank is equal to that of almost all the provincial heads of Directorates but usually lower than that of most heads of central directorates,[1] is the head of all district level officers.[2] They perform their duties under the dual control and supervision of the D.O. and the higher level (i.e. divisional and provincial or central level) officers of their respective Directorates. Though these district level officers look to the superior officers of their respective Directorates for guidance and though a tension exists between them and the D.O., their functions and activities are in varying degrees influenced and controlled by him. His control over other officers is indispensable for coordinating their activities.[3]

These officers normally have no need for direct contact with the Secretariat. But if it becomes necessary they are supposed to contact the Secretariat either through their respective heads of the Directorate or through the D.O. who, unlike other district level officers, has such direct contact.

The D.O. and the Secretariat. Their is no separate or special Directorate to control and supervise the functions of the D.O. In the district he is, in fact, the direct representative of all the Secretariat Departments. All the Secretaries, whose official rank is higher than that of the D.O., send to him necessary instructions and directives with regard to their respective departments. Though he has direct contact with all the Secretariat Departments, he is required to deal with the following frequently: Establishment Division/Services and General Administration (S & G.A.), Home, Local Government, Revenue, and Planning. In Bangladesh and (former and present) Pakistan his promotion, transfer, etc. are controlled by the Establishment Division and

[1] The "Warrant of Precedence" notified in the *Pakistan Gazette*, Extraordinary, No. 21-2-61—public, dated the 7th March, 1963.

[2] A. H. Aslam, *The Deputy Commissioner* (Lahore, 1957), p. 16. (Originally it had been a disseration submitted to the Department of Political Science, University of Punjab, in partial fulfilment of the degree of Master of Arts.)

[3] See below, chap. vi.

the S. & G. A. department respectively.[1] In (former and present) Pakistan unlike other Secretariat Departments, the head of the S. & G. A. Department is the Chief Secretary himself. In fact he is the provincial head of all the D.O.s. As he is a very busy officer and has to deal with many other matters, the sole responsibility of one of the two Additional Chief Secretaries is to assist him in respect of the functions of the S. & G. A. Depart ment.[2] In Bangladesh, where, as noted above, the post of the Chief Secretary has ceased to exist from 1971, the Secretaries of Establishment and Cabinet Divisions and the Principal Secretary to the Prime Minister perform most functions that were previously performed by the Chief Secretary in order to exercise control and supervision over D.O.s

The D.O. as the Two-Way Channel of Communication. The D.O. is not only the "most important link in the long official chain stretching from the villages to the central cabinet"[3] but as the principal officer of the government and the head of all governmental agencies in the district he "serves as a multi-purpose link between the people and the government."[4] It is through him that "the government maintains contact with the people."[5] He serves as a two-way channel of communication between them. On the one hand he explains the government's policies and programmes to the people and on the other the views and problems of the people to the government. That is why he is frequently and variously called the 'eyes', the 'ears', the 'arms' and the 'tongue'

[1] In (former and present) Pakistan Establishment Division, which is located in the central Secretariat, does not directly come into contact with the D. O. and vice versa. Its counterpart in the provincial Secretariat is S & G. A. department which directly deals with the matters concerning public services and general administration (Including district administration) in the province. After the emergence of Bangladesh as a separate and independent state the provincial Secretariate and its S & G. A. department were raised to the status of central Secretariate and Establishment Division respectively. Now the Establishment Division performs the functions of the S & G. A. department in the former East Bengal Secretariate and those of the Establishment Division of (former and present) Pakistan.

[2] *Report of the Provincial Reorganisation Committee*, p. 28.

[3] *First Five Year Plan*, p. 101.

[4] Aslam, *op. cit.*, p. 16.

[5] *First Five Year Plan*, p. 101.

of the government. He is even regarded as "the hyphen that joins, and the buckle that binds the Government and the people."[1]

The D.O. is assisted by Additional D.O.s, Assistant Commissioners and Deputy Magistrates (Bangladesh)/Extra Assistant Commissioners (Pakistan).

District and Sessions Judge

The highest judicial authority in the district is the District and Sessions Judge. He is completely independent of the control and supervision of the D.O. to whom he is equal in official rank. He performs his duties under the control and supervision of the High Court. In (former and present) Pakistan the High Court, which is the highest judicial authority in the province, performs its functions under the general supervision of the Supreme Court, the highest judicial authority in the country. In Bangladesh, where there is no Supreme Court at the present moment (1972), the High Court is the highest judicial authority in the country. The draft constitution proposes that there shall be a Supreme Court for Bangladesh comprising the Appellate Division and the High Court Division. The former will hear appeal from judgement from the latter.[2] There will be no separate High Court.

The Division

"For the purpose of convenience of supervision the districts are grouped into Divisions."[3] In Bangladesh and Pakistan there are 4 and 13 (before 1969, 12) divisions respectively.[4]

[1] Quoted in Minhajuddin, "Some Aspects of District Administration" in Inayatullah (ed.), *District Administration in West Pakistan* (PARD, Peshawar, 1964) (It is a collection of papers presented at a symposium held on district administration at the PARD, Peshawar, in April, 1964.) [Hereafter cited as Inayatullah (ed.), *D. A. in W. P.*], p. 31.

[2] See articles 94(1) and 103(1) of the draft constitution in *The Bangladesh Observer*, Oct. 14, 1972.

[3] Outline of District Administration in Bengal (Govt. of Bengal, Home Department, Calcutta, 1944) (NIPA, Dacca, Reprint No. 113) (cyclostyled), p. 2.

[4] *Census of Pakistan, 1961*, vol. 2, p. I—21, vol. 3, p. I—33.
There were three divisions in East Bengal. One of the divisions namely Rajshahi (which had consisted of 8 of the then 17 districts) was very big because immediately after partition (1947) a few districts (or part thereof) which had been the part of the Presidency Division of Calcutta were added

At the head of the division there is an officer called the Divisional Commissioner "who has certain statutory powers but whose duties are mainly advisory and supervisory. He has no responsibility for the day-to-day administration of the districts in his Division."[1] He supervises and coordinates the functions of the D.O.s in his division and also those of the officers of different Directorates who are stationed at the divisional headquarters for supervising and coordinating the functions of the district level

---

to it. In 1960 the *Report of the Provincial Administration Commission* recommended that 5 of the 8 districts should constitute the Rajshahi division and the rest of the 3 districts and one of the districts of Dacca division should constitute a new division called Khulna. (pp. 21-23.) The recommendation was accepted by the then central cabinet. (*Cabinet Decisions*, p. 3.)

In West Pakistan there had been 10 divisions. According to the recommendations of the *Report of the Provincial Administration Commission* (pp. 55-58, 85-86), which had been accepted by the then central cabinet (*Cabinet Decisions*, pp. 5-6.), two new divisions, namely Karachi and Sargodha, were created in early 1960s. While Sargodha division was created for the sake of administrative convenience, some special factors led to the creation of Karachi division. A short history of Karachi will give us an idea of these special factors. On July 23, 1948, an area of 612 square miles (Karachi city and the surrounding areas) was carved out of the district of Karachi and was designated as the 'Federal Capital' under the administration of the then central government. Later in April 1952 it was given the status of the Chief Commissioner's province. In July 1959 the central capital was shifted to Rawalpindi. (*Census of Pakistan, 1961*, vol. 3, p. I-33.) Then it was given the status of a division. Karachi division consisted of the former capital area, Karachi district and Lasbella district. It was (and is) the smallest division in terms of area. (*Ibid.*) In 1970 West Pakistan was split up into four provinces namely the Punjab, Sind, Baluchistan, and the N. W. F. P. ("Quarterly Review of Administrative Affairs: April-June, 1970" in *Administrative Science Review*, NIPA, Dacca, vol. iv, no. iii, Sept. 1970, p. 65.) Now Karachi city is the capital of the province of Sind. The area of the Karachi division has not undergone any change. Both provincial and divisional headquarters are located in the Karachi city. In 1969 former princely states namely Amb. Dir, Swat, and Chitral were converted into districts and a new division namely Malakand division, consisting of these new districts and Malakand agency, was created. (*Ibid*, vol. iii, no. iv, 1969, p. 109.)

[1] Outline of District Administration in Bengal, p. 2.

officers of their respective Directorates.[1] The Commissioner acts as a supervisory authority mainly because a "Division is much too large an area to be an effective unit of administration."[2]

As is the case with the D.O., his promotion, transfer, etc. are mainly controlled and supervised by the Establishment Division (Bangladesh)/S. & G. A. Department (Pakistan).[3] The official rank of the Commissioner is higher than that of the Secretaries in the provincial Secretariat with the exception of a few Secretaries of very important departments such as Home, Finance, etc., to whom he is equal in rank. His rank is also equal to that of the joint Secretary in the central Secretariat.[4]

There are some differences between the role of the Commissioner in Bangladesh and that of his counterpart in Pakistan, the reason for which may be traced in the administrative history of British India. The Commissioner in Non-Regulation Provinces (e.g. Punjab, N.W.F.P.) was required to exercise rigid and close control and supervision over different aspects of administration in the districts in his division and over the D.O.s who, as noted in chapter i, enjoyed enormous discretionary powers. But in Regulation Provinces (e.g. Bengal), in which, as noted above, the D.O.s had much less discretionary powers

[1] Formerly the jurisdictions of the regional officers of different Directorates did not always conform to the divisional jurisdiction because each department used to determine the jurisdiction of its regional officers. As a result the jurisdiction of a regional officer of one directorate also used to vary from that of a regional officer of another Directorate. So it was very inconvenient for the Commissioner to coordinate their functions. Thus the *Report of the Provincial Administration Commission* recommended that the jurisdiction of all regional officers should conform to the divisional jurisdiction. (pp. 99, 102.) According to this recommendation the jurisdictions of the regional officers of most Directorates with the exception of a few were reorganised towards the beginning of the 1960s in order to make them conform to the divisional jurisdiction.

[2] *Rowlands Report*, para. 114(1).

[3] Also see above, pp. 120-121. In both Bangladesh and Pakistan the Board of Revenue also controls and supervises the revenue functions of the Commissioner and the D.O. (See below, chap. iv.)

[4] Also see the discussion on Public Services (below).

and were required to discharge their responsibilities within a relatively rigid framework of rules and regulations, the Commissioner was mainly concerned with the revenue side of administration and, to some extent, with the affairs of local bodies though he exercised some general control and supervision over other aspects of administration in the districts. Such a difference persisted during the post-partition period. Later, with the increasing importance of development functions, the introduction of "Basic Democracies" and the lessening importance of the revenue function,[1] the Commissioner in East Bengal was gradually required to give more and more attention to other aspects of administration. Moreover, during the post-1958 (the year in which first Martial Law was declared) period the increasing centralisation of administration at the central headquarters further accelerated this process because the central government, as noted above, was always dominated by the West Pakistani politicians and administrators who were thus more familiar with the pattern of administration in West Pakistan. They wanted the Commissioner in East Bengal to exercise more control over D.O.s. But yet the Commissioner in West Pakistan figured much more prominently in district administration than his counterpart in East Bengal.

Moreover during the period between 1955 and 1970 several factors, discussed below, further added to the powers and importance of the Commissioner in West Pakistan. Unification of all the provinces of West Pakistan into one province made it "a province of long distance."[2] Moreover, Lahore, the provincial capital, was so located in a corner of the province that many districts were far away from it. At the time of unification it was, therefore, felt that the position of the Commissioner as a supervisory authority should be further strengthened. It was also felt that the people who were living in far-flung places would find it difficult if they were required to approach the authority at the provincial headquarters for less important matters. It was, therefore, decided that some extra powers and authority should be

[1] See below, chap. iv. [2] *Council Report on West Pakistan*, p. 13.

delegated to the Commissioner as well as to the D.O.[1] Towards the beginning of the 1960s the extension of the Frontier Crimes Regulation (FCR)[2] to the whole of West Pakistan with certain modifications, made it incumbent on the Commissioner to exercise more rigid control and supervision over criminal administration in the districts. So the Commissioner in West Pakistan figured very prominently in the field of criminal administration of the districts. Although in 1969-70 West Pakistan was divided into four provinces and FCR was withdrawn, the Commissioner still continues to enjoy some of the powers gained in the 1950s and 60s.

After having made a survey of district administration in British Bengal the Rowlands Committee had concluded that "in many instances the Commissioner is a mere post office"[3] and that by occupying "a halfway position"[4] between the government and the D.O., he had created an unnecessary administrative "bottleneck."[5] The Committee had, therefore, recommended that the post of the Commissioner should be abolished.[6] After much discussion at the governmental level the post had not been abolished.

Sub-Division in Bangladesh

For administrative convenience and decentralisation each of the 19 (before 1969, 17) districts in Bangladesh except two (Tangail and Patuakhali) is divided into several sub-districts called sub-divisions.[7] Each sub-division is in charge of a Sub-Divisional Officer (S.D.O.) who works under the direct control and supervision of the D.O.[8] In each district one of the sub-divisions in which the district headquarters are located is called the *sadar*

[1] B. A. Kureshi, "Coordination of Administration at the Divisional Level" in Rafiq Inayat (ed.), *op. cit.*, p. 25. Also see Wilbur, *op. cit.*, p. 261.

[2] See below, chap. iv.

[3] *Rowlands Report*, para. 114 (iii).

[4] *Ibid.*, para. 113.

[5] *Ibid.*, para. 114 (iii).

[6] *Ibid.*, para. 113.

[7] Before 1969 Tangail and Patuakhali were sub-divisions of Mymensingh and Barisal districts respectively. They were made districts in 1969. Now each of them is an 'one sub-division district'. Before 1969 Bogra was the only district in East Bengal which was not divided into sub-divisions. In the early 1970s Bogra was divided into sub-divisions.

[8] Outline of District Administration in Bengal, p. 4.

sub-division.[1] In Bangladesh there are 55 (before 1971, 54)[2] sub-divisions including 19 *sadar* sub-divisions.[3] Either an Assistant Commissioner or a Deputy Magistrate is appointed as the S.D.O. He is assisted by several Deputy Magistrates who according to their seniority are called the 2nd Officer, 3rd Officer, 4th Officer and so on.

As the headquarters of the district and those of the *sadar* sub-division are located in the same town, the *Sadar* Sub-Divisional Officer is overshadowed by the presence of the D.O. and, therefore, the importance and influence of the former are lessened to a great extent. But the Sub-Divisional Officer of an outlying sub-division is the "miniature Deputy Commissioner."[4]

[1] Since Tangail and Patuakhali districts are not divided into sub-divisions, the area of each of these two districts is same as that of its *sadar* sub-division. For example, the area of the Tangail district is coterminous with that of *sadar* Tangail sub-division. Same is the case in Patuakhali. So each of these districts is also a *sadar* sub-division and in each of them there is a D.O. as well as a *sadar* S.D.O. who assists the former (i.e. D.O.).

[2] In the early 1970s a new outlying sub-division namely Jaipurhat was created in Bogra district.

[3] In a few districts the area of the *sadar* sub-division is very large. Each of the big *sadar* sub-divisions is split up into two parts, each under the control of a separate S. D. O. If each of those big *sadar* sub-divisions which are split up into two parts, is regarded as two sub-divisions, then there are 60 (before 1971, 59) sub-divisions in Bangladesh. But usually a *sadar* sub-division, whether divided into two parts or not, is not regarded as two sub-divisions. In different official maps (for example, the map incorporated in the *Report of the Provincial Reorganisation Committee*, part II) each of the *sadar* sub-divisions has been shown as one sub-division. Usually both of the *sadar* sub-divisional officers act independently of each other, but one of them is regarded as junior to the other. The headquarters of the two *Sadar* S.D.O.s are located in the same town and their offices in the same building. But it appears that the *Census Report* (1961) regarded each of those *sadar* sub-divisions which are divided into two parts as two sub-divisions. According to this report there were 59 sub-divisions in 1961. (*Census of Pakistan, 1961*, vol. 2, pp. I-21-22.)

[4] Masihuzzaman, "How Pakistan is Governed" in *Pakistan Quarterly*, vol. xiii, nos. 2 & 3, 1965, p. 126. Of course in his article, Mr. Masihuzzaman has not mentioned anything about the difference that exists between the *sadar* sub-division and the outlying sub-division and between the *sadar* S.D.O. and the outlying S.D.O. But his above mentioned comment applies only to the outlying S.D.O.

In his sub-division he enjoys almost the same prestige and influence as the D.O. Like the latter he is an all-purpose officer in his sub-division and his functions range from the maintenance of law and order and revenue administration to the community development and the welfare of the people. Of course, though he exercises most of the powers of the D.O. within his sub-division his statutory powers are less than those of the latter.[1] All his powers, other than those given to him by various enactments,[2] come to him as delegated powers from the D.O. and he exercises them on his behalf. The former to a considerable extent relieves the latter from the burden of judicial duties, routine work and supervisory functions.[3] A considerable volume of work is disposed of at the sub-divisional officer level. The main purpose of the sub-division is to decentralise district administration and to bring the administrative machinery closer to rural people so that their grievances and difficulties may easily be known and redressed.[4] Thus the administrative machinery at the sub-divisional headquarters may be regarded as an extension of the administrative machinery which is located at the district headquarters. The sub-division is one of the most important layers of district administration.

Almost all the Directorates have their officers at sub-divisional headquarters. They work under the dual control and supervision

1 The following statutory powers of the D.O. are not exercised by the S.D.O.: the issue of gun licenses, passports and domicile certificates, appointment of staff etc. (Muhite, D. C.'s Office, p. 3.)

2 He enjoys statutory powers with regard to rent control, finance tax, magisterial and judicial functions, matters concerning local bodies, and some other matters. (*Ibid.*, p. 3.)

3 *Pro. Adm. Com. Report*, p. 189.

4 Mainly for these reasons sub-divisions were created in British Bengal during the second half of the last century. [*Report on the Administration of Bengal*, 1871-72 (Calcutta, 1872), p. 76.] A *Report* held that "no distribution of the superior machinery of government will be effective unless we have sufficient inferior instruments." (*Ibid.*, p. 75.) The *Report* proposed several measures to strengthen administration in the sub-division and to make the S.D.O. a "real representative" (p. 75) of the D. O. (*Ibid.*, pp. 75-77.)

of the Sub-Divisional Officer and the district level officers of their respective Directorates.

The sub-division also serves as "a good training ground for young officers before being given independent charge of a district".[1] Moreover, the high density of population in Bangladesh has further heightened the importance and usefulness of the sub-division especially in this country. Had there been no sub-divisions it would have been difficult for the D.O. in Bangladesh to handle the problems of the vast population.[2] We have already noted that in March 1972 it was declared that all the sub-divisions would be made districts. However, it was not declared whether new sub-divisions would be created within new districts. If no new sub-divisions are created, then in the future there will be no sub-divisions in Bangladesh.

Thana

In Bangladesh each sub-division is divided into several *thanas* (literally meaning 'police station'). There are 411 *thanas* in Bangladesh.[3] As the name indicates, *thanas* were originally created for organising police administration mainly in rural areas. A few police officers and a small police force under the command of a sub-inspector were stationed at the *thana* headquarters.

Formerly the departments, with the exception of a few, such as general administration, revenue, registration, etc., did not usually appoint their officers below the sub-divisional level unless there were special reasons, and the jurisdictions of the officers of the above-mentioned departments (except police) did not

1 *Pro. Adm. Com. Report*, p. 189. Mr. Philip Mason also said "He is a lucky young man who could stay in one sub-division for two or three years. He would learn in the second year what mistakes he had made in the first...He would have learnt the groundwork of his profession and whatever else might happen later he had something firm to build on. But far too often he would be tempted by some meretricious offer to forfeit experience that could never be replaced and then he would have to make each mistake at least once more." (Woodruff, *op. cit.*, p. 87.)

2 We shall later find that till very recently the sub-division was not at all important in district administration in Pakistan.

3 *Census of Pakistan, 1961*, vol. 2, p. I—19.

always conform to *thana* jurisdiction. Later, in the course of our discussion we shall see that towards the beginning of the 1960s the government began to undertake massive rural works programmes and decided that the administrative machinery of various departments, which were connected with development activities, should be extended down to the *thana* level. As a result, the officers of various 'nation building' departments were gradually posted at the *thana* level and their jurisdictions also conformed to the *thana* jurisdiction.[1] Thus at the *thana* level another important layer of district administration was created in the 1960s.

In the *thana* the most important officer is the Circle Officer (C.O.) who works under the direct control and supervision of the S.D.O.[2] Before the 1960s the C.O.'s jurisdiction used to extend over an area called 'circle' which covered two to three *thanas*. But for the purpose of launching massive rural works programmes, the government decided in 1961 to appoint one C.O. per *thana* and to abolish 'circles'.[3] His primary responsibility is to guide the

1 See below, chap. v.

2 The factors that were responsible for the creation of the post of the C. O. are discussed in the following passages:
The Royal Commission upon Decentralisation (1909), held that "In Bengal and Eastern Bengal we were much struck by the fact that, owing to the absence there of charges corresponding to the *tahsil* of other provinces, the direct contact of the administration with the people is mainly through the police. The unsatisfactory character of this situation was generally admitted". (*Report*, para. 601.) It recommended that either the number of sub-divisions should be increased to a large extent or the sub-divisions should be divided into circles each of which would be in the charge of a Sub-Deputy Magistrate—Collector. It preferred the "latter course." [para. 601 (i).]

Later the *Levinge Report* discussed this problem in detail and held that there was a "need of an executive agency subordinate to the Sub-Divisional Officer". (p. 19.) It recommended the creation of the post of the Circle Officer who would serve as a link between the Sub-Divisional Officer and the village communities, carry out some miscellaneous functions and supervise local bodies at the village level. (pp. 75-76, 101, 103-108.) The post of the Circle Officer was created in 1919. [S. G. Hart, *Self-Government in Rural Bengal* (Calcutta, 1927), p. 6.]

3 Memo. No. G. A. VIII/1236 (90), Dec. 23, 1961 (Govt. of E. Bengal) There were 127 circles. (*Ibid.*) In 1945 the *Rowlands Report* had firs

local bodies at the lower levels and to supervise their development activities.[1]

Unlike the D.O. and the S.D.O. he has no official control over other *thana* level officers. But he is supposed to keep himself informed of the activities of other departments in the *thana*. Moreover, he has to coordinate their functions. This he can do only through persuasion and through local bodies' meetings. As the representative of the S.D.O. he has fairly considerable influence and prestige in the *thana* which enable him to exert some influence and pressure over other officers. But he cannot impose his views on them against their wishes. If any officer refuses to accept his suggestion or opinion he has no alternative but to refer the matter to the S.D.O. who, as we have already noted above, has control over other officers operating within his jurisdiction.

The C.O. is, in fact, a development officer. Unlike the D.O. and the S.D.O. he has no responsibility for the maintenance of law and order and the collection of land revenue. Of course, he is required to keep the D.O. and the S.D.O. informed about general conditions pertaining to revenue and law and order affairs. Though he is mainly a development officer he also performs a host of other functions as directed by the Sub-Divisional Officer. A fairly considerable amount of his energies and time is spent in answering questions and in giving information demanded by the S.D.O. and the D.O.[2] In fact the C.O. is their main source of rural information. He sends a monthly report to the Sub-Divisional Officer.[3]

---

recommended that "Circle Officers should be increased to one per *thana*" in view of the increasing rural development activities. [*Rowlands Report*, para. 83 ; also see para. 82(1).]

[1] The following circulars of the Department of Local Government explained his functions in the light of the changes in the field of rural development: No. S-VI/2E-4/62/143(80), Feb. 26, 1962; No. BD/S-VI/2E-4/62/ 403(80), June 8, 1962; No. GA/ -40/65-161, Feb. 11, 1965.

[2] M. Anisuzzaman, *The Circle Officer: A Study of his Role* (NIPA, Dacca, 1963), p. 4.

[3] Department of Local Government, Memo. No. GAL-40/65-161, Dacca, February 1, 1965.

Before 1962 his monthly tour diary was sent to the D.O. through the S.D.O. Now he is required to send it to the S.D.O. only.[1] And if there is anything important in the diary the latter informs the D.O. about it. The tour diary provides the S.D.O. with much information about rural life.

Sub-Division in Pakistan

We have already noted that sub-divisions, which were created long before partition, figure very prominently in district administration in Bangladesh and that a considerable volume of work is disposed of at this level. But until very recently the sub-division was not at all important in district administration in Pakistan. It is now gradually gaining importance there. At the time when the *Report of the Provincial Administration Commission* (1960) was being written there were only 40 sub-divisions in West Pakistan of which 20 were in Sind, 14 in the Punjab, 5 in the N.W.F.P. and only one in Baluchistan.[2] The Provincial Administration Commission wrote:

> "We consider that efficient administration at district level will be facilitated by strengthening the administration lower down. To secure this object it would be fit and proper if the sub-divisional system is strengthened and extended to areas where it does not exist at present. Apart from other advantages this will result in the creation of an effective administrative unit even closer to the people than the district and will relieve the District Officer of a great deal of routine work."[3]

It further recommended that the big *tehsils*[4] should be converted into sub-divisions and small *tehsils* should gradually be "formed into sub-divisions according to a phased programme extending over a period of ten years."[5] At the end of 1963 the number of sub-divisions in West Pakistan was 86.[6] The remaining *tehsils* are gradually being formed into sub-divisions. From the early 1960s the enormous increase in rural development programmes

[1] Anisuzzaman, *op. cit.*, p. 20.
[2] *Pro. Adm. Com. Report*, p. 189.
[3] *Ibid.*, p. 189.
[4] Sub-units. (See below, pp. 133-134.)
[5] *Pro. Adm. Com. Report*, p. 189.
[6] Masihuzzaman, *Pakistan Quarterly*, p. 125.

has also further added to the importance and necessity of sub-divisions in Pakistan.[1]

There is no *sadar* sub-division in Pakistan. The head of the sub-division in Pakistan (except Sind) is called the Sub-Divisional Magistrate (S.D.M.).[2] The post of the S.D.M. is held by an Assistant Commissioner or an Extra Assistant Commissioner (E.A.C.). He is assisted by several E.A.C.s. In many places where there are no sub-divisions, the D.O., whose functions and official status and rank are same as those of the D.O. in Bangladesh, is also required to perform some additional functions, which are discharged by the S.D.O. in Bangladesh.

Tehsil/Taluka

While in some places in Pakistan (excepting Sind) ***Tehsils*** are the component parts of districts, in some other parts they are the component parts of sub-divisions.[3] In Sind, where each and every district is divided into sub-divisions, *talukas* are the component parts of sub-divisions.[4] The *tehsils/talukas* were originally created as units of revenue administration. Later, the officers of some other departments were gradually posted at the *tehsil/taluka* level. The most important officer is the chief revenue officer who is respectively called *Tehsildar* and *Mukhtiarkar* in *tehsil* and *taluka*.[5] Like the C.O. in Bangladesh, he does not have any control over other officers in the *tehsil* or *taluka*. But being the representative of the D.O. (or the S.D.M., if there is any) and being the oldest government functionary in the area, he enjoys fairly considerable influence and prestige. Like the C.O., he

[1] M. M. Qurashi, "The Role of a Sub-Division" in the Rural Works Programme Supplement, published in *The Pakistan Times* (Lahore, March 7, 1966).

[2] In Bangladesh and Sind he is called Sub-Divisional Officer (S.D.O.).

[3] This is mainly because, as we have already noted, in some districts or in part thereof, there are no sub-divisions. There are also some sub-divisions each of which consists of only one *tehsil*, i.e. the jurisdiction of the former is coterminous with that of the latter.

[4] In 1961 there were 211 *Talukas/Tehsils/sub-Tehsils* in West Pakistan. (*Census of Pakistan, 1961*, vol. 3, pp. I—34-35.)

[5] *Census Report, 1961*, p. I-34.

provides the D.O. (and the S.D.M.) with necessary information about different aspects of rural life and administration. But in respect of other functions his role is different from that of the C.O. In addition to his revenue duties, the *Tehsildar* also acts in the capacity of a second-class Magistrate.[1] Unlike the C.O., he is not much concerned with development activities. For undertaking the responsibility of supervising development activities in *tehsils* or *talukas* the post of Development Officer was created in the 1960s. But the prestige and influence of the Development Officer are much less than those of the C.O. Thus in the rural areas of Bangladesh the C.O., i.e. a development officer, is the principal government functionary, whereas in those of Pakistan the *Tehsildar* or *Mukhtiarkar*, i.e. a revenue officer, is the principal government functionary.

Below the *thana/tehsil/taluka* level there are some units each consisting of a number of villages. These units have been separately created by different departments for organising their respective affairs in rural areas. The jurisdiction of one unit usually does not conform to that of another.[2]

Political Agencies

The "tribal areas of the...N. W. F. P. form a separate class and administration, if any, consists of a loose type of political control".[3] The special character or pattern of administration of Six districts in the tribal areas, each of which is called 'political agency', makes them different from the districts in "settled areas".[4] A brief discussion of the social condition of the

[1] M. Hasan Khan, Duties and Functions of Tehsilder (an unpublished dissertation submitted to the Department of Political Science, University of Punjab, in partial fulfilment for the degree of Master of Arts, 1957), p. 20.
The revenue functions of the *Tehsilder/Mukhtiarkar* are discussed in detail in chapter iv of this book.

[2] See below, chap. iv. Also see charts i and ii, pp. 135, 136.

[3] *Pro. Adm. Com. Report*, p. 192.

[4] The term "settled areas" is usually used to indicate the difference between the tribal areas and non-tribal areas. The districts in non-tribal areas are also called "settled districts".

CHART I

BANGLADESH

ADMINISTRATIVE UNITS

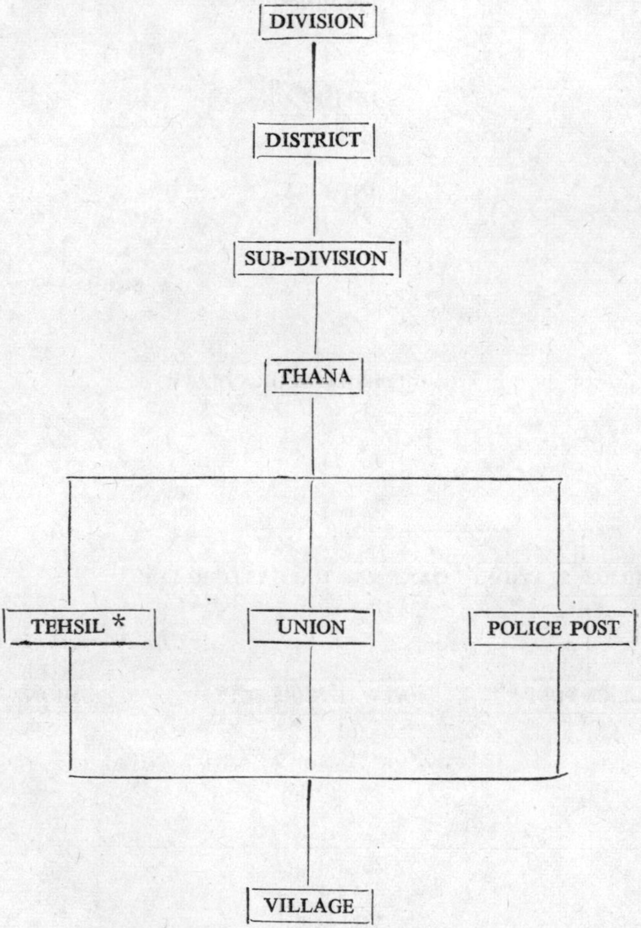

* Land Revenue Administration Unit.

CHART II

PAKISTAN

ADMINISTRATIVE UNITS

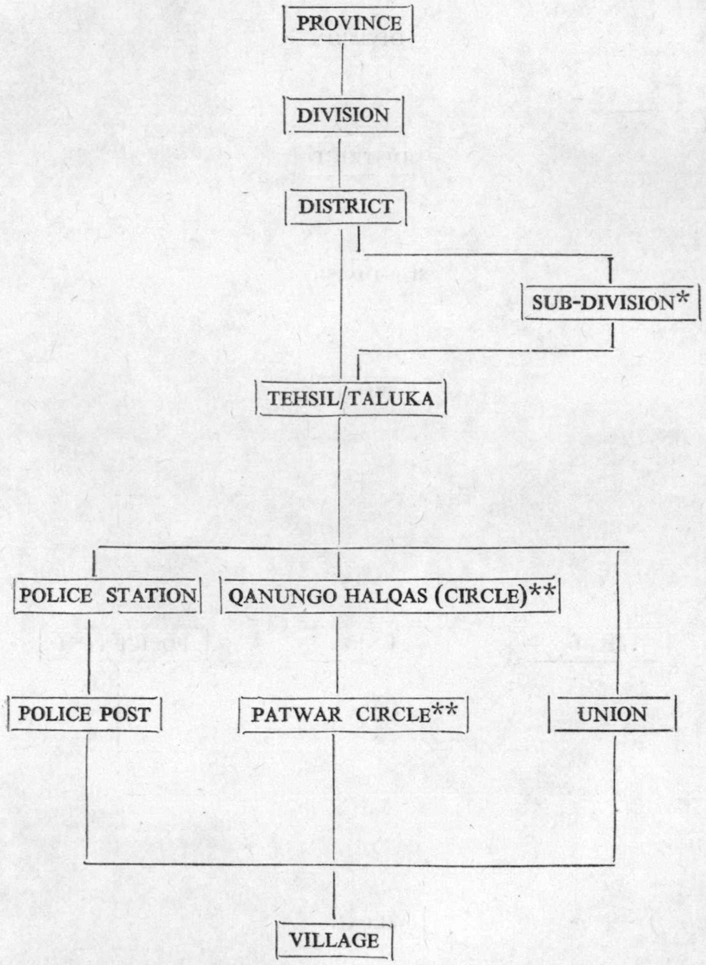

* In some areas of Pakistan there is no sub-division.
** Land Revenue Administration Units.

CHART III

PAKISTAN

(FORMER AND PRESENT)

ORGANISATIONAL AND FUNCTIONAL RELATIONSHIP BETWEEN THE HIERARCHY OF THE MAIN ADMINISTRATIVE BRANCH AND THAT OF A DIRECTORATE

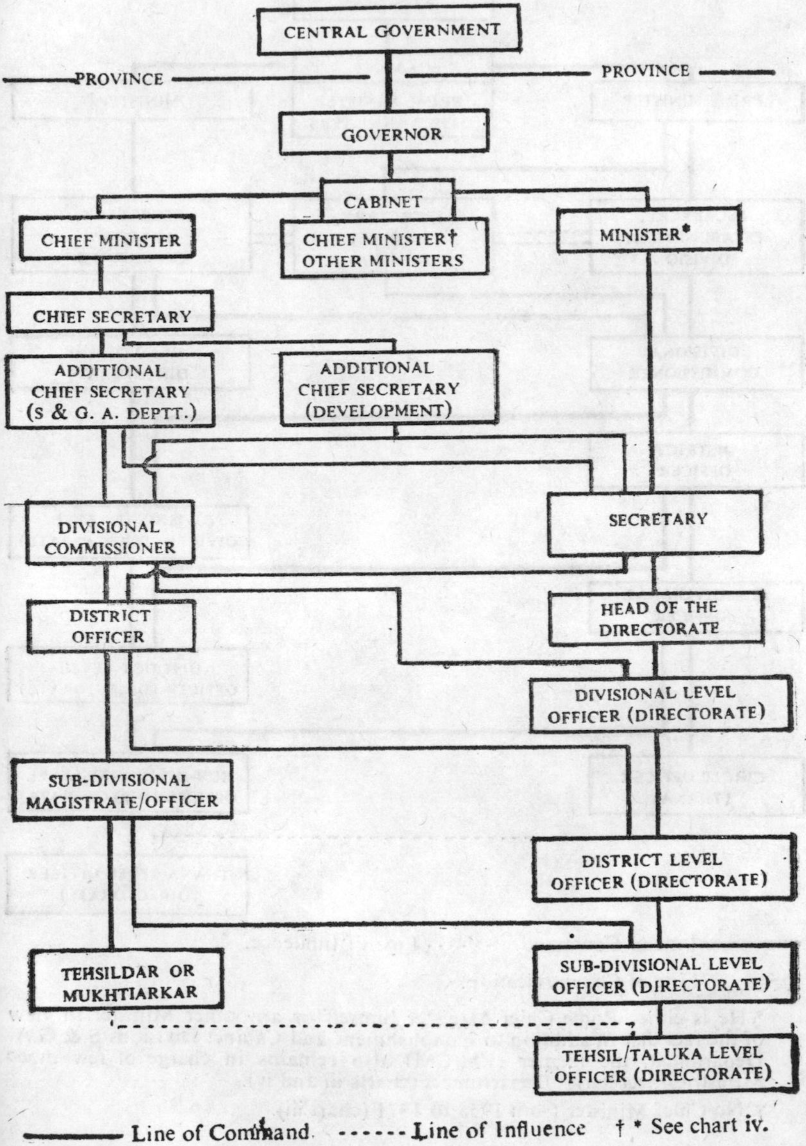

CHART IV

BANGLADESH

ORGANISATIONAL AND FUNCTIONAL RELATIONSHIP BETWEEN THE HIERARCHY OF THE MAIN ADMINISTRATIVE BRANCH AND THAT OF A DIRECTORATE

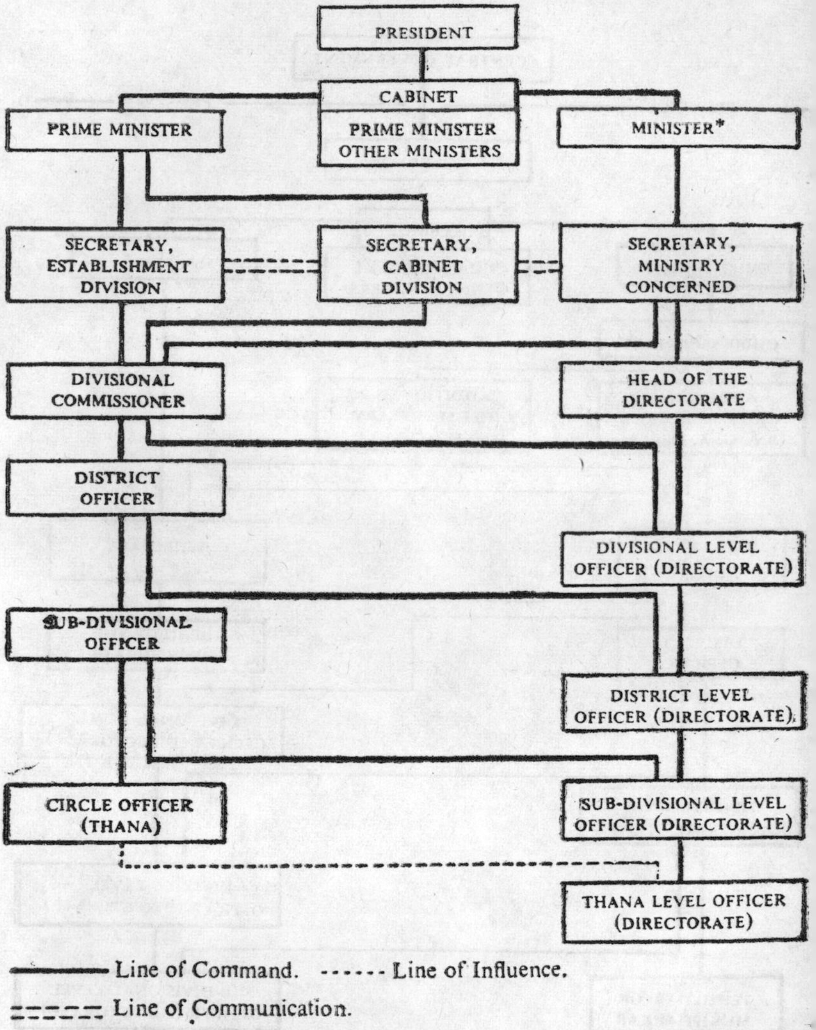

* He is either Prime/Chief Minister himself or any other Minister in view of the fact that in addition to Establishment and Cabinet Divisions/S & G.A. Department, the former (PM/CM) also remains in charge of few more Ministries/Secretariat Departments (charts iii and iv).

† No Chief Minister from 1958 to 1971 (chart iii).

tribal areas will give us some idea of the reasons that led to the introduction of a different type of administrative system in these areas.

The north western part of the N. W. F. P. is an "isolated area which has traditionally scorned the refinements of the outer world and contact with the rest of South Asia".[1] This region is mostly mountainous and barren and is inhabited by tribesmen devoted to their own way of life.[2] They "are independent, orthodox Muslims with immense pride in their own culture and respected as fighters".[3] By nature they are militant and aggressive. From their early boyhood they get training in rifle shooting from their parents and become expert marksmen. No one is required to have a licence for possessing fire arms. A visitor in the tribal areas will find[4] that every person, no matter whether he is old or young, is carrying a rifle. The Simon Commission's following account of the tribal areas is still valid to a considerable extent:

> "Beyond the locus of the military roads[5]...the tribesman does what is right in his own eyes, without being hampered by police *sepoys* or the code of Criminal Procedure. He lives inside his fortified farmstead with his womenkind, cultivates by primitive methods a limited strip of ground, maintains a constant state of feud with many of his neighbours, knows that if he shoots his enemy neither the frontier authorities nor the British courts are likely to interfere."[6]

In many places the tribesmen have gradually changed their nature and are now quite peaceful. But still in some places a

[1] James W. Spain, "Pathans of the Tribal Area" in Stanley Maron (ed.), *Pakistan: Society and Culture* (Human Relations Area Files, New Haven, 1957), p. 135.

[2] *Pro. Adm. Com. Report*, p. 192.

[3] Braibanti, *Research*, p. 187.

[4] As did the present writer.

[5] For example, the road through the Khyber which runs from Peshawar to the Afgan frontier, a distance of 34 miles, through the grimmest of bare mountains, is well guarded for the protection of travellers.

[6] *Simon Report*, vol. i, p. 319. Of course, attempts are made to catch the murderers with the help of tribal leaders and they are tried through the *Jirga* (council of tribal elders) system. The *Jirga* system is discussed later in chapter iv.

traveller or an officer is required "to keep his ears open and run the risk every day of the knife or bullet of a fanatic".[1] For example, in North and South Waziristan travellers and officials usually do not move without armed guards. In a few areas the tribesmen live a pastoral rather than a highly agricultural life.

These tribal areas were "not controlled by the British, but their affairs were administered loosely by political agents through a variety of systems ranging from those allowing complete autonomy to those in which various laws of the 'settled' areas were applicable".[2] The British Government also did not collect revenue from tribal areas because the "acceptance by the Pathan of control through a Political Agent essentially depends upon the fact that he is not called upon to pay any taxes".[3] The British policy was not to interfere in the internal affairs of the tribes and to leave the responsibility of administering the tribal areas to the tribal chiefs because any attempt to improve the administrative pattern in these areas could lead to serious bloodshed. After partition the government of former Pakistan also followed the policy of non-interference in tribal areas for the same reason.

Because of the backwardness and the tribal character of these areas it is not possible to introduce a formally organised administrative and legal system there. These areas are administered partly by the administrative and legal system which is in operation in other parts of Pakistan but mainly by tribal laws based on tribal customs, usages and values of tribal honour and retribution. There is an institutional blend of these two systems.[4]

The constitution (1962) of former Pakistan declared that no laws passed by the central or provincial legislature would apply to a tribal area or to any part of a tribal area unless the President or the Governor so directed.[5] The President or the Governor could, with respect to any matter within the legislative competence of the central or provincial legislature, make

1 Woodruff, *op. cit.*, p. 154. This comment is still valid in many places of tribal areas.

2 Braibanti, *Research*, p. 187.

3 *Simon Report*, vol. i, p. 319.

4 Braibanti, *Research*, p. 187.

5 *1962 Constitution*, Art. 223(i).

regulations for a tribal area or any part thereof.[1] A special statute called the Frontier Crimes Regulation (F. C. R.) of 1901 is in force in tribal areas. This Regulation lays down the broad outline and determines the general pattern or nature of administration in tribal areas. But the nature of the internal working of the administration, which depends on local tribal customs and usages, varies from place to place.

Each political agency is in charge of an officer who, as noted above, holds the same official rank as that of the D.O. and whose designation is Political Agent. He is assisted by an Assistant Political Agent, an Assistant Political Officer and other subordinate staff. A few departments have their representative officers in the agency, the functions of whom are coordinated and supervised by the Political Agent.[2] Officers of all ranks are interchanged between political agencies and 'settled districts'.

There is no separate officer in the Political Agency to hold the post of the District and Sessions Judge. The Political Agent usually combines the functions of the District Magistrate, the Collector[3] and the District and Sessions Judge in his person.[4] Of course, the nature of his functions in these capacities varies widely from that of the functions of the officers who hold these posts in 'settled districts.' He is required to discharge these functions mainly in collaboration with tribal leaders and the *Jirga* (council of tribal elders).[5] Another important characteristic of the tribal areas is that the jurisdictions of the Supreme and High Courts do not extend over these areas.[6]

1 *Ibid.*, Art. 223(2). "The President may at any time, by order, direct that the whole or any part of a Tribal Area shall cease to be a Tribal Area." [*Ibid.*, Art. 223(3).]

2 *Census Report of Tribal Agencies, 1961* (Karachi, n.d.), pp. I—6, 52, 81, 115. (Hereafter cited as *Agencies Census Report.*)

3 His role as collector is not very important because, as noted above, in most tribal areas no revenue is collected.

4 *Agencies Census Report*, pp. I-81, 65, 115, 164.

5 See below, chap. iv.

6 *Pro. Adm. Com. Report*, p. 209.

The Political Agent provides the liaison between the tribes in his agency and the Government. Each tribe, the "political importance" of which "is generally determined by its fighting capacity" and numerical strength, is divided into sub-tribes, sections, sub-sections and families or houses.[1] Each tribe, or sub-tribe or section has control over a defined territory. All these tribal tiers are under the control of a number of tribal chiefs called *maliks* who are responsible to the Political Agent for the affairs of the territories which are under their respective control. The tribal chiefs to a varying degree serve as the intermediaries between the Political Agent and the tribal people. The primary responsibility of the Political Agent is to convey the policies and aims of the government to the tribal leaders and then to ensure their implementation with the consent and cooperation of these leaders.[2] No doubt with the passage of time the tribal areas are in a process of change and, as a result, the role of the Political Agent is also gradually undergoing a change. But still his role is "more political and diplomatic than administrative" and "is associated with verbal jugglery and manoeuvres".[3]

The names of the six political agencies are Khyber, Malakand, Mohamand, Khurram, North and South Waziristan. There are also certain strips of tribal territories along the settled districts of Hazara, Dera Ismail Khan, Kohat, Bannu and Peshawar, which are under the general political charge of the respective Deputy Commissioners of these districts.[4] When each of these Deputy Commissioners deals with the administration of the strip of tribal territory attached to his district, he acts not in the capacity of Deputy Commissioner but in that of Political Agent.

Before 1970, the pattern of administration of the princely states (Amb, Dir, Swat, and Chitral) in tribal areas was very different from that of the administration of other parts of the tribal areas. In "reality their internal administration....remained outside the conventional district system" and was "entirely in the hands of

[1] Kunwaer Idris, "An Introduction to the Administrative Set-Up in a Political Agency" in Inayatullah (ed.), *D. A. in W. P.*, p. 21.

[2] *Ibid.*, p. 20. [3] *Ibid.*, p. 23. [4] *Pro. Adm. Com. Report*, p. 191.

ruling feudal chiefs".[1] In these "states the authority of the feudal ruler (variously designated *Wali*, *Nawab*, *Mim*, *Khan*, *Nizam*) is paramount although contact with the ruler and the bureaucracy of Pakistan is maintained through a political agent usually in residence in an adjacent area".[2] For example, contact with the feudal rulers of the states of Chitral, Swat and Dir was maintained by the Political Agent of the Malakand agency.[3] While commenting on the princely states in the N. W. F. P., Professor Mahmood Hussain said in the Constituent Assembly of former Pakistan "We have dealings with one single individual who looks after law and order and who practically does exactly the same thing in the states which all the Maliks (tribal chiefs) do in the tribal regions."[4]

Sometimes after the promulgation of the second Martial Law (1969) in former Pakistan, the princely states were converted into districts and the rulers were stripped of their powers.[5] Malakand agency was made a division which included Chitral, Swat, Dir and those areas which had formerly been the parts of the Malakand agency. Amb was included in the Peshawar division.

Increasing Volume of Work and the Changes in the Framework of the D. O.'s Office

From the early period of British administration, the functions and activities of district administration began to increase. The

[1] Braibanti, *Research*, p. 184. [2] *Ibid.*, p. 185.

[3] Malakand agency consisted of the following areas: (1) Malakand Protected Area and other parts of Malakand (Bejaur and Utmankhel). (2) Dir State, (3) Chitral State and (4) Swat State. (*Agencies Census Report*, p. I—2). The official headquarters of the Political Agent was in the Protected Area. His functions and position in the Protected Area and other parts of Malakand were more or less similar to those of the Political Agents in other agencies. But in respect of these states he was nothing more than a liaison officer and got nothing to do with the internal administration.

[4] *Constituent Assembly of Pakistan Debates*, March 28, 1951, pp. 531-532, quoted in W.A. Wilcox, *Pakistan: The Consolidation of a Nation* (London, 1963), p. 152.

[5] "Quarterly Review of Administrative Affairs in Pakistan" (July-Sept. 1969) in *Administrative Science Review*, vol. iii, no. 4, December, 1969, p. 109. S. Hussain, "Dir —From State to District" in *Pakistan Times*, Sept. 19,1969. S. Hussain "The Problems of Chitral " in *Ibid.*, Sept. 17,1969.

increase did not come in a rush but in haphazard uneven instalments which correspondingly increased the pressure of the work of the D.O. because the over all responsibility for the new and added functions naturally fell on him as he was the head of the administration. From time to time such subordinate administrative units as *tehsil*, *taluka*, sub-division, circle, etc. and new subordinate posts were created and the number of officers was increased in order to give him some relief from the heavy burden of work.

The posts of Deputy Magistrate and Joint Magistrate were created in the second quarter of the last century.[1] One of the reasons for appointing the officers of specialised departments in districts mainly in the second half of the last century was to enable the D. O. to give more attention to more important aspects of administration. But still the volume of work of the D.O. continued to increase with the result that he and his subordinates became over worked.

> "Towards the close of the Viceroyalty of Lord Curzon, it became increasingly apparent that the Lower Provinces generally and Eastern part of Bengal particularly were administratively starved...civil servants... were generally tied to their desks...And while Eastern Bengal was so scantly manned, the whole of the Lower Provinces needed a larger administrative staff."[2]

It became increasingly difficult for the D. O. and his immediate subordinates to go on extensive tours and to become thoroughly acquainted with different problems and with the remotest parts of the district.[3] The post of Circle Officer was created, the number of Deputy and Sub-Deputy Magistrates was increased and in big districts one Additional D.O. was appointed to assist the D. O.[4]

1 Lovett, *op. cit.* (1818-1858), p. 25.

2 H. V. Lov tt, "District Administration in Bengal: 1858-1918" in H. H. Dodwell (ed.), *op. cit.*, p. 252. Hereafter cited as Lovett, *op. cit.* (1858-1918).

3 *Levinge Report*, pp. 1, 18-20.

4 We have already noted the factors (p. 130, fn.2.) that led to the creation of the post of the Circle Officer. Discussion with a few retired officers who worked during the prepartition days, has enabled the present writer to know about the increase in the number of officers and the appointment of Additional D. O. in big districts.

The strength of the ICS cadre was also increased.[1] But the volume of work continued to increase very fast from the beginning of the 1920s. The Acts of 1919 and 1935 which introduced constitutional reforms both at the central and the provincial levels and the increasing importance of rural development[2] required the D. O. to

> "add to his innumerable duties, the maddening and infructuous business of answering questions, whether put down for formal answer in the House or sent informally direct, the host of subjects included under the heading of Rural Development and the labour of persuading where he had been used to command. It was not surprising that he did not always find it possible to check land records as he used to do, that cases were taking longer and longer to be settled".[3]

In the mid-1940s the *Rowlands Report* took this problem into serious consideration and concluded that "only a superman could bear"[4] the responsibility which had been entrusted upon the District Officer from time to time and that necessary steps must be taken in order to enable the D. O. to play his role effectively and efficiently. The report held that the most important step in the direction of solving this problem was to provide him with adequate additional staff "both as to quality and quantity".[5] We have already noted in this chapter that the *Rowlands Report* divided the functions of the D. O. under five broad headings. The report recommended that in those districts where the work was heavy each of the five groups of functions should be in the charge of a separate officer directly responsible to the D. O.[6] and none of them must be "an independent authority".[7] These officers would carry maximum possible delegation of authority from him. It was also pointed out by the report that he could be relieved of "duties which he can shed without detriment to and indeed to the

[1] Woodruff, *op. cit.*, p. 303.
[2] See below, chap. v.
[3] Woodruff, *op. cit.*, p. 303.
[4] *Rowlands Report*, para. 89.
[5] *Ibid.*, para. 92.
[6] *Ibid.*, para. 94.
[7] *Ibid.*, para. 97. The D.O., as noted above, had already been assisted by several Deputy and Sub-Deputy Magistrates. But the report was of the opinion that in addition to these officers, there should be five officers of the status of Additional District Officer or Senior Deputy Magistrate in order to help him in supervising the functions of other officers.

advantage of the discharge of his main functions".[1] It held that some of his judicial functions could be transferred to the District and Sessions Judge.[2] Finally, it held that another way in which relief could be given to the D.O. was to give him greater measure of delegated authority on a variety of matters which had no great financial or administrative significance. He should be authorised to dispose of those matters on the spot instead of entering into correspondence with the government[3] because such correspondence used to consume "a disproportionate amount of his time and energy".[4]

1947-1955. Although the importance and the usefulness of these recommendations were appreciated by the government no major steps were taken to implement them mainly because of unsettled conditions and upheavals that preceded and followed the transfer of power. In (former) Pakistan there was a serious shortage of trained and qualified officers. Moreover, the immediate post-partition period witnessed large-scale transfer of population and the disruption of trade and commerce, channels of communications etc. There was also the pressing need to establish new central and provincial governments.[5] As a result of all these factors, the government could not give attention to administrative reforms. Of course, from the late-1940s the number of Deputy and Sub-Deputy Magistrates/Extra Assistant Commissioners began to increase slowly. But the D. O.'s office remained seriously understaffed and thus efficiency of district administration continued to suffer.

After the abolition of the *Zamindari* system in East Bengal in 1950 the government began to acquire gradually *Zamindari* estates. As a result, the D.O. in the capacity of the Collector, as we shall see in chapter iv, had to undertake a stupendous task of reorganising the revenue system in his district. This considerably added to his burden. In the mid-1950s, as we shall see in chapter v, the government was about to launch development programmes on a large scale. The D. O. was supposed to organise, supervise an

[1] *Ibid.*, para. 92. [2] *Ibid.*, para. 102(a). [3] *Ibid.*, paras. 103 and 275
[4] *Ibid.*, para. 92. [5] *First Five Year Plan*, p. 7.

coordinate the development activities. But he had neither time nor adequate high-ranking staff. The Gladieux Report held that "the historic law and order, magisterial and revenue functions ... are so absorbing that most district officers find it almost impossible in the absence of top staff assistance to operate as a general stimulator and coordinator on development".[1] Moreover, visits by Ministers and other dignitaries, which considerably increased after partition, consumed a fairly considerable amount of his time.[2] As a result of these factors he "played but a minor role in the development programme thus far".[3] The major recommendations of the Gladieux Report, which were almost identical to those of the *Rowlands Report* and the purpose of which were to enable the D. O. to spend adequate time and energy to furthering the cause of development, were that the D.O. should be assisted by an Additional District Magistrate to render him necessary help in performing his duties with regard to law and order, administration of criminal justice, etc., a Chief Revenue Officer to help him in revenue matters, a general Administrative Officer to help him in performing general management duties such as treasury work, the issue of gun licenses and other permits etc. and in supervising the multifarious duties of subordinate staff, and a Development Officer to act as the chief assistant to the D.O. in the field of development.[4] The report also held that the D.O. could be relieved of a considerable part of his burden by broad delegation of authority and by improving the internal organisation of his office.[5]

1955-1960. In the mid-1950s the D. O. was relieved of a part of his judicial responsibilities[6] and some routine works. In 1956 an Additional Collector[7] was posted in almost all the districts of East Bengal.[8] No other major steps were taken during this period.

[1] Reorganisation of Pakistan Government for National Development (cyclostyled) (Gladieux Report) (Planning Board, Govt. of former Pakistan, Karachi, May 1955), p. 81.

[2] *Ibid.*, p. 82. [3] *Ibid.*, p. 81. [4] *Ibid.*, p. 83.

[5] *Ibid.*, p. 84. [6] See below, chap. iv.

[7] Now called the Additional Deputy Commissioner (Revenue).

[8] A. M. A. Muhith, "Political and Administrative Role in East Pakistan's Districts" in *Pacific Affairs*, vol. XL, nos. 3 and 4, fall and winter, 1967-68,

In fact, the shortage of high ranking officials and political instability stood in the way of administrative reform.

The second half of the 1950s witnessed a substantial addition to the burden and responsibility of the D. O. following the large increase in, and the specialisation and diversification of, government work. Several factors were responsible for such changes: *The First Five Year Plan* (*1955-1960*) and the *Village AID First Five Year Plan* (*1955-56—1959-60*) were being implemented during this period.[1] The acquisition of *Zamindaries* in East Bengal, which, as noted above, had begun in 1950, was completed in 1956. Thus millions of people in East Bengal became the direct tenants of the government and it became necessary for the district revenue organisation to collect land revenue directly from them and not from the *Zamindar* intermediaries.[2] The introduction of the new system of local bodies in 1959, as we shall see below, brought the D. O. and his staff much closer to these bodies and made it incumbent on them to participate in the activities of these bodies much more directly than before. By the end of the 1950s the administration in districts reached a state of chaos and confusion. According to the estimate of the D.O. of Dinajpur (in East Bengal), made in 1960, work in some sections increased from 300% to 900%.[3] Of course, the Additional Collector relieved the District Officer to a considerable extent from the burden of revenue work

---

p. 281. The appointment of the Additional Collector was, in fact, caused and warranted by the abolition of the *Zamindari* system in East Bengal.

1 See below, chap. v. 2 See below, chap. iv.

3 *Report of the Implementation Sub-Committee on the Reorganisation of District Offices* (Dacca, Nov. 1960), para. 6(1). Hereafter cited as *Implementation Sub-Committee's Report* (*District*).

The increase in the revenue work was the problem of District Administration mainly in East Bengal. But in other fields of district administration the increase in the volume of work was almost the same in both the areas. Of course, as most districts in East Bengal had vast populations the increase of work in other fields made the problem in East Bengal more acute than that in West Pakistan. In West Pakistan some land reforms were introduced in 1959 which increased the revenue work to some extent. But a considerable part of the increased revenue work was not of permanent nature.

during that period. But in the face of the magnitude of the entire volume of increased work in different fields of district administration the help rendered to him by the Additional Collector was not of great significance.

The administration at the district and at the higher levels had already been over centralised.[1] The sharp increase in the volume of work during the second half of the 1950s further aggravated the problem to a considerable extent. It not only caused delay in the working of administration at different levels of the province but made it difficult for the high ranking officials to supervise the functions of their subordinates. Thus it was observed that

> "matters of even a trivial nature reach the highest levels for decision or intervention. The irony of it is that over-centralisation exists side by side with inadequate supervision and control by the higher levels of administration in matters of real importance. There is an increased dependence on the petty officials whose importance and power in the eyes of the local people have grown out of proportion to his responsibility".[2]

It was felt that "lack of proper supervision" was the "main cause" of the "deterioration of district administration".[3]

In 1960 the Provincial Administration Commission pointed out that in the preceding years the most difficult problems that the government faced in its attempts for decentralisation were the unwillingness of high ranking officials to part with their powers on the one hand and on the other the reluctance of subordinate officers to take responsibility. In the case of the former unwillingness to delegate powers resulted partly for the desire to retain authority and patronage and partly from lack of faith in the ability of subordinates to take sound decisions. And on the other hand the fear that mistakes and errors of judgement would be

1 We have noted that in the mid-1940s the *Rowlands Report* had already mentioned about overcentralisation. The following example will illustrate the extent of overcentralisation at the district level: The D.O. is required personally to see and approve or disapprove the leave application of the *Patwari* (this post exists in Pakistan only) whose jurisdiction extends over a few villages only and who is six or seven layers down in the revenue hierarchy. (Gladieux Report, p. 82.)

2 *Pro. Adm. Com. Report*, pp. 3-4.

3 *Implementation Sub-Committee's Report* (*District*), para. 6(1).

followed by severe punishments made the subordinates reluctant to accept responsibilities.[1] "The interplay of these two factors not only leads to serious delay in the execution of governmental programmes and gives a look of sluggishness to the entire machine but involves the hierarchy in matters of such details that larger issues of real significance begin to receive inadequate attention."[2]

It was also felt that the continuation of ancient procedural requirements consume an enormous amount of time of the D.O. and his high ranking subordinates and imposed on them an intolerable burden of detailed and routine work.[3] A report observed that "the District Officer is saddled with various routine work and office files".[4]

Since 1960. The beginning of the 1960s witnessed some administrative reforms of considerable importance which were the results of the recommendations of the Reports of the Provincial Administration Commission, the Provincial Reorganisation Committee, the Implementation Sub-Committee on the Reorganisation of Provincial Administration and the Implementation Sub-Committee on the Reorganisation of District Offices.[5]

[1] *Pro. Adm. Com. Report*, p. 95. The Commission discussed this problem with reference to all the departments.

[2] *Ibid.*, p. 95.

[3] The nature of the routine work may be illustrated by the following example: The D.O. or the Additional D.O. was required to sign not only the originals but also all the copies of different notices for requisition and acquisition of immovable properties. Sometimes copies of one notice used to run into hundreds. If a Deputy Magistrate was empowered to sign the copies on behalf of the D.O., a lot of his time could be saved.

[4] *Implementation Sub-Committee's Report* (*District*), para. 8.

[5] The Provincial Reorganisation Committee and other two Sub-Committees were offshoots of the Provincial Administration Commission. The Commission mainly laid down broad principles or outlines for future administrative reform on the basis of which the Committee and the Sub-Committees worked out the details.

These reforms may also be regarded as the result of the fact that the Martial Law regime was very eager to make a favourable impression on the minds of the people and to justify the illegal and unconstitutional method by which it had overthrown a constitutional system. It had, therefore, set up a number of Commissions and Committees in order to introduce some reforms which could serve as a means of propaganda.

The first two reports laid great emphasis on the maximum decentralisation of authority and responsibility. They recommended that adequate legal, executive and financial powers should be delegated to the officers working at different administrative layers of the province and that they should be assigned with well defined authority[1] so that they could deal with "day to day requirements of the people on the spot"[2] without making unnecessary reference to higher authorities. Keeping the problems of decentralisation, that the government had faced in preceding years, in mind the authors of the *Report of the Provincial Administration Commission* pointed out that.

> "It is...essential to ensure that delegation of authority should not be merely nominal but effective and should be built deep in the organisation. To this end it has to be impressed on the superior officers that delegation is not an abdication of responsibility but only an enlargement of it and that 'it is only by the development of competence below that high responsibility can be upheld.'"[3]

In accordance with these recommendations, considerable powers and responsibility were delegated to the officers working at different administrative levels of the province.[4] On the recommendations of the Implementation Sub-Committee on Reorganisation of District Offices, the D.O. was relieved of many routine works[5] and significant changes were also introduced into the framework of the District Officer's office. It was decided by the government that in those districts where the volume of work was heavy, his functions would be grouped into three divisions

1 For details of the recommendations see *Pro. Adm. Com. Report* (pp. 92-94) and the *Report of the Provincial Reorganisation Committee*, part ii (paras. 152-159, 197-207).

2 *Pro. Adm. Com. Report*, p. 94. 3 *Ibid.*, pp. 95-96.

4 *Report on the Implementation Sub-Committee on the Reorganisation of Provincial Administration* (Dacca, 1960), pp. 2-3. Subsequent years again saw further decentralisation of powers and authority.

5 *Implementation Sub-Committee's Report* (*District*), para. 8, appendix, paras. 2, 15. (The decisions of the government on the recommendations of this report were incorporated in the appendix.) For example, Deputy Magistrates were empowered to dispose of some routine matters such as the issuing of requisition and derequisition notices, the signing of cheques for payment of compensation, house rents, etc. (*Ibid.*, appendix, para 15.)

each under the charge of an Additional District Officer.[1] So there would be three Additional D.O.s, namely Additional Deputy Commissioner (General), Additional Deputy Commissioner (Development) and Additional Deputy Commissioner (Revenue), who would respectively assist the D.O. in matters concerning general administration (including law and order affairs), development activities and revenue administration. Each of the three divisions of functions would be split up into several groups. A Deputy Magistrate would be in charge of one or more groups depending on the load of work in the district concerned.[2]

Accordingly the framework of the D.O.'s office was reorganised in the early 1960s.[3] So in those districts where the load of work was heavy there were three Additional D.O.s and in other districts two.[4] But formerly there had been one Additional D.O. in bigger districts and none in smaller ones. Only very big districts like Mymensingh, Barisal etc., or very important districts like Dacca, had had two and occasionally three Additional D .O.s.[5] But now

[1] *Ibid.*, para. 10, appendix, para. 4. This recommendation of the Sub-Committee was rather an elaboration of the comment of the *Report of the Provincial Administration Commission* that the D. O. should be equipped with "adequate staff". (p. 182.)

[2] *Implementtation Sub-Committee's Report* (*District*), para. 11, Appendix, para. 4.

[3] The discussion of the framework of the D.O.'s office is based on that of the D.O.s office in East Bengal. The arrangements of the D.O.s' office in West Pakistan were more or less the same. But as the districts in West Pakistan widely varied from region to region so in certain regions there were differences. Usually the number of Additional D.O.'s varied depending on the load of work.

[4] *Actual Distribution List of Officers*, (Corrected up to December, 1964.) (published quarterly by the Govt. of the then East Bangal, Dacca.) In some districts the importance of the functions belonging to one of the three divisions was not very great. In those districts the designation of the officer in charge of that division of functions was Joint Deputy Commissioner, i.e. holding a lower rank than that of the Additional Deputy Commissioner. In East Bengal, only one district (i.e. Chittagong Hill Tracts), which was an exception, had only one Additional Deputy Commissioner. (*Ibid.*)

[5] *Actual Distribution Lists of Officers.*

most districts in Bangladesh have two or three Additional D.O.s.[1] Thus the D.O. is now considerably relieved of his burden. But, still he is one of the most over-burdened officers. It is also generally felt that the number of Deputy Magistrates/E.A.C.s should be increased because they are overworked. An increase in their number will not only further relieve the D.O. of his less important work but also increase the efficiency of administration and accelerate the speed of administrative work in the district.

One of the major consequences of the increase in the volume of work, of diversification of functions and of the consequent increase in the number of officers operating at various layers of district administration is that the D.O., who, as noted in chapter i, had a very close and intimate contact with the rural people, has gradually lost such contact with them.[2] In Bangladesh and Pakistan, as in India,

> "Today it is probably true to say that the senior district official is more aloof and out of touch with the general public than was his British predecessor. The old-style British District Officer spent anything up to half the year in camp, from September to May. It is easy to ridicule the almost Mughal style in which he moved: the elaborate camp, the ceremonial entry into a village on horseback, surrounded by a posse of notables; the inspection of village accounts and the hearing of disputes under the banyan tree.... He [the villager] was able to receive the *hakim* [the ruler i.e. D.O.] on his own native ground, he could speak to the great man face to face; he was able to make proposals or register grievances and expect an answer. If all this has become an anachronism, it has not been replaced by anything new; there is just a vacuum.
>
> "Today, few District Officers go out on lengthy tours. Certainly, they are tied to headquarters by all the reports they have to compile and the ministers and other visitors whom they have to please. So today's inspections are perfunctory and unsatisfactory. There is no leisurely entry into the village demesne on horseback, giving time for the village folk to absorb their visitor into their own environment. He arrives, in a storm of dust in a jeep, a visitor from another world, and he keeps his other-world aura with him. There is a hasty walk around, a conference

[1] This comment is made in early 1973.

[2] Of course, some other factors (e.g. social, political and economic changes, the increasing importance of local and political leaders etc.) are also partially responsible for this.

with the leaders, a propaganda speech, a cup of tea, and he is off to another village and another."[1]

Local Bodies

Introduction. At the time of partition there were District Board at the District level,[2] Union Board (E. Bengal)/Panchayat (W. Pakistan) at the village level[3] and the Municipal Board in urban areas. And there were no local bodies in backward areas.[4] The District Board and the Union Board/Panchayat were classified as rural local bodies and the Municipal Board as an urban local body. The majority of members of the District and the Municipal Boards were elected and the rest nominated.[5] The Union Board/

1 Hugh Tinker, "Authority and Community in Village India" in *Pacific Affairs*, vol. 22, no. 4, 1959, pp. 369-370.

2 The jurisdiction of the District Board extended over the entire district excluding those urban areas where there were Municipal Boards. In the Sylhet district of East Bengal there was no District Board. There were four local Boards—one in each sub-division. [*Note on Reorganisation of Local Bodies in the Province* (*S. D. Khan Report*) (Dacca, 1957), para.28.]

3 The jurisdiction of the Union Board/ Panchayat usually extended over a few villages. In Sylhet district there were no Union Boards. There were the following local bodies in a number of villages: Village Authorities and Circle *Panchayats*. (*Ibid.*, paras. 77, 88.)

4 There were no local bodies in Chittagong Hill Tracts District in East Bengal (*Ibid.*, para. 13.), Baluchistan (except in Quetta Town), political agencies and the former princely states (except in Bahawalpur state where there were a few *Panchayats*, which, of course, had only a formal existence) in West Pakistan.

In West Pakistan there were some areas which held a midway position between very backward areas and 'advanced' areas. In these areas there were some local bodies called Town Committees and Notified Area Committees which were mainly nominated bodies and their functions were more or less similar to those of the Municipal Board. The composition of these bodies did not undergo any significant change during the period between 1947 and 1959.

5 The proportion of the elected members to nominated members varied from region to region. In East Bengal three-fourths of the members of the District Board and of the Municipal Board were elected, the rest nominated. (*Ibid.*, paras. 15, 37.) Of course, in Dacca and Chittagong districts, four-fifths of the members of the Municipal Board were elected. (*Ibid.*, para. 37.)

Panchayat consisted of elected members only.[1] The elected members of all the local bodies were elected on the basis of restricted franchise.[2] Each local body elected one Chairman (or President) and one (or two) Vice-Chairman (or Vice-President) from amongst its (elected) members[3] except in the Punjab where the Chairmen of most District Boards were the D.O.s. During the period between 1947 and 1959 the system of nomination was gradually abolished in most local bodies and in most regions with the exception of some ; the official chairmen of the District Boards in the Punjab were replaced by the elected non-official chairmen; and adult franchise was also introduced in local bodies' elections.[4] Unlike other local bodies, the system of direct election of the President and the Vice President of the Union Board was introduced in 1956.[5]

[1] In 1945 the *Rowlands Report* had recommended that the system of nomination should be abolished in all the local bodies [paras. 373, 389.] but the system had been abolished only in the Union Board in 1946. Before that one-third of the members of the Union Board had been nominated by the D.O.

In the *Panchayat* the system of nomination had been abolished much earlier. (Siddiq, Local Govt., p. 18.) Both before and after partition the *Panchayat* election result was required to be confirmed by the D.O. in the case of minor *Panchayats* and by the Government in the case of major *Panchayats*. [*The Pak-Punjab Panchayat Reorganisation Report* (*Masudul Hasan Report*) (Lahore, 1954), p. 17.]

[2] Every adult person who paid certain rates or taxes or had some educational qualification was eligible to vote and to become a member (*S. D. Khan Report*, paras. 16, 38, 62.)

[3] Of course, the Government reserved the right to appoint the Chairman or Vice-Chairman. (*Ibid.*, para. 19.)

[4] *PARD* (*Peshawar*) *Report No.* 9, p. 24. *An Analysis of the Working of Basic Democracy Institutions in East Pakistan* (Comilla, 1961) (A report prepared by the PARD, Comilla. Hereafter cited as *An Analysis of BD*), pp. 79. This report has also briefly discussed the rural local bodies that existed immediately before the introduction of the "Basic Democracies". This report does not give a very clear idea of the working of the "Basic Democracy Institutions" because it is based on the working of these institutions during the first year when they were still in their infancy. The report is a good theoretical analysis of the role that these institutions were supposed to play in the field of rural development.

[5] *Ibid.*, p. 7.

These local bodies had powers to levy taxes, rates, tolls, road and public works cesses and to realise fees etc. They also received modest government grants.[1]

The local bodies were supposed to perform those functions which were likely to "promote health, comfort and convenience of the public".[2] Their main functions were to make provision for and to maintain water supply, sanitary and drainage systems, roads, culverts, small bridges, dispensaries, primary schools, burial and cremation grounds, to take the necessary measures for the prevention of epidemics and infectious diseases, to register births and deaths, etc.[3] These were more or less the common functions of all local bodies. In addition to these functions a Municipal Board was also required to perform some other functions appropriate to an urban body. It was supposed to prescribe building line and street alignment, to supervise and control slaughter houses, market places, etc., to improve slum areas and to perform some other functions. In addition to development functions, which were their main responsibilities, the Union Boards were also required to perform some petty judicial duties and to maintain and supervise *Chowkidars* and *Dafadars* (Village Watchmen and Head Watchmen).[4]

The Divisional Commissioner, the D.O. and the S.D.O. could control, supervise and direct the functions and activities of the local councils. The Officer[5] had powers to modify or reject the budget of a local council, to inspect any work that had been undertaken by it and all books, proceedings, records, etc., that were in its possession, to suspend its resolutions or prevent it from doing any act which he thought was likely to cause injury or annoyance to the public or lead to a breach of the peace, to act in default and to exercise control over many other aspects of local councils.[6] The Provincial Government could supercede or dissolve

[1] *Ibid.*, p. 8. Also see below.
[2] *S. D. Khan Report*, para. 25.
[3] *An Analysis of BD*, pp. 8, 10, 11.
[4] *Ibid.*, p. 12.
[5] In some cases the Divisional Commissioner, in some cases the D.O. and in some cases the S.D.O. exercised these powers.
[6] *S. D. Khan Report* has discussed in detail the powers in respect of control and supervision that were exercised by officers over bodies (Paras. 26-27, 48-50, 70-76.)

a District Board and a Municipal Board and the Divisional Commissioner a Union Board.[1] In practice the Provincial Government or the Divisional Commissioner used to take such actions against a local body after having consulted the D.O. or according to his suggestion.

Effectiveness of Union Boards and Panchayats. So far as effectiveness was concerned, the position of the District and Municipal Boards in East Bengal was more or less the same as that of the District and Municipal Boards in West Pakistan. Later we shall be able to assess the extent of their effectiveness when we discuss in this chapter the degeneration of local bodies in (former) Pakistan. But a separate discussion of the Union Boards in East Bengal and the *Panchayats* in West Pakistan is necessary because there was a world of difference between them.

Though some attempts had been made to establish local bodies at the village level during the second half of the last century, it had been towards the very beginning of the 1920s that local bodies at the village level had been set up on a well organised basis in various provinces of British India. And the "most complete system of 'rural authorities' was established in Bengal".[2] "Out of all the provinces, only in Bengal did the new village government begin to operate before the commencement of Dyarchy."[3] Since then the Union Boards had been playing an important role in contributing to rural development and in arousing political interest among the rural people of Bengal.[4] While discussing local bodies at the village level the Simon Commission in 1930 had commented that "Development is promising and has gone furthest in the United Provinces, Bengal and Madras."[5] From the following comment of the *Rowlands Report* (Bengal) (1945) it appears that the Union Boards had continued to have a fairly good record: "The Union Boards seem to us the most promising of these institutions. We

[1] *Ibid.*, paras. 27, 51, 74.

[2] Tinker, *Foundations*, p. 116.

[3] *Ibid.*, p. 118.

[4] The role that they had played in arousing political interests is discussed in chapter vii.

[5] *Simon Report*, vol. i, para. 347.

visualise these Boards as becoming definitely a more active agent in the development work both in the activities they undertake and in their influence on village life."[1]

Although after partition all the local bodies in (former) Pakistan began to degenerate for several reasons, which are discussed later in this chapter, the Union Boards in comparison with other rural local bodies remained effective. In 1955 the Gladieux Report commented that "East Bengal has probably gone farthest in local organisation by virtue of its complete coverage of the Province with Union Boards each embracing 10 to 15 villages."[2]

While the Union Board was an active body in East Bengal, its counterpart in West Pakistan called *Panchayat* was almost inactive. The *Panchayat* system was in force only in the West Punjab and Bahawalpur state.[3] And in other parts of West Pakistan there were no local bodies at the village level. There were about 20,000 villages in the West Punjab. But the number of *Panchayats* was only 4,500 which covered about 7,000 villages. "Out of these *Panchayats*, most *panchayats* exist merely on paper."[4] A report on the Panchayat system held that

> "About 2000 Panchayats do not work. In actual fact, therefore, there are working panchayats for one fifth of the total number of villages in the province. Most of the landlords oppose the extension of the panchayat system to their villages, for they are afraid that in the event of the establishment of a Panchayat, there will be a diminution of their social power. Most of the villagers avoid the system, for they feel that the Panchayats would mean more obligations and taxes. Party faction is a common evil in our rural life. When panchayats are set up in party faction ridden villages, party strifes and disputes are carried to the panchayats. Panchayats are thus brought to disrepute. . . In such circumstances no serious attempt is made to develop the panchayat system...no one in the rural areas takes the Panchayat seriously".[5]

---

1 *Rowlands Report*, para. 86.

2 Gladieux Report, p. 91. Of course, it may be noted that the Chittagong Hill Tracts District, as we have already mentioned, did not have local bodies.

3 *Proceedings of the Local Government Seminar, 1956* (Lahore, 1957), p. 91. (Hereafter cited as *Local Govt. Seminar Proceedings.*)

4 *Local Government Reforms Committee: First Interim Report* (Lahore, 1951) (The committee was set up by the Government of the Punjab), p. 18.

5 *Masudul Hasan Report*, p. 5.

Various reports and the local government seminar strongly recommended the introduction of the Panchayat in every village or a group of villages.[1] But no serious effort was made. For the reasons mentioned above, the functions of the Panchayat were hardly performed. Thus the rural people in West Pakistan was almost completely unfamiliar with local self-government. One Officer, therefore, rightly observed that "Unions are a familiar unit of development for East Pakistan, not so in the West. In East Pakistan the Local Governments have operated at the Union and the District levels. In West Pakistan they have usually operated at the District level."[2]

Degeneration of Local Bodies. After partition (1947) the local bodies in (former) Pakistan began to degenerate very rapidly. Several factors were responsible for this:

Formerly persons who had found it difficult to secure a prominent place in higher politics had taken an interest in the affairs of local bodies. After partition the number of the prominent leaders decreased and as a result the competition for a prominent place in national or provincial politics was not as stiff as it had been. So the persons who had formerly participated in the activities of local bodies began to move towards provincial and central politics. And their places in the local bodies were taken by persons of much less ability.

Moreover, increasing urbanisation and industrialisation attracted not only the labour class but also the more educated and enterprising people from rural areas into the towns. As a result, rural local bodies were denuded of talent. The "mobility of educated people towards urban areas...left few able people...to participate in local affairs".[3]

1 *Ibid.*, p. esp. 2. *Local Government Reforms Committee: First Interim Report*, pp. 17-20. *Report of the Local Self-Government Committee* (Karachi, 1954) (The committee was appointed by the government of Sind), pp. 4-7. (Hereafter cited as *Report of the Local Self-Government Committee, 1954.*) Gladieux Report, pp. 96-98. *The Local Government Seminar Proceedings*, p. 187. *The First Five Year Plan*, p. 105.

2 Masihuzzaman, *Pakistan Quarterly*, p. 126.

3 A. T. R. Rahman, "Working of Basic Democracies" in the *Proceedings of*

After partition the government faced economic, political and administrative problems of immense magnitude. The immediate concern of the government was to undertake the stupendous task of tackling and solving these problems. Local bodies instead of getting the special attention of the government, received less and less attention.

Local bodies had always suffered from lack of finance. In 1930 the Simon Commission had commented that "It is a commonplace of administration in India that financial resources are generally quite inadequate to meet needs and this is especially true in local self-government."[1] After World War II, its financial condition had further deteriorated mainly because prices had begun to rise very rapidly. The *Rowlands Report* had observed that because of "rising prices", "the inelasticity of resources" and "the failure to realise in full even those cesses which are due", local bodies had become seriously handicapped financially.[2] After partition prices continued to rise with the result that the financial position of local bodies continued to deteriorate further. Inadequacy of funds further contributed to their degeneration.

In pre-partition days when non-officials had become the chairmen of local bodies, the standard of efficiency of these bodies had begun to decline. Moreover, the officials also had begun to exercise less control and supervision over these bodies which also added to their increasing inefficiency.[3] After partition officials developed a tendency to remain aloof from the activities of local bodies as far as possible which further aggravated the situation. The absence of effective official supervision and guidance rendered these bodies almost wholly ineffective.

The growing popular demand "to curtail the powers and authority of the officials" over the local bodies and the "increased

---

The Third All Pakistan Political Science Conference, 1962 (Karachi, March 1965), p. 253.

1 *Simon Report*, vol i, para. 354 ; also see para. 349.

2 *Rowlands Report*, para. 394 ; also see para. 367.

3 *Simon Report*, vol. i, para. 351. *Report of the Local Self-Government Committees, Sind, 1943.*
(Karachi, 1945), paras. 114-117.

preoccupation of the district authorities with their other duties" were the main factors responsible for "a rapid relaxation of official supervision".[1] We have already discussed in detail the second reason, i.e. the increased preoccupation of the district authorities.[2] The first reason may be further illustrated below: Members of higher local bodies became increasingly eager to free themselves from official control. They demanded that local bodies be made powerful units of local administration. From time to time the pre-eminence of the officials in local administration was criticised in various reports, by political parties and by the speakers at the Local Government Seminar.[3] As a result the officials became

[1] *First Five Year Plan*, p. 104.

[2] See above: "Increasing volume of work and the changes in the framework of the D.O.'s Office", pp. 144-154.

[3] The views expressed in different reports, in the Manifesto of a political party and in the Local Government Seminar may be quoted here:

"This Committee is of the opinion that if democracy is to be broad based, it must be national as well as local. Local Government should, therefore, represent a substantial measure of local self-government and must be something different from the decentralised activity of the state. In any democratic constitution it is necessary that a permanent and commodious repository of local power shall be maintained as an alternative to the undue extension of the bureaucratic arm of the State and as a means of providing the widest opportunity for a practical education in political responsibility." (*Local Government Reforms Committee: First Interim Report*, pp. 12-13.) The report also held that the position of the D.O. in relation to local bodies was "inconsistent with democratic principles". (*Ibid.*, p. 11.) This aspect of local administration has been discussed in *ibid.* (p. 9 to 17.) It may be noted that all the members (except the Secretary to the committee) of this committee were non-officials and most of them were the influential members of local bodies: for example, Mayor, Lahore Corporation and the Chairmen of District and Municipal Boards. Another report, namely the *Report of the Local Self-Government Committee, 1954*, was also in favour of lessening the powers of officers. But this report was not so radical in its approach as the former one. (pp. 2, 18.) (Also see *Masudul Hasan Report*, pp. 17-18.)

The Muslim League Manifesto declared that "In principle the Muslim League stands for the very widest extension of local self-government on the model of the parishes and communes of America. It is not logical or possible to have democracy at the apex sustained by bureaucracy at the base; and in fact democracy should be most extensive where it comes closest in touch with the ordinary life of the common man. In practice

careful in exercising their control and supervision over local bodies. They did not like to be embarrassed by political and public criticism which usually followed an action against a local body by an officer. Thus maladministration, corruption, nepotism, inefficiency and serious default in the performance of some essential services became the common characteristics of local bodies. And when the picture of maladministration in any local body became too apparent to be ignored, the officers used to recommend to the provincial government the supersession of the body or the withdrawal of functions. As a result, the supersession of local bodies or the withdrawal of functions became more frequent in the post partition period. Government officials were appointed to perform the functions of the superseded local bodies. These bodies were superseded much more frequently in West Pakistan than in East Bengal. In the latter though several Municipal Boards were superseded after partition, the supersession of District and Union Boards was rare.

The *First Five Year Plan* was not in favour of supersession of local bodies and the appointment of officials in place of the superseded bodies for performing their functions.[1] But it was in

---

this implies that we must train our people for local self-government in all directions, so that decisions which are now bureacraticallv taken and executed by Deputy Commissioners and Superintendents of Police should be arrived at and taken responsibility for by the elected representatives of the people." (Quoted in *Local Government Reforms Committee: First Interim Report*, p. 13.) Of course, in practice the Muslim League Government did not follow the above mentioned principles or policies. Many local bodies were superceded during the period when Muslim League was in power. In some cases the political interests of the Muslim League itself were responsible for the supersession of these bodies. (See below.)

It was held in the *Local Govt. Seminar* that some sections of different local government acts gave the District Officer "unnecessary" and "arbitrary" powers and that the "interference thus caused results in inefficiency and delay". (pp. 91-92.) It may be noted that this seminar was organised and mainly attended by the members of local bodies who divided themselves into several groups such as the District Board Group, the Municipal Group, the Panchayat Group, etc.

1 "The extension of bureaucratic control will tend to kill initiative, inhibit leadership and prevent self-help enterprise among men and women all over

favour of official guidance and supervision. It, therefore, held that

> "District Officers and Commissioners possess powers which should enable them to intervene when signs of abuse and maladministration first appear without waiting until a serious situation develops. They can issue directives and set aside decisions which involve palpable injustice or clear abuse of power. Prompt exercise of these prerogatives in lieu of supersession or withdrawal of functions would constitute a salutory check on the administration of local bodies and render supersession or withdrawal of functions largely unnecessary."[1]
>
> "The approach must be one of guiding and helping the local bodies so as to make them effective instruments of administrative and social progress and not one of curtailing their scope and crippling them for the sake of efficiency."[2]

The discussion of inadequate official supervision and control over local bodies is not very relevant to Union Boards. They used to receive considerable official attention. The Circle Officer whose primary responsibilities and duties were to look after the Union Boards and who was supposed to spend a considerable part of his time and energies in guiding and helping these bodies used to exercise considerable control over them. Moreover, the members of the local bodies at the village level were not as influential as those of Municipal and District Boards. As a result, the official supervision and control over Union Boards did not warrant much criticism or attention from influential or politically oriented people of the district such as lawyers, contractors, businessmen, etc.

---

the country...The lack of confidence in local bodies displayed by the Provincial Governments in frequently superseding them, in withdrawing functions from them, shakes their self-confidence as well as public confidence in them. This is a blow to the progress of democracy which must be avoided." (*First Five Year Plan*, p. 104.)

1 *Ibid.*, p. 104.

2 *Ibid.*, p. 104. A similar view was expressed by another report. It held that "Government must and would provide adequate supervision and guidance whenever it is necessary but to provide for the total abolition of any self-governing unit will be inconsistent with our firm conviction that responsible self-government is an extremely slow growing plant and it calls for infinite patience on the part of those who nourish it." (*Report of the Local Self-Government Committee, 1954*, p. 18.)

Of course, though in many cases maladministration was responsible for supersession of local bodies, it was not the cause in every case. Sometimes supersession resulted from political factors.[1] If the henchmen of those who were in powers at the provincial level were in a minority in a District Board or were not on good terms with those who controlled or dominated the Board, they often pressed their leaders or Ministers to supersede the Board on the excuse of inefficiency and maladministration. On some occasions they were successful in their efforts. On the other hand, if these henchmen were in a majority in a District Board usually the election was not held in time in that District and the members continued to hold office for an indefinite period even if the performance of the Board was not at all satisfactory. All these factors further accelerated the process of degeneration of local bodies.

From 1959. In October 1959 the Martial Law regime abolished all the rural local bodies by a presidential decree and introduced a four-tier system of local bodies called "Basic Democracies".[2] Under the new system there were Union Council/Town Committee/Union Committee, *Thana/Tehsil* Council, District Council and Divisional Council at the union, *thana/tehsil*, district and divisional levels respectively. While the Union Councils were formed in rural areas, the Town/Union Committees were formed in urban areas only. In April 1960 the urban bodies, i.e. the Municipal Boards, were abolished and new municipal bodies called Municipal Committees were set up[3] in urban areas with large or fairly large populations. The composition, organisation and other features of the local bodies are explained in tables viii, ix, x, xi.

1 One report also indirectly expressed the same view while discussing the powers of supersession. It held that "We do not want that Government should continue to be embarrassed by powers which it may under certain circumstances be compelled to ulilize under political pressure." (*Report of the Local Self-Government Committee, 1954*, p. 18.)

2 *Basic Democracies Order* (Govt. Publication, 1959). Hereafter cited as *B.D. Order*.

3 *Municipal Administration Ordinance, 1960*. (Hereafter cited as *Municipal Ordinance*.)

TABLE VIII

DIFFERENCE BETWEEN THE UNION COUNCIL, THE TOWN COMMITTEE AND THE UNION COMMITTEE

Union Council

The jurisdiction of the Union Council extended over a group of villages usually with a population of about 10,000 but sometimes ranging between 4,000 and 15,000.[1] Union Councils had replaced Union Boards/ *Panchayats*.

Town Committee

A Town Committee was constituted in an ordinary town with a population not exceeding 14,000 (or in some cases 15,000).[2] It may be said that it was constituted in a rural area with some urban characteristics. In some places they had replaced small Municipal Boards.[3]

Union Committee

A Union Committee was constituted in a city or a big town.[4] In every city or big town there was a Municipal Committee and the Municipal area was divided into a number of unions for each of which there was a Union Committee. It may be said that "A Union Committee serves as a territorial sub-committee of the Municipal Committee."[5]

Notes on table VIII

Thus, while the Union Council and the Union Committee were purely rural and urban bodies respectively, the Town Committee occupied a midway position between them. A member of a council/committee represented approximately 1,000 people but sometimes the number of persons represented by one member varied from 800 to 1,400 persons. Of course, this principle was not always followed in the case of Union Committees.

[1] *A Guide to Basic Democracies* (Karachi, 1960?), p. 10. (Hereafter cited as *B.D. Guide*.)

[2] *Ibid.*, p. 32. [3] *Ibid.*, p. 34. [4] *Ibid.*, p. 32.

[5] Malik Md. Siddiq, "Pakistan" in *Local Government in the 20th Century* (International Union of local Authorities, Hague, 1963), p. 309.

TABLE IX

COMPOSITION OF UNION, THANA/TEHSIL, DISTRICT AND DIVISIONAL COUNCILS AND TOWN/UNION COMMITTEE

Union Council and Town/Union Committees

CHAIRMAN	VICE-CHAIRMAN (From 1963)	CONTROLLING AUTHORITY	SECRETARY
Elected from amongst the members	As for Chairman	E. Beng: Sub-Divisional Officer (Union Councils) District Officer (Town/ Union Committees)* W. Pak: District Officer*	Appointed by the Council. Performed clerical functions
MEMBERS: All the members were elected directly—adult franchise.			

*The Provincial Government was the Controlling Authority of those Union Committees which were within the municipal and cantonment areas of Dacca, Karachi and Lahore.

Thana/Tehsil Council

CHAIRMAN	VICE-CHAIRMAN (From 1963)	CONTROLLING AUTHORITY	SECRETARY
Sub-Divisional Officer. Where there was no sub-divisional Officer *Tehsildar* was the Chairman.	Circle Officer (Only in E. Bengal)	District Officer	E. Beng: No Secretary. But in practice C. O. acted as Secretary. W. Pak: Development Officer.
MEMBERS: (a) All the Chairmen of Union Councils and Town Committees (not less than 50% of the total members). (b) Not more than 50% of the total members were officials (usually *thana/tehsil* level officers).			

District Council

CHAIRMAN	VICE-CHAIRMAN (From 1963)	CONTROLLING AUTHORITY	SECRETARY
District Officer	Elected from amongst the non-official members.	Divisional Commissioner	Assistant Director of 'Basic Democracies'*
MEMBERS: (a) Not less than 50% of the total members were indirectly elected by an electoral college consisting of only the Chairmen of Union Councils and Town/Union Committees. (b) Not more than 50% of the total members were officials. (Usually all the Sub-Divisional Officers within the district and most district level officers.)			

TABLE IX (CONTD.)

Divisional Council

CHAIRMAN	VICE-CHAIRMAN	CONTROLLING AUTHORITY	SECRETARY
Divisional Commissioner	No Vice-Chairman	Provincial Government	Director (in W. Pak.)/Deputy Director (in E. Beng.) of 'Basic Democracies.'*
MEMBERS: (a) Not less than 50% of the total members were non-officials. The non-official members of the Divisional Council from a district were indirectly elected by an electoral college consisting of the indirectly elected members of the District Council of that district. (b) Not more than 50% of the total members were officials (usually all the District Officers within the division and most divisional level officers.)			

Notes on table IX

*The Director or Deputy Director and the Assistant Director of 'Basic Democracies' were the staff officers of the Divisional Commissioners and the District Officers respectively.

A considerable part of the table is prepared on the basis of *B.D. Order*. Some information (*e.g.* information about Secretaries) was collected during interviews.

TABLE X

THE METHODS OF SELECTING THE MEMBERS OF THE RURAL LOCAL BODIES IN THE LATE-1950S

When the system of "Basic Democracies" had been first introduced in 1959 the Methods of selecting the members had been different from those which have been described in table IX. The earlier methods are discussed in this table.

Union Council and Town/Union Committee

(a) Not less than 50% of the total members had been elected directly on the basis of adult franchise. (b) Not more than 50% of the total members had been appointed from amongst the non-officials by the District Officer in West Pakistan and by the Sub-Divisional Officer in East Bengal with the prior approval of the District Officer.

Thana/Tehsil Council

(a) All the Chairmen of Union Councils and Town Committees (not less than 50% of the total members). (b) Not more than 50% of the total members had been appointed by the District Officer (with the prior approval of the Divisional Commissioner) from amongst the officials as well as from non-officials.

TABLE X (CONTD.)

District Council

(a) Not less than one half of the total members had been appointed by the Divisional Commissioner (after having consulted the District Officer) from amongst the non-officials. At least 50% of the non-official members, i.e. the 25% of the total members, had been appointed from amongst the Chairmen of Union Councils and Town/Union Committees.
(b) Not more than one half of the total members had been officials (all the Sub-divisional Officers within the district and most district level officers).

Divisional Council

(a) At least one half of the total members had been appointed by the provincial government (after having consulted the Divisional Commissioner) from amongst the non-officials. Not less than 50% of the non-official members, i.e. the 25% of the total members had been selected from amongst the Chairmen of Union Councils and Town/Union Committees.
(b) Not more than one half of the total members had been officials (all the District Officers within the division and most divisional level officers).

TABLE XI

COMPOSITION OF THE MUNICIPAL COMMITTEE

Chairman

The Chairman was an official appointed by the government. In big cities where the load of work was heavy an officer was appointed as full time chairman. For example, there was a full time chairman for the Dacca Municipal Committee which was and is a very large and important municipal body. But in smaller cities and towns one of the officers performed the functions of the chairman in addition to his other duties. For example, the chairman of the Pubna Municipal Committee (the municipal body of a district town in East Bengal) was the Additional Deputy Commissioner. In those sub-divisional towns, where there were Municipal Committees, usually a Deputy-Magistrate acted as the Chairman and also performed his other duties.

Vice Chairman

Every Municipal Committee elected one of its non-official members as the Vice-Chairman. He was also the ex-officio member of the District Council. Though he was a non-official he was regarded as an official member of the District Council because he held this position in the District Council by virtue of his position as the Vice-Chairman of the Municipal Committee.

TABLE XI (CONTD.)

Controlling Authority

The Divisional Commissioner. The Controlling Authority of a few important Municipal Committees was the Provincial Government.

Members

(a) All the Chairmen of Union Committees were usually the members of the Municipal Committee. [Art. 3(15) of the *Municipal Ordinance, 1960*, calls them" elected members" of the Municipal Committee.] Article 9(a) of the *Municipal Ordinance* held that the number of "elected members" of the Municipal Committee "shall in no case exceed thirty". Thus if the number of the Union Committees in a city or town was more than 30 then all the Union Committees were grouped into 30 groups and each of them returned one member to the Municipal Committee.

Both officials and non-officials were also appointed as the members of the Municipal Committee usually by the Controlling Authority. The number of the official and appointed non-official members did not exceed the number of "elected members".

The Controlling Authority. The Controlling Authority had considerable powers to take the necessary actions if he thought that "anything done or intended to be done by or on behalf of a local council is not in conformity with the law or is in any way against public interest".[1] He had authority to quash the proceedings, to suspend the execution of any resolution passed or order made by the local council, to prohibit the doing of anything proposed to be done and to require the local council to take such steps as might be specified.[2] He had the power to act in default.[3] The Chairman of a Union Council or a Town/Union Committee could be suspended by the Controlling Authority.[4] The provincial government could supersede Divisional and District Councils and some special Municipal and Union Committees[5] and the Divisional Commissioner other councils and Committees.[6]

1 *B.D. Order*, Art. 74.

2 *Ibid.*, Art. 74.

3 *Ibid.*, Art. 75.

4 *Ibid.*, Art. 78A.

5 Special Municipal and Union Committees were those which were within the Municipal and Cantonment areas of Dacca, Karachi and Lahore.

6 *B.D. Order*, Art. 78. These Provisions of the *B.D. Order* also "apply to Municipal Committees". (*Municipal Ordinance*, Art. 110.)

In practice these powers were seldom exercised by a Controlling Authority. It did not become necessary for him to exercise external control over a local council by taking resort to the powers vested in him as the Controlling Authority because he was in an advantageous position to exercise internal control over a local council. We have already noted that the official chairman of each higher council or committee was the direct subordinate to the Controlling Authority[1] of that council or committee and that the official chairmen of higher councils were the administrative and executive heads of their respective areas and enjoyed enormous power and status. Thus it was not very difficult for the official chairman to influence the decision of the local body. Moreover, as noted above, the Secretary to a higher council who had control over the internal administration of the council was a government official and was a direct subordinate to the official chairman, and he exercised his functions under his control and supervision.[2] Thus we find that the official control over the higher councils as well as the higher committees was both extensive and intensive. Though the Union Council and the Town/Union Committee were wholly elected bodies, they were required to perform their functions under the close supervision and control of officials[3] and the respective higher councils and committees, the

[1] The Chairmen of Divisional, District and *Thana/Tehsil* Councils and Municipal Committees were the direct subordinates to the Controlling Authorities of those bodies.

[2] A government circular describes the (Deputy) Director and the Assistant Director of Basic Democracies (i.e. the Secretaries to the Divisional and the District Councils respectively) as the "staff officers" of the Divisional Commissioners and the District Officers respectively "in all matters with which the Basic Democracies are concerned". [No. GAI-40/65-161, dated Dacca, 11th Feb. 1965 (Services & General Administration Department, Govt. of the then East Pakistan).] We have already noted that though the Circle Officer was the Vice-Chairman of the *Thana* Council, he in practice acted as its Secretary. The Development Officer who was the Secretary to the *Tehsil* Council was the direct subordinate to the District Officer (or the Sub-Divisional Magistrate, if there was a sub-division).

[3] Of course, the Union Committee was subject to less official control than the Union Council and the Town Committee.

Chairmen and Secretaries of which, as noted above, were officials. To an extraordinary degree they were financially dependent on the officials who had powers and authority to withhold grants which constituted the major part of their income. Moreover, the development plans of each council were subject to the approval of a committee consisting of officials.[1]

But it would be wrong to say that the non-official members were not in a position to exercise some influence over the officials. No doubt, officials were in an advantageous position to maintain firm control over the administration of various councils but a close study of different aspects would reveal that the non-official members were in a position to exercise some influence in one way or another over the officials and that politically oriented local leaders were gradually emerging.[2]

Functions. The functions of the District Council, the Union Council and the Municipal Committee were the same as those of the earlier local bodies i.e. the District, the Union and the Municipal Boards respectively.[3] But as the District and the Union Councils were required to undertake the responsibility for executing community development programmes, the volume of their functions and activities increased to a great extent.[4] Initially it was not envisaged that the *Thana/Tehsil* council should be entrusted with any specific functions and it was regarded as a coordinating body. But later we shall see that subsequently the *Thana* Council was entrusted with considerable responsibility with regard to the execution of community development programmes and came to be regarded as one of the

[1] See below, chap. v. [2] See below, chap. vii.

[3] This conclusion has been drawn after having compared the functions of the pre-58 local bodies and those of the post-58 local bodies. The functions of the Union and the District Councils have been discussed respectively in the third and the fourth 'schedules' incorporated in the *B.D. Order* and those of the Municipal Committee in part iv of the *Municipal Ordinance*. The functions of the pre-58 and the post-58 systems of local bodies were also briefly discussed in the *Joint Report of the BNR and the PARD*, pp. 10, 11, 13, 14, 15, 17.

[4] See below, chap. v.

most important councils in the four-tier system of local bodies.[1] The Divisional Council did not have any specific functions to perform and was regarded as a coordinating body. But in practice it was not required to perform any important functions even in the field of coordination. In fact, it was a superfluous body which did not have much utility. The Union Committee usually performed those functions which were delegated to it by the Municipal Committee. The functions of the Town Committee were largely on the lines of those assigned to the Municipal Committee. Here it may be mentioned that so far as the maintenance of law and order and general administration were concerned the local bodies did not have any authority.

Both nation building departments (i.e. directorates) of the government and local bodies had concurrent jurisdictions. While the former undertook heavy and important development and welfare works, the latter undertook relatively minor and less important development and welfare works.[2] (Sometimes the former supervised the works of the latter and gave them technical or specialised assistance and advice.) Thus development or welfare works could be divided under two headings: (i) Works performed by the nation building departments and (ii) Works performed by the local bodies. The volume of works performed by the former was much more than that of works performed by the latter.

Sources of incomes. The sources of incomes of various councils and committees are explained in table xii on page 173.

[1] See below, chap. v.

[2] For example, long highways and bridges, multi-storied buildings, etc. were constructed by the 'Roads and Buildings' Department. Similarly, all important educational institutions such as colleges, high schools, technical institutions, etc. and important and big hospitals, medical centres, etc. were set up and supervised by the Education and Health Departments respectively. On the other hand, primary schools, dispensaries, etc. were usually set up and supervised by the local bodies. The Education and Health Departments also had authority to supervise these institutions.

TABLE XII[1]

THE SOURCES OF THE INCOMES OF LOCAL BODIES

Union Council	(i) Taxes, rates, fees, loans, etc. (ii) 6.25% of the land revenue collected by the government from its area. (iii) Large grants from the government and the higher councils.
Thana/Tehsil Council	No power to levy taxes or rates. Large grants from the government and the higher councils.
District Council	Same as the Union Council.
Divisional Council	No power to levy taxes or rates. Modest government grants.
Municipal and Town Committee	(i) Taxes, rates, fees, loans, etc. (ii) government grants.
Union Committee	No powers to levy taxes or rates. The budget of the Municipal Committee made provision for the works of the Union Committee.

Two important features of the sources of income of the rural local bodies were that (i) the government grants increased to an extraordinary degree[2] and (ii) the district and the Union Councils were given much wider powers to levy taxes. Two factors were mainly responsible for this increase in grants and powers to levy taxes: the political motive of the Ayub regime[3] and the increase in the volume and importance of community development programmes.[4]

[1] The table is prepared on the basis of information obtained from *An Analysis of BD*, pp. 19, 21, 23, 26 and *B. D. Guide*, pp. 22-24, 34.

[2] Average amount of grants for each Union Board/Council—1957-58: Rs. 72.32; 1964-65: Rs. 3724.93. (Source: M. Rashiduzzaman, "A Comparative Study—Union Boards and Union Councils" in *The Morning News*, Dacca, Nov. 6, 1966.) Grants for District Boards/Councils—1957-58: 3.41%; 1965-66: 39.48% [M. Rashiduzzaman, "A Comparative Study of District Boards and District Councils" (typed.)] These figures were based on a sample survey made in East Bengal by Dr. Rashiduzzaman of the Department of Political Science, University of Dacca.

[3] See below, chap. vii.   [4] See below, chap. v.

A typical characteristic of the "Basic Democracies" system was that 80000 (later 120000)[1]. "Basic Democrats" (i.e. all the members of Union Councils and Town/Union Committees) constituted the electoral college for electing the President of the country and the members of both National and Provincial Assemblies. The system of "Basic Democracies", which disfranchised the entire adult population of former Pakistan and thus deprived them of their right directly to elect their parliamentary representatives, was very unpopular especially in East Bengal. It was widely believed and felt that the system had been deliberately brought into existence by the Ayub government, which avoided direct election on the basis of adult franchise, for the purpose of giving itself an appearance of being a democratically elected government and keeping itself in power for an indefinite period.[2] Thus, especially in East Bengal there was a serious lack of public respect for and confidence in those bodies. As a result, the very fact that the "Basic Democrats" constituted the electoral college seriously undermined the position and functions of the "Basic Democracies" institutions as local self-government institutions.

Finally, we may now repeat some points in table xiii in order to compare and contrast the pre-58 and the post-58 systems of local bodies with each other. (See below, p. 175.)

So far as the composition of the District and the *Thana/Tehsil* councils and that of the Municipal Committee and the nature of official control and supervision over local bodies were concerned, the post-58 system, generally speaking, was more or less similar to the system that had been in operation in the period that had preceded the 1919 Act or, more appropriately speaking, in the last century. In the early 1920s a diarchic form of administration had come into operation at the district level because of the provision that the District Board in most provinces of British India could be allowed to elect one of its non-official members as its Chairman. The diarchic system, which had been partially

1 *The Guardian* (London, Nov. 14), 1968.

2 For further illustration of this comment see below, chap. vii.

TABLE XIII

COMPARISON BETWEEN THE PRE-58 AND THE POST-58 SYSTEMS OF LOCAL BODIES

PRE-58 SYSTEM	POST-58 SYSTEM
1. At union (mainly in E. Beng.) and District levels and in urban areas.	1. At union, *thana/tehsil*, district and divisional level and in urban areas.
2. Not in backward areas.	2. In all areas.
3. Members of most local bodies: non-officials only—directly elected—adult franchise.	3. Members of Union Councils and Town/Union Committees: non-officials—directly elected—adult franchise. Members of other Councils and Committees: Not more than 50% were officials and not less than 50% were non-officials; non-officials were indirectly elected by an electoral college.
4. Non-official Chairman or President.	4. Union Council and Town/Union Committee: non-official Chairman. Other Councils and Committees: official Chairman.
5. Less official control and supervision	5. More official control and supervision.
6. Modest government grants.	6. Large government grants.
7. Limited taxing powers.	7. More taxing powers.
8. Comparatively less rural development works.	8. Comparatively more rural development works.
9. Did not form Electoral College.	9. Electoral College for electing Assemblies and the Head of the State.

representative in character, came to an end with the introduction of the post-58 system of local bodies.

The Future System of Local Bodies in Bangladesh

In January 1972 the Government of Bangladesh dissolved the post-1958 system of local bodies i.e. "Basic Democracies".[1] It was declared that (i) the Union Council, (ii) the Union Committee, (iii) the Town Committee, (iv) the *Thana* Council,

[1] President's Order no. 7 of 1972, *The Bangladesh Gazette*, Extraordinary, January 20, 1972.

(v) the District Council, and (vi) the Municipal Committee would be replaced by (i) the Union *Panchayat*, (ii) the *Nagar Panchayat*, (iii) the *Shahar* Committee, (iv) the *Thana* Development Committee, (v) the *Zilla* Board, and (vi) the *Paura Shava* respectively,[1] that there would be no local body at the divisional level, and that a Committee or an Administrator would be appointed in order to make provision for the performance of the functions of each dissolved local body till such time as new local bodies were established under the laws to be made by the legislature of Bangladesh. Since then appointed administrators, who are officials, have been performing the functions of the dissolved local bodies. Now (mid-1973) it is felt that soon the new system of local bodies will be introduced in this country and that the new bodies will consist of elected non-official members and presidents/chairmen. Unlike the former system, the officials will not be made ex-officio members and presidents/chairmen of these bodies.

Public Services

Introduction. In former Pakistan there was a large number of public services each with a separate name. Professor Braibanti observed that the "structural organization of the public services of Pakistan is one of the most complicated of any bureaucratic system in existence."[2] The services were divided by both horizontal and vertical lines. By horizontal lines they were classified into four classes, namely class I, class II, class III and class IV, according to the degree of importance of the work performed and the nature and the scale of responsibility undertaken by each of the services.[3] By horizontal lines the members of these four classes were also divided into two groups, namely gazetted officers

1 *Ibid.* And President's Order no. 17 of 1972, *The Bangladesh Gazette*, Extraordinary, February 29, 1972. Also see President's Order no. 110 of 1972, *The Bangladesh Gazette*, Extraordinary, September 11, 1972.

2 Braibanti, *Research*, p. 132.

3 M. A. Chaudhuri, "The Organisation and Composition of the Central Civil Services in Pakistan" in *International Review of Administrative Sciences*, vol. xxvi, 1960, no. 3, p. 281.

and non-gazetted officers.[1] The members of all class I services and most class II services were gazetted officers whose appointment, transfer, retirement, dismissal, etc. were notified in the government gazette.[2] They held higher posts and were entrusted with higher responsibilities in respect of administration and management. The members of class III were petty or clerical staff who performed less important or routine work under the supervision of the members of the class I and class II services. The class IV employees were manual workers such as peons, bearers, orderlies, night guards, etc., who performed petty jobs.[3]

By vertical lines the public services were divided into a large number of individual services such as (i) Civil Service of Pakistan, (ii) Pakistan Foreign Service, (iii) Police Service of Pakistan, (iv) Pakistan Audit and Accounts Service, (v) Pakistan Taxation Service, (vi) Pakistan Customs and Excise Service, (vii) Post and Telegraph Service, (viii) Central Engineering Service, (ix) Provincial Civil Service, (x) Provincial Health and Medical Service, (xi) Provincial Engineering Service, (xii) Provincial Agricultural Service, and many other services.[4]

The first eight services were central superior services and the rest the provincial services. The central superior services were class I services and their members were class I officers from the first day of their appointment. Most of the provincial services, with the exception of one or two (e.g., Provincial Civil Service) were class II services.[5] Thus the members of most of the provincial services began their official career as class II officers. Of course, later when they were promoted to senior positions they became class I officers, though they were not the members of the

[1] Masihuzzaman, *Pakistan Quarterly*, p. 126.

[2] M.W. Abbasi, *Civil Service in Pakistan* (Pakistan Administrative Staff College, Lahore, n.d.) (Text of a talk delivered by Mr. Abbasi, Principal Pakistan Administrative Staff College, at the NIPA, Lahore), p. 4.

[3] M.A. Chaudhuri, *op. cit.*, p. 281.

[4] For the names of other important services, see Braibanti, *Research*, p. 136. Also see Masihuzzaman, *Pakistan Quarterly*, p. 127.

[5] In British India and in the first decade of former Pakistan, the Provincial Civil Service was a class II service.

central superior services. The recruitment of most members of central superior services i.e. services was made directly. Only very small number of officers of class II services were occasionally promoted to these services. Both the methods of direct recruitment and promotion from lower services were followed in selecting the members of class II services.[1] Direct recruitment to any service was made on the basis of competitive examination or selection test conducted by the Federal or Provincial Public Service Commission.[2]

The Civil Service of Pakistan (CSP). The Civil Service of Pakistan was the most important service in (former and present) Pakistan. It was also very important for any study of district administration. It was the successor of the Indian Civil Service (ICS) which, according to Sir Erik Franklin, "was the most distinguished Civil Service in the world".[3] On the Civil Service of Pakistan, Professor Braibanti commented that it was "one of the greatest institutions of governmental leadership in the world".[4]

He also held that the "nation must depend to an extraordinary degree on the intellectual and administrative competence of carefully trained generalist executives, namely the Civil Service of Pakistan, to operate government and to give intellectual direction to the new synthesis of governmental power which is being inevitably created".[5] The Civil Service of Pakistan far from including all the civil employees of the government consisted of

1 M.A. Chaudhuri, *op. cit.*, p. 282.

2 Public Service Commissions were autonomous bodies. The different aspects of the Commissions' functions, position, structure, etc. have been discussed in Braibanti, *Research*, pp. esp. 119-131. There is also a discussion on Commissions in Ahmed Rabbani, "Recruitment and Selection in Pakistan" (Cyclostyled) (A paper presented at the Seminar on Development Administration, Pakistan Administrative Staff College, Lahore, n.d.), pp. 2-6.

3 Quoted in Braibanti, *The Civil Service of Pakistan*, p. 258.

4 Ralph Braibanti, "Working Paper on Course of Study at the Civil Service Academy of Pakistan (Tentative Draft, March 21, 1961, Cyclostyled). (This paper was prepared when Professor Braibanti was the Chief Advisor to the Civil Service Academy, Lahore.) (NIPA, Dacca, Reprint No. 17, August 1964), p. 7.

5 *Ibid.*, p 2.

a very limited number of officers called CSPs. On January 1, 1966 there were only 482 CSPs including 62 probationers.[1] Among the class I services it was the topmost service and occupied a special position within the public services.[2] Such terms as the elite of bureaucracy, the *corps d'elite*, the premier service, etc. were applied to it. It could be compared with the Administrative Class in Great Britain. But while the members of the Administrative Class did not work at the local level, CSP officers were spread all over the country and were also stationed at the central and the provincial headquarters. It was really the "pivotal service around which the entire administrative edifice centre and province is organised".[3] Two-thirds of the posts of Secretaries, Joint Secretaries and Deputy Secretaries of the Central Secretariat and three-fourths of the 'Cadre Posts' in the province such as Chief Secretary, Additional Chief Secretaries, the members of the Board of Revenue, Divisional Commissioners, Secretaries, D. O.s, Joint Secretaries, Additional D. O.s, Deputy Secretaries and some other higher posts were reserved for CSP officers and the rest of the above mentioned posts for other services[4] (mainly the Provincial Civil Service and

[1] *Gradation List of the Civil Service of Pakistan* (Corrected up to January 1, 1966) (Rawalpindi) (Gradation List is published annually). Here it may be mentioned that except under very exceptional circumstances, the officers of class II services and other class I services were never promoted to the Civil Service of Pakistan. Members of this service were always recruited directly. Immediately after partition only a very few officers of the provincial civil service were promoted to this service and immediately after the declaration of the first Martial Law in 1958, few army officers were appointed in that service.

[2] Muneer Ahmad, *The Civil Servant in Pakistan* (Karachi, 1964), p. 21. This is primarily a study of the attitudes of the public servants in former Pakistan. The term 'the Civil Servant' in the title does not mean the CSP only, but any civil employee—CSP or non-CSP.

[3] M.A. Chaudhuri, *op. cit.*, p. 283.

[4] See following notifications (and the schedules attached with the notifications) of the Establishment Division of the Cabinet Secretariat, Govt. of the then Pakistan : No. F. 25/12/51-SE9, Karachi, Ist June, 1954 ; No. 25/12/51-SE9, Karachi, 21st June, 1954. Of course this criterion for filling the above mentioned posts in the Central Secretariat did not apply to those posts reserved for the officers who belonged to what was called

Secretariat Service). One third of the posts of the Judges of the Supreme and the High Courts and those of the District and Sessions Judges were to be filled by CSP officers and the rest of these posts by the members of the Provincial Civil Service (Judicial) and those of the Bar.[1] Though the bulk of the CSP officers worked in the Secretariats and in the administrative branch of district administration some of them also occupied higher posts in other governmental agencies.[2] Of course, almost all the posts in most Directorates were held by the officers of other services which had been created for various Directorates. For example, the higher posts (at various levels) in the Directorates of Education, Police and 'Roads and Buildings' were filled by the members of the Educa-

---

'Economic Pool' (earlier called Finance and Commerce Pool). The purpose of creating the 'Economic Pool' was to draw economic financial talents from various services into a common cadre. Sixty per cent of the posts of the 'Economic Pool' were reserved for the CSP officers.

The number of the CSP officers was much less than the number of the posts reserved for them. Thus many posts reserved for them were filled by the members of other services. These posts would be filled by the CSPs on a long-term basis through annual recruitment on the basis of open competitive examinations.

1 *Ibid.* For the reason mentioned above, all the judicial posts reserved for the CSP officers were not filled by them.

2 Often the following important posts in other governmental agencies were also filled by the CSPs: Chairman, Water and Power Development Authority; Director, National Institute of Public Administration; Principal, Administrative Staff College; Chairman, Industrial Development Corporation; Director General, Investment Promotion and Supplies Department; Chairman (and some Members) of Agricultural Development Corporation; Chief Controller of Imports and Exports; Chief and Deputy Chief Economists, Planning Division; Director of Audit, Defence Services; Director, Guddu Barrage; Chairman, Small Industries Corporation; Chairman, Dacca or Karachi or Lahore or Chittagong Development Authority; Director, Labour; Director, Commerce and Industries; Collector of Customs; Director, Mineral Development; Registrar, Co-operative Societies; Director, Bureau of National Reconstruction; Collector of Central Excise; Project Director, Gulam Mohammad Barrage; Chairman (and some Members), Road Transport Corporation; Director, Bureau of Statistics; Director, Academy for Rural Development and many other posts. (Source: *Gradation Lists of the Civil Service of Pakistan.*)

tion, the Police and the Engineering Services respectively. Thus, we find that the services to which most officers of Directorates belonged were different from the services to which the officers of the Secretariat Departments belonged.[1] Of course, there were some Directorates such as the Directorates of 'Commerce and Industries' and Co-operative Societies, etc. for which no 'superior services' were created. Most higher posts in such Directorates were held by the CSP officers as well as by the members of the Provincial Civil Service.

The Civil Service of Pakistan was an "all-purpose" and "all-Pakistan" service, the members of which were required to serve anywhere in the country. As the members of an "all-Pakistan" service, they moved from province to province, from province to centre and vice versa. As the members of an "all-purpose" service, they moved from one type of work to another, from one department to another, they moved from the district to the Secretariat or a Directorate and vice versa, during the course of their official career. On the other hand, the members of each of the other services performed the functions which the name of their service indicated and usually remained in the Directorate, for which the service was created, throughout their official career.

On completion of the pre-service training, a CSP officer invariably began his official career in district administration as the S. D. O. (E. Beng.)/ S. D. M. (W. Pak.) of an outlying subdivision. Table xiv will give an idea of the nature of the mobility of a CSP officer.

Thus, we find that the CSP officers had a dual role. On the one hand, they served as the executive arms of the government deployed in the field and on the other hand, in the Secretariat they took part in the process of policy making. The frequent interchange of the CSP officers (as well as of the members of the Provincial Civil Service) between the district and the Secretariat and the feeling that they belonged to the same service brought the D. O. and the higher

[1] We have already noted that most of the top posts in the Secretariat Departments were held by the CSP officers and some by the members of the Provincial Civil Service and of the Secretariat Service.

TABLE XIV

THE NATURE OF THE MOBILITY OF A CSP OFFICER

Part I

Sub-Divisional Officer/Magistrate←→Assistant Political Agent←→Section Officer (both central and provincial Secretariats)←→Other posts, the official status of which was equal to that of above mentioned officers.

↓

Part II

Additional Deputy Commissioner←→Additional Political Agent←→Deputy Secretary (Provincial Secretariat)←→Other posts, the official status of which was equal to that of above-mentioned officers.

↓

Part III

Deputy Commissioner←→Political Agent←→Joint Secretary (Provincial Secretariat)←→Deputy Secretary (Central Secretariat)←→Other posts, the official status of which was equal to that of above mentioned officers.

↓

Part IV

Secretary (Provincial Secretariat) (the rank of which was higher than that of Deputy Commissioner but lower than that of Divisional Commissioner)*←→other posts, the official status of which was equal to that of above-mentioned officers.

↓

Part V

Divisional Commissioner←→Secretary (Provincial Secretariat) (the rank of which was equal to that of Divisional Commissioner)*←→Joint Secretary (Central Secretariat)←→Other posts, the official status of which was equal to that of above mentioned officers.

↓

Part VI

Additional Chief Secretary (Provincial Secretariat)←→Additional Secretary (Central Secretariat)←→Other posts, the official status of which was equal to that of above mentioned officers.

↓

Part VII

Chief Secretary (Provincial Secretariat)←→Secretary (Central Secretariat)←→High Commissioner/Ambassador←→Other posts, the official status of which was equal to that of above-mentioned officers.

For some explanatory comments on table XIV, see below, p. 183.

staff of the Secretariat closer to one another and as a result they were influenced by one another's views and a mutual respect and understanding developed between them. These factors further strengthened to an extraordinary degree the legal relationship that already existed between the D. O. and the Secretariat.[1] Later

Some Explanatory Comments on Table XIV (p. 182)

For example, Mr. B, a CSP officer who held the rank of SDO/SDM might or might not be required to move from one post to another post mentioned in the first part of the table. In the course of his movements, he might or might not be required to hold the same post twice or thrice or even more. Later on when he held higher posts (mentioned in the subsequent parts of the table) the nature or pattern of his mobility was same. Of course, on very rare occasions one might find some minor deviations from the usual procedure.

Of course, the nature of the mobility of the CSP officers who were working in the judicial branch was different. When a CSP officer who held the post of or equal to that of the SDO was due for promotion, it was decided whether he would be transferred to the judicial branch or to the administrative branch. If he was selected for the judicial branch he was promoted to the rank of Additional District and Sessions Judge and usually he remained in the judicial branch throughout his official career. On the other hand, if he was selected for the administrative branch, he was promoted to the rank of Additional D.O. or Deputy Secretary to the provincial government or to that of some other post which was equal to these two posts. After this decision, an officer was not usually interchanged between the administrative and the judicial branches. Of course, occasionally officers were interchanged between these two branches of government. But this was not the usual procedure.

CSP officers were interchanged between the administrative branch in districts and the Provincial Secretariat much more frequently than between other governmental agencies. Of course, after becoming the Secretary to the provincial Government, an officer was not appointed to any post in the district because the rank of Secretary was higher than that of D.O. Of course, later a Secretary might be appointed as Divisional Commissioner and thus he might again come into close contact with district administration.

* Before 1961 the official status of provincial Secretaries was higher than that of the D.O., but lower than that of the Divisional Commissioner. Then the government decided that the status of the Secretaries of a few important departments, such as Home, Finance, etc., would be upgraded. So, after 1961 there were some Secretaries in the provincial Secretariat, the official status of whom was equal to that of Divisional Commissioners, or Joint Secretaries in the Central Secretariat.

[1] Earlier in this chapter we have already noted that in the district the D.O. is the representative of all the Ministries/Secretariat Departments and

we shall see in the chapter (iv) on the 'Problems of Coordination' in districts that this close relationship was a very important source of his influence which he could and, in fact, did exert on the officers of various Directorates stationed in his district, for coordinating their activities. Such a close relationship was indispensable and very useful for better and coordinated administration in districts.

Calibre of CSP Candidates. The members of the Civil Service of Pakistan were selected on the basis of competitive examinations conducted by the Federal Public Service Commission. Only those candidates who occupied top places in the list of the successful candidates were selected for the Civil Service of Pakistan. The basic idea of the examination was based on "Macauley's famous assertion that the persons who excel over others in academic learning also excel over them in other walks of life".[1]

Most of the bright students after having completed an Honours or Master's degree sat for the Superior Service Examination in the hope of joining the Civil Service of Pakistan[2] because, as noted above, it was the most prestigious service in the country, the assignments given to the CSPs were of higher and more responsible nature ; most key posts which carried greater influence and status were reserved for them; the CSP officers had better prospect of climbing up to the heights of the public services[3] and

---

that as a result direct contact exists between him and the Secretariat.

The above discussion will serve as the background of chapter vi, in which the problems of co-ordination in district administration is discussed.

[1] Muneer Ahmad, *op. cit.*, p. 216.

[2] The parents of the students also usually insisted that they should try to join the Civil Service of Pakistan. Professor Braibanti commented that "In India, Pakistan, Ceylon and Burma, for example, an ambitious mother's wish for her son was not that he enters politics, law, medicine or teaching, but rather that he enters the higher civil service." Braibanti, "Administrative Modernisation" in Myron Weiner (ed.), *Modernisation* (New York, 1966), p. 168.

[3] An efficient CSP officer who had began his official career as the SDO or SDM could rise to such exalted positions as the Chief Justice or Justice of the Supreme Court or of the High Court, or the High Commissioner/ Ambassador or the Chief Secretary to the provincial government or the

they enjoyed many privileges and facilities such as rapid promotion and better pay scale, accommodation, service conditions etc.

But in spite of the fact that the bright students tried to join the Civil Service of Pakistan the overall standard of the service and the calibre of the members seriously deteriorated since partition in 1947.[1] The calibre of the members of the Indian Civil Service (ICS) was very high. The "ICS tradition was leavened by intellectuality"[2] and this tradition has become a legend. Many ICS men were well known as philosophers, historians and scholars

> "whose craftmanship and devotion to learning was reflected not only in prescribed census and settlement reports but in 'extra curricular' enterprises as well. In the work of these men there was attention to meticulous classification of data, integrated social and economic studies which would satisfy the canons of rigorous empiricism, earthly humanitarian scholarship attuned to the homely requisites of village uplift yet guided by uncommon missionary dedication and meticulous compilation...... of such precision that they remain today documents of legal standing for local administration."[3]
>
> "...the intellectual tradition of the ICS was no mean obscurantism or sterile pedantry; at its worst it was dilettantism but at its best it was marked by an eclectic quality, an imagination, and a vision worthy of the greatest respect".[4]

But the Civil Service of Pakistan was not able to maintain that intellectual standard. Of course, a few CSP officers who joined the service since partition were exceptionally brilliant. But the calibre and academic standard of most members of the service were average in comparison with those of most members of the Indian Civil Service. The Federal Public Service Commission which was consistently concerned with the deterioration in the calibre and standard of candidates, deplored "the absence of original thinking and critical faculty, poor spelling and grammar,

---

Secretary to the central government or the Head of a governmental agency, or of a corporation (e.g. Industrial Development Corporation) comparatively at an early age.

[1] See the comment of the Federal Public Service Commission (below).

[2] Ralph Braibanti, "Reflections on Bureaucratic Reform in India" in Ralph Braibanti and Joseph J. Spengler (eds.), *Administrative and Economic Development in India* (Durham, 1963), p. 24.

[3] *Ibid.*, pp. 24-25.

[4] *Ibid.*, p. 24.

superficiality and immaturity of judgement"[1]. The Commission held that the decline of intellectual and academic standards and political and social disarticulation after partition were responsible for the decline of the standard of candidates. Moreover, before partition many bright students from Great Britain and all over British India had sat for the Indian Civil Service Examination and as a result only those candidates who had been exceptionally bright could get into the service.

The decline of the standard of the service had much more seriously affected the working of district administration than that of the administration at the higher levels because at these levels some members of the Indian Civil Service were working.[2] Thus, in the mid-1950s the *First Five Year Plan* commented that "Barring a few outstanding exceptions, there has been a noticeable deterioration in the quality of district personnel in recent years, owing to the general shortage of mature and experienced administrators, made more acute by withdrawals to the Secretariat."[3]

Of course, it should be admitted that though the overall standard of the Civil Service of Pakistan seriously deteriorated, most of the best available young talents in the country joined this service, that the calibre of CSP officers, with some exceptions, was better than that of the members of other services and that in the face of adversity, chaos and confusion, they rendered much valuable service to the country which deserved recognition.[4]

[1] Braibanti, *The Civil Service*, p. 280.

[2] On January 1, 1966 some 50 former members of the Indian Civil Service were in the Civil Service of Pakistan. (*Gradation List of the Civil Service of Pakistan*, corrected upto January 1, 1966.)

[3] *First Five Year Plan*, p. 101. The penetration of the Indian Civil Service by Muslims was very insignificant. In 1947 the strength of the ICS cadre was 1157 of which 52% were British, 39% Hindu and only 9% Muslim. (Braibanti, *Reflections on Bureaucratic Reform in India*, p. 21.) As a result, the number of ICS officers was very insignificant in former Pakistan. Thus it was felt that the vacuum created in the Secretariat should be filled in as far as possible with these handful of officers.

[4] Wilber, *op. cit.*, p. 274.

The Provincial Civil Service (PCS)[1]. The Provincial Civil Service is also important for any study of district administration. Like the Civil Service of Pakistan, it was also an all-purpose service. But it was not an all-Pakistan service though sometimes a few posts in the central secretariat were held by them. They were "meant for the provincial administration."[2] Thus the members of the Provincial Civil Services of East Bengal and West Pakistan worked in their respective provinces. The main purpose of having this service was to recruit candidates for filling the posts of Deputy Magistrates (E. Beng.)/Extra-Assistant Commissioners (W. Pak.).[3] The bulk of PCS officers worked in these capacities. Like CSP officers they also moved from district to Secretariat or other governmental agencies and vice versa but not as frequently as CSP officers. A small fraction of higher posts and relatively "less important positions in general administration are given to the officers of the cadre of Provincial Civil Service".[4] They were not promoted to higher ranks as quickly as CSP officers. In 1966 the age of most PCS officers in East Bengal who held the posts of S.D.O. and D.O. ranged from the mid-30s to 55 and from the mid-40s to 55[5] respectively[6]. And the age of almost all CSP officers in East Bengal and West Pakistan who held these two posts in 1966 ranged from the mid-20s to the late 20s and from the early-30s to the mid-30s respectively.[7] Only a limited number of PCS officers who

[1] In former East and West Pakistan the Provincial Civil Service was respectively called East Pakistan Civil Service (EPCS) and Provincial Civil Service (PCS). In this book Provincial Civil Service (PCS) will be referred to as the common name for both the services.

[2] A. Rashid, "Deputy Commissioner: Justification and Role in a Welfare State" (cyclostyled) (A paper read at the Seminar on Development Administration held at Pakistan Administrative Staff College, Lahore, n.d.), p. 5.

[3] On entering the service PCS officers were first appointed as Deputy Magistrates/Extra Assistant Commissioners.

[4] Muneer Ahmad, *op. cit.*, pp. 202-203.

[5] The age of retirement was 55.

[6] *The Civil List* (Dacca, 1966) (*The Civil List* is published after every two years). The age of PCS officers in West Pakistan who held these posts was also more or less same.

[7] *Gradation List of the Civil Service of Pakistan* (corrected up to January 1, 1966).

proved to be efficient were appointed as S.D.O. and D.O. Only a few of them who were considered very bright and efficient were promoted to a rank higher than that of the D. O. or the Joint Secretary to the provincial government.

A considerable proportion of the members of the Provincial Civil Service was recruited through competitive examinations conducted by the Provincial Public Service Commission and the rest by promotion from other subordinate services. Though the pattern of the Provincial Civil Service examination was almost the same as that of the central superior Service examination, there was a world of difference between the calibre of a PCS officer who entered the service after partition and that of a CSP officer. But in pre-partition days the calibre and academic standard of a considerable number of the members of the Provincial Civil Services, for example those of the Bengal Civil Service, had been very high,[1] though not as high as those of the members of the Indian Civil Service. But after partition the gap between the calibre of PCS officers and that of CSP officers widened to an extraordinary degree. No doubt, as noted above, the calibre of PCS officers also went down, but the deterioration of the calibre of CSP officers was much greater than that of CSP officers. Several factors were responsible for the sharp fall in the standard of the Provincial Civil Service. In pre-partition days those who had failed to join the Indian Civil Service or Indian Police or Accounts Service had tried to join the Provincial Civil Services of their respective provinces. Moreover, as only a small number of candidates had got the opportunity to get into central services because of very stiff competition,[2] many persons who had sat for the Provincial Civil

[1] After partition a few members of the Bengal Civil Service, as noted above, were absorbed into the Civil Service of Pakistan. Some members of the Bengal Civil Service who were still in the provincial Civil Service were holding higher posts such as those of the Divisional Commissioners, the Secretaries to the Provincial Government and heads of other governmental agencies.

[2] We have already noted the factors which were responsible for the stiff competition in the Indian Civil Service Examination. The same factors were responsible for the stiff competition in the Audit and Accounts Service Examination and especially in the Indian Police Service Examination.

Service examination had also been bright. But after partition the prospect and scope in some other services and also in private enterprises gradually increased. As a result, career in the Provincial Civil Service was not so favoured in the post-partition period.

The deterioration of the standard of the Provincial Civil Service also seriously affected the efficiency of district administration because, as noted above, all the posts of Deputy Magistrates/ Extra Assistant Commissioners were filled by the PCS officers. The D. O., the Additional D.O. and the S.D.O. depended to a considerable extent on them for running administration efficiently.

Here it may be mentioned that a CSP D. O. (or Additional D.O. or S.D.O.) enjoyed much greater prestige and position than his PCS counterpart. The former derived his influence and prestige not only from his legal or statutory powers but from the very fact that he was the member of the premier and the most sought-after service in the country, the members of which, as noted above, held most of the key posts in the administrative hierarchy stretching from the centre down to the sub-divisional level. As a result, the former was in a much more advantageous position to exercise greater influence and control over both officials and non-officials than the latter.

Future Changes in the Public Service System

After liberation, the Government of Bangladesh appointed a Services Reorganisation Committee to look into various aspects of public services and to recommend about the structure and the pattern of the future public service system in Bangladesh. Recently, the Committee has submitted its report to the government. It has not yet been made public (mid-1973). But it is widely believed that the Committee has made some radical recommendations and that the public service structure will undergo radical changes in Bangladesh in the near future.

The structure and other aspects of the public service system in former Pakistan, which we have discussed above, have not undergone any change in present Pakistan. It is also strongly felt that in the foreseeable future no significant change will take place there.

CHAPTER IV

TRADITIONAL FUNCTIONS

The discussion of the traditional functions of district administration may be arranged under the following three headings : (a) Law and Order or Criminal Administration, (b) Revenue Administration and (c) General Administrative or Miscellaneous Functions.

LAW AND ORDER OR CRIMINAL ADMINISTRATION

Introduction

"[The maintenance of law and order is] the primary concern of every civilised government, irrespective of every other consideration. But law and order are two different terms...[For example,] a person may make a speech or write a pamphlet which offends the law but which does not lead to disorder. A government would, therefore, be failing in half of its duty if it ignores such a speech on the ground, for instance, that although a month has passed since the speech was made or the pamphlet written, nothing untoward has happened. It is overlooked that this attitude offends the majesty of law and gradually comes to bread contempt in the minds of the speakers, writers and a multitude of readers... Since this ultimately recoils on the 'order' situation, it is well for the administrator to bear in mind that people should be disciplined to keep within the bounds of law".[1]

In (former and present) Pakistan, at the provincial level the head of the matters concerning law and order is the Home

[1] *Munir-Kayani Report*, p. 288. (For further discussion see below, pp. 34-35.) this comment was made by Mr. Justice Munir and the late Mr. Justice Kayani in view of the fact that from the early 1950s the *Ulema* in West Pakistan, who were religious fanatics, began to deliver inflammatory speeches in religious and public meetings and to write inflammatory pamphlets in order to stir hatred and bitterness in the minds of the general people against the *Ahmadi* sect but the administrative authority did not take any firm action to prevent the *Ulema* from doing so with the result that a section of the orthodox people gradually develop a very hostile and militant attitude towards the *Ahmadi* sect which ultimately resulted in very serious anti-*Ahmadi* riots in various places of West Pakistan in 1953.

Minister.[1] He is assisted by the Chief Secretary and the Home Secretary. The "Chief Secretary is in charge of 'public tranquility', and for police matters...the secretarial work is dealt with by the Home Secretary, who acts as the Chief Secretary's assistant in the sphere of law and order."[2] The head of the police Directorate is the Inspector General of Police (I.G.) who is subordinate to the Home Secretary. The nature of the relationship between the Home Secretary and the I.G. is more or less similar to that of the relationship between the head of a Secretariat Department and the head of a Directorate.[3] At the central level also the head of the matters concerning law and order is the Home Minister. Here it may be mentioned that unlike some African countries there are no two separate police forces i.e. the central or federal and the provincial or local police forces. There is only one police force namely provincial police force the hierarchy of which stretches from the provincial headquarters down to the village level.[4] The central government's policies and decisions in regard to matters concerning law and order are executed through the provincial government. The law and order matters are usually regarded as provincial subject.

As Bangladesh is not divided into provinces, the question of central or provincial police force does not arise. After the emergence of East Bengal as a separate and independent state of Bangladesh, the former provincial police force of East Bengal became the central or national police force. So, in Bangladesh also there is only one police force the hierarchy of which stretches from the central headquarters down to the village level.[5] As there is no province and consequently no Chief Secretary, Home Secretary to the (central) Government of Bangladesh

[1] From 1947 to 1958, when parliamentary form of government was in operation, home portfolio was usually held by the Chief Minister and from 1958 to 1972, when there was non-parliamentary form of government, it was usually held by the Governor.

[2] *Munir-Kayani Report*, p. 288.

[3] See above, chap. iii.

[4] For an idea of police hierarchy in (former and present) Pakistan see below, chart v.

[5] See below, chart vi.

looks after the matters concerning law and order and assists the Home Minister. The Head of the police force is also called the Inspector General of Police (I.G.). So far as the nature of his theoretical relationship with the Home Secretary is concerned, there is no basic difference between Bangladesh and Pakistan.

In both Bangladesh and (former and present) Pakistan the district is the 'basic' and the 'focal' unit of criminal administration. In his capacity as District Magistrate, the D.O. is "the ultimate authority in the district responsible for law and order".[1] He is "the head of criminal administration in the district."[2] As District Magistrate his powers are two-fold. Firstly, he has control over the police force operating within his jurisdiction and secondly, he is the direct head of all Magistrates in the district.

Before going into the details of the law and order aspect of district administration it may be mentioned that "Broadly speaking, law and order has two aspects viz (i) maintenance of public peace and (ii) investigation and trial of criminal cases."[3]

[1] *Pro. Adm. Com. Report*, p. 186.

[2] *Punjab Police Rules, 1934*, vol. i (Lahore, 1934), paras. 1, 2. In pursuance of the decision (June 23, 1960) of the central Cabinet [see *Decisions of the Cabinet on the Report of the Provincial Administration commission* (Karachi, 1962), p. 24. Hereafter cited as *Cabinet Decisions*.] the then Provincial Government in East Bengal decided on July 8, 1960 to incorporate this section of the *Punjab Police Rules, 1934* into the *Police Regulations of Bengal, 1943* (Calcutta, 1943. Reprinted in Dacca in 1958) which are now in force in Bangladesh. This section of the *Punjab Police Rules* was numbered as section 15(a) of the *Police Regulations of Bengal*. [see Minutes of the Meeting of the Panel (of officers) on Law and Order (cyclostyled), Dacca, July 8, 1960.] Later we shall see that in pursuance of the above mentioned decision of the central Cabinet some sections of the Police Regulations in West Pakistan [after the integration (1955) of West Pakistan into one province most sections of the *Punjab Police Rules* were applied throughout West Pakistan] were incorporated into the *Police Regulations of East Bengal* and vice versa. Here it may be mentioned that the purpose of the two sets of Regulations had for long been the same. Now the very language used, as we shall see below, became identical or almost identical.

[3] *Pro. Adm. Com. Report*, p. 184.

District Officer's Control over the Police

The Superintendent of Police (S.P.) is the "executive head"[1] of the police force in the district, but the D.O., who "is primarily responsible for the good order of the district and the efficient working of the police",[2] is the overall head of the police force in his district.[3] As such "the Superintendent of Police is subordinate to him."[4] He and his force are "under the command of the Magistrate of the District"[5] (i.e. District Magistrate). The following few passages quoted from various Police Regulations will further illustrate the legal nature of the relationship between these two officers :[6]

> "[The S.P.]...is responsible, subject to the control and direction of the District Magistrate, for the proper performance by officers subordinate to him of all preventive and executive duties".[7]

---

[1] *Punjab Police Rules, 1934*, para, 1.8. *Police Regulations of Bengal, 1943*, para. 16(a). (Numbered and incorporated in 1960. See Minutes...Panel on Law and Order, p. 5.)

[2] The Punjab Government Consolidated Circular No. 2 (Corrected up to January 11, 1939), para, 13, quoted in the *Council Report for West Pakistan*, p. 15. *Police Regulations of Bengal, 1943*, para, 15(b). (Numbered and incorporated in 1960. See Minutes...Panel on Law and Order, p. 5.)

[3] The paragraph 13 of the Punjab Government Consolidated Circular No. 2 declared that "In all districts of the Punjab, the District Magistrate is the head of the police Department." (Quoted in the *Council Report for W. Pak.*, p. 15.) Thus we find that while in one document the S.P. is called the "executive head" (see above, p. 193) of the police force, in another document the D.O. is called the "head" of the police force. This appears to be somewhat confusing and vague. This vagueness may be cleared by pointing out that while the S.P. is the immediate departmental head of the police force [It may be mentioned that before 1960, in East Bengal the *Police Regulations of Bengal* called the S.P. the "immediate head of the police force of the district" (see para. 15a of the unmodified 1958 reprint edition of the *Regulations.*)], the D.O. is the overall head or the overlord of the police force.

[4] *Police Regulations of Bengal*, para. 15(a). (Incorporated in 1960. See Minutes...Panel on Law and Order, p. 5.)

[5] *The Bombay District Police Act, 1890* (Later in Sind it was called Sind District Police Act), quoted in *Council Report for W. Pak.*, p. 15.

[6] Later we shall see that in practice the nature of their relationship is not exactly the same as stated in the legal provisions of different Police Regulations.

[7] *Police Regulations of Bengal*, para. 16(b). [Before 1960 the number of the

"[Though the]...administration of the police force is vested in the Superintendent of Police...he is expected to place himself and his force at the disposal of the District Magistrate as an effective instrument in the maintenance of law and order".[1]

"The police force is the instrument provided by the Government to enable him [D.O.] to enforce his authority and fulfil his responsibility for the maintenance of law and order. The police force in the district is, therefore, placed by law under the general control and direction of the District Magistrate [[2]] who is responsible that [sic] it carries out its duties in such a manner that effective protection is afforded to the public against lawlessness and disorder."[3]

"In all that affects the relations between the police and the public or the keeping of the public peace, the District Magistrate must be consulted [by the S.P.] and his orders complied with."[4]

"The primary duty of the Superintendent of Police is to afford the District Magistrate the utmost possible assistance, both himself and through the police under his command, in the preservation of the peace and the prevention or detection of crime. He shall keep in close and constant personal touch with the District Magistrate and shall keep him fully and promptly informed, both by personal conference and by written reports, of all matters relating to crime and public order. While it is his duty to initiate action by the police in such matters, he must keep the District Magistrate informed and be guided by his orders."[5]

---

paragraph was 15(a). In 1960 it was renumbered. See Minutes...Panel on Law and Order, p. 5. Before 1960 the wording of the para was slightly different.]

[1] *Police Regulations of Bengal*, para. 16(c). (Incorporated in 1960. See Minutes ...Panel on Law and Order, p. 5.)

[2] The Police Act of 1861, on the basis of which all provincial police regulations were subsequently formulated, had first declared that the S.P. and his force would perform their functions "under the general control and direction" of the D.O. [See the Police Act, 1861 in *The Unrepealed General Acts of the Governor General in Council: From 1834 to 1872*, vol. i (Calcutta, 1928 edition), sec. 4.] It may be mentioned here that the S.P. was first appointed in 1861. Before that the *Darogha* (the Officer in charge of a police station) was directly responsible to the D.O. [For a brief discussion of the difference between the police administration in the pre-1861 period and that in the post-1861 period see Philip Woodruff, *The Men Who Ruled India: The Guardians* (London, 1963 edn.), pp. 51-54.]

[3] *The Punjab Police Rules*, para. 1.15. *The Police Regulations of Bengal*, para. 15(c). (Incorporated in 1960. See Minutes...Panel on Law and Order, p.5.)

[4] *Punjab Police Rules*, para. 1.15. *Police Regulations of Bengal*, para. 16(e). (Incorporated in 1960. See Minutes...Panel on Law and Order, p.6.)

[5] *Punjab Police Rules*, para. 1.16. Almost similar views have been expressed in the *Police Regulations of Bengal*, para. 21(a). [See Minutes...Panel on

> "[It is also the responsibility of the D.O. to]...exercise constant supervision over the prevention and detection of crime for the proper conduct of which he is ultimately responsible. An important part of his duties is to inspect the Police Stations of his district at regular intervals".[1]

But the D.O. has no authority to interfere in matters concerning the internal administration, discipline, economy and training of the force.[2] The S.D.O. exercises "more or less the same authority" over the Sub-Divisional Police Officer (Deputy or Assistant Superintendent of Police) "as is exercised by the District Magistrate over the Superintendent of Police."[3] In short, we may say

---

Law and Order, p. 5. Before 1960 the para. no. was 16(a). See 1958 reprint edition of the *Regulations*.]

[1] *Police Regulations of Bengal*, para. 17. (See Minutes...Panel on Law and Order, p. 6. Before 1960 the para no. was 19. See 1958 reprint edition of the *Regulations*.) Similar views have also been expressed in the *Punjab Police Rules*, para. 1.15.

While inspecting a Police Station the District Officer is supposed to "give special attention to

(i) "the general diary and the manner in which it is written up;
(ii) "the recording of vital statistics;
(iii) "the proper working of the Arms Act;
(iv) "the general state of crime in the Police-Station [each Police Station has jurisdiction over an area] and any reasons for its increase or decrease;
(v) "whether the Sub-Inspector [a Sub-Inspector is in charge of each Police Station] appears to have a proper knowledge of his duties, whether he is in touch with the respectable inhabitants of his charge, has acquired local knowledge, and takes an interest in his work;
(vi) "whether the police station officials appear to be working properly and have a proper knowledge of their duties and the neighbourhood;
(vii) "whether the police station has been regularly and properly inspected" (by other high ranking officials i.e. the Sub-Divisional Officer, the Superintendent of Police, the Additional Superintendent of Police, the Deputy or Assistant Superintendent of Police etc.). (*Police Regulations of Bengal*, para. 17. See Minutes...Panel on Law and Order, p. 6. Before 1960 the para. no. was 19. See 1958 reprint edition of the *Regulations*.)

[2] *Police Regulations of Bengal*, para. 16(a). [See Minutes...Panel on Law and Order, p. 5. Before 1960 para no. was 15(b). See 1958 reprint edition of the *Regulations*.] *Punjab Police Rules*, para. 1.15.

[3] *Police Regulations of Bengal*, para. 22. (See Minutes...Panel on Law and Order, p. 10. Before 1960 the para no. was 23. See 1958 reprint edition of the

that legally police force in the district is supposed to perform its duties under the control and supervision of the magistracy (i.e. the D.O., the Additional D.O.s, the S.D.O.s and other subordinate Magistrate).

No doubt, the Police Regulations clearly establish the authority and control of the D.O. over the S.P. and his force. But there is a good deal of vagueness about the exact nature of the relationship between these two officers and about the exact nature of the authority and control that the former is supposed to exercise over the latter. Such vagueness has often resulted in clashes between the D.O. and the S.P. and has minimised to a considerable extent the effectiveness of the authority and control of the former over the latter. The provision that the police force should perform its functions "under the general control and direction" of the D.O. is capable of interpretation in different ways. And in practice, it is interpreted in different ways. The police authority interprets it in such a way as to enable itself to enjoy as much independence from the control of the magistracy as possible. While the latter tries to maintain his control over the former, the former tries to assert its independence. Moreover, the provision that the D.O. should not interfere in the internal administration of the police force appears to be in conflict with the spirit or implications of other provisions of the Police Regulations. The prevention and detection of crime, the relation between the police and the public, the maintenance of public peace, all the responsibilities of the D.O., are closely connected with the internal administration of the police force. The efficiency or inefficiency, the discipline or indiscipline, the conduct and behaviour of the police force in one way or another are bound to affect these aspects of criminal administration. Thus, in practice it is not possible to discharge effectively the responsibilities entrusted to the D.O. by the provisions quoted above, unless he has effective control over the internal administration of the police force. It is argued by the police that if such

Regulations. Before 1960 the wording of the para was also slightly different.)

authority is given to the D.O. he would meddle unnecessarily with the details of police matters which would hamper the police administration. But, as the maintenance of law and order is only one of the several important functions of the D.O., even if he were to be given complete authority over the internal administration of the force, he would be unlikely to meddle unnecessarily with the details of internal administration because he would not have adequate time to do so. But such authority would enable him to exercise more control over the subordinate police officers which is essential for effectively discharging his law and order responsibilities. Moreover, it would make him more effective as a 'check' on 'police excess'. We shall later see that an effective 'check' on 'police excess' is much more essential in this part of the world than in more advanced countries.

Police Officers are very jealous about the supremacy of the magistracy over the police force. They argue that the supervisory control exercised by the magistracy over the police force is completely unnecessary and causes delays and interference in normal police functions. The hostility towards the magistracy and the tendency to bypass it as far as possible were also the characteristics of police attitudes in British India. This point may be illustrated by the fact that while making it emphatically clear that the S.P. was "subordinate" to the D.O. paragraph 13 of the Punjab Government Consolidated Circular no. 2 (1939) declared that "the idea, which has on occasions been advanced, that the Superintendent of Police is officially the head of an altogether separate department is entirely opposed to the principles on which the police force was constituted".[1]

Though the notion of police independence was sometimes expressed in British India, the D.O. at that time was able to

[1] Quoted in *Council Report for W. Pak.*, p. 15. In 1960 the Provincial Administration Commission expressed almost similar views. It held that "the important point is that the police force in the district is not 'another' department of government but the field arm of the District Magistrate himself in the sphere of law and order". (*Pro. Adm. Com. Report*, p. 187.) For a similar comment of another report in East Bengal see below, p. 11, fn. 2.

exercise more or less firm control over the S.P. and his force. Of course, the extent of such control varied from province to province. But since partition (1947) such attitudes in police departments have increasingly become more common and the control of the D.O. over the police has weakened. The extent of such change is not same in Bangladesh and Pakistan.

Pakistan. Especially in the Punjab the police were less subject to the control of the magistracy than their counterparts in most other parts of British India.[1] But after partition (1947) the situation began to deteriorate in the Punjab as well as in other parts of West Pakistan. One author held that

> "The situation has become worse after partition. All political parties depend more on the police for aggrandizement of their policy. Thus the police has become more powerful. The Superintendent of Police and the Deputy Commissioner have become two separate heads of the district and a sort of dyarchy has come to work in the district. It is said that the Superintendent of Police can often defy the Deputy Commissioner with impunity. Also the Magistracy, which is supposed to command the police, is reported in cases to have become afraid of police... The Government depend more on the police than on the Civil Service and consider the police to be more reliable. [He also holds that] the Inspector-General of Police, who is supposed to be under the Home Secretary, has due to changes in the political structure, traditionally become more powerful than the Home Secretary. The police organisation is directed more from the provincial capital than by the Deputy Commissioner in the district. In theory, the Deputy Commissioner is the head of the police in the district, but in actual practice he cannot wield strong control over the police. In many cases, the police do not worry much about him."[2]

One officer, recalling earlier days of his career (but writing when he had himself become a D.O.), described in the following passage

[1] Aslam, *op. cit.*, p. 50. This generalisation did not fully apply to Sind and Baluchistan, but it was more or less true of the N.W.F.P. whose administrative pattern closely followed that of the Punjab. We have also noted that until the very beginning of this century it had been a part of the Punjab.

Mr. Aslam implied that the local conditions and the nature of the people of the Punjab prompted the Government to make the police less subject to the supervisory control of the magistracy and to make it a powerful organisation without being subject to too many checks. (*Ibid.*, p. 50.)

[2] *Ibid.*, pp. 50-51. This comment made in the mid-1950s is still valid.

(which will further illustrate the point) the conversation between himself and his own D.O. who was not at all satisfied with the district police administration:

> "Sir, you are the administrative head of District Police and you can cope with such situation. He grinned saying, 'you are a child. If I take firm action to-day the police will not spare me tomorrow.' I smiled and kept quiet as at that time I did not fully comprehend the wisdom of that prescription of tact and the luxury of becoming deaf, dumb and blind in the sense that the Chinese monkeys were."[1]

Bangladesh. In British Bengal, which, as noted above, had more developed administrative tradition of a Regulation Province and where the officers were required to work under relatively rigid and elaborate rules and regulations,[2] the D.O. could maintain a comparatively firm control over the police force in his district. After partition, although several factors[3] gradually began to weaken his position vis-a-vis the S.P.,[4] he could still exercise a fair

[1] Sardar Hizbullah, "District Administration and Development" (Cyclostyled) (A paper read at the Seminar on Public Administration organised by the Pakistan Academy for Rural Development, Peshawar, in March 1962), p. 7.

[2] See above, chap. ii, p. 97 and chap. i (especially see the comment of the *Levinge Report*, quoted on page 33.)

[3] These factors are more or less similar to those factors which have weakened the position of the D.O. vis-a-vis heads of other departments in the district since partition. (See below, chap. vi.)

[4] In the *Report of the East Bengal Police Committee, 1953* (Dacca, 1954) (Hereafter cited as *East Bengal Police Committee's Report*) it was commented that "we have reason to think that the police...do not like this control [i.e. D.O.'s control] over them and it does not appear that the District Magistrates are at present exercising the general control which under the Police Regulations, Bengal, they are required to exercise...In...certain cases...the Superintendents of Police went out of their way to ignore the District Magistrate. This tendency on the part of the police officers is, to say the least, deplorable and is totally inconsistent with the basis of the police administration itself, namely, discipline. Every officer of the Government must realise that he is only a part of the entire machinery and if the Regulations require that he should subordinate his views to those of another officer even of another department, it is his duty to act in accordance with the Regulations. Resentment against any control which under the Rulees is exercised by others indicates utter lack of sense of responsibility and a false notion of one's own dignity. A Superintendent of Police should realise

degree of control and influence over the police force. But in October 1961 the central government decided to divest the D.O. of his power to write the annual confidential report on the activities and efficiency and the nature of the cooperation received by him from the S.P.[1] with the result that the position of the D.O. vis-a-vis the S.P., as we shall see below, was weakened to a very great extent.

It is not very clear why the decision was taken. It is widely believed that the then Home Minister of the central government, Mr. Zakir Husain, who previously had been the Inspector General of Police in East Bengal, was at least partially responsible. It is well known that he always maintained a strong feeling and sympathy for his own department and service and always tried to strengthen the position of the police vis-a-vis the magistracy.[2]

---

that he is not the officer solely responsible for the preservation of the peace in the district, but that the District Magistrate is the officer on whose shoulders that responsibility has been thrown. That being so, any tendency on the part of the Superintendents of Police to ignore the District Magistrates should be firmly put down...It is our considered opinion that the Government should make it clear that...any tendency in spirit or in letter to ignore the District Magistrate will be viewed with grave displeasure." (*Ibid*, para. 133.) Such tendency, which was increasingly gaining ground at that time, is now much more pronounced and widespread and has become part and parcel of the S.P.'s attitude towards the D.O.s.

[1] Central Govt. to Provincial Govts., letter no. 27/CF/59-iv, dated August 1, 1962.

[2] This generalisation may be at least partially substantiated by the fact that so far as the powers and position of the D.O. and the S.P. were concerned Mr. Husain, who was a member of the East Bengal Police Committee, 1953, opposed some of the views of the President (who was a Judge of the Dacca High Court and later became the Chief Justice of the same court and then the Governor of East Bengal) and all other members of that committee who were in favour of strengthening the position of the D.O. vis-a-vis the S.P. A few passages quoted below from the report of that Committee will illustrate this point. While recommending that the "Superintendent of Police should not have the power of transferring a Sub-Inspector, if the District Magistrate had objections to such a transfer," the Committee noted that "Mr. Zakir Husain, however, is against the proposed change in the present procedure of transfers of officers in charge of police stations." The Committee further added that Mr. Zakir Husain thought that "In making this recommendation, the majority of the Committee have laid down an 'extraordinary proposition.'" The Committee argued that the "majority of

Thus it was quite likely that he as the Home Minister of the central government exerted his influence to divest the D.O. of his power

---

the Committee feels that Mr. Zakir Husain has not given his full consideration to the recommendation they have made. They have not laid down any extraordinary proposition. On the other hand, they have reached this conclusion after a careful consideration of this question." About another remark of Mr. Husain, the Committee observed that "we have no material before us justifying that remark". (*East Bengal Police Committee's Report*, paras. 141-144.) In another place the Committee held that "Mr. Zakir Husain however, while agreeing with the majority of the Committee that the rural police should be integrated into the regular police is of the view that the power of appointment and dismissal of the village Constable should vest in the Superintendent of Police and not in the District Magistrate. At present, the *chaukidar* (rural police) is appointed by the District Magistrate on the recommendation of the President, Union Board, and the latter can dismiss him with the approval of the District Magistrate...It is true that the Superintendent of Police has power of appointment and dismissal in the case of regular Constables and it may be said that when the rural police is integrated with the regular police he should logically have the same power over the Village Police. But the fact remains that a substantial part of the cost of the maintenance of the Village Police is still to be borne by the Union Boards. That being so, we think that the powers of appointment and dismissal should vest in the District Magistrate, who has control over the Boards, and not in the Superintendent of Police. Mr. Zakir Husain says that the cost of maintenance of the regular police is also met by the villager, but in this he overlooks the fact that the villager pays a special tax for the Village Police while he does not pay a similar tax specially for the regular police. This difference we have kept in view." (*Ibid.*, para. 153.)

Mr. Husain maintained a distrust of the local and political leaders. The following passage will further illustrate this point: Mr. Husain argued "I feel that the Committee have overlooked this sound principle [i.e. the principle of non-interference in the internal police administration] in recommending the arrogation of power by District Magistrate over transfer of police officers without realising their full implications. In practice what is likely to happen when a proposal goes to the District Magistrate for the transfer of the officer in charge will be as follows. Interested 'popular representatives' whose behests the officer in charge will find difficult to carry out, will find excuses for running to the District Magistrate carrying tales and poisoning his ears against the officers and the District Magistrate will find it difficult to disbelieve or disoblige such 'popular representatives'. Thus a chain of intrigues will start in the district with no end in sight. The officers would in the result begin to look more to [the] District Magistrate than to the Superintendent of Police for their safety against such

to write the annual confidential report on the S.P.[1] Probably some other factors were also responsible for this decision: It is well known that in former Pakistan the central government was always dominated by the West Pakistani politicians and we have already noted that in West Pakistan the police was (and is) more trusted than the civil service by the politicians, that towards the end of the 1950s the central government assumed more control over the decision making process of the provincial government and that the latter, in fact, became the agent of the former. The centralisation of control over the decision making process, perhaps, partially caused this decision. It was also widely believed that political motives of the Ayub government were responsible to a considerable extent for the decision.

---

intrigues which will undermine all discipline on which the police administration rests." (Minute of dissent by Mr. Zakir Husain in *Ibid.*, p. 64.) Mr. Husain's argument does not seem plausible. It is difficult to accept the argument that on hearing complaints from 'popular representatives' the D.O. would form a biased opinion about the police officer concerned without making a formal or informal inquiry about the conduct of the officer. Moreover, Mr. Husain cannot expect that in this part of the world where the people are overwhelmingly illiterate and are not conscious of their rights, a 'let alone' policy about the police administration should be followed and that there should not be a comparatively neutral administrative authority to whom complaints could be made against the police so that he could look into the matter (for detailed discussion see below, pp. 18-19.) Mr. Husain's argument that for the D.O. it would be "difficult to...disoblige such 'popular representatives'" is also not plausible. If a D. O. has to yield against his wishes to a pressure of such a 'popular representative' then the latter must be a very powerful leader who has strong influence over Ministers. In that case the police will become more susceptible to the pressure of such a person. In fact, the D.O. and the superior Civil Service have always enjoyed greater influence and authority than the police to withstand as far as possible such pressure.

1 Mr. Husain's efforts were probably further aided by the fact that the then Chief Secretary to the Govt. of East Bengal was a member of the Police Service of Pakistan who previously had been the Inspector General of Police in East Bengal. It may be pointed out that in the administrative history of Bengal and perhaps in that of the whole Sub-Continent, he was the first member of the Police Service to occupy such a vital and exalted administrative post. Before partition this post was usually held by ICS officer and since partition by the CSP officer.

Though the provincial government was mainly responsible for the maintenance of law and order the above mentioned decision was taken by the central government.[1] A member of the Board of Revenue commented that

> "It is not, therefore, understood how the central government could issue a directive that the Deputy Commissioner should cease to write the annual confidential report on the Superintendent of Police. It does not appear that the central government gave any opportunity to the provincial government to express its views on this subject which properly falls within the sphere of provincial responsibility."[2]

It was argued that while the D.O. was directly responsible for the maintenance of law and order he was deprived of the main source of his control and influence over the police force which was the most important agency for the purpose of maintaining law and order and through which he was to execute most of his decisions concerning law and order matters and to obtain a good deal of information on the basis of which he could take most of such decisions. "Fullest cooperation of the S. P. is necessary in playing this vital rolc of maintaining law and order in the district."[3] But being deprived of his authority to write the confidential report on this officer he could not "pull his full weight on the police...nor can he exercise his powers given to him by the Police Regulations".[4] In fact the order of the central government

1 Formerly criminal administration had been listed as a provincial subject and thus the maintenance of law and order hed been the sole responsibility of the provincial government. But in the 1962 constitution there was no list of provincial subjects though there was a schedule of central subjects. In fact, the provincial government acted as the agent of the central government. Thus, sometimes it was argued that for law and order matters the central government was also indirectly responsible. This was a controversial topic though in practice most law and order matters were dealt with by the provincial government.

2 The letter (no. 1-MSA/65, dated Feb. 2, 1965) written by a Member of the Board of Revenue, the then Govt. of East Bengal, to the Additional Chief Secretary to the then Govt. of East Bengal.

3 The letter (no. 4-CSL/65, dated March 9, 1965) written by a Member of the Board of Revenue, the then Govt. of E. Bengal to the Additional Chief Secretary to the then Govt. of E. Bengal.

4 Letter no. 1, MSA/65, dated Feb. 2, 1965 (see above, fn. 2).

"unwittingly served as a wedge between the D.C. [i.e. D.O.] and the S.P.".[1] As a result, there was "no sense of cohesion and oneness between the executive and the police force which existed in the law and order machinery before".[2] The situation could be compared with "something like two swords in one scabbard".[3] Such a situation was "certainly not conducive to good administration".[4] The D.O. in discharging his law and order functions had to depend to a considerable extent on the "goodwill"[5] and the "mercy"[6] of the S.P. "Unless he [the latter] is on good terms with the D.C. he can find out convenient excuses for the delay in enforcing an order."[7] Sometimes the orders of the D.O. were not properly executed. The weakening of his position vis-a-vis the S.P. correspondingly weakened his control and influence over the subordinate police officers. In view of the increasingly deteriorating situation the then Government of East Bengal wrote to the central government that

> "It is, therefore, considered essential that the S.P. should in actual practice be made the immediate subordinate of the D.C. giving him unflinching loyalty and support. In order that he may get the willing cooperation and loyalty of the S.P. this government feels that he should be given the power to write the confidential report on the S.P."[8]

---

[1] *Ibid.* [2] *Idid.*

[3] Letter no. 4, CSR/65, dated March 9, 1965. As a result of the withdrawal of this power from the D.O. some S.P.s even developed the idea that they were "independent" of the direct control of the D.O. and that the latter "should seek their assistance in the manner in which such assistance would be sought from the officers of other governmental departments in his capacity as a coordinator". In this connection it may be mentioned that "the relationship between the D.C. and the S.P. stands on a different footing from that between the D.C. and other district level officers". Because though the D.O. had always been the head of other departments in the district and though with the increase in the importance of development functions he became equally responsible for development works, he in discharging his development functions was "essentially a co-ordinator". [The letter (no. GA VI-148-64-46-C dated Dec. 4, 1965) from the Additional Chief Secretary (E. Bengal) to the Cabinet Secretary (Central Government).]

[4] The letter no. 4, CSR/65, dated March 9, 1965. [5] *Ibid.*

[6] The letter no. GA VI-148-64-46-C dated Dec. 4, 1965.

[7] The letter no. 4, CSR/65, dated March 9, 1965.

[8] The letter no. GA VI-148-64-46-C dated Dec. 4, 1965.

But the central government did not give its approval.

It may be mentioned that though in the course of last 25 years the control and influence of the D.O. over the S.P. have lessened to a considerable extent in Bangladesh, the former can exercise greater control and influence over the latter than those exercised by his counterpart in Pakistan. The difference between the nature of the relationship between these two officers in Bangladesh and Pakistan is most probably the result of some differences that, as noted in chapter ii, exist between the administrative as well as cultural and social traditions of the two countries.

Some Comments on the Problem

It is widely believed and felt that in the sub-continent the police has always maintained a 'typical police mentality' and that 'police excess' has been one of the characteristics of police administration and that in the foreseeable future there is little hope that this situation will undergo rapid and radical change. On the other hand the D.O. and the S.D.O., who are, in fact, semi-judicial authorities (see below), have always been required to act as checks on the police authorities and to protect the common people against 'police excess'. In a society, as we have already briefly mentioned, in which the people are overwhelmingly illiterate, are not conscious about their rightful position in the society and do not have the courage to protest against 'police excess', such protection is much more essential than in advanced societies. It is, therefore, essential that the police authority should perform its functions under the strict control and supervision of a general administrative or semi judicial authority. Under the present administrative system traditionally the D.O. (and the S.D.O.) is the most appropriate and suitable functionary to act as supervisory authority over the police for several reasons. Firstly, as the administrative head of the district (and the sub-division) he has relatively close contact with different sections of the society, especially with local elites[1] who constitute a very important

[1] i.e. Political and social leaders or workers, local educationists, lawyers, doctors, local journalists, big farmers, local businessmen and industrialists, landed "aristocrats" etc.

source of information concerning different aspects of the district ranging from social, political, economic conditions to police, development, revenue and general administration. Secondly, as the head of the magistracy he has close association with the Magistrates who try criminal cases and thus in the course of formal and informal discussions with these Magistrates he can and does form an impression about the nature of the handling of the criminal cases by and about the conduct of the subordinate police officers.[1] Thirdly, as the overall head of the police force he has also direct and close contact with the police officers who explain police matters from their point of view. In this connection it should be also taken into consideration that though he is the overall head of the police force, he is not one of them and that, thus, unlike other police officers, he is not likely to develop a biased departmental feeling and to become a party to the police organisation. He, therefore, has the advantage of reviewing the police administration with an open mind and from both within and without. From the foregoing discussion we find that he gets information about the police force from various and diversified sources and thus, he is in a position to weigh and compare information. He is, therefore, in a more advantageous and impartial position than any other high ranking police officers to make a fair assessment of the integrity and efficiency of a police working within his jurisdiction.[2]

[1] Later in this chapter we shall see that he also enjoys the judicial powers of a first class and/or 'section 30' Magistrate though he seldom tries or does not try cases especially in Bangladesh. For a long time it has been suggested that in order to introduce complete separation of powers at the local level the Magistrates who try criminal cases should be placed under the administrative and supervisory control of the District and Sessions Judge. In future this step may be taken. In that case some administrative arrangements may be easily made to enable the D.O. (and the S.D.O.) to come into close association with these Magistrates and to have half-yearly or quarterly reports from them. In these reports the Magistrates will be able to record the impressions which they form about the police officers during trial.

[2] We have already noted that Mr. Zakir Husain was haunted by the fear that the popular representatives would poison the ears of the D.O. against the subordinate police officers. (See above, p. 200, fn. 2. This comment is

Thus, we find that the D.O. should have full control over the police force operating within his district. But we have already noted that as a result of several factors, in practice his position vis-a-vis the S.P. has weakened to a great extent. Now even if he is given the power to write the annual confidential report on the S.P. he will not be able to assert his full control over the police force though such power will enable him to regain some control and influence over the force. In view of the increasing independence and assertive attitude of the police authority, much more effective and strong measures are necessary for strengthening the D.O.'s position. In the present environment, which has been undergoing considerable and rapid changes since partition (1947), the vertical structure of the police force under the command of a Chief i.e. the Inspector General of Police, who is assisted by Deputy Inspector Generals of Police (each is in charge of the force in a division or range) the number of whom has increased during the last three decades, is in fact the main source of the influence and the assertive attitude of the police force. Some people believe that the vertical structure of the police force should undergo radical change. They feel that the police functionaries above the district level should be abolished, that the S.P. and other police officers in the District should be made directly responsible to the D.O. and through him to the Home Secretary and the Home Minister, and that the D.O. should have the power to take necessary disciplinary actions against the subordinate police officers. They also feel that though the transfer of police officers from one district to another should be made by the Home Minister, the transfer of subordinate police officers within the district should be made by the D.O. They also think that a police intelligence bureau, more or less similar to Scotland Yard or the F.B.I., may be set up at the central/provincial level for assisting the district police in investigating difficult cases but it should not have any administrative or supervisory control over the district police.

on page 201.) But from our foregoing discussion we find it difficult to accept his view.

Though these suggestions are very radical they do not seem to be illogical or impractical. Such steps will definitely put a check on the increasing independence of the police department and will subject it to adequate magisterial control. But under the present circumstances there is no possibility that in the foreseeable future such radical changes of the century-old structure and pattern of police administration will be introduced. If no such steps are taken then strong disciplinary action should be taken against those police officers who try to ignore the D.O. In practice, of course, it will be very difficult to take such action during a period of social, political and administrative tensions.[1] But, if the growing independence of the police department is not checked, then there is a danger that a police *raj* will come into existence especially in rural and semi-urban areas.

The police authority and those who are not in favour o strong magisterial control over the police argue that whether or not the D.O. will be able to exercise adequate control over the police force in his district depends to a considerable extent on his personality. No doubt, it is true. Personality always plays a very vital role in human relationships. But there are also many other factors which are also no less important in determining the nature of such relationships. Moreover, in a status oriented society, which, as we have just said, is under the strain of social, political and administrative tensions, the importance of personality is not always very great. Thus, some effective administrative measures are necessary for strengthening the position of the D.O. vis-a-vis the police force. The Provincial Administration Commission while commenting on the relationship between the D.O. and the S.P. already pointed out that "we are fully conscious of the fact that a great deal will depend on the ability and personality of the District Magistrate himself...[but] it is necessary that the relationship should be defined and not left to the accident of personality".[2]

1 The impact of social, political and administrative tension on administration is discussed in chapter vi.

2 *Pro. Adm. Com. Report*, p. 187.

D.O. as the Head of the Magistracy

In his capacity as District Magistrate the D.O. is the head of the district magistracy which comprises the D.O. himself, the Additional D.O.s, the S.D.O.s and a number of subordinate officials called the 'Deputy Magistrate and Deputy Collector' (Bangladesh)/Extra Assistant Commissioner (Pakistan). According to their judicial powers to try less important criminal cases, all these officers are classified into four classes of Magistrates, namely 'Section 30', Class I, Class II and Class III Magistrates. The nature and extent of judicial powers of these four classes of Magistrates may be illustrated by table xv.

Though the D.O. and the S.D.O. are the heads of the magistracy in the district and in the sub-division respectively, they have no authority to interfere in the proceedings of the court or in the judicial decisions of these Magistrates.[1] They mainly exercise administrative and supervisory control over the Magistrates. For example, it is their responsibility to distribute cases among these Magistrates, and to see that they dispose of the cases regularly, and that whether there are arrears of cases etc. The D.O. or the S.D.O. may also require a Magistrate to perform such magisterial duties as to preside over a mobile court constituted by the former in order to check traffic irregularities, to record the dying declaration of a person who is dying as a result of some injury etc. He may also require a Magistrate to lead a police force (or he may lead it himself) while executing a search or arrest warrant if it is of some special importance or while making a raid against some anti-social activities or while handling a situation resulting from breach of peace such as riots, student or labour disturbances etc. These Magistrates also assist the D.O. and the

(*Contd. on p. 215.*)

[1] Of course, the D.O. or the S.D.O. has the authority to withdraw any case from the court of any Magistrate subordinate to him and may inquire into or try the case himself or refer it for inquiry or trial to any other Magistrate. [*The Code of Criminal Procedure*, sec. 528(a).] Usually a case is transferred from the court of one Magistrate to that of another Magistrate if one of the parties in the case submits an application for transfer of the case from the court of that Magistrate. Such transfer is granted only if the party concerned can give reasonable and adequate reasons for applying for such transfer.

TABLE XV

JUDICIAL POWERS OF THE MAGISTRATES. HIGHER JUDICIAL AUTHORITIES WHO HEAR APPEAL AGAINST THEIR JUDICIAL DECISIONS.

Magistrates	Sentences that they may pass	Appeals against their judicial decisions are heard by the
Section 30 (Pak. only)	Imprisonment—not exceeding 7 years and other powers of a 1st Class Magistrate.[1]	(i) High Court: if the term of imprisonment exceeds 4 years. (ii) District and Sessions Judge: if it is less than that.[2]
Class I	(i) Imprisonment—not exceeding 2 years. (ii) Fine—not exceeding 1000 Tk./Rs. (iii) Whipping.[3]	District and Sessions Judge.[4]
Class II	(i) Imprisonment—not exceeding 6 months. (ii) Fine—not exceeding 200 Tk./Rs.[5]	*Pakistan:* District Officer. He may get it heard by a 1st Class Magistrate.[6]
Class III	(i) Imprisonment—not exceeding 1 month. (ii) Fine—not exceeding 50 Tk./Rs.[7]	*Bangladesh:* Upto 1958 the procedure was same as that in Pakistan and since March 1958, District and Sessions Judge. He may get it heard by an Assistant Sessions Judge.[8]

[1] *The Code of Criminal Procedure* (1898), secs. 30,34. [2] *Ibid.*, sec. 408. [3] *Ibid.*, sec. 32. [4] *Ibid.*, sec. 408. [5] *Ibid.*, sec. 32. [6] *Ibid.*, sec. 407. [7] *Ibid.*, sec. 32.
[8] *Ibid.*, sec. 407. This section was amended by the East Pakistan Ordinance no. xii of 1958 known as the Code of Criminal Procedure (East Pakistan Amendment) Ordinance, 1958. See *The Dacca Gazette* (Extraordinary), Monday, March 3, 1958. In 1945 the *Rowlands Report* had already recommended that the D.O.'s judicial power to hear appeal against the decisions of the 2nd and the 3rd Class Magistrates should be transferred to the District Judge. [*Rowlands Report*, para. 102(a).]

General Notes on Table XV

In Bangladesh there is no Section 30 Magistrate. Even the D.O. in this country does not enjoy the power of a Section 30 Magistrate. The provision for Section 30 Magistrate was made for Non-Regulation Provinces. (See the note at the end of section 34 of the *Code of Criminal*

(*Contd. on page 213*)

CHART V

BANGLADESH

ORGANISATIONAL AND FUNCTIONAL RELATIONSHIP BETWEEN VARIOUS HIERARCHIES OF FUNCTIONARIES WHICH DIRECTLY OR INDIRECTLY DEAL WITH THE MATTERS RELATING TO LAW AND ORDER AND ADMINISTRATION OF JUSTICE IN THE COUNTRY

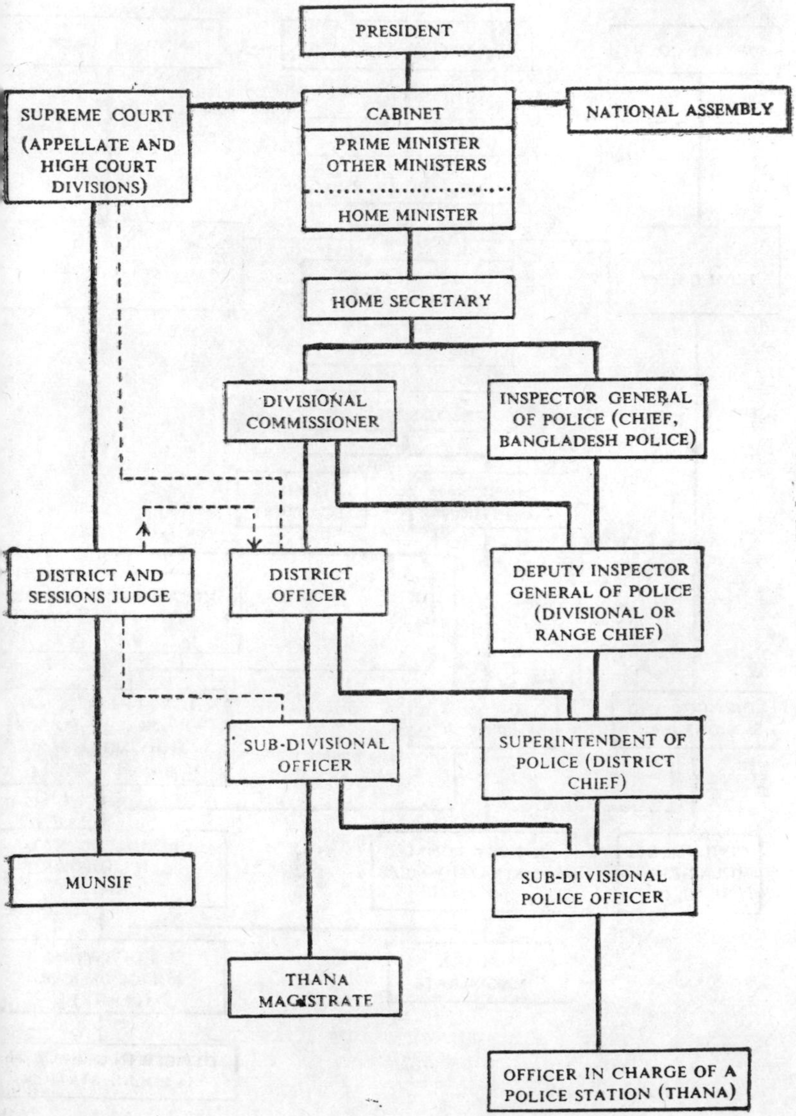

CHART VI

PAKISTAN
(FORMER AND PRESENT)

ORGANISATIONAL AND FUNCTIONAL RELATIONSHIP BETWEEN VARIOUS HIERARCHIES OF FUNCTIONARIES WHICH DIRECTLY OR INDIRECTLY DEAL WITH THE MATTERS RELATING TO LAW AND ORDER AND ADMINISTRATION OF JUSTICE IN EACH PROVINCE

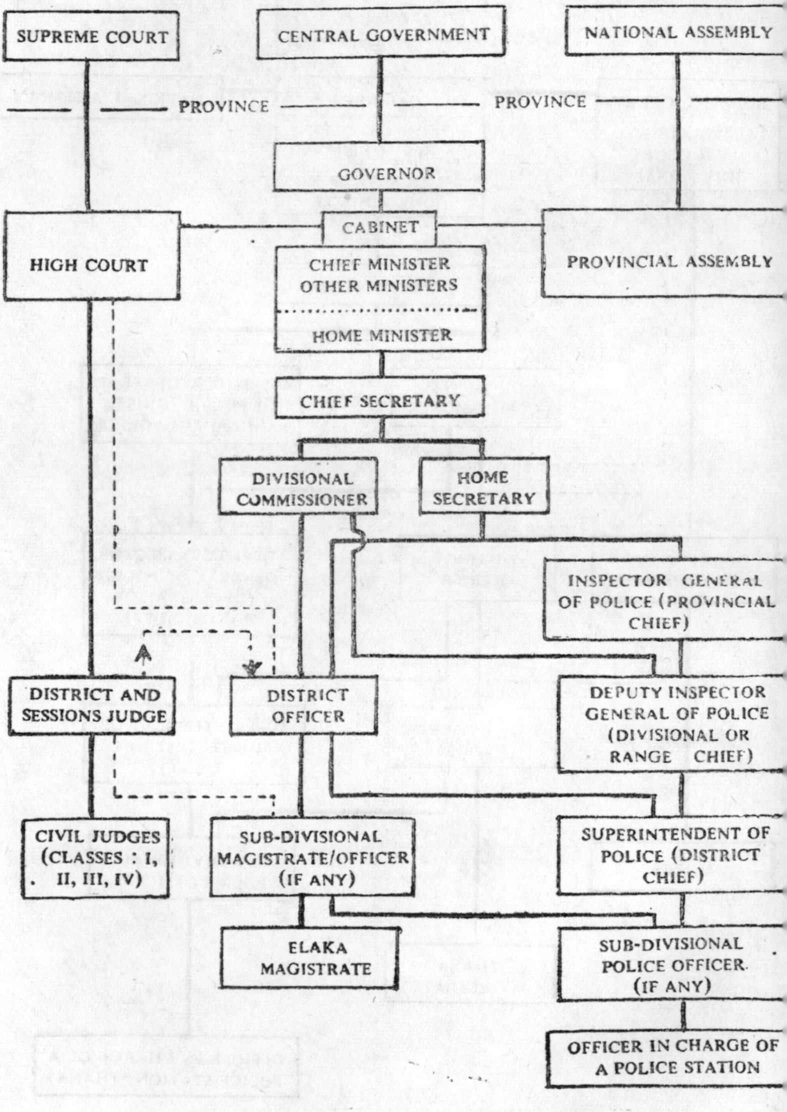

(Contd. from page 210)

Procedure.) But, as we have noted in chapter i, British Bengal, the part of which now constitutes Bangladesh, was a Regulation Province.

As is the case in regard to other Section 30 Magistrates, if the D.O. tries a case in the capacity of a Section 30 Magistrate and sentences the accused to imprisonment, for less than four years, appeal against his decision is also heard by the District and Sessions Judge whose official rank is same as that of the D.O. It means that when the latter acts in judicial capacity, he does not enjoy any special privilege.

Notes on Charts V and VI

Charts V and VI give an idea of the nature of the relationship that exists between the judiciary, the administrative cum magisterial and the police hierarchies in Bangladesh and (former and present) Pakistan respectively.

So far as the administration of justice and the matters concerning law and order are concerned, the central government of (former and present) Pakistan do not directly come into the picture. But in Bangladesh, where there is no province, the central government directly deals with them.

Home Minister. That member of the Cabinet who deals with the matters concerning law and order is called Home Minister or the Minister of Interior.

Home Secretary. The official status of the Home Secretary to the central government (i.e. the government of Bangladesh or that of former and present Pakistan) is higher than that of the Home Secretary to the provincial government (e.g. the former government of East Bengal or the government of the Punjab etc.). The official status of the provincial Home Secretary is equivalent to that of the Joint Secretary to the central government and also to that of the Divisional Commissioner.

Judiciary and Magistracy. ------ This line indicates that though higher judicial authorities hear appeal against the judicial decisions of Magistrates, they do not exercise any administrative control and supervision over them.

Chart V shows that theoretically the higher judicial authorities in Bangladesh have powers to hear appeals against the judicial decisions of the District Officer. But, in practice, the question of hearing such appeals does not arise in view of the fact that the District Officer in Bangladesh does not try any case though he has the powers of a First Class Magistrate. But, in Pakistan he tries criminal cases as First Class and Section 30 Magistrates. The appeals against his judicial decisions are, therefore, heard by higher judicial authorities in Pakistan.

In Bangladesh, while (the High Court Division and the Appellate Division of) the Supreme Court and the District and Sessions Judge try both civil and criminal cases, the Magistrates and the Munsifs try criminal and civil cases respectively. The District and Sessions Judge is usually assisted by the Additional District and Sessions Judges and the Subordinate and the Assistant Sessions Judges, the number of whom depends on the volume of work in the district concerned. The Additional District and Sessions Judge possesses all the judicial powers of the District and Sessions Judge. The powers of the

Assistant Sessions Judge in Bangladesh are same as those of the Section 30 Magistrate in Pakistan. The Assistant Sessions Judge also holds the post of the Subordinate Judge and in that capacity also tries civil cases. But all Subordinate Judges are not Assistant Sessions Judges. Only those Subordinate Judges who have served in that capacity for sometime (i.e. who are fairly senior) are given the powers of an Assistant Sessions Judge (i.e. the power to sentence a guilty person to undergo rigorous imprisonment upto a period not exceeding seven years).

What has been said about Bangladesh also applies to Pakistan with some exceptions. For example, in (former and present) Pakistan there is separate High Court which is the highest judicial authority in a province. In Pakistan the counterparts of the Subordinate Judge and the Munsif are Civil Judges. There are four classes of Civil Judges, namely class I, class II, class III, class IV. In Bangladesh the Subordinate Judge and the Munsif have been functioning since British period. In Pakistan (especially in the Punjab and the N.W. F.P.) the powers of the Assistant Sessions Judge are, in fact, exercised by the Section 30 Magistrate. So, while in Bangladesh these powers are in the hands of judicial authorities, in Pakistan they belong to the executive cum administrative authorities.

The offices of the Section 30 Magistrate and the *Elaka* Magistrate have never existed in Bangladesh/East Bengal/British Bengal (in this century). Of course, in British Bengal occasionally some Magistrates were vested with the powers of Section 30 of the code of criminal procedure for sometime only. Such measures were usually temporary arrangements. But, it was never the usual and normal practice here. The office of the *Elaka* Magistrate is completely unknown in this part of the sub-continent. The office of the *Thana* Magistrate was introduced here for the first time in the late-1960s.

Divisional Commissioner. We have noted above that in Bangladesh the Divisional Commissioner has never been required to make himself closely associated with the law and order aspect of the administration. But in Pakistan he has been required from early British period to take direct and keen interest in this aspect of administration.

Police. The Superintendent of Police is assisted by Additional Superintendents of Police, Deputy Superintendents of Police, the number of whom depends on the volume of work in the district.

The post of the Sub-Divisional Police Officer is held by a Deputy or Assistant Superintendent of Police.

A senior Sub-Inspector of Police remains in charge of a *Thana* (Police Station). He is assisted by a few Sub-Inspectors of Police, Assistant Sub-Inspectors of Police and a small police force. The Police Stations are grouped into circles. An Inspector of Police remains in charge of a circle whose main responsibility is to inspect and supervise the police stations within his jurisdiction and to coordinate their functions. The circle is not an important unit of police administration. A Police Station is divided into police posts each in charge of a Head Constable or a Police Sergeant (mainly in big cities like Dacca, Lahore, etc.) or an Assistant Sub-Inspector of Police.

S.D.O. in the performance of their executive, administrative and revenue functions (see below). In performing all these functions they remain under the direct control and supervision of these two officers whose order they are bound to carry out. And these two officers find no difficulties in exercising control over these subordinate officers because, unlike the police officers (and the officers of other departments) they are their direct subordinates and they write annual confidential reports on the activities of these officers.

"Conditions Requisite for Initiation of Proceedings". Criminal cases are initiated in one of the following three ways: The D.O., the S.D.O. and any other Magistrate who has been especially empowered, may take cognisance of any offence "(a) upon receiving a complaint of facts which constitute such offence; (b) upon a police report of such facts; (c) upon information received from any person other than a police officer, or upon his own knowledge or suspicion, that such offence has been committed".[1]

So far as different stages of the trial of criminal cases are concerned, there are some differences between Bangladesh and Pakistan. In the former, cases are usually initiated in the court of the S.D.O. Some of the cases are tried by the S.D.O. himself and rest of the cases are distributed by him among other Magistrates subordinate to him.[2] But the D.O. in this country neither tries cases (see above) nor usually takes cognisance of offence.

1 *The Code of Criminal Procedure*, sec. 190(a). Even if a case has resulted not from a police report but from one of the other factors mentioned above, the officer, who has taken the cognisance of the offence, may direct the police to investigate the matter and submit a report.

2 We have already noted in chapter iii that like the D.O., the S.D.O. is an all-purpose officer and the administrative and executive head of the area which has been placed in his charge and that he is required to perform a large number of diverse functions. Thus, he does not have time to try more than a few criminal cases. So far as the trial of criminal cases is concerned, his primary responsibility is to take cognisance of offences and then to distribute them among other Magistrates. If he is away from the sub-divisional headquarters on tour, the Magistrate who is called the Second Officer performs this responsibility of the S.D.O.

Even if he comes to know or suspects that a crime has been committed, he usually passes an order directing the S.D.O., within whose jurisdiction the offence has been or is suspected to have been committed, to take the necessary action for initiating and trying a case. Thus, we find that so far as the initiation and trial of criminal cases and their distribution among other Magistrates are concerned, in Bangladesh the D.O. in practice does not come into the picture. It is the S.D.O. who plays the prominent role in this respect and relieves the D.O. from the burden of judicial functions. Of course, in doing so he remains in close touch with the D.O. who maintains an overall supervision over the magistracy in the district.

But in most parts of Pakistan the procedure is different from that in Bangladesh.[1] In this country especially in the Punjab and the N.W.F.P., a number of police stations are grouped into what is called *elaka*. For each *elaka* there is an *Elaka* Magistrate who has the power to take cognisance of an offence. Usually the criminal cases originating within the jurisdiction of an *Elaka* Magistrate are tried by him. But if he does not have adequate judicial powers to impose adequate punishment upon an accused person in a case, then after the preliminary hearing the case is transferred to the court of a Magistrate who enjoys higher judicial powers and who may reside at the District headquarters. In many places of Pakistan the D.O. or the Additional D.O. tries some cases. Sometimes he also distributes cases among other Magistrates and, if necessary, transfers cases from the court of one Magistrate to that of another Magistrate. If any part of a district constitutes a sub-division then sometimes the S.D.M. may also be required to discharge some of these responsibilities. Thus we find that so far as different stages of criminal cases are concerned the D.O. or the Additional D.O. in Pakistan is required

[1] We have already noted in chapter i that Pakistan consists of four provinces and several former princely states of British India, the administrative legacies and the pattern of administration of which were not completely uniform. Thus the procedure that is followed at different stages of criminal cases is not only different from that which is followed in Bangladesh but is not also exactly uniform throughout Pakistan. The discussion in this paragraph is on the broad general pattern.

to play a more active and direct role than his counterpart in Bangladesh who mainly acts as a supervisory authority in this respect. Thus the latter can and does devote more time and energy to administrative and executive functions and to development works.

The full trial of less important criminal cases is held in the courts of Magistrates and appeals against their decisions are heard by higher judicial authorities (Bangladesh)/by both higher judicial and magisterial authorities (Pakistan).[1] But in both Bangladesh and Pakistan only the preliminary hearings of serious criminal cases are held in the courts of the Magistrates and after preliminary hearings if they come to the conclusion that there are sufficient evidences, they commit these cases to Sessions[2] where the District and Sessions Judge, who has powers to award maximum sentence (i.e. life imprisonment or transportation and death sentence),[3] try them.[4]

For a long time it has been strongly suggested that the executive arm of the government should be divested of its power to try less important criminal cases. It is argued by those who are in favour of such separation that it is an universally accepted fact that the executive authority should not be entrusted with judicial powers and that the union of such powers in the person of the same officer shakes the confidence and faith of the people in the courts of the Magistrates. Those who are not in favour of such separation of powers argue that the situation is not yet ripe for such separation and that the conditions (that we have noted in chapter i) which made it essential that these powers should be

[1] For further illustration see above, charts V and VI and table XV.

[2] *The Code of Criminal Procedure*, sec. 206. This section has laid down broad principles only.

[3] A death sentence passed by the District and Sessions Judge or the Additional District and Sessions Judge is subject to the confirmation of the High Court. (*Ibid.*, sec. 31.)

[4] As there is no Section 30 Magistrate in Bangladesh, those cases, which are tried by the Section 30 Magistrate in Pakistan, are committed to sessions in Bangladesh. In this country these cases are tried by the Assistant Sessions Judge.

united in the persons of the D.O. and his subordinates have not yet undergone significant changes. They also argue that such separation might so undermine the prestige and authority of the D.O. and the S.D.O. that they might find it difficult to perform their executive and administrative functions effectively. Thus they think that if these officers are divested of their judicial powers the law and order aspect of district administration might suffer a setback. But nowadays it is increasingly and widely believed that the social and administrative conditions have undergone considerable changes in the course of this century, that the question of separation of these powers should now be reviewed in the light of the changed conditions and that these arguments against such separation are no longer valid in Bangladesh and in relatively advanced areas of Pakistan.

One of the directive principles of the 1956 constitution of former Pakistan was that the "State shall separate the judiciary from the executive as soon as practicable".[1] Following this directive principle of the late constitution the government of East Bengal passed an Act in November 1957 in order to divest the executive arm of judicial powers though, as we shall see later, in practice the Act was not implemented. The Act declared that besides the High Court there would be two types of criminal courts in East Bengal, namely the Courts of Sessions and the Courts of Magistrates,[2] that there would be two kinds of Magistrates namely Judicial Magistrates (1st, 2nd and 3rd classes) and the Executive Magistrates (D.O., Additional D.O., S.D.O. and Special or Subordinate Executive Magistrates),[3] that the District and Sessions Judge would not only hear appeals against the decisions of Judical Magistrates but they would also exercise full administrative and supervisory control over them and that the D.O. and the S.D.O. would no longer exercise any control and supervision over the

[1] *1956 Constitution*, art. 30.

[2] East Pakistan Act XXXVI of 1957, Code of Criminal Procedure (East Pakistan Amendment) Act, 1957 in *The Dacca Gazette* (Extraordinary), Monday, Nov. 11, 1957, sec. 3.

[3] *Ibid.*, sec. 4.

Judicial Magistrates who would not perform any administrative and executive functions. In the performance of administrative and executive functions the D.O. and the S.D.O. would be assisted by the Special or Subordinate Executive Magistrates.

It was also provided in the Act that "the aforesaid Act shall come into force in such areas and on such date as the Provincial Government may, by notification in the official Gazette, specify in this behalf".[1] But the provisions of the Act, as we have already mentioned, were not translated into practice. Shortage of officers was one of the reasons for not taking any step for separating these powers. Moreover, at that time the government was not willing to undertake the task of reorganising the pattern and structure of district administration which would have inevitably resulted from such separation. Finally, opinion was still divided on the question as to whether the time was ripe for such separation, although on paper powers were completely separated. Later, the Law Commission of 1958-59 also strongly recommended that these powers should be completely separated in practice and that the Magistrates should be classified into Judicial Magistrates and Executive Magistrates.[2] But no steps were taken to implement these recommendations. On the contrary, the government entrusted its executive arm in West Pakistan with more judicial powers.[3]

Some Concluding Comments. In the preceding pages we have examined the position of the D.O. as the head of the police force and that of the Magistracy in the district and have noted that so far as the administrative and supervisory aspects are concerned his control over the magistracy is adequate but his control and influence over the police force have lessened to a great extent and are completely inadequate. But in order to discharge his

[1] *Ibid.*, sec. 1 (3).

[2] *Report of the Law Reform Commission, 1958-59* (Karachi, 1959), p. 23. (Hereafter cited as *Law Reform Commission's Report.*)

[3] For the discussion on the extension of the jurisdiction of the Frontier Crimes Regulation to 'settled districts' of West Pakistan and the subsequent modifications of this Regulation in these districts, see below.

responsibility in regard to law and order it is much more essential that he should have much greater control and influence over the police force than over the Magistracy. It is generally felt that on the one hand, he should be divested of his authority to exercise administrative and supervisory control over the magistracy because such authority, as noted above, might prejudice the impartial administration of justice; and on the other hand, his full control and authority over the police force should be effectively and adequately established. The Provincial Administration Commission commented that "Regardless of what decision is taken by Government on this issue [i.e. the separation of judiciary from the executive], we consider that to enable the District Magistrate to discharge his responsibility in regard to law and order, his control over the police must be made effective."[1]

Some of the Very Important Powers of the District Officer for Maintaining Public Peace and Tranquility

If there are serious riots or disturbances or if it is apprehended that there is every likelihood of a serious breech of peace it is the D.O. (or S.D.O.) who takes the decision as to what steps should be taken in order to restore or maintain public tranquility. He may impose a curfew or he may take any or all of the following steps: he may prohibit processions, meetings, assemblage of more than a certain number of persons, say five, in certain areas, the use of loud speakers or microphones, movement of people or plying of vehicles on certain roads or in certain areas, carrying of weapons or dangerous instruments or materials, etc.[2] At the time

[1] *Pro. Adm. Com. Report*, p. 184. In its report the Commission very precisely referred to the question of the separation of judicial and executive powers (only 3 sentences) and did not make any comment on whether or not these powers should be separated. Of course, from their writings it appears that they were inclined to prefer that the D.O. might be allowed to continue to enjoy judicial powers to try criminal cases and to act as the head of the magistracy. But the first part of the comment ("Regardless of what decision is taken by the Government on this issue"), which we have quoted above in the text, clearly indicates that they did not feel that judicial powers and his position as the head of the magistracy were very essential for discharging his responsibility in regard to law and order.

[2] He takes such a decision under the authority of section 144 of *The Code of*

of a serious disturbance usually the D.O. (or S.D.O.) and the S.P. (or S.D.P.O.) remain present at the scene.[1] If the mob becomes violent the D.O. (or S.D.O.) makes the decision whether the police should open fire, or make bayonet or *lathi* (big bamboo stick of one or two inches diameter) charge or use tear gas etc.

If the D.O. or the S.D.O. comes to know that a person or a group of persons is doing something (e.g. delivering inflammatory speeches or writing inflammatory pamphlets or books) which might ultimately cause a riot or disturbances, it is one of his most important law and order responsibilities to take necessary steps to prevent the person or persons concerned from doing so. In order to protect the community against anticipated crime or breach of peace, he may also require a person who is suspected of being a "Bad Character" or who is a habitual offender or who is likely to do something unlawful, to show cause why he should not be ordered to execute a bond, with or without sureties, for keeping peace or good behaviour. He may finally order him to sign the bond.[2]

Political Agencies and Other Tribal Areas

We have already noted in chapter iii that the political agencies, which are very backward tribal areas of Pakistan and which are inhabited by the militant and orthodox tribesmen, are almost completely isolated from the rest of the world and that the D.O. who is called the Political Agent exercises loose control over his jurisdiction and maintains liaison between the government and the tribal chiefs who, in fact, administer the internal affairs of their

---

Criminal Procedure. (No appeal may be made to higher judicial authorities against such a decision.) If these powers are misused then sometimes it results in a heated debate on the floor of the Assembly. (See *N.A.P. Deb.* Aug. 1, 1963, vol. ii, no. 39, pp. 2431-2438.)

1 For some instances or description of disturbances or riots see *Munir-Kayani Report*, part vi and the *Report* written by a Judge, Dacca High Court after having made an enquiry into an incident which had resulted in police firing on the mob in the Sylhet district. (published in *The Dacca Gazette*, Extraordinary, Dec. 3, 1958,) (Also see Woodruff, *op. cit.*, pp. 257-266.)

2 *The Code of Criminal Procedure*, secs. 107, 110. If he is finally ordered to execute a bond he may appeal to higher judicial authorities.

tribes.[1] There is no codified law for these areas. The Frontier Crimes Regulation (FCR) of 1901 lays down some broad principles of administration of justice. The tribal laws and customs, in fact, serve as the basis of administration of justice in these areas.

The FCR also extends over most of Baluchistan,[2] which is primarily a tribal region and a considerable part of which is also officially classified as tribal or special areas. In most of Baluchistan the regular codes of "settled areas" are also in force. Thus in these areas there is a dual legal system; both FCR and the regular codes of "settled areas" are operating simultaneously.[3]

Under the FCR of 1901 the D.O. has the discretion to decide whether a case (civil or criminal) should be tried by a regular court or it should be referred to a tribunal called *Jirga*[4] which is "a Council of three or more persons [i.e. tribal chiefs] convened according to the Pathan, Biluch or other usage, as the Deputy

1 For detailed discussion see chapter iii, pp. 134, 139—143.

2 Later we shall see that in 1963 the FCR was extended to other districts of West Pakistan with certain modifications of some of its provisions but in Baluchistan and in political agencies of N.W.F.P. (including certain strips of tribal regions attached to five settled districts of the N.W. F.P.) the FCR remained in force without such modifications. (see below.)

3 *Pro. Adm. Com. Report*, pp. 199-200, 206. *Law Reforms Commission's Report*, p. 105. Of course, in Kalat division (which was called the Baluchistan States Union consisting of former princely states in Baluchistan before the integration of West Pakistan into one province in 1955) though the civil, criminal and penal codes are modelled on corresponding codes of "settled areas", there are some differences between the former and the latter. (*Law Reforms Commission's Report*, pp. 103-4.) The provincial Administration Commission commented that the "administrative system of Kalat Division is something of a hotchpotch. Some features of regular administration have been grafted on to the...[Kalat] system. The position has been made worse by the bad draftsmanship of Codes." (*Pro. Adm. Com. Report*, p. 205.)

4 The Frontier Crimes Regulation (FCR), 1901, secs. 8(1), 11(1). Full text of the Regulation has been incorporated at the end of the *Report of the Frontier Regulations Enquiry Committee, 1931* (*Niamatullah Committee Report*) (Calcutta, 1931), see appendix iv(2). So far as the civil cases are concerned those disputes which are likely to cause bloodfeud or murder or culpable homicide not amounting to murder or mischief or breach of peace are referred to *Jirgas*. [FCR, sec. 8(1).]

Commissioner may in each case direct".[1] In political agencies the cases are referred to *Jirga*. In normal practice, in 'A areas' (i.e., some townships, cantonments, railway lines and stations and *Bazaar* areas) of Baluchistan the cases are tried by regular courts and in 'B areas' of Baluchistan the cases are referred to *Jirgas*.

"The tribunal styled as 'Council of Elders' plays an important part in the trial of civil and criminal cases."[2] The following comment of the Simon Commission will give some idea of the background and the nature of and the government policy towards the *Jirga* system especially in political agencies:

> "there is a system of traditional indigenous justice administered by tribunals called *Jirga*. The essential point to bear in mind is that the *Jirga* system has its origin in tribal custom, and is recognised and applied by the tribesmen themselves in areas where the agents of the Government make no attempt to intervene. The system, in a carefully regulated form is, however, preserved and made use of under the authority of the Government... in the area of tribal tracts. The Code governing the use of *Jirgas* is, to be found in the Frontier Crimes Regulations, 1901... But in applying it [i.e. FCR] to the Political Agencies, the Government...makes it plain that it has no intention of interfering with or undermining in any way the influence, responsibility, or authority of the tribal *Jirgas*, or of disturbing the practice under which the Elders of the community concerned are ordinarily required themselves to deal with tribesmen who have committed offences".[3]

The *Jirga* is under no obligation to follow any enacted laws while conducting its proceedings and, in fact, comes to its conclusions on the basis of tribal values and customs. No lawyer is allowed to appear at any stage of a *Jirga* trial—whether of a civil or criminal nature. The *Jirga* places its finding before the D.O. and may also add a recommendation as to punishment.[4] He has the authority to

1 *Ibid.*, sec. 2(a).

2 *Niamatullah Committee Report*, p. 24.

3 *Simon Report*, vol. i, para. 362. These comments are still valid especially in political agencies and other very backward tribal areas. (By 'very backward tribal areas' the present writer means those tribal areas where the contact of the tribal people with other parts of the country is very insignificant, where the tribal bonds are very strong, where the people fanatically and very rigidly follow the tribal values and customs and where the hold of the tribal chiefs over their peoples is very strong.)

4 The maximum punishment that can be awarded for any serious offence

accept and act upon the finding and the recommendation as to punishment or to reject them or to take some other steps that are permitted by the FCR.[1] If he does not have special reasons to think that the finding of the *Jirga* should not be relied upon the usually accepts and acts upon it. Especially in very backward tribal areas (e.g. political agencies) he rarely interferes with the finding and recommendation of the *Jirga*. The High and the Supreme Courts do not have any jurisdiction over the cases tried under the provisions of the FCR. Thus, no appeal against the decisions of the *Jirga* and the D.O. may be made to these highest judicial authorities in the country.[2] Of course, it is allowed to petition the Divisional Commissioner to exercise his prerogative to review the order made by the D.O. under the FCR. Even if no such petition is made to him he "may call for the record of any proceeding under this Regulation and revise any decision, decree, sentence or order given, passed or made therein".[3]

(i.g. murder), when investigated by a *Jirga*, is fourteen years rigorous imprisonment. In the FCR there is no provision for death sentence. [FCR, sec. 12(2).]

[1] On receipt of the finding of the *Jirga* the D.O. may take the following decisions :

Civil Cases [Sec. 8(3) of FCR]	Criminal cases [Sec. 11(3) of FCR]
(a) May remand the case for the *Jirga* for a further finding; or (b) may refer it to another *Jirga*; or (c) may refer the parties to the civil courts; or (d) may pass a decree in accordance with the finding of the *Jirga* "or of not less than three-fourths of the members thereof on any matters stated in the reference"; or (e) may declare that further proceedings under this section are not required.	(a) and (b) Same as civil cases; or (c) May acquit or discharge the accused person or persons or any of them; or (d) may, in accordance with the finding of any matter of fact of the *Jirga* or of "not less than three-fourths of the members thereof, convict the accused person or persons or any of them of any offence of which the facts so found show him or them to be guilty".
(Usually the decision of a *Jirga* in a very backward tribal area is unanimous.)	

[2] *Ibid.*, sec. 48. [3] *Ibid.*, sec. 49.

The system of trial by *Jirga* has been operating for a long time because it is generally believed that if justice is administered through regular courts it will be difficult to find witnesses. The witnesses are likely to be reluctant to give evidence before a court of law which is a strange body to them. There may not be any witnesses at all. As the family and tribal feuds follow more or less predictable and understandable courses or patterns, the basic assumption is that when a crime is committed usually the guilty person is known though there may not be any witness to the crime. And the tribal chiefs of the area concerned either know about the factors that are involved in the incident and the guilty person or come to know about them without much difficulty. Moreover, even if there is some evidence in a case it may not be "sufficient for conviction in a court of law" or it may not be "accepted as reliable by a court of law." So "the case is likely to collapse in a court of law for want of sufficient or reliable evidence".[1]

In political agencies if someone commits a murder for the sake of what is called 'pathan honour' he will not hesitate to confess it before a *Jirga* but before a court of law he will not do so. On the other hand, he will try to produce false evidences before the court. It is mainly because while the court of law has no other alternative but to sentence him according to the provisions of the penal code the *Jirga* will try to arrive at a settlement between two parties (i.e. the families or clans or tribes of the murderer and the murdered person). Such settlement is essential in order to bring a family or tribal feud to a permanent end and to establish peace. Only such a settlement can terminate the feud. The following example given by Sir Olaf Caroe, who was the Chief Commissioner of Baluchistan and the last Governor of the British N.W.F.P. will further illustrate these points:

> "Let us suppose that case A arises out of a blood-feud, and that Shirin Khan has shot and killed Anwar in revenge for the murder of Shirin's brother by Anwar's uncle. According to Pathan custom Shirin only did what honour requires. If Shirin were brought before the ordinary courts

[1] *Niamatullah Committee Report*, p. 3.

> which administer a system of law repugnant and incomprehensible to him, knowing that his conviction would probably result in his going to the gallows for doing his duty, he would do everything he could to evade 'justice'. Among other things a host of perjured witnesses would be produced in his defence. But if brought before a *Jirga*...he would proudly admit, indeed claim, that he had done what honour required.[[1]] The business of the *Jirga* would then be to arrive, if possible, at a settlement which will terminate the feud, either by payment of blood-money, or by giving of girls in marriage—a very common method of composing a feud...—or by some other expedient such as requiring Shirin and the rival party to enter into bonds to keep the peace, backed by substantial sureties. There would be no penalty enforced by the State. [Sir Olaf further added that] The point to realise is this. Pathan custom requires the satisfaction of the aggrieved rather than the punishment of the aggressor. The law as we understand it concentrates as against the aggressor, and compensation for the aggrieved hardly enters the picture. The Pathan in fact treats crime as a kind of tort."[2]

But if someone commits a murder not for the sake of what is called 'Pathan honour' but for some other reason, which according to pathan tradition and custom, is not a 'just reason' then such a murder will be considered 'an unjustifiable murder' by the pathan community. In such a case the *Jirga* "might recommend the highest possible term of imprisonment, fourteen years".[3] Such a crime will be condemned by the pathan community and the murderer and his family or clan will not receive the support or sympathy of the community.

After the annexation of these areas to the British Indian Empire towards the end of the 1840s a regular judicial system was introduced. But this regular judicial system, as Sir Olaf commented,

> "with its lawyers and its appeals and its European scale of crime values, was hopelessly out of accord with Pathan sentiment...the law frequently outraged strongly held convictions...it imposed sanctions or penalties

1 Like Sir Olaf the Simon Commission also had commented that "It is significant that there is less challenge of notorious facts, and more frequent admission of the truth, before *Jirgas* than in ordinary courts where professional advocates are engaged." (*Simon Report*, vol. i, para. 362.)

2 Olaf Caroe, *The Pathans: 550 B. C.—A. D. 1957* (London, 1958), pp. 354-5.

3 *Ibid.*, p. 355. (Sir Olaf has given two more examples. See cases 'B' and 'C' in *Ibid.*, p. 355.)

> not justified by custom. The whole thing, for years, was a garment that did not fit. [Thus]...in 1872 a positive attempt was made to relax this inelasticity by the introduction of the Frontier Crimes Regulation".[1]

The FCR of 1872 was later replaced by the FCR of 1901.

From our foregoing discussion we find that the trial by *Jirga* is "in accordance with ancient tribal tradition" and "has the practical advantage of securing decisions on the spot with the help of those who are likely to have the best knowledge both of the actual incident and of local custom".[2]

What has been said in preceding paragraphs about the utility of the *Jirga* system and the logic behind it is valid only in very backward tribal areas such as political agencies. But the general attitude towards the *Jirga* system in other FCR areas, which with the passage of time have undergone some social, political, economic and educational transformations, has now changed to a fairly considerable extent.

The Quetta-Kalat Laws Commission of 1958, which "saw no merit in continuing the *Jirga* system in Quetta and Kalat",[3] was "definitely of the opinion that this system of laws was outmoded and should be scrapped in toto".[4] Later the Pakistan Law Reforms Commission of 1958-59 found that the opinion "on the desirability or otherwise of retaining *Jirga* trials is sharply divided".[5] On the one hand the intelligentsia, the commercial class and members of the legal profession in the 'settled areas,' who gave instances of abuse of powers under the FCR by the administrative officers, "all made a dead-set against the continuance of the *Jirga* law"[6] and on the other hand, "those residing in rural areas or having tribal associations are generally in favour of the retention of the system, provided that certain abuses that have crept into the system are removed".[7] The Commission also observed that "an underlying

1 *Ibid.*, pp. 352-3.

2 *Simon Report*, vol. i, para. 362.

3 Ralph Braibanti, *Research on the Bureaucracy of Pakistan* (Durham, 1966), p. 195. (Here it may be mentioned that these two divisions—Quetta and Kalat—cover almost the whole of Baluchistan.)

4 *Law Reforms Commission's Report*, p.107.

5 *Ibid.*, pp. 107-8.

6 *Ibid.*, p. 108.

7 *Ibid.*, p. 108.

current of dissatisfaction with the scheme of things prevailing under the system is becoming visible".[1] It further added that "the old tribal bonds which spelled success for the *Jirga* are loosening and individualism is daily gaining more and more ground".[2] The Commission was of the opinion that the *Jirga* system should be changed and that "steps should be taken to provide a regular judicial administration"[3] in those areas which were "favourable to change"[4] because of their "educational, social and economic development".[5] But at the same time the Commission also felt that the *Jirga* system should be retained in "certain areas."[6] It held that

> "in the present conditions, it seems unavoidable to continue the *Jirga* system wherever conditions do not yet justify a change. This would be necessary to satisfy the people who still retain tribal loyalties and consider that their tribal customs should be preserved. Progressive laws cannot outpace social progress."[7]

In these areas there are also other difficulties in replacing the *Jirga* system by the regular judicial and magisterial systems. Such replacement will naturally minimise to a considerable extent the authority and influence of the tribal chiefs who will, therefore, bitterly resent any attempt at such a replacement. In such areas it would be almost impossible to make the regular judicial and magisterial systems work and to run the general administration against the opposition of these tribal chiefs who have virtually full control and enormous influence over their tribes. The Pakistan Law Reforms Commission remarked:

> "We recognise that administration in these areas cannot be run at present without the help of the tribes resident therein, which means, in practice, the assistance of Chiefs of these tribes. This would imply that if this system of administration is to continue, the *Jirga* system which is an integral part of the tribal system, would also have to be maintained".[8]

---

1 *Ibid.*, p. 108. Some people also think that the structure of tribal responsibility has deteriorated in many places and that the tribal administration in those areas is characterised by the tyranny of tribal chiefs.

2 *Ibid.*, p. 108. 3 *Ibid.*, p. 109. 4 *Ibid.*, p. 108.

5 *Ibid.*, p. 108. 6 *Ibid.*, p. 108. 7 *Ibid.*, pp. 108-9.

8 *Ibid.*, p. 109.

When the Commission held that the *Jirga* system should be retained in "certain areas" it did not specifically name any particular areas. By "certain areas" it probably meant political agencies and a few other very backward tribal areas. No doubt, in other tribal areas the way of life has undergone some changes but in most areas of political agencies it has changed very little and the process of change is very slow. The *Jirga* system is probably the most suitable and the most practical system for administering justice in political agencies.

Extension of the FCR to Other Areas

One of the terms of reference of the Pakistan Law Reforms Commission was to examine the *Jirga* system and its "extension to suitable areas".[1] While the Commission observed that "However, it is for serious consideration whether the areas in which the Frontier Crimes Regulation is now in force should not be further curtailed, in view of changed conditions", it made it emphatically clear that there was, "in our opinion, no case for extension of the *Jirga* system to other areas at all".[2] But soon after the publication of the report of the Commission the jurisdiction of the FCR was extended to a number of districts in 1960. In 1962 the Governor of West Pakistan was empowered to extend its jurisdiction at his own discretion to the whole of West Pakistan. In the same year he extended its jurisdiction to certain districts of the province.[3]

The arguments, that were put forward in favour of such extension, were that it suited the genius of the people, that the modern system of trial by courts of law was expensive, complicated and unsuitable for most people, that the system of administering justice should not only be simple and inexpensive but should be based on the values paramount in society. It was argued that it was "futile" to apply western legal norms to "litigation arising from totally different societal values".[4] It was

> "among vigorous peoples who have a strong faith in their own traditional institutions...that you will find the strongest demand for restoration of their original institutions. There is nothing superficial about

[1] *Ibid.*, p. 1. [2] *Ibid.*, p. 109. [3] Braibanti, *Research*, p. 190.
[4] *Ibid.*, p. 192.

this desire. It is nothing more or less than a groping for the true roots of their being, as individuals and as a nation...It is the natural cry of a strong organism to be connected once again with its original and proper roots... A first requisite for this purpose is to search for the true roots of the nation's being...[It was further added that] Not all the maxims upon which British legal concepts are based are universally true. A good many are opposed to basic concepts in vogue for twenty centuries and more in the countries of the Middle East, to which we in this country are by religion and culture, most closely allied. To ensure that the maximum good in the national character is produced, it is necessary to pay full attention to 'the eternal source of all legality', so that in a real sense 'the law may grow out of the society.'"[1]

The comments of Sir Olaf Caroe, made in his book *The Pathans*, are often cited in favour of the arguments for the retention and the extension of the *Jirga* system. Sir Olaf commented in his book that "It is an obvious principle that the law should in some sense grow out of the society; it should be a projection of the common personality. The law of one civilisation cannot be applied to a society with utterly different standards without the most dire results".[2] But Sir Olaf's comments in another place suggest that he advocated the *Jirga* system only for backward tribal areas, that he did not advocate this system for relatively advanced areas and that he would like to see the *Jirga* system replaced by the regular system in those areas which had already undergone adequate social change. The following passage from his written memorandum addressed to the Quetta-Kalat Laws Commission of 1958 will illustrate these points:

"My own opinion is that an entirely fresh line of distinction should be drawn in Baluchistan. It should be decided which, if any, region outside the towns, cantonments are ripe for regular administration, and which are still in a tribal condition analogous to what exists on the North-West Frontier. In the first, which might for instance include the plains, part

[1] A.R. Cornelius, "Restoration of Judicial Responsibility to People" in *The All-Pakistan Legal Decisions* (journal section), vol. xv, 1963, pp. 12-13. Though here Mr. Justice Cornelius, the then Chief Justice of former Pakistan, argued in favour of the *Jirga* system, in another place he criticised the attitude of the officers who on the grounds of expediency avoided the jurisdiction of regular courts and referred cases to *jirgas*. (See below, p.48.)

[2] Caroe, *op. cit.*, p. 355. Chief Justice Cornelius also quoted this passage in support of his views. (*op. cit.*, p. 9.)

of Sibi and the open country round Quetta and Pisin, police should be set up and the regular law administered. In the second, the Frontier Crimes Regulation or something like it, should be kept. [He further stated that] Here I would repeat the suggestion that the social, administrative and jurisprudential situation in present day Baluchistan be reviewed, and the territory divided into categories for (a) regular, (b) tribal management. [He further added that] At the same time I make the admission in conclusion that in my opinion the British Administration in their time in Baluchistan were too static in their treatment of these problems. The acceptance of the standards, of a simple tribalism is not enough. There is need to pose a challenge. In Baluchistan we left to our successors much of what we left undone."[1]

Criticism of the Extension. The extension of the FCR to "settled areas", which entrusted the government and its executive arm with arbitrary powers and made them the arbiters to decide whether a case should be tried by a regular court of law or should be referred to a *Jirga*, was widely and strongly criticised. The critics "denounced the extension with vigor, asserting that it meant retrogression to 'primitive' norms for persons who had long lived under Western criminal law".[2] It was pointed out that "the British system is universally regarded as one of the best systems of justice".[3]

One of the "potential" effects of such an extension was "the use of FCR jurisdiction as a means of deprivation of public liberties by avoiding due process of law and judicial review...Another aspect of potentially oppressive use of the FCR was the broad discretion in which was imbedded the right of the deputy commissioner to assign a case to a *Jirga* rather than leave it for trial by ordinary courts."[4] Mr. Justice Cornelius, the then Chief Justice of Pakistan, "suggested" that on the grounds of expediency "the jurisdiction of ordinary courts was being avoided to an increasing extent by assignment of cases to *Jirga*."[5] In the Nawab Gul case the Chief Justice, therefore, "deplored the reference of accused persons to a *Jirga* when there appeared to be no case against

[1] Quoted in *Law Reforms Commission's Report*, p. 109.

[2] Braibanti, *Research*, p. 191.

[3] *Ibid*., p. 193.

[4] *Ibid*., p. 191.

[5] *Ibid*., p. 192.

them."[1] Critics also strongly objected to section 40 of the FCR which empowered the D.O. to require a person, who in his opinion was likely to commit a serious crime or to cause a breach of peace, to execute a bond, with or without sureties, for good behaviour or for keeping peace. "This made it possible to suppress public liberties arbitrarily without due process of law."[2] The critics also felt that "one of the reasons for the government's decision" to extend the jurisdiction of the FCR was "the immense police powers inherent in this provision" of the Regulation.[3]

One of the most vital criticisms was that most characteristics of the tribal way of life which had been responsible for the introduction of the *Jirga* system to tribal areas and also for its success in these areas were not the characteristics or at least the significant characteristics of the way of life of the people of the "settled districts" to which the FCR had been extended. Of course, previously many characteristics of the way of life in these districts had been somewhat similar to the characteristics of tribal or clannish way of life. But with the passage of the time, it changed to an enormous extent. Though the tribal or clannish bonds and customs continued to influence, in varying degrees, social life, their importance had been lessening. Unlike the chiefs in tribal areas, usually the persons who used to sit in the *Jirga* of the settled or semi-settled districts neither enjoyed loyalties and special respects of the local inhabitants nor had they any strong influence or control over them. Moreover, unlike the chiefs in tribal areas, the former usually had no close and intimate contact with the latter and were not likely to be thoroughly acquainted or aware of the various aspects and the background of a crime committed in their areas because unlike those in tribal areas family feuds and other quarrels did not usually follow understandable and predictable patterns or courses in "settled" or "semi-settled" areas. Unlike the tribal people, the inhabitants of these areas, who had more contact with neighbouring areas or other parts of the country and who became accustomed to the system of trial by regular courts

[1] *Ibid.*, p. 190. [2] *Ibid.*, p. 190. [3] *Ibid.*, p. 190.

of law, were not likely to have much faith in and respect for the *Jirga* and its decision.

We may summarise the arguments against the extension of the FCR to other areas by saying that though strong tribal and clannish affinities were characteristics of a considerable part of the "settled areas" of West Pakistan there were enormous differences between the way of life in these areas and that in tribal areas, that, therefore, the *Jirga* system was not likely to work satisfactorily and successfully in the former areas though it proved to be a suitable and practical system in the latter areas, and that such extension entrusted the government and its executive arm in "settled" and "semi-settled" areas with virtual arbitrary powers which did not in any way come under the review of the judiciary.

Modification of the FCR. In April 1963 some provisions of the FCR were modified and then its jurisdiction was extended to the whole of West Pakistan except to political agencies, the Quetta and Kalat divisions (i.e. almost whole of Baluchistan), Lasbella district of the Karachi division, the Nasirabad sub-division of the Jacobabad district and certain strips of tribal regions in the N.W.F.P.[1] In these areas (i.e. political agencies and other areas mentioned above) the FCR of 1901 remained in force without any modification.[2] A few important provisions of the

[1] The West Pakistan Criminal Law (Amendment) Act, 1963, published in *Gazette of Pakistan* (Extraordinary), April 19, 1963. Later published in pamphlet form with the following title: *The West Pakistan Criminal Law (Amendment) Act, 1963 (Act VII of 1963) and The West Pakistan Criminal Law (Amendment Rules, 1963)* (corrected up to 1st October, 1965) (Lahore, 1965) (Hereafter cited as *W. Pak. C. L. Act, 1963*), see sec. 1 (2) and the 3rd schedule. Original sub-section 2 of section I was substituted by the W. Pak. Ordinance no. XLIV of 1963 and the 3rd schedule was also added by the same ordinance. (See the footnote of the above mentioned pamphlet.)

[2] Of course, in Pakistan there are a few pockets of backward areas (e.g. the areas which are called "Excluded Areas") in which neither the regular laws nor the modified or the unmodified FCR are in force. Usually these areas have been administered by separate regulations. Sometimes some regular laws of "settled areas" have also been extended from time to time to some of these areas. The administration in these areas is almost as backward as

modified form of the FCR (i.e. The West Pakistan Criminal Law Act of 1963), which operated in the "settled" areas of West Pakistan, is discussed below:

It was not the D.O., but the Divisional Commissioner who made the decision whether it was "expedient in the interest of the justice, that the question of guilt or innocence"[1] of any person or persons (excepting public servants[2]) accused of any of the specified offences should be referred to the decision of a tribunal.[3] In making such a decision the Commissioner took the suggestion of the D.O. into serious consideration and usually his suggestion was accepted. The tribunal consisted of four members and a president who must have the powers of an Additional D.O. or a S.D M. or a Section 30 Magistrate.[4] The four members were appointed by the D.O. from a panel of 60 to 100 persons appointed by the Commissioner for each district in his division. While appointing these members to the panel he, according to the instruction of the Act, was supposed to take their "integrity, education and social status" into consideration.[5] The recommendation of the D.O., who had much more knowledge of the

that in tribal areas though usually the administration in the former is, relatively speaking, more developed than that in the latter. "The Excluded Areas represent a kind of intermediate stage between 'special areas' [i.e. tribal areas] and the areas under normal administration." (*Pro. Adm. Com. Report*, p. 209.) For example, Upper Tanawal (204 square miles and approximately 50 thousand population) is an "Excluded Area". (For a brief discussion of the administration of these areas see *ibid.*, pp. 213-217.) When we shall later discuss the pattern of administration of the Chittagong Hill Tracts district in Bangladesh which is also an "Excluded Area", we shall have some idea of the pattern of administration in "Excluded Areas."

1 *W. Pak. C. L. Act, 1963*, sec. 3(1).

2 If a public servant is accused of an offence, the permission of the government is necessary before taking such a decision. [*Ibid.*, sec. 3(3).]

3 A number of sections of the Panel Code (1860), Sea Customs Act (1878), Land Customs Act (1924) and Prevention of Corruption Act (1947) were listed in the first schedule of *ibid.* If a person is accused of an offence under any of these sections the Divisional Commissioner could take such a decision. [*Ibid.*, sec. 3(3).]

4 *Ibid.*, sec. 4(a).

5 *Ibid.*, sec. 5.

local people and the local elite, was usually accepted by the Commissioner when he appointed members to the panel. Lawyers were also allowed to attend the proceedings of the tribunal in defence of the accused person or persons.

On receiving the finding from the tribunal, the decisions that the D.O. could take under the West Pakistan Criminal Law Act of 1963 were more or less similar to those[1] that his counterpart in the FCR area could take under the FCR of 1901.[2] As under the FCR, the maximum punishment that the former could award was fourteen years rigorous imprisonment,[3] and appeal against any of his decision under this Act could be made only to the Divisional Commissioner.[4]

Some Comments. The modification of some provisions of the FCR did not alter the fact that the government and its executive arm in the "settled areas" of West Pakistan enjoyed enormous arbitrary powers, and that the Supreme and the High Courts continued to be deprived of any jurisdiction over cases that were referred to such tribunals.

In early 1969, the Ayub regime was replaced by Yeahya regime which repealed with effect from the 1st of December, 1969 the West Pakistan Criminal Law (Amendment) Act of 1963 i.e. the modified form of FCR of 1901.[5] Of course, the unmodified FCR of 1901 continued to be in force in political agencies and some other tribal areas, about which we have discussed above.[6]

From our foregoing discussion we find that from the point of view of administration of justice, Pakistan may be divided into three regions. Firstly, under the unmodified FCR of 1901 the *Jirga* system alone is in operation in political agencies and in some strips of tribal areas in N.W.F.P.[7] Secondly, both regular courts of law and *Jirga* system are operating concurrently in certain areas

[1] See above, p. 224. [2] *W. Pak. C. L. Act, 1963*, sec. 10.

[3] *Ibid.*, sec. 11. [4] *Ibid.*, secs. 18-19.

[5] *Pakistan Observer* (Dacca), December 2, 1969. New ordinance was entitled Criminal Law (Amendment) Act (Repeal) Ordinance, 1969. (*Ibid.*)

[6] See above, p. 233. [7] *Ibid.*, pp. 221-2, 233; also see chap. iii.

(e.g. almost whole of Baluchistan, and Lasbella district and Nasirabad sub-division of Sind).[1] Of course, in some of these areas, the regular laws are slightly different from those of "settled areas."[2] Thirdly, the regular courts of law alone are in operation in "settled districts". Of course, from 1963 to 1969, both regular courts of law and special tribunals, which were in fact modified form of *Jirga* were functioning concurrently in these areas.[3] But, in Bangladesh regular courts of law alone are administering justice in all the districts of Bangladesh except one (i.e. the Chittagong Hill Tracts district which is very sparsely inhabited by tribal people and is classified as an "Excluded Area").[4]

[1] *Ibid.*, pp. 221-2, 233. [2] *Ibid.*, p. 222 fn. 3. [3] *Ibid.*, pp. 233-236.

[4] We have already noted in chapter iii that though in terms of area the Chittagong Hill Tracts district is the second biggest district in Bangladesh, in terms of population it is the smallest district, that it is mostly covered by hills and jungles and that it has inherited the administrative tradition of a Non-Regulation Area. Unlike the tribal people of Pakistan, the people of this district, who are also tribal people, are not militant but peaceful and law abiding. The people of this district lead a simple life and there is little crime and litigation among them. The administration of this district is run according to the Chittagong Hill Tracts Regulation of 1900 (which only lays down some broad principles of administration of justice) and the rules made thereunder. The Panel Code, the Evidence Act and the Code of Criminal Procedure are also applicable to this district in so far as they are not inconsistent with the provisions of the Chittagong Hill Tracts Regulation and the rules made thereunder. The tribal cases as well as civil cases are decided on the basis of tribal customs and traditions though in the event of a civil case sometimes some provisions of regular civil laws and codes are also taken into consideration. There are no *Munsifs*. The S.D.O. and his subordinates i.e. the Deputy Magistrates, try both criminal and civil cases as well as tribal cas.s. The tribal chiefs and the tribal headmen also try tribal cases. [*District Census Report: Chittagong Hill Tracts, 1961* (Dacca, 1963), p. I—8.] The lawyers are not allowed to take part in the proceedings of a court. The D.O. also acts as the District Judge. In that capacity within his district he is the highest judicial authority in respect of civil and tribal cases having both original and appellate jurisdictions. But he does not act as the Sessions Judge. (Of course, like other D.O.s in Bangladesh he enjoys the powers of a 1st class Magistrate but usually he does not try any criminal cases though he supervises the working of the criminal administration and the functions of other Magistrates.) It is the Divisional Commissioner of the Chittagong division, whose official seat is at the headquarters of the Chittagong district which is adjacent to Chittagong

In order to compare the position of the D.O. in Bangladesh with that of his counterpart in Pakistan, a few points pertaining to his judicial powers may be repeated in the following table:

TABLE XVI

COMPARATIVE STUDY OF D.O.'S JUDICIAL POWERS IN BANGLADESH AND PAKISTAN

BANGLADESH	PAKISTAN
Regular Laws and Codes	*Regular Laws and Codes*
He enjoys the powers of a 1st Class Magistrate: maximum punishment—2 years rigorous imprisonment (In practice he does not try any case)	Usually he enjoys the powers of a Section 30 Magistrate: Maximum punishment—7 years rigorous imprisonment.
He does not have power to hear appeal	He can hear appeal against the decisions of 2nd and 3rd Class Magistrates
Higher judicial authorities have powers to hear appeals against his judicial decisions	Higher judicial authorities have powers to hear appeal against his judicial decisions
Special Regulations	*Special Regulations*
There is no special regulation except in Chittagong Hill Tracts district. He can try all types of civil cases and petty criminal cases.	In FCR area he takes decisions in respect of all types of civil and criminal cases : Maximum punishment—14 years rigorous imprisonment.
	Higher judicial authorities have no power to hear appeal against such decisions

Hill Tracts district (see the map at the end of the book), who acts as the Sessions Judge of the Chittagong Hill Tracts district. In that capacity he has both original and appellate jurisdictions in respect of criminal cases. (*Pro. Adm. Com. Report*, p. 210.) But in practice he does not try a case at the initial stage. He tries only those cases which are committed to sessions and hears appeals against the decisions of other Magistrates in criminal cases. He has the authority to impose the maximum sentence, i.e. the death sentence. One of the interesting points is that while the jurisdictions of the Supreme and the High Courts do not extend over the tribal areas of Pakistan, they extend over the Chittagong Hill Tracts district. The High Court Division and the Appellate Division of the Supreme Court of Bangladesh have the authority to hear appeals against the decisions of the Divisional Commissioner and the D.O. when they act as the Sessions Judge and the District Judge respectively.

Thus we find that so far as the administration of criminal justice is concerned there is an enormous difference between the position of the D.O. in Bangladesh and that of his counterpart in Pakistan.

LAND REVENUE ADMINISTRATION

Introduction

The revenue department is the only important department which does not have separate high ranking field officers. It is the D.O. himself and his immediate subordinate officers who act as the high ranking field officers of the revenue department.[1] It is mainly because, as we have noted in chapter i, modern district administration in the sub-continent and the office of the D.O. had their origin in revenue administration and in the office of the Collector respectively.

Pakistan. The pattern of land revenue administration is not uniform throughout Pakistan. We have noted in chapter i that at the time of partition West Pakistan inherited both the *Ryotwari* (i.e. Munro system) and the *Mahalwari* land revenue system. While the former system, which is now called the Sind system, is in force in Sind, former Khairpur state, and the Nasirabad sub-division of Baluchistan, the latter system, which is now

1 Of course the revenue department has its own petty revenue officers who under the control and supervision of the D.O. and his subordinates, perform their functions at the lower levels of district administration (see below).

Here it may be mentioned that the D.O. is responsible for the collection of land revenue but not for taxes on industries, business and other personal incomes. The Income-tax Officer, who is a member of the Taxation Service and who is posted at the district headquarters, checks the accounts of the people concerned and makes assessment. He is responsible to see that the taxes are regularly paid to the district treasury. If anyone fails or refuses to pay, he refers the matter (called certificate case) to the D.O. who then takes necessary administrative and judicial measures in order to realise the amount. The Income-tax Officer is assisted by a few Inspectors. His functions are supervised by the Assistant Commissioner of Income-tax who remains in charge of the income-tax administration in a group of districts. The Commissioner of Income-tax is the Administrative head of the income tax department. Income-tax is an important source of income of the government. This department performs its functions under the control of the Ministry of Finance.

called the Punjab system, is in force in other areas of Pakistan.[1] Under the Sind system the settlement is made with the *ryot* (tenant) who is directly responsible for the payment of land revenue, while under the Punjab system the settlement is made with the *Mahal* (village community) which pays the land revenue to the government through the village headman.[2] (For detailed discussion see below.)

Bangladesh. At the time of partition the land revenue system in East Bengal was completely different from both the Sind and the Punjab systems. We have noted in chapter I that in 1793 Cornwallis introduced permanent settlement or *Zamindari* system in Bengal and that under this system the D.O.'s major responsibility was to see that fixed land revenues were regularly collected from some intermediaries called *Zamindars*. Thus, the revenue work was not heavy in Bengal and "all that the Collector [i.e.D.O.] needed was some clerical assistant for the preparation of demand lists and the maintenance of *tauzi* i.e. registers of revenue accounts".[3] He was also assisted by one or two Deputy Collectors.

[1] Of course, in some tribal areas no land revenue system has been in force from the British period. We have already noted in chapter iii that the Simon Commission mentioned that the tribal people accepted the government control through the Political Agent on the condition that they would not be required to pay any revenue. (see above, chap. iii.)

[2] The Sind and the Punjab systems of land revenue are administered according to the provisions of the Bombay Land Revenue Code of 1879 and the Punjab Land Revenue Act of 1887 respectively. The Punjab Land Revenue Act of 1887 is in force in the former Bahawalpur state, N.W.F.P. and Baluchistan with certain modifications. (*Council Report for W. Pak.*, p. 10.)

[3] *Pro. Adm. Com. Report*, p. 175.

The comment of the Provincial Administration Commission, in fact, gives a misleading impression about the extent of simplicity of the revenue functions in E. Bengal. The revenue function of the D.O. in E. Bengal was no doubt much simpler than that of his counterpart in other places. But it was not so simple as it appears to be from the comment of the Commission. The land revenue not only included fixed revenue to be collected from the *Zamindars* but also the following incomes : collection from government estates, sale process of waste land, redemption of land tax, recoveries on account of survey, settlement charges, recovery of cost of maintenance of boundary pillars, rent and cesses on lands, recoveries

In 1950, as we have already noted in chapter iii, the *Zamindari* system was abolished by the Tenancy Act of 1950. The system which replaced it is more or less similar to the *Ryotwari* or Sind system. We shall later see that as a result of this abolition a fairly long hierarchy of new revenue functionaries were created below the district level.

The Board of Revenue (Provincial)

Under the Revenue Minister the Board of Revenue (provincial), which consists of three members, is the highest land revenue authority and in each province of (present and former) Pakistan. In 1955 when all the provinces and the former princely states in West Pakistan were integrated into one province, the then highest revenue authorities, namely the Financial Commissioners in the Punjab and Bahawalpur and the Revenue Commissioners in the N.W.F.P., Sind and Baluchistan, were replaced by the Board of Revenue (provincial).[1] But it was in 1772 that the Board of Revenue (provincial) was first established in British Bengal, part of which now constitutes Bangladesh.[2]

The Board of Revenue (provincial), which is the "Executive Head" of the land revenue administration, exercises superintendence and control over all revenue functionaries. It acts as the "chief adviser" to the Cabinet for policies in respect of all land revenue and agrarian matters, as an "expert body for making

of overpayments, collection of payments for services rendered by the government for improvement of lands or for similar reasons etc. [*Civil Budget Estimates for the year* 1939-40 (Alipure, Calcutta, 1939), pp. 3-4.] Thus in his capacity as the Collector he was not only responsible for supervising regular collection of fixed land revenue but also for supervising these aspects of land revenue administration. We shall later see that he was (and is) also the Revenue Judge.

1 Such replacement was recommended in 1955 in the *Council Report for W. Pak.*, p. 10.

2 The Board of Revenue in British Bengal was reconstituted in 1822 by the Bengal Board of Revenue Regulation, again in 1850 by the Bengal Board of Revenue Act and finally in 1913 by the Bengal Board of Revenue Act. [*Report of the Land Revenue Commission: East Pakistan* (Dacca, 1959) (Hereafter cited as *1959 Revenue Commission Report*), para 88.]

rules" and regulations, subject to the approval of the government, for prescribing "uniform standards and procedures" in order to "regulate the disposal of revenue matters and the powers and duties of Revenue Officers",[1] as co-ordinating agency in all matters relating to land management and administration with the authority to call from other departments necessary reports and information in respect of these matters.[2] Above all, it is the highest revenue court for revenue cases (i.e. mutation, partition etc.). Sometimes it is argued that the judicial and revenue functions vested in it should be separated. But in 1960 the Provincial Administration Commission pointed out that

> "There is an interdependence of judicial and executive functions in revenue administration and any artificial separation of the two would be ill-advised. Revenue courts are only revenue officers functioning in a quasi-judicial capacity and it is necessary that this inter locking of the two functions should also exist at the highest executive and judicial levels for revenue matters in the province."[3]

There is no Revenue Directorate. Of course, the Board of Revenue (provincial) may broadly be regarded as the Revenue Directorate because a part of its functions is more or less similar to the functions of a Directorate. But there is a world of difference between the nature of the relationship that exists between the Board of Revenue (provincial) and the Revenue Department in the Secretariat. We have already noted in chapter iii that the head of a Secretariat Department, i.e. the provincial Secretary, usually holds a higher and more preeminant position than the Head of the provincial Directorate and that the former enjoys great influence especially in the policy making aspect. But the official status of the Members of the Board of Revenue (provincial) is, on the contrary, much higher than that of the Secretary of the Revenue Department in the provincial Secretariat.[4] The members

[1] *Pro. Adm. Com. Report*, p. 165. [2] *Ibid.*, p. 165.

[3] *Pro. Adm. Com. Report*, p. 164.

[4] We have noted in chapter iii that the official status of the Secretaries of only six Secretariat Departments is equivalent to that of the Divisional Commissioner. The Revenue Secretary is not one of them. So, his status is also lower than that of the Divisional Commissioner.

play a much more prominent role in the process of policy making and execution. The Secretary serves as the channel of communication between the Revenue Minister and the Board of Revenue.

Besides the Board of Revenue (provincial) in each province, there is also a Central Board of Revenue at the central level of (former and present) Pakistan. While the former looks after the matters concerning land revenue, agricultural income-tax etc., the latter deals with general income-tax, customs and other revenue matters. After the emergence of Bangladesh as a separate independent state, a National Board of Revenue with all the powers and functions of the Central Board of Revenue of (former and present) Pakistan was appointed. The Board of Revenue (provincial) also continued to operate simultaneously. But recently (early 1973) the Government of Bangladesh has decided to abolish it and to entrust its powers and functions on the Revenue Department in the Secretariat (i.e. Revenue Ministry), and National Board of Revenue. As there is no province in Bangladesh, it is generally felt that there is no point in having a separate provincial Board of Revenue.

Divisional Commissioner

"The main duty" of the Divisional Commissioner, whose post was created in 1829, "was to help the Board of Revenue in the close supervision of the land revenue administration in the district, and some supervisory and appellate powers of the Board of Revenue were transferred to the Commissioner".[2] We have already noted in chapter iii that in British Bengal and during the early post-partition period the Divisional Commissioner in East Bengal was mainly concerned with the revenue side of district administration though he exercised some general control and supervision over other aspects of it; whereas in those parts of British India which later constituted West Pakistan and which had been Non-Regulation Provinces, the Divisional Commissioner was equally concerned with almost all the aspects

1 *The People* (Dacca), March 4, 1973.

2 *1959 Revenue Commission Report*, para. 99.

of district administration. But from the middle of the 1950s, in East Bengal also the Divisional Commissioner was required to give more and more attention to other aspects of district administration and during the last decade he gave much less attention to revenue administration.[1] Recently (early 1973), the Bangladesh Government has decided to relieve the Divisional Commissioner of the responsibilities in regard to revenue matters.[2]

Collector

The D.O. in his capacity as the Collector is required to act as (i) a collector of land revenue, water dues etc., (ii) a recorder of agricultural statistics, (iii) a "guardian" and registrar of the rights in the soil enjoyed by private persons, (iv) "a prompter of the stability and improvement of the landed property", (v) a "custodian of state property", and (vi) a Judge of the revenue cases.[3] But later we shall see that in practice he does not directly perform these functions, that he simply maintains an overall

[1] The East Pakistan Land Revenue Commission of 1959, which was of the opinion that the Divisional Commissioner, who had been "originally" and "primarily meant for the land revenue administration" (*Ibid.*, para. 103) should be required to give adequate attention to land revenue administration, held that the "Commissioners of Divisions are at present by-passed in many matters concerned with land revenue administration. The Board of Revenue often correspond with the District Officers [D. O., Additional or joint D.O.s (Revenue). See below] who again reply direct to them. This practice may be justified in case of urgency. But even in such cases copies of the correspondence should pass through the Commissioner. Copies of all returns of collection etc., should be sent to the Commissioner, who should review the same and send his own comments thereon to the Board of Revenue, with a copy to the District Officers. He should take an active interest in, and should be made responsible for, land revenue administration in his Division. He should inspect each District [Revenue] Office once a year and each Sub-division [Revenue] Office once in two years." (*Ibid.*, para. 109.) But as a result of an enormous increase in the volume of other and new functions and the lessening importance of revenue function (see below), nowadays in practice the Divisional Commissioner is not required to give more attention to land revenue administration.

[2] *The People* (Dacca), March 4, 1973.

[3] *Punjab Land Administration Manual* (Lahore, 1960) (First edn. 1908) by James M. Douie. p.1. Same in Bangladesh and in other parts of Pakistan.

control and supervision over the revenue machinery in the district and that the Additional or Joint D.O. who is directly subordinate to him mainly performs these functions.[1] In performing these functions the Additional or Joint D.O. is assisted by a fairly long hierarchy of revenue functionaries.[2] The Revenue Deputy Collector (Bangladesh)/the Extra Assistant Commissioner (Revenue) (Pakistan), who is posted at the district headquarters is his main lieutenant.

The revenue function is not only the oldest function of the D.O. but once it was one of two most important functions, the other being law and order. He used to devote a great deal of time and energy to revenue administration which always received his special and personal attention. The extent of his ability to administer revenue matters efficiently was one of the most important criteria by which his competence as a D.O. was measured. Several factors were responsible for the paramount importance of revenue administration: Firstly, land revenue used to be the principal source of revenue receipts of the provincial government. Secondly, land revenue administration enabled the D.O. and his subordinates to come into the closest contact with the rural people who constituted the bulk of the population of the country and to learn about the conditions and problems of the remotest part of the countryside. The revenue hierarchy was, in fact, considered the central channel of communication between the people and the government. Thirdly, land revenue administration affected to an enormous extent the interest and the well being of the bulk of the population of the sub-continent (which was primarily an agricultural country) who were almost wholly dependent on the land for their livelihood.[3] Fourthly, the office of the Collector was a great source of his influence and prestige. He could easily bring his pressure to bear upon the landed "aristocrats" either to keep a

[1] Of course, if there is no Additional or Joint D.O. in any district the D.O. of that district is required to spend a good deal of time and energy in order to supervise land revenue administration. Nowadays, the Additional or Joint D.O. is not posted only in those districts (the number of which, of course, is not very large) in which the load of work is not very heavy.

[2] See below, chart iv.

[3] See above, chap i.

check on their arbitrary and tyrannical dealings with their tenants or to make use of their influence at the time of emergency (e.g. communal riot, or dispute between hostile groups etc.). The Simon Commission commented that "as Collector, he has numerous sources of influence that can be brought to bear in the right quarter".[1]

But from the post-war period the large increase in and the specialisation, diversification and modernisation of governmental functions, the mushroom growth and expansion of development activities, the rapid urbanisation and industrialisation[2] minimised to an enormous extent the importance of land revenue administration.[3] The Collector also found "his hands too full with a great variety of urgent problems to find sufficient time and energy to devote to revenue administration".[4] Moreover, from the 1950s and the 60s the percentage of land revenue in the provincial budget continued to decrease very fast mainly as a result of the increase in incomes from other sources.[5] The percentage of land revenue was, therefore much less than before. Such decrease further lessened the importance of land revenue administration to a considerable extent. So far as the D.O. in East Bengal was concerned the importance of land revenue administration was also eroded by the lessening importance and influence of the *Zamindars* and finally by the abolition of the *Zamindari* system in 1950. Because, on the one hand, it was not necessary for him to act as a check on the excesses of *Zamindars* and, on the other hand, they did not have any significant influence which he could make use of at the time of emergency e.g. riots etc.[6] (Later we shall see

[1] *Simon Report*, vol. I, para. 320.

[2] Of course, still it is primarily an agricultural country. But in comparison with the past it is now fairly industrialised and urbanised.

[3] Of course, the process of these changes began long before the war. But it was during the post-war period that this process became further accelerated.

[4] *The Government Estates Manual, 1958* (Dacca, 1958), p. 2. (Hereafter cited as *Estates Manual.*)

[5] The decrease in the percentage of land revenue in the provincial budget is shown in tables xv and xvi and in charts vii and viii.

[6] Of course, from another point of view the abolition of the *Zamindari* system

that in Bangladesh the recent decision of the authority to perpetually exempt those persons who have less than 25 *bighas* of land from paying land revenue, further lessened its importance to an enormous extent.)

The D.O. was thus expected to give more and more attention to the welfare and development functions and to other important aspects of district administration. He was under no obligation to deal directly with or to give close attention to revenue matters. Moreover, most D.O.s were not interested in revenue administration. The impression obtained by the present writer was that especially the young D.O.s consider revenue work 'dull', 'boring', and of 'routine nature' and that they tried to avoid it as far as possible.[1] In East Bengal the Land Revenue Commission of 1959, which said that according to "the present arrangement...the Collector is to exercise overall supervision over land revenue administration",[2] found that "Supervision is exercised by

(*Contd. on p. 251*)

increased the importance of land revenue administration because of the fact that millions of people became the direct tenants of the government and that it became necessary to reorganise revenue administration in the light of the new responsibility.

1 They find law and order, development and general administrative functions more exciting and interesting than the revenue function. It is also interesting to note that when an officer is appointed as an Additional D.O., he prefers to work in the capacity of the Additional D.O. (General) or in that of the Additional D.O. (Development), but not in that of the Additional D.O. (Revenue).

2 *1959 Revenue Commission Report*, para. 108. The above comment of the Commission was the factual statement of the then administrative arrangement. This comment was not intended to mean that the Commission also wanted that the D.O. could now simply exercise "overall supervision over revenue matters". This Commission was mainly composed of senior revenue officers who had worked in district administration when revenue function had been considered one of the most important functions. As a result, these officers had some bias towards the revenue function and were revenue oriented officers. It appears from their writings in the report that they were not very happy with the idea that the D.O. should remain contended with what was called "overall supervision" of revenue matters and that they were of the opinion that the D.O. should become very closely associated with land revenue administration. (*Ibid.*, esp. para. 103.) For their views about the role of the Commissioner see above, p. 243, fn. 1.

TABLE XVII

LAND REVENUE

BRITISH BENGAL/EAST BENGAL

Figures are in thousand takas/rupees

YEARS	TOTAL REVENUE RECEIPTS	LAND REVENUE	% OF LAND REVENUE
1870-71	15,34,72	4,04,15	26.3
1880-81	17,31,54	3,73,61	21.6
1890-91	19,03,17	3,82,79	20.1
1900-01	23,08,12	4,09,00	17.7
1910-11*	25,19,11	5,07,42	20.1
1920-21	11,28,04	2,90,31	25.7
1930-31	10,96,54	3,29,48	30.0
1940-41	14,66,52	3,67,90	25.1
1960-61	47,53,00	10,83,00	22.7
1961-62	73,88,00	14,55,00	19.7
1962-63	76,49,00	7,66,00	10.0
1963-64	95,88,00	13,00,00	13.5
1964-65	1,10,14,00	12,15,00	11.0
1965-66	1,17,94,00	13,43,00	11.4
1966-67	1,27,23,00	14,37,00	11.3
1967-68	1,49,96,00	18,00,00	12.0
1968-69	1,42,76,00	13,73,00	9.6
1969-70	1,68,83,00	15,00,00	8.8
1970-71**	1,78,91,00	15,00,00	8.3

* 'East Bengal and Assam' and West Bengal. ** Budget Estimate.
Source: See below, p. 248.

TABLE XVIII

LAND REVENUE

BRITISH PUNJAB/WEST PAKISTAN

Figures are in thousand takas/rupees

YEAR	TOTAL REVENUE RECEIPTS	LAND REVENUE	% OF LAND REVENUE
1870-71	3,85,09	2,13,43	55 4
1880-81	3,03,90	2,04,95	67.4
1890-91	6,98,36	2,24,47	32.1
1900-01	9,53,45	2,42,80	25.4
1910-11	7,10,76	2,80,40	39.4
1920-21	11,94,03	2,83,26	23.7
1930-31	11,81,84	4,88,13	41.3
1940-41	12,23,47	4,67,19	38.2
1960-61	79,30,00	16,13,00	20.3
1961-62	89,72,00	14,42,00	16.1
1962-63	1,26,44,00	14,55,00	11.5
1963-64	1,54,38,00	15,51,00	10.0
1964-65	1,76,58,00	15,14,00	8.6
1965-66	1,70,89,00	11,39,00	6.6
1966-67	1,78,30,00	17,10,00	9.5
1967-68	1,93,65,00	17,82,00	9.2
1968-69	1,87,40,00	16,68,00	8.9
1969-70	2,15,87,00	16,70,00	7.7
1970-71**	1,87,21,00	20,66,00	11.0

** Budget Estimate.

Source (Tables xv and xvi) :

Tables xv and xvi and charts vii and viii have been prepared on the basis of the figures available in annual issues of the *Civil Estimates of Provincial Governments* (Published by the Govt. of British India), *Pakistan Budgets* and *Pakistan Economic Survey* (Published by the Govt. of former Pakistan. See the volumes for the above mentioned years).

CHART VII.

LAND REVENUE PERCENTAGE
BRITISH BENGAL/EAST BENGAL

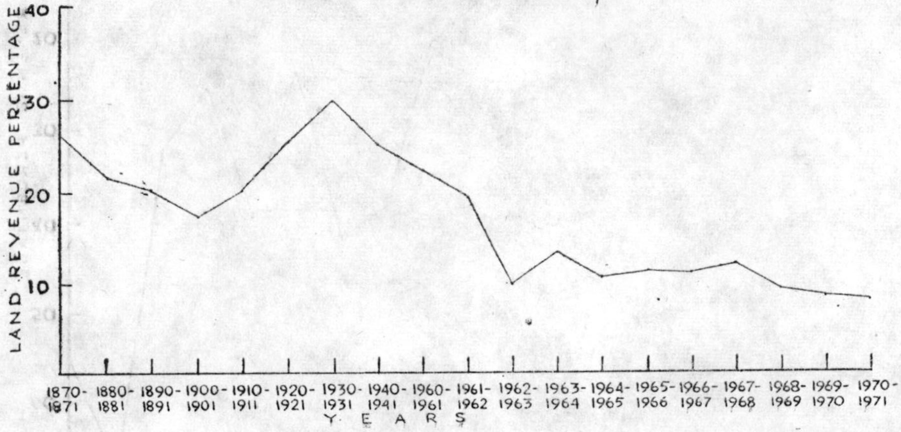

CHART VIII

LAND REVENUE PERCENTAGE
BRITISH PUNJAB/WEST PAKISTAN

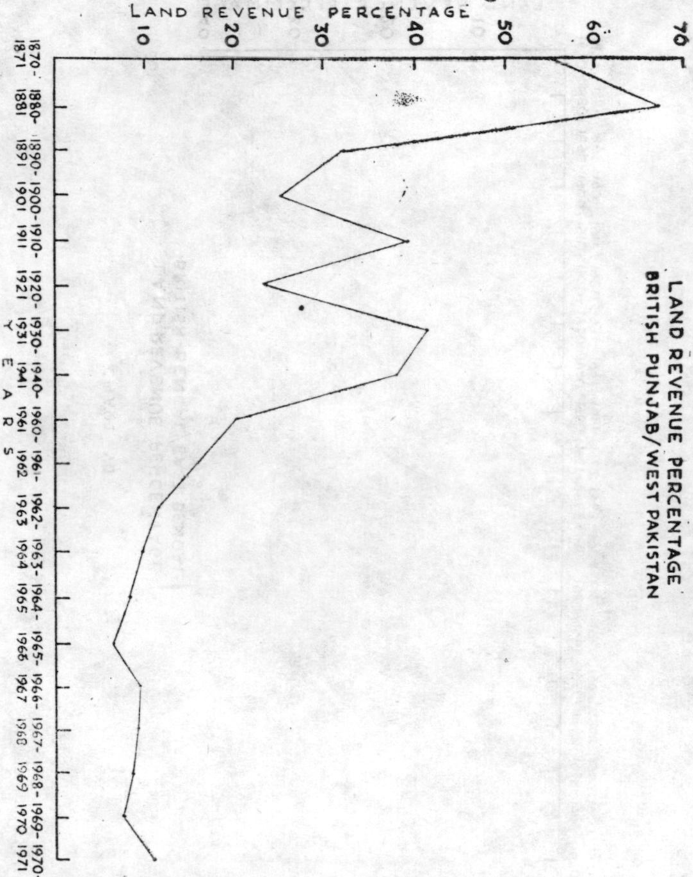

each Collector according to his own interpretation of the words 'overall supervision'. In some districts, Collectors take some interest in land revenue administration while in other districts they do not take any appreciable interest."[1] The indifferent attitude of the D.O. towards the land revenue administration enabled the revenue machinery in the districts to perform its functions almost like a separate department.[2] Usually the Additional or Joint D.O. (Revenue) corresponded "direct with the Board of Revenue".[3] Some held that the direct communication between the former and the latter was partly the result of administrative convenience. As the D.O. usually took little or no interest in revenue matters and as the Additional or Joint D.O. (Revenue) dealt with them directly, if letters were sent by the latter to the Board of Revenue through the former in most cases he would simply forward them to the Board. Thus it was argued by some that direct communication saved time. The general view was that he should directly communicate with the Board, but the D.O. must be kept well informed of important aspects of land revenue administration because the ultimate responsibility was on him. In 1963 a Revenue Committee, appointed by the Government of East Bengal held that he "should keep the Deputy Commissioner informed of all important correspondence with the Board of Revenue and also of all important orders and circulars by the Board. He should also invariably forward to the Commissioner copies of all the letters he addresses direct to the Board of Revenue".[4] It was generally felt that if the D.O. was kept informed it would be possible for him, if he found it necessary, to step in and to take decisions himself. It appeared

1 *Ibid.*, para. 108.

2 Those departments are regarded as separate departments, the functions of which are not the direct responsibility of the D.O. and the heads of which perform their functions under the dual control of the D.O. and the divisional and provincial/central officers of their respective Directorates.

3 *1959 Revenue Commission Report*, para. 95 (f).

4 *Report of the Land Revenue Administration Enquiry Committee: East Pakistan, 1962-63* (Dacca, 1963), para. 33. (Hereafter cited as *1963 Revenue Committee Report.*)

to be sound and logical opinion. But, the important point was that whether or not he would keep the D.O. informed depended to a considerable extent, as we have noted, on the desire of the D.O. himself. If he wanted to be informed regularly he could direct the Additional or Joint D.O. (Revenue) to do so. Usually the latter would comply with such direction in view of the fact that he was the direct subordinate of the former.[1]

Some young officers felt that as the revenue function had lost its importance it should be separated from the general administrative and executive function of the government, that a separate land revenue service and a revenue directorate should be created, that a separate revenue district officer should be appointed and that he like other district level departmental heads should work under the general control and supervision of the D.O. Moreover, it was also argued that as the land revenue system of the sub-continent was very complicated as well as very cumbersome, a thorough study of the system and adequate revenue experience was necessary in order to acquire a thorough knowledge of the details of different aspects of the revenue system and that such knowledge was indispensable to run land revenue administration efficiently and to act as a revenue Judge. In the past an officer had usually acquired such knowledge because he had usually spent a very considerable part of his career in district administration and also because he could devote a considerable part of his time and energy to revenue work. But later, with the

[1] Unlike the relationship between the District Officer and other district level departmental heads which was usually strained by serious administrative tension (see chap. vi), the relationship between the D.O. and the Additional or Joint D.O. was a harmonious one. Both of them belonged to the same service (i.e. erstwhile provincial or central civil service) and to the same hierarchy (i.e. the administrative and executive hierarchy). Thus a 'we' feeling developed between them. The latter was the direct subordinate of the former on whose reports and comments his prospects in government service depended to a considerable extent. Moreover, if a hitch developed between them the latter, unlike a district level department officer who in the event of a hitch with the D.O. usually got the full support of his divisional and provincial/central heads, could not in normal circumstances expect to get any such support from a higher officer. Under such circumstances usually the latter would not and did not disregard the wishes of the former.

expansion of the Secretariat and other government functionaries, the mobility of the officers between the administrative and executive branch of district administration and other government organisations increased and promotions also became more frequent. As a result, usually an officer did not have long uninterrupted spells of district administration. If a revenue service and a revenue hierarchy were created, a revenue officer would deal with no other aspects of administration except the revenue aspect and he would remain in the department throughout his career. Thus, he could gain adequate knowledge of the details of land revenue administration. Moreover, in the modern age it did not seem to be a sound principle that the chief administrative and executive head of the district should be burdened with the responsibility of supervising land revenue administration.

Against this suggestion it was argued by the revenue oriented officers that land revenue administration, as we have noted, enabled the D.O. and his high ranking subordinates to come into close contact with the rural population and to have a better knowledge of rural conditions and problems. But these advantages could only be realised by a degree of devotion to revenue matters which became increasingly unattainable in the post-war period because of the reasons mentioned above.[1] In fact, such knowledge of rural conditions and problems could be gained through other means. The new community development function and his close contact with local bodies, which was in fact the result of this function, could and, in practice, did serve this purpose. Moreover, the gradual improvement of communications and increased mobility between rural and urban areas also made it easier for the D.O. to gain some knowledge of rural conditions from other sources.

The separation of the revenue function from the administrative and executive functions would not have uniform impact on district administration in both Bangladesh and Pakistan. In Pakistan where the landed "aristocrats" are the vested interests and the

[1] See above, pp. 245-250.

most dominant and prominent figures in local areas, such separation would very adversely affect district administration and the overall position of the D.O. We have already noted in chapter ii that the tenants and the poor peasants in Pakistan are very much oppressed by the landed "aristocrats", many of whose activities amount to serious criminal as well as civil offences, and that the position of the tenants may be compared with that of serfs. The union of revenue and law and order powers in the person of the D.O., the influence and the prestige that he enjoys and large powers of patronage that he wields, enable him to maintain some control and to exercise considerable influence over these landed "aristocrats". The separation of revenue powers from other powers of the D.O. would weaken his position vis-a-vis the landed "aristocrats". But in Bangladesh such separation would not seriously affect district administration and the overall position of the D.O. mainly because the *Zamindari* system was abolised long ago. Perhaps, such separation would rather modernise and rationalise district administration and the office of the D. O. in Bangladesh.

Here it may be mentioned that the question of separation of the revenue hierarchy from the administrative and executive hierarchy was not a widely discussed topic and that no report or document, as far as the present writer is aware, did not discuss such a proposal. Some young officers thought of such separation. Of course, now the question is being seriously considered in Bangladesh in view of the fact that exemption of land revenue in many cases, as we shall see below (p. 267), has reduced the importance of land revenue administration to an extraordinary degree.

Sub-Divisional Officer

Like the D.O., the S.D.O. is the overall head of revenue functionaries operating within his jurisdiction but in practice he exercises nominal control and supervision over them. Like the former, the latter gives more attention to important aspects of administration, i.e. development, law and order, the affairs of local bodies etc. In regard to revenue matters he is especially assisted by a Deputy Magistrate cum Deputy Collector.

Tehsildar (Punjab System Area)/Mukhtiarkar (Sind)

In Pakistan the *tehsil* (Punjab, N.W.F.P., Baluchistan)/ *taluka* (Sind) is a very important unit of land revenue administration. The *Tehsildar/Mukhtiarkar* is the head of land revenue administration in the *tehsil/taluka*. He supervises and directs the working of subordinate revenue functionaries within his jurisdiction. He is responsible for the preparation, maintenance and checking of *Jamabandi* (record of rights), for keeping and checking accounts, for supervising the collection of land revenue in the *tehsil/taluka*, for the preparation and timely submission of returns etc. He also tries petty revenue cases. He is also in charge of the sub-treasury located in the *tehsil/taluka*. He is assisted by one or two *Naib* (Deputy) *Tehsildar*/Head *Munshi*.[1] At the district headquarters the facts and figures in regard to land revenue are prepared on the basis of those supplied from different *tehsil/taluka*.

Sub-Divisional Manager (E. Bengal)

Though the Sub-Divisional Manager was posted at the subdivisional headquarters, he could be regarded as the counterpart of the *Tehsildar/Mukhtiarkar*. Boardly speaking, his functions[2] were similar to, though less important than, those of the *Tehsildar/ Mukhtiarkar*. But so far as prestige and influence were concerned there was an enormous difference between the Sub-Divisional Manager in East Bengal and the *Tehsildar/Mukhtiarkar* in West Pakistan. While making a comparison between the latter and the Circle Officer in Bangladesh we have already noted in chapter iii that in Pakistan the former is the oldest and the most important functionary in the *tehsil/taluka*, that within his jurisdiction he acts as the representative of the D.O. or the S.D.M. (if there

[1] M. Hasan Khan, "Duties and Functions of Tehsildar", an unpublished dissertation submitted in partial fulfilment of the degree of Master of Arts to the Punjab University (Lahore, 1957), pp. 11-17. "Machinery For Revenue Administration in Former Sind Area" (cyclostyled), a study note prepared by the Civil Service Academy, Lahore, for the CSP probationers of 1964, pp. 2-4. (Hereafter cited as CSP Academy's Note on Revenue Administration in Sind.)

[2] *1959 Revenue Commission Report*, para. 95. *1963 Revenue Committee Report*, para. 20.

is any) and that traditionally he enjoys a very preeminent position in the eyes of the local inhabitants. All these factors collectively contribute to his importance and influence. But the post of the Sub-Divisional Manager, which was a petty and non-gazetted post, was created in the 1950s after the abolition of the *Zamindari* system. Moreover, as he was posted at the sub-divisional headquarters, he was not only overshadowed by the presence of such a high ranking all-powerful officer as the S.D.O., but also by that of other important officers, e.g. Magistrates, the Sub-Divisional Police Officer, the Assistant Engineer, etc. While he was an almost completely unknown figure at the sub-divisional headquarters, the *Tehsildar/Mukhtiarkar* was (and is) the most prominent officer at the *tehsil/taluka* headquarters. The office of the Sub-Divisional Manager, as we shall see below, was abolished in the late-1960s.

Lowest Revenue Functionaries

> "[In Sind] So far as the field work [1], which is primarily done by the *Tapedar*, is concerned, the Supervisory *Tapedar* is another officer who is the most important one. Actually he is promoted from senior-most *Tapedars* and put in charge of a Circle. It is his duty to see that the team of *Tapedars* working under him does its job according to the desired standard and in time. Therefore, if a Supervisory *Tapedar* is slack, the work of the *Tapedars* is bound to go in arrears. Experienced Revenue Officers generally keep a strict eye on the work of Supervising *Tapedars* to ensure that they exact work from the *Tapedars*."[2]

In Bangladesh and in the Punjab system area of Pakistan, while the counterparts of Supervisory *Tapedar* are Circle Officer (Revenue) (Bangladesh) and *Girdawar* or Field Kanungo (Punjab), those of *Tapedar* are *Tahsildar* (Bangladesh) and *Patwari* (Punjab).[3] Here it may be noted that there is a world of difference between the *Tehsildar* in Pakistan and the *Tahsildar* in Bangladesh.

[1] Field work includes the preparation and maintenance of record of rights and accounts, the inspection of field, keeping of the records of crops, revision of maps, making a record of mutation, partition etc. It is on the basis of these facts and figures that the record of rights and accounts at higher levels are prepared.

[2] CSP Academy's Note on Revenue Administration in Sind, p. 2.

[3] See below, charts ix, x, pp. 259-260.

We have already noted above[1] that the *Tehsildar* in Pakistan is a very important and old revenue functionary who holds a fairly higher position in the revenue hierarchy in the country.[2] But the *Tahsildar* in Bangladesh, the post of whom was created in the 1950s, is nothing but a petty clerk who is, relatively speaking, a very new functionary and occupies the lowest position in the revenue hierarchy[3] in the country. The functions of the lowest revenue functionaries in Bangladesh and in the Punjab are more or less similar to those of their respective counterparts in Sind, i.e. the Supervisory *Tapedar* and the *Tapedar*. The only major difference is that the *Tapedar* in Sind and the *Tahsildar* in Bangladesh not only perform field work but also collect land revenue from each tenant. But in the *Mahalwari* or the Punjab system area, where there is joint liability of all the tenants of a village for the land revenue payable for all the lands in the village and where, as noted above, the settlement is not made with the individual tenant but with the *Mahal* (village community or estate) as a whole, the *Patwari* simply does 'field work', but does not collect land revenue from each tenant. It is the *Lambardar* (Village headman) who collects the land revenue from all the tenants belonging to the village community and deposits the collected amount to the sub-treasury located at the *tehsil* headquarters.

After the abolition of the *Zamindari* system in East Bengal it was suggested in the early 1950s that the *Lambardari* system of the Punjab should be introduced for the collection of land revenue. But an experienced senior revenue officer who had very intimate knowledge of the rural Bengal opposed the suggestion in 1952 and rightly pointed out that

> "(i) The genius and tradition of the people of East Pakistan are different from those in West Punjab. In West Punjab there are strong tribal and clannish affinities, but such affinities do not exist in East Pakistan. (ii) There is no joint liability for the rent of all lands in the entire village in East Pakistan as in West Punjab. (iii) People of East Pakistan are too

[1] See above, pp. 255. [2] See below, charts ix, p. 259.

[3] See below, charts ix and x, pp. 259-260.

individualistic and democratic to tolerate bossing over by the village headman. (iv) It will be very difficult to get the right type of men for the work in every one of the 56,000 villages in East Pakistan."

He concluded by saying that it "would not be successful" in East Bengal.[1] As a result, no further attempt was then made to introduce the system in East Bengal. In the middle of June 1959, "the East Pakistan Land Revenue Commission" visited West Pakistan and discussed with the then Governor of West Pakistan, the land revenue administration in East Bengal.[2] From their discussion with him the Commission felt that the *Lambardari*

"system...succeeded in West Pakistan mainly because of two important provisions of law, namely, (i) joint liability of all tenants of a village...(ii) Liability of the defaulting tenant or any other tenant of the village, including the *Lambardar*, to be arrested and detained in custody by the gazetted *Tahsildar* for the recovery of arrears of the land revenue."[3].

The Commission pointed out, as Mr. Ishaque had done in 1952, that

"There is no joint liability in East Pakistan and there has never been any such joint liability here. Villagers in East Pakistan are not prepared to accept joint liability. This is the main reason why the Cooperative Movement has not been successful here. The introduction of joint liability about rent by legislation, which will radically change the land tenure system in East Pakistan may, we fear, create great dissatisfaction and unrest in the minds of tenancy."[4]

(*Cont. on p. 261*)

---

[1] Quoted in *1959 Revenue Commission Report*, para. 116. He was Mr. Ishaque, the then Member of the Board of Revenue and the State Purchase Commissioner who had been an ICS and who from the very beginning of the 1940s to the mid-40s had come into close contact with the rural life of British Bengal in the capacity of the Commissioner (i.e. Head) of the Directorate of Rural Reconstruction.

[2] Here it may be mentioned that the Governor of West Pakistan, Mr. Aktar Husain, who had been a member of the former ICS, at that time also happened to be the Chairman of the Provincial Administration Commission and that of the Land Reforms Commission of West Pakistan. At that time both of these Commissions were making their survey.

[3] *1959 Revenue Commission Report*, para. 119 (i,ii). (It may be mentioned that the concept of joint liability had existed in those areas long before it became a part of legal provisions.)

[4] *Ibid.*, p. 32. *The Report of the Provincial Administration Commission*, the Chairman of which, as noted in footnote 2 on this page, was the

(*Cont. on p. 260*)

CHART IX

PAKISTAN
(FORMER)
HIERARCHY OF LAND REVENUE ADMINISTRATION

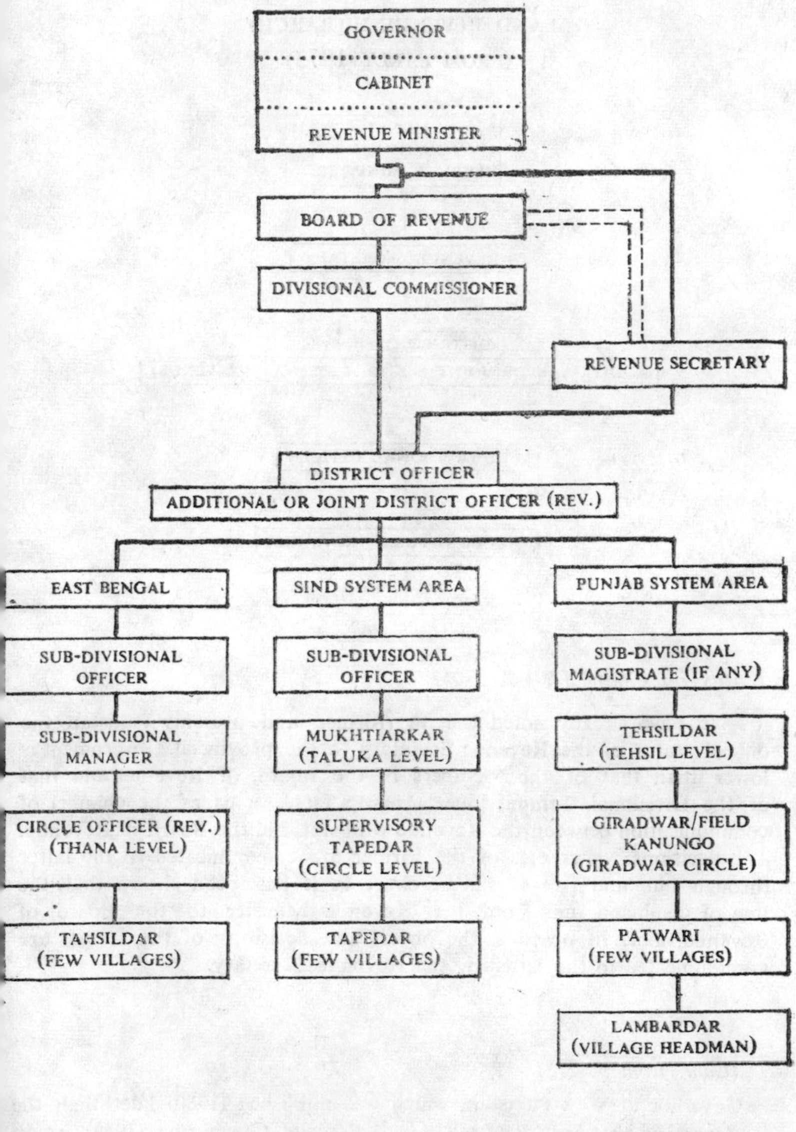

For notes on chart ix see next page.

CHART X

BANGLADESH

LAND REVENUE HIERARCHY

(FROM EARLY 1973)

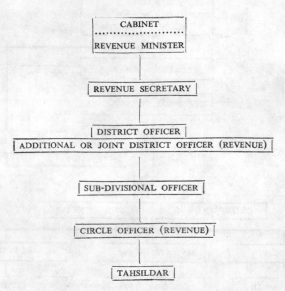

CABINET
....
REVENUE MINISTER

|

REVENUE SECRETARY

|

DISTRICT OFFICER

ADDITIONAL OR JOINT DISTRICT OFFICER (REVENUE)

|

SUB-DIVISIONAL OFFICER

|

CIRCLE OFFICER (REVENUE)

|

TAHSILDAR

Notes on Chart IX (p. 259)

We have already noted that in (former and present) Pakistan the official status of the Revenue Secretary to the provincial Government is lower than that of the Members of the Board of Revenue and that of the Divisional Commissioner. He, in fact, serves as the channel of communication between the Revenue Minister and the Board of Revenue. The decisions, views etc. of the former are communicated to the latter through him and vice versa. In chart ix it has been shown that the line of command runs from the Revenue Minister to the Board of Revenue, but, in practice, the orders and decisions of the former are communicated to the latter by the Revenue Secretary.

(*Cont. from p. 258*)

Governor of West Pakistan, which was published (1960) later than the *Report of the East Pakistan Land Revenue Commission* (1959), again recommended that the *Lambardari* system should be introduced in East Bengal. (*Pro. Adm. Com. Report*, p. 177.)

Finally the proposal for collecting land revenue through village headman was, therefore, dropped. In fact, most people felt that any attempt to introduce the *Lambardari* system in East Bengal would be ridiculous.

In addition to these functionaries there is a Superintendent of Accounts (Bangladesh)/*Sadar Kanungo* (Pakistan) in each district. His main function is to audit regularly the offices of subordinate revenue functionaries. The Superintendent of Accounts also acts "as a sort of Financial Adviser to the Additional Collector".[1] So far as the auditing is concerned he is assisted by a number of auditors (Bangladesh)/Field *Kanungo* (Pakistan).

Bangladesh: Maladministration at Lower Levels

After the abolition of the *Zamindari* system in 1950 the Government gradually began to acquire *Zamindari* estates. But in the mid-50s it decided that the acquisition of all the *Zamindari* estates must be completed by April 1956. As a result, suddenly millions of people became the direct tenants of the government with the result that the revenue department had to shoulder the responsibility of thoroughly reorganising and expanding the revenue machinery within a short period. As a consequence, the revenue machinery was reorganised and expanded in a haphazard manner.[2] In order to man all the posts of Sub-Divisional Manager, Circle Inspector and *Tahsildar*, which had been created during the first half of the 1950s, a huge number of persons were appointed hurriedly within a very short period. In early 1956, 5,500 *Tahsildars* and Assistant *Tahsildars* and 300 Circle Inspectors were appointed.

> "As it always happens when a large number of men are appointed quickly, these appointments were made without proper examination of the qualifications of these men and their suitability for the posts and without any scrutiny as to their background regarding honesty and integrity. Favouritism and nepotism by the politicians...played a great part in the selection of a large section of these officers."[3]

---

[1] *Estate Manual*, para. 10.

[2] *1959 Revenue Commission Report*, paras. 17-18.

[3] *1963 Revenue Committee Report*, para. 14.

While the Sub-Divisional Managers had insignificant revenue background, the Circle Inspectors and the *Tahsildars* "generally speaking... had no revenue background and very little knowledge about revenue law and the work they were expected to do".[1] While the *Tahsildars* received no training before they joined,[2] the Sub-Divisional Managers and the Circle Inspectors received "nominal training" for a period of $2\frac{1}{2}$ months in revenue law and survey.[3] When the newly created or extended part of the revenue machinery began to function all these officers, as we shall see later, were found to be completely incompetent. The Sub-Divisional Manager was "unsuitable for responsible work entrusted to them." Most of them lacked "experience, initiative and imagination"[4] and did not have " the necessary personality and strength of character to be able to supervise and control"[5] the revenue functionaries working at lower levels. There was "considerable lack of efficiency"[6] among the *Tahsildars*. They were "low paid"[7] and "comparatively small men"[8] who were vested with "considerable power to do good or bad to the tenants".[9] Thus, it was

> "necessary that there should be constant and effective supervision of their work by responsible officers, who can command their respect, in order to keep them honest and efficient. Slackness of supervision not only leads to corruption and to harassment of the public but also appreciably affects collection of Government demands."[10]

---

[1] *Ibid.*, para. 16. Also see *1959 Revenue Commission Report*, para. 95(b).

[2] *1963 Revenue Committee Report*, para. 15.

[3] *Ibid.*, para. 16.

[4] *1959 Revenue Commission Report*, para. 95(d).

[5] *1963 Revenue Committee Report*, para. 20.

[6] *1959 Revenue Commission Report*, para. 95(b).

[7] *1963 Revenue Committee Report*, para. 19.

[8] *1959 Revenue Commission Report*, para. 106.

[9] *1963 Revenue Committee Report*, para. 19. Also see *1959 Revenue Commission Report*, para. 106. (Above comments imply that in a poor and status oriented society if low paid petty officials are entrusted with considerable powers especially revenue powers and if there is no strict supervision of their work, they usually become oppressors and corrupt.)

[10] *Ibid.*, para. 106.

The Circle Inspectors whose "primary duties are to inspect and supervise the works of *Tahsildars*"[1] were, in fact, intended to work in such a way as to "keep them in the right path".[2] They "themselves knew less about revenue work than the *Tahsildars*. Moreover, they had not the personality to be able to control the *Tahsildars* even when they found the *Tahsildars* going wrong."[3] As a result, the "*Tahsildari* system began to acquire many vices".[4] The higher revenue functionaries, i.e. the D.O., the Additional D.O.(Revenue), the S.D.O and the Revenue Deputy Collector (stationed at the district headquarters), who were busy and overworked, could not maintain a strict and close watch on these newly created revenue functionaries.[5] In short, "the main defect of this system was the lack of strict supervision of the work of the *Tahsildars*, Circle Inspectors and Sub-Divisional Managers".[6] The total effect of "this lack of supervision and the initial mistake of appointing a number of incompetent men without proper enquiry about their antecedents"[7] was a hopeless situation of chaos and confusion. As a result, the government suffered heavy financial losses and the poor tenants who constituted the bulk of the population of East Bengal were harassed and often required to pay more than they should have done. The corrupt petty revenue functionaries caused great hardship to poor tenants[8] The Land

[1] *Ibid.*, para. 95(c).

[2] *1963 Revenue Committee Report*, para. 19.

[3] *Ibid.*, para. 19. [4] *Ibid.*, para. 21.

[5] Moreover, the D.O. and the S.D.O., as noted above, were not interested in revenue matters.

[6] *1963 Revenue Committee Report*, para. 19. [7] *Ibid.*, para. 21.

[8] These points may be further illustrated by the following passages:

"In course of our tours we have inspected many *Tahsil* offices and had discussions with all classes of people about the working of the *Tahsildari* system. Everywhere we heard severe condemnation of this system. It was said that the *Tahsildars* are generally corrupt and rude to the ordinary classes of tenants, that no rent can be paid in reasonable time without illegal gratification. It was alleged that a large number of mutation cases and applications for splitting up of the holdings were pending in every

Revenue Administration Enquiry Committee of 1963 clearly and aptly pointed out that they were "of the opinion that immediate and effective steps should be taken to prevent further deterioration of revenue administration in the country". It further added that

---

Tahsil office, mainly because these cases are never taken unless the *Tahsildar* and Circle Inspector are paid illegal gratification. It was further alleged that the *Tahsildars* treated the Government *Khas* (owned) lands as their personal property and let these out in *barga* [to allow some one to cultivate the land in return of half the share of the crops] surreptitiously for their personal gain. We were told in many places by the ordinary people that the *Tahsildars* are really *Zamindars* in a new garb with all their oppressions and that they are all the more powerful and dangerous as they have the authority of Government behind them." (*Ibid*., para. 23.)

"In almost all the memoranda and replies to Questionnaire received by us from the educated section of the public, there is similar condemnation of the *Tahsildar* as a class. We were satisfied that there is considerable truth in these allegations." (*Ibid*., para. 24.)

"In course of our inspection of the *Tahsil* offices we found slackness on the part of *Tahsildars* everywhere. We found almost in all the *Tahsil* offices we visited that Register II (Tenants' Ledger) had never been kept up-to-date. In some offices, collections made more than 1 year ago had not been entered in Register II. In no office (except in Noakhali district) the Defaulters' List (Return III) had been ever prepared, though this Return had to be prepared before issuing requisitions for certificates which must be based on this Return. This had swelled the number of certificates [i.e. certificate cases which are started in order to realise revenues from the defaulters] unnecessarily...the total amount covered by the pending certificates is much more than the total amount of arrears of rent, cess, etc. This is evidently due to the fact that certificates have been filled in many cases for rents which have been already paid." (*Ibid*., para. 25.)

"The Return I, prescribed in the Government *Estates Manual*, shows the demand, collection and balance, as well as amounts credited into the treasury during the whole Revenue year. An important part of the work in connection with this return is the verification report of the Treasury Officer regarding the amounts credited into the Treasury. It is our experience that in no office in the province is this Return compiled nowadays. This leaves the door wide open for defalcation of Government money by the *Tahsildars*. There have been actually many cases of defalcation of Government money by the *Tahsildars* every year since 1956 involving several lakhs of rupees every year." (*Ibid*., para. 27.)

"The inefficiency of the *Tahsildars* has also been reflected in the unsatisfactory state of collection of Government revenue every year since 1956." (*Ibid*., para. 28.)

it was "the duty of the Government to see that revenue administration which affects almost every person in the country should be free from corruption and free from unnecessary difficulties".[1] The 1959 and the 1963 reports on land revenue administration in East Bengal recommended that the non-gazetted post of the Sub-Divisional Manager should be abolished and that a Revenue Deputy Collector, who was a Grade I officer of the then East Pakistan Civil Service, should be placed in charge of the revenue administration in the sub-division, that he would, as the Sub-Divisional Manager used to do, perform his functions under the general control and supervision of the S.D.O.[2] The Sub-Divisional Manager was not immediately replaced by the Revenue Deputy Collector because of the shortage of officers. In the late 1960s the post of the Sub-Divisional Manager was abolished. Since then, in respect of revenue matters the S.D.O. has been assisted by a Deputy Magistrate-Deputy Collector. In the late 1950s and the 60s it was generally felt that the revenue machinery should be properly reorganised at the sub-divisional headquarters because it would be much more convenient to administer land revenue matters from the sub-divisional level than from the district level. After the abolition of the *Zamindari* system the village and the *thana* became the focal points of revenue administration and the sub-divisional level was much closer to the *thana* and the village than the district level which was, so far as the *thana* and the village were concerned, too high a level.

[1] *Ibid.*, para. 29.

[2] *Ibid.*, para. 32. [This report also recommended that he should be given the status of the Additional Sub-Divisional Officer (Revenue). (*Ibid.*, para.32.)] *1959 Revenue Commission Report*, para. 107.

Here it may be mentioned that the post of the Sub-Divisional Manager was created as a temporary measure because sufficient high ranking officials of the then East Pakistan Civil Service were not available at that time. Before the publication of the 1959 and the 1963 reports, the Government *Estate Manual* declared in 1958 that "Until officers of requisite seniority are available, the work in a sub-division will be looked after by the Sub-Divisional Manager, working under the general supervision of the Sub-Divisional Officer." (para. 7.)

When the government had had to deal with a number of *Zamindars*, the district was the most suitable unit of revenue administration. But when the government was directly dealing with the millions of tenants of very densely populated districts in East Bengal, the sub-division would have been most suitable as the fundamental unit for supervising and administering land revenue matters.

So far as land revenue administration in the *thana* was concerned, the 1959 and the 1962 reports recommended that the non-gazetted Circle Inspectors should be replaced by the gazetted Grade II officers of the then East Pakistan Civil Service and that the designation of these gazetted officers should be Circle Officer (Revenue).[1] This recommendation was not immediately implemented mainly because of the shortage of officers. Only in big *thanas* Circle Officer (Revenue) was posted. Later Circle Officer (Revenue) was gradually posted in most *thanas*.

The reports also recommended that necessary arrangements should be made in order to give adequate and comprehensive revenue and settlement training to all officers connected with land revenue administration.[2] The 1963 report further recommended that a strict and close watch should be maintained on the working of the *Tahsildars*, that if "a reasonable complaint of corruption or misconduct"[3] was received against any *Tahsildar* or Assistant *Tahsildar* strict disciplinary measures should be taken against him, that the Circle Officer (Revenue) should have "the power to suspend" and to "inflict minor punishment"[4] on a *Tahsildar* or any other subordinate revenue functionary and that the Revenue Deputy Collector should have the authority to "inflict all sorts of punishment except 'dismissal' and 'removal from service'"[5] on a *Tahsildar* or Assistant *Tahsildar*. Most of the above recommendations were implemented with the result that the standard of land revenue administration improved to some extent, but it conti-

[1] *1959 Revenue Commission Report*, para. 106. *1963 Revenue Committee Report*, para. 30.

[2] *Pro. Adm. Com. Report*, p. 177. *1959 Revenue Commission Report*, para. 127, appendices B and C. *1963 Revenue Committee Report*, paras. 15-16.

[3] *Ibid.*, para. 30. [4] *Ibid.*, para. 30. [5] *Ibid.*, para. 32.

nued (and still continues) to suffer from inefficiency, corruption and other serious defects.

In August 1972 the Government of Bangladesh declared that if the total area of agricultural land held by a family did not exceed twenty five standard *bighas,* such family would be exempted from payment of land revenue in respect of such lands.[1] Insignificant percentage of the families in Bangladesh have twenty five or more *bighas* of land. Moreover, some of these families have already divided their respective lands among their respective relations in order to avoid the payment of land revenue. Now, only an insignificant percentage of families will pay land revenue with the result that the importance and the volume of land revenue work will reduce to a point which will be absolutely insignificant and negligible. So, it is generally felt that in the future the lower positions in the revenue hierarchy might be abolished or their number might be drastically curtailed and each of them might be placed in charge of the revenue matters of much larger area. One of the reasons for the abolition of the Board of Revenue was the insignificant and negligible importance of land revenue administration. Mainly for the same reason the Divisional Commissioner has also been relieved of his responsibility in regard to this matter.

The recent decision of the Government of Bangladesh to give exemption in respect of land revenue has been welcome mainly for two reasons. Firstly, it is felt that from the point of view of rural economy the decision has been good. Secondly, the mergin between the government's income from this source and its expenditure on revenue administration was very small.

From the preceding discussion we find that in Bangladesh the importance of land revenue is insignificant and negligible, but in Pakistan it is, relatively speaking, an important aspect of district administration. It is generally felt that its lessening importance is increasingly enabling district administration in Bangladesh to give more and more attention to more important aspects of

[1] President's Order no. 96, *The Bangladesh Gazette* (Extraordinary), 15.8. 72.

administration, e.g., welfare and development activities. Its lessening importance therefore increasingly modernising district administration in Bangladesh.

GENERAL ADMINISTRATIVE OR MISCELLANEOUS FUNCTIONS[1]

General administration includes a vast range of diversified activities and responsibilities. The D.O. is responsible for ensuring that these functions are properly performed either by himself or by other officers subordinate to him. In some cases he is indirectly responsible and in some other cases directly responsible.

Food control and supply, rationing, rent control, rehabilitation of refugees, civil defence, government publicity, census, the campaign against anti-social activities, the campaign in favour of welfare and development activities and the general welfare of the district are part of his overall responsibility. He is responsible for making arrangements for providing accommodation for government employees in the district and for this purpose or for any other administrative reasons (e.g. emergency) he has the authority to requisition houses. One of his very important responsibilities is to make arrangements for conducting local council and assembly elections in his district. If a foreign or national dignitary visits his district he has to make arrangements for his reception and to organise appropriate ceremonies.

He also performs many other ceremonial functions. He is frequently invited to many social ceremonies as the chief guest. He addresses various types of meetings. He cuts tapes and inaugurates, for example, industrial or agricultural fairs, cattle shows, exhibitions, schools, colleges, hospitals, roads, bridges etc. He frequently presides over prize-giving ceremonies of different institutions. He also acts as the Chairman or the President of many autonomous and semi-autonomous institutions in his district. In these capacities he is required to spend some time and energy. The following is the list of those autonomous or semi-autonomous bodies in the Khulna district in Bangladesh of which the D.O., Khulna, is either Chairman or the President :

[1] Also see below, appendices C and D.

Chairman, Board of Trustees, Syedpur Wakf Estate,
,, Central Cooperative Bank,
,, Central Cooperative Fishermen's Society,
,, Government Employees Housing Cooperative Society,
,, Collectorate Employees Housing Cooperative Society,
,, Baitul Falah.
President, District Sporting Association,
,, Social Youth Welfare Council,
,, District Inter-Schools Sports Association,
,, District Boy Scouts Association,
,, District Red Cross Society,
,, Governing Body, Khulna Degree College,
,, Managing Committee of Khulna Zilla School,
,, Governing Body of Khulna Girls' College,
,, Managing Committee of Coronation Girls' High School,
,, District Primary Education Office,
,, Managing Committee of Women Industrial School,
,, Maheswarpasha Arts School,
,, Stadium Committee,
,, U. F. D. Club,
,, Zonal Land Allocation Committee,
,, Site Selection Committee,
,, Self-Help Centre Committee,
,, State Orphanage Committee,
,, District Arts Council,
,, Soldiers, Sailors and Airmen's Board,
,, Housing and Settlement Allocation Committee,
,, District Anti-Smuggling Coordination Committee,
,, Urban Community Development Board,
,, Maternity and Child Welfare Centre.

He is primarily responsible for ensuring that arrangements are made for celebrating state occasions (e.g. Independence Day). During such occasions he presides over state ceremonies and takes the salute of the armed force, police force, boy scouts, girl guides, etc.

One of his general administrative responsibilities is to coordinate the functions of different government departments, local councils and other semi-governmental institutions. Such coordination is mainly required in the field of development activities. Different aspects of this role are discussed in detail in chapter vi.

The D.O. is frequently required by the government to provide it with information on a variety of subjects ranging from political and administrative conditions of the district to social, cultural and economic conditions. It is also his responsibility to keep the government regularly informed about changes and developments in his district. The government also requires him to give his comments or opinion on various issues. He appoints many petty officials. State titles are confirmed on the people of his district mainly on the basis of his recommendations. He issues a number of different types of permits and licences.

It is also his general administrative responsibility to visit other governmental or semi-governmental offices and such institutions as schools, colleges, etc. occasionally in order to see whether they are functioning properly. He has authority to inspect all works and projects of these departments and institutions and to suggest measures for the improvement of their working.[1] Of course, he has no authority to interfere with the technical aspects and internal administration of any department.

One of his most important general administrative responsibilities, no less important than his development, law and order, revenue, and any other general administrative functions, is his responsibility to take measures if there is an emergency e.g. cyclone, flood, famine, earthquake, epidemic etc. During such emergencies (and also during the visit of a foreign or national dignitary or for some other administrative purpose, e.g., election) he has the full authority to requisition not only the transport or other possessions of other departments but also the services of the officers of these departments. He acts as the captain of a combined

[1] *Report of the Provincial Re-Organisation Committee*, part II, para. 15 (iii). Also see Additional Chief Secretary's memorandum no. IC-20/62, May 18, 1962 (Govt. of the then E. Pakistan, S. & G.A. Department).

operation team consisting of his immediate subordinates (i.e., the Additional D.O.s, S.D.O.s and the Magistrates) and the officers of other departments. He has also the authority to close down schools, colleges etc. and to convert them into relief or refugee camps.[1] If the emergency is of a very serious nature the government provides him with additional officers from the Secretariat, Directorates and other districts.

The following example will give some idea of the steps taken at the time of an emergency: Rampur village, which is very close to the district headquarters of the Comilla district in Bangladesh, was struck in April 1961, by a tornado and hailstorm which caused the death of four persons and much property damage. After having received the information, the S.D.O. of the south *sadar* sub-division of the Comilla district[2], in whose jurisdiction the Rampur village was situated,

> "immediately rushed to the village. On his way he informed the police and took some constables with him from Kandirpar police outpost. The time was 1 a.m. (4th April) ...S.D.O. gave the following report of his visit: 'Then we (I and Additional S.D.O. and some other persons) proceeded to that area. We went to South Rampur and we had a round of the whole village and some neighbouring villages...We discussed with the people."[3]

At about 3 a.m. the S.D.O. returned to Comilla.[4] At about 6 a.m. he again went to Rampur with the D.O. The D.O. gave the following account of his visit and of the relief measures:

> "Early in the morning I was informed about 6 a.m. I left immediately along with S.D.O. and Civil Surgeon and went to the spot, met

[1] Some of his emergency powers are briefly discussed in the *Provincial Re-Organisation Committee Report*, part II, para. 15(v) and in the Additional Chief Secretary's Memorandum (see preceding footnote).

[2] We have already noted in chapter iii that the sub-division in which the district headquarters are situated is called the *Sadar* sub-division.

[3] Edgar A. Schuler and S.M. Hafeez Zaidi, "Response To Village Disaster: Tornado and Hailstorm At South Rampur, Comilla" in *Inside the East Pakistan Village—Six Articles* (Asian Studies Papers, Asian Studies Center, Michigan State University, 1966), pp. 50-1.

[4] Comilla is also the name of the town in which the headquarters of the Comilla district and the Comilla *sadar* sub-division are located.

the people, saw the damaged houses, talked to the local people and the Chairman of the Co-operative Society, visited the house where the death occurred. The bodies were still there. I encouraged the people and sympathized with them. An Ansar (auxiliary force) officer was deputed by S.D.O. when he went last night to help and to estimate the loss and damage. He made a list of all houses and the nature and extent of damage. He gave me a report in the morning when I reached there. He made a list of houses damaged, but it was incomplete. So in the morning I deputed Sub-Divisional Relief Officer to make a complete list and at the same time arranged for free distribution of rice to those people who had their paddy damaged. Immediately some free rice was given the same day to the needy people by the S.D.O. And at the same time, when I came back [to Comilla] I sent information by wire to Government to sanction house building loans, house building grants and relief rice, etc. When the sanction came in a day or two, it was distributed through Relief Officer. Civil Surgeon was consulted whether any step should be taken. He said—no need, because of recent inoculation. The storm-affected area is so restricted, and that also reduced danger of epidemic. I generally exhorted them not to depend too much on relief. Rehabilitation of houses depends mostly on labour. The houses fall but can be re-erected. The people should try to help themselves, but ask for help if needed. Similarly, free rice only for those in need. About drinking water, most of the tubewells were all right. I checked that; 2 or 3 were working."[1]

A report on the relief measures taken in the Chittagong district in Bangladesh during an emergency of a very serious nature resulting from an extremely severe cyclone, which is incorporated in the book as appendix D, will give us further insight into the emergency function of district administration.

[1] Quoted in E.A. Schuler and S.M.H. Zaidi, *op. cit.*, p. 51. The accounts of the District Officer and the Sub-Divisional Officer quoted by the authors of the article were taken down during interviews. They also quoted the accounts of many other officers. They held that "If there are any errors in the quoted passages they are the responsibility of the writers rather than the informants, for we did not have time to check with them in all cases." (*Ibid.*, p. 45.)

Here it may be mentioned that the emergency in Rampur village was not of a serious nature. If the Rampur Village were situated in an outlying sub-division, the D.O. would not have gone there immediately. The S.D.O. who enjoyed (and enjoys) all the emergency powers of the D.O. would have dealt with the matter. Later the D.O. might or might not pay a casual visit. As the village was very close to the district headquarters, he went there. He commented that "Actually it was not absolutely necessary for me to go there." (*Ibid.*, p. 51.)

The responsibility of the D.O. extends not only to dealing with an emergency but also to taking precautionary measures if he apprehends that some emergent situation is going to arise.

The general administrative or miscellaneous functions of the Sub-Divisional Officer of an outlying sub-division are similar to those of the District Officer.

From our foregoing discussion we find that while the importance of law and order and general administrative functions has not undergone any significant change, that of land revenue function has reduced to an enormous extent. In the following chapter we shall discuss development function, which is one of the most important, and comparatively new, functions of district administration.

CHAPTER V

DEVELOPMENT FUNCTION

Introduction

During the last two decades or so the concept of community development[1] has added a new dimension to the development functions of district administration in Bangladesh and Pakistan. The concept had its origin in the post-war period.[2] In the late 1940s and in the 50s the British Colonial Office, the US International Cooperation Administration (ICA) and the UNO encouraged the under-developed countries to take an interest in community development. As a result, the concept of community development gradually emerged as a universal phenomenon in the under-developed world. The impact of this universal phenomenon was strongly felt in former Pakistan from the mid-1950s and especially from the early 1960s. And district administration was required to undertake the new responsibility of community development. Here it may be mentioned that in many quarters there is a wrong notion that the concept of community development is something novel in Bangladesh, India and Pakistan. In fact, although the name is new the idea is quite old in these countries.

> "The origin of the idea of Community Development may be traced to the initiative of British officials in northern India who endeavoured to bring about 'village uplift', to Rabindranath Tagore, who hoped to

---

1 The UNO defined community development as "the processes by which the efforts of the people themselves are united with those of the governmental authorities to improve the economic, social and cultural conditions of communities, to integrate these communities into the life of the nation and to enable them to contribute fully to national progress". [Quoted in Jack D. Mezirow, *Dynamics of Community Development* (New York 1963), p. 10. (Hereafter cited as Mezirow, *Dynamics*.)

2 The term community development entered international parlance in 1948 when the Cambridge Conference on African Administration, organised by the British Colonial Office, substituted it for "mass education". (*Ibid.*, p.9.)

recreate a sense of community in his experiments in Sriniketan in East Bengal; and to James Yen, who returned from Yale to north China to fight Four Fundamental Weaknesses of Chinese life (ignorance, poverty disease and social disintegration) by a programme of mass education."[1]

In the early stages of British administration in the sub-continent the basic principle was that the main concern of district administration should be the maintenance of law and order and the collection of revenue.[2] Rural development was regarded as a heresy practised by crazy District Officers. But it

> "was not unknown. It might have been secondary or sporadic or extra-curricular. It might have been a personal fad or hobby to ease boredom. [[3]] But it was not unknown for collectors [i.e.D.O.s] in their devotion to good government to go beyond their book of words. The ideal set to the Collector and the powers invested in him made this inevitable."[4]

Gradually it became part of their official duties.

We have already noted in chapter I that in the second half of the last century the local bodies, which were headed by the D.O.s or their subordinates, were introduced in this sub-continent and were entrusted with the task of laying roads, looking after sanitary measures, providing drinking water, spreading primary education

1 Hugh Tinker, *Ballot Box and Bayonet* (London, 1964), p. 105.

2 See above, chap. iii.

3 Mr. Philip Mason also observed that "every man had his *shauq*, his pet enthusiasm, and very often two, of which one was pure recreation and the other philanthropy. There was Brown, whose hobbies were tigers and embankments to store water in the rains; Smith who would go miles for a snipe and planted all the roads in every district he was ever in with double avenues of trees; and Jones, who was building hospital when he wasn't pigsticking.

> 'Why is my district death-rate low?'
> said Banks of Hezabad,
> 'Well, drains and sewage-outfalls are
> my own peculiar fad'.

And because of their fads, their humour and their tolerance, many district officers were not merely much less intolerable than might have been expected but were looked on with real affection by the people of their districts." (Woodruff, *op. cit.*, p. 96.)

4 M.A. Pai, "The Emerging Role of the Collector" in *The Indian Journal of Public Administration*, vol. viii, no. 4, 1962, p. 481.

etc. But even outside the sphere of local bodies' activities the concept of rural welfare and development began to gain importance and official attention. Towards the end of the last century and the beginning of the present century government gave "attention on the social milieu of crop yield"[1] in order to face the famine situation. In 1904 the Cooperative Credit Societies Act was passed and from then onward D.O.s led by Malcolm Darling and Strickland began to take an interest in the cooperative techniques for solving the problems of village communities. Although the cooperative movement, for a variety of reasons, did not produce the results expected, much useful and beneficial work was done through it.[2] From the beginning of the 1920s relatively much more direct and concentrated efforts were made in the field of rural development.[3] Here it may be mentioned that the governments of various provinces owed to F. L. Brayne, who from 1920 as the D.O. of Gurgaon district in the Punjab made a determined and remarkable effort for more than seven years in order to improve the rural life of the district, the methods and principles of organised rural development. His work in the Gurgaon district "provides one of the most interesting chapters in rural development on the sub-continent. His village uplift programme was the first large-scale rural development scheme and the most important to be launched by the government under the British rule."[4] The Royal Commission on Agriculture in India observed that they were "favourably impressed with a striking attempt" that was being made by Brayne in order to improve the socio-economic conditions of the rural people in the Gurgaon district and they strongly recommended that his methods and principles of rural development should be followed in other

1 Braibanti, *Research*, p. 200.

2 Roedad Khan, "The Deputy Commissioner's Place in the Village-AID Pattern" in *Village AID in West Pakistan* (Collection of some papers presented at various seminars on Village AID) (Lahore, Feb. 1957), p. 5[illegible]

3 See foreword written by Sir Malcolm Hailey for F.L. Brayne's *Village Uplift in India* (Gurgaon, 1927).

4 Mezirow, *Dynamics*, p.18.

parts of the sub-continent.[1] In fact, the influence of his village uplift programme on the subsequent rural development programmes in different parts of the sub-continent was "marked and lasting".[2] In fact, the foundation of the modern concept of community development in India, Bangladesh and Pakistan were laid by him. Many of the methods and the principles which are now practised and encouraged not only in Bangladesh, India and Pakistan but also in many other under-developed countries by the community development people, were formulated and advocated by him.[3]

The rural development programme was first organised in the Punjab in 1923. The example of the Punjab was followed by the Central Provinces (1930), then by the United Provinces and finally by Bombay (1933) and Bengal (1936).[4] The rural development

[1] *Report of the Royal Commission on Agriculture in India* (London, 1928), p. 502.

[2] C.F. Strickland, "Voluntary Effort and Social Welfare" (hereafter cited as Strickland, *Voluntary Effort*) in Blunt (ed.), *Social Service*, p. 391. Sir Sikander Hyat Khan, the Chief Minister of the Punjab observed in the mid-1930s that "by dint of perseverence and practical sympathy, he has almost single-handed set up a new tradition". [See foreword written by Sir Sikander Hyat Khan for F.L. Brayne's *Better Village* (Madras, 1937).]

[3] Brayne wrote a number of books and pamphlets on the methods and principles of rural development that he had followed in the Gurgaon district. Especially his *Village Uplift in India* and *Better Village* give a fairly exhaustive account of such methods and principles.

[4] Tinker, *Foundations*, p. 208. For a brief account of the development and working of rural development administration in different provinces see Strickland, *Voluntary Efforts*, pp. 392-394. In 1937/38 Strickland wrote that "in the last three years the Government of India has set aside large sums (nearly £3,000,000) for grants to provincial Governments in aid of rural improvements". (*Ibid.*, p. 394.) The provincial governments themselves also began to allocate more finance for rural developments. Moreover, local subscriptions for development works were also raised. In order to reorganise the curriculum for the ICS probationers in such a way as to make them familiar with the social and rural welfare activities in the sub-continent, a committee was set up in 1936 under the chairmanship of Sir Atul C. Chatterjee. For the same purpose another committee was appointed in 1937 under the chairmanship of Sir Edward Blunt. The recommendations of both the committees were accepted by the Government. [Blunt (ed.), *Social Service*, preface, p. iii.]

movement received further impetus after the introduction of provincial autonomy in 1937.[1] In October 1938 Sir Edward Blunt wrote "At the present time, processes of uplift—both rural and urban, both economic and social—are being carried out in all provinces, which are engaging the attention both of official and non-official agencies."[2] Of course, later the rural development movement suffered some set back as a result of the difficulties and problems caused by World War II and its aftermath.

Here it may be mentioned that as early as the 1890's Nobel Prize winner Rabindranath Tagore, the famous Bengali poet, had urged reconstruction of the village and his essays on this theme "are an eloquent philosophical justification of the virtues of rural life".[3] In fact, he had pioneered the history of rural development in the sub-continent though his efforts had remained confined to limited areas. "His establishment of several institutes after 1914 was a landmark."[4] His best known institute had been founded at Sriniketan in East Bengal in 1921 which had operated for more than 30 years and served 85 villages.[5] He had set a noble example in Bengal. Thus, we find that "while in Bengal the chief impetus for rural improvement came from rumination and poetic inspiration and from outside government initiative; in the Punjab the movement was from within government and was characterised by programs of action by energetic, practical British administrators"[6] (especially F.L. Brayne, Malcolm Darling and C.F. Strickland).

[1] Haridawar Rai, "The Changing Role of the District Officer (1860-1960)" in *The Indian Journal of Public Administration*, vol. ix, no. 2, 1963, p. 127.

[2] Blunt (ed.), *Social Service*, preface, p. v.

[3] Braibanti, *Research*, p. 200.

[4] Mezirow, *Dynamics*, p. 16. One of the most important institutes had been established in Santiniketan. "His programs at Santiniketan and at Sriniketan were efforts in which he has sought to practice what he had advocated." (Braibanti, *Research*, p. 200.) For other unofficially organised rural and social welfare programmes see Strickland, *Voluntary Efforts*, pp. 380-390.

[5] Mezirow, *Dynamics*, p. 16.

[6] Braibanti, *Research*, p. 201.

From the foregoing discussion we find that the idea of community development is not novel in this sub-continent though, as we shall see below, from the mid-1950s community development has gained considerable importance and prominence and its scope has widened very extensively.

First Phase of Community Development in the post-47 period : Village Agricultural and Industrial Development (Village AID or V-AID): 1953—1961.

In the immediate post-47 period community development did not receive serious attention of the then government mainly because its immediate concern, as noted in chapter iii, was to deal with the problems and unsettled conditions that followed the transfer of power. It was from the early-1950s that community development gradually began to receive attention. The community development programme, namely V-AID, was first introduced in 1953.[1] Of course, it came into full operation in 1954/55. It was considered as "the means for bringing better living standards and a new spirit of hope [and] confidence to the villages, where...about 90 per cent of the people of the country live".[2] The Prime Minister of former Pakistan in his letter to the Chief Ministers of East Bengal and West Pakistan observed that it was "the first determined effort" on the part of the government "to tackle the multifarious problems which daily confront the vill-

[1] The V-AID programme was based on the recommendations of the Sufi Committee. In 1951 a group of 5 officials of the Agricultural Department headed by Mr. Sufi, the then Deputy Secretary to the Ministry of Food and Agriculture, Government of former Pakistan, visited the USA and spent four months under the auspices of the US ICA. During that four months they studied the agricultural extension services in the USA. On their return they submitted a report on the basis of their experience in the USA. [See "The Sufi Report" in *Village AID: Some Articles and Reports* (Lahore, Dec. 1960), p. 11.] Substantial help in the form of commodities and training of personnel was received by the Government of former Pakistan from the US ICA. The establishment of the academies, where the V-AID staff received training, was financed in part by the Ford Foundation. (Braibanti, *Research*, p. 202.)

[2] *The First Five Year Plan*, p. 16.

agers".[1] The primary aim of the V-AID programme was to "foster effective citizen participation in the rural self-help projects"[2] in the fields of agriculture, health and sanitation, adult literacy, primary education, cottage industry, minor irrigation and reclamation, secondary road construction, cooperative societies, village social and recreational activities etc. The V-AID programme sought to accomplish this aim or goal through

> "a process of education, based upon discussion and planned community action, designed to assist villagers to acquire the attitudes, concepts and skills prerequisite to their effective democratic participation in the solution of as wide a range of development projects as possible in an order of priority determined by their increasing level of competence. The basic assumption is that by helping villagers acquire a greater confidence in themselves and their government servants, precision in using scientific methods of community problem solving, competence in using cooperative methods of discussion and action and skill in resolving social conflict, their development efforts will be enhanced and existing conditions of apathy, over-dependence on authority, fear of change and factionalism will be overcome. Through this educational process and with the coordinated extension information programmes of the technical agencies of government, villagers are encouraged to re-order the priority of their projects in accordance with government targets and programmes."[3]

The V-AID Administration and Personnel. For the purpose of V-AID administration each district was divided into a number of "development areas." At the district and the "development area" levels V-AID Advisory Committees were formed, the composition of which may be illustrated in tables[4] xix and xx.

The main function of the Committees was to serve as a coordinating body and to review the V-AID work periodically.

[1] The letter of the Prime Minister of former Pakistan to the Chief Ministers of East Bengal and West Pakistan, dated Oct. 13, 1955 quoted in *Village-AID: Five Year Plan*, 1955-56—1959-60 (Karachi, 1956) (Hereafter cited as *V-AID Plan*), p. iv.

[2] Jack D. Mezirow and Frank A. Santopolo, "Five Years of Community Development in Pakistan" in *Village AID: Some Articles and Reports*, p. 115. (Hereafter cited as Mezirow and Santopolo, *Community Development*. The authors of the article were Community Development Advisors, US Operation Mission to former Pakistan.) The aim of the V-AID programme is discussed in detail below.

[3] *Ibid.*, pp. 115-116.

[4] *V-AID Plan*, pp. 19-20.

TABLE XIX

COMPOSITION OF DISTRICT V-AID ADVISORY COMMITTEE

Chairman:	D.O.
Secretary:	Senior Development Officer.
Members:	All S.D.O.s, district level heads of nation building departments, all V-AID Development Officers and two Village Council members per "development area".

TABLE XX

COMPOSITION OF V-AID DEVELOPMENT AREA ADVISORY COMMITTEE

Chairman:	D.O. or S.D.O.
Secretary:	V-AID Development Officer.
Members:	Representatives of the nation building departments operating below the district level. V-AID Supervisors and Workers, Chairmen of all Village Councils, and the representatives of the interested local groups who were usually selected by the Development Officer.

The D.O. was made "responsible for the successful implementation of the V-AID programme within his district".[1] In the mid-1950s the *First Five Year Plan* pointed out that from now onward one of the principal concerns of the D.O. would be V-AID.[2] His main responsibility in respect of V-AID was to supervise the working of the V-AID organisation and to ensure the coordination between it and the technical departments.[3] One author held that

> "Village-AID programme is a mission and the Deputy Commissioner is the head of the mission in the district. He must infuse in all, with whom he may come into contact, whether officials or non-officials, the noble purpose of the mission. And if this has been done vigorously half of the Deputy Commissoner's job is accomplished."[4]

In the sub-division the role of the S.D.O. was similar to that of the D.O. But later we shall see that in practice the D.O. and the

[1] The Prime Minister's letter in *ibid.*, p. iv.

[2] *First Five Year Plan*, p. 102.

[3] Said Ahmad, "The Deputy Commissoner's place in the Village AID Pattern" in *Village AID in West Pakistan*, pp. 81-82.

[4] M.A. Haq, "The Deputy Commissioner as the Coordinator at the District Level" in *ibid.*, p. 68.

S.D.O. did not play a significant role in respect of the V-AID, especially in East Bengal.

The "development area", composed of approximately 150 villages with a population of roughly 150,000, was made the basic unit for administering the V-AID programme.[1] The "development area" was in charge of a Development Officer. In East Bengal and West Pakistan respectively 2 and 3 supervisors worked under the guidance and control of the Development Officer. Although initially it had been designed that one of the Supervisors would be a woman, only in a few areas women Supervisors were appointed mainly because of the paucity of women staff.

The V-AID Worker was "the spearhead of this programme."[2] In East Bengal and West Pakistan respectively 20 and 30 V-AID workers were posted in a "development area" each responsible for five to eight villages. In each "development area" 5 to 10 women V-AID workers, depending on their availability, were posted.[3]

When the V-AID programme was first launched in the mid-1950s the *V-AID Plan* drew the following picture of a V-AID worker:

> "The Village-AID Worker is a multipurpose development worker... Instead of a representative of each nation-building department approaching a villager—and they would become a multitude—the Village AID worker goes to the villages as a single point contact equipped with multipurpose developmental responsibility representing the educational arm of such departments. [It was also pointed out that] Although employed by Government, the Village AID Worker is not an 'officer' but a 'worker'—a servant of the people. He has no regulatory or enforcement powers over the villagers... His approach is one of persuasion not coercion in planning and in action."[4]

Of course, in practice, as we shall see below, the V-AID Worker did not behave and act in the way expected by the *V-AID Plan.*

[1] Mezirow and Santopolo, *Community Development*, p. 116.

[2] *V-AID Plan*, p. 24. There was a striking resemblance between the V-AID Worker and Brayne's Village Guide. (See Brayne's *Village Uplift*, pp. esp. 39-40.)

[3] Mezirow and Santopolo, *Community Development*, p.116.

[4] *V-AID Plan*, pp. 24-25.

On completion of one-year training the V-AID Worker was sent to villages.[1]

V-AID Approach. It was thought that replacement of many old and outdated techniques and methods practised by the villagers with modern and improved techniques and methods would solve many village problems. There were many old methods and techniques which had very little value and merit but the village people were used to them and had been practising them since their boyhood. So they used to consider them the best methods and techniques. Thus, it was felt that until and unless the usefulness of modern methods and techniques could be demonstrated in villagers' farms or homes and proved to be better than old techniques and methods it was quite unlikely that they would accept and practise them. Thus, the V-AID programme was based on the assumption that if the usefulness of a method or technique could be successfully demonstrated to a villager then "he will not only adopt the practice or skill himself but will become the best agent for its propagation in the village. The role of the V-AID Worker here is obvious; he must be able to teach the skill or practice to the villagers and help them to demonstrate it themselves and to their neighbours."[2]

One of the important functions of the V-AID worker was to form a Village Council in the village, but no hard and fast rules and regulations were provided for this purpose. Of course, a broad outline was suggested by the *V-AID Plan*. It was held that it would not be possible for the worker to organise a Village Council within a short time. It was suggested that at first he should try to become thoroughly acquainted with the villagers and to gain their acceptance and confidence. He should try to find or develop local leadership. Then he should bring the prominent and influential local persons together. Thus it was expected that through this slow

[1] Several V-AID Institutes were set up in which the V-AID Workers received their training. Their training course included agriculture, animal husbandry, cooperative techniques, health and sanitation, human relations (individual relations and group relations), home economics, etc. (*Ibid.*, p. 141.)

[2] *V-AID Plan*, p. 41.

process a Village Council should be formed, the membership of which should be drawn from different interests and classes of the village. "A council may be regarded as a formal or visual result of a period of informal working with individuals and small groups until they feel the need for coming together."[1] And it was also made clear that "in any case the Village Councils are completely non official bodies and consist of the recognised leaders of the village who serve on a voluntary basis".[2] As there was no method of organising the Village Council the process of organisation varied widely from place to place considerably depending on the attitude of the V-AID Worker, the Supervisors and the Development Officer. In many areas the youth organisation called *Chand Tara* Clubs (Moon and Star Clubs) were organised by the V-AID workers in order to encourage social and recreational activities.

The Planning and the Execution of Projects. The process of planning was based on the assumption that "there must be some needs which were felt and acknowledged by the villagers and on which they were willing to work".[3] The first stept of the V-AID worker in the direction of preparing a development plan for the village was to encourage the local leaders to discuss between themselves their problems and unsatisfactory conditions and the underlying reasons for them. His primary concern was to stimulate their thought and action and to sustain their interests.[4] He then "helps the group to pinpoint some problem which promises relatively quick results, which involves a number of people in its achievement, is within the capacity of the villagers to accomplish and is easily seen and recognised as a product of group effort".[5] But in practice the process of planning varied from region to region.[6] In many cases the V-AID worker did not take the

1 *Ibid.*, p. 27. 2 *Ibid.*, p. 28. 3 *Ibid.*, p.28.

4 Said Khan, "Evaluating Operational Procedure in the Development" in the *Report of All-Pakistan Seminar on Village Agricultural and Industrial Development Programme* (held at Dacca from May 18 to 23, 1959) (Karachi, 1960), pp. 53-54. (Hereafter cited as *Report on All Pakistan Seminar on V-AID.*)

5 *V-AID Plan*, pp. 27-28. 6 Mezirow, *Dynamics*, p. 211.

trouble to undergo such a lengthy process of planning. After some discussion with village leaders the plans were usually prepared by the V-AID Worker, the Supervisors and the Development Officer, then the formal consent of the Village Council was obtained. All development plans prepared at the village level were presented to the Development Area Committee, the Chairman of which, as noted above, was either the D.O. or the S.D.O. Of course, in many cases they did not attend meetings. This committee could approve or disapprove the plans with or without necessary modifications or readjustments. It was usually expected that the cost of each project should be borne by the villagers' contributions of cash, materials and labour. In cases where adequate local resources were lacking the committee sometimes gave financial grants upto the extent of the 50% of the total estimated cost.[1] Under V-AID programme usually big projects were not undertaken. Such projects as approach or feeder roads, repair or construction of small school or dispensary buildings, improved sanitary arrangements, filling useless village ponds, digging of village wells etc. were included in village development plans. The projects were implemented by the Village Council aided by the V-AID worker. The Development Officer and the Supervisors supervised the execution of the projects and guided the Village Council and the V-AID Worker.[2]

Termination of the V-AID Programme. With the introduction of the system of "Basic Democracies" in 1959, the new military government of former Pakistan decided to integrate the V-AID programme with it.[3] Finally, in 1961 the termination of the programme was declared. Here it may be mentioned that ministerial and administrative changes and reorganisation, administrative indecision and the curtailment of technical and financial assistance by the foreign missions slowed down rural development

[1] Mezirow and Santopolo, *Community Development*, p. 119.

[2] S. Khan, *Evaluating Operational Procedure*, p. 55.

[3] *Basic Democracies: NDO-BD Integration and Training Programs* (Ministry of Health and Social Welfare, Karachi, n.d.), p.1.

in former Pakistan during the period between late-1959 and 1962.[1]

V-AID Aim. The philosophy of the V-AID programme was very close to the idea of those who regard community development as mainly a programme of social or cultural education. The V-AID programme which was mainly "an instrument for producing sociological change",[2] primarily aimed at the social, moral and cultural development of the rural people. No doubt, the material development (e.g. construction of roads, bridges etc.) of the rural areas was also its aim but, relatively speaking, it was of secondary importance. Its principal aims were to give the villager confidence, to stimulate in him a desire for better living and to show him how to improve his economic condition by using improved and modern methods and techniques of agriculture, poultry farming etc. so that they might satisfy his new desire.[3]

The V-AID programme devoted a considerable amount of its energies to bringing "change in the ways and attitudes of people",[4] to teaching them the ideas of better living and to improving their civic sense. It sought to "develop human potentialities that is the resources of the mind."[5] One author who was in the V-AID organisation observed that

> "The entire programme of V-AID is a programme of education in the broad sense of the term of the concept. Sustenance of the programme can only be expected if and when the people can become conscious of their rightful position in a community and this sense can only be inculcated through education... The purpose of Information and Education is to approach the masses and create in them the desire and ability to make effort themselves to get rid of poverty and insecurity, dirt and disease, stagnation and inertia and to occupy rightful place in the community."[6]

---

1 Mezirow, *Dynamics*, pp. 118-119.

2 Paul S. Taylor, "Observations and Critique on the V-AID Programme in Pakistan" in *V-AID: Some Articles and Report*, p. 79.

3 S.S. Choudhury, "Media of Mass Education" in the *Report on All-Pakistan Seminar on V-AID*, p. 101.

4 Taylor, *op. cit.*, p. 79.

5 M.A. Haq, Comment made during the discussion on topic no vii: "Evaluating V-AID Publicity" in *Report on All-Pakistan Seminar on V-AID*, p. 105.

6 S.S. Choudhury, *op. cit.*, p. 101. The methods or media that were adopted

But the aim of the Rural Works Programme which succeeded the V-AID programme, was different. Relatively speaking, the Works Programme was not a programme of education in the sense the V-AID programme was. Of course, under the Works Programme the members of the local council received some training and rural people occasionally received some information about new methods of and new ideas about agriculture, sanitation etc. But the primary aim of the Works Programme was the material improvement of the rural areas. Its main target was to construct networks of roads and highways, bridges, embankments etc. Both heavy and minor construction works were included in the Works Programme's plans which were formulated at different levels: district, *thana/tehsil* and union levels. But we have already noted that the V-AID programme had not undertaken heavy construction works and that a V-AID plan, which usually had covered a very limited area, had been formulated at the village level.

A Brief Survey of the V-AID Programme. The original idea of the V-AID programme was that the V-AID personnel should become the extension agents of all nation building departments. But instead of playing the role of extension agents they alone took up the responsibility of rural development ignoring other departments and sometimes even in rivalry with them. The departments also became vindictive and jealous and frequently stood in the way of the progress of the V-AID programme. They often did not support the programme with supplies and services with the result that successful demonstration of modern methods and techniques was not always possible on the part of the V-AID personnel.[1]

---

to communicate new ideas and techniques to rural people were broadly classified into the following 5 groups: (i) Literary—booklets, pamphlets etc., (ii) Audio—radio, tape recordings, gramophone etc., (iii) Visual—silent films, displays of slides through projectors, posters etc., (iv) Audio-Visual —talking films etc., (v) Folk Art—songs, dramas etc.

[1] *The Comilla Rural Administration: History and Annual Report*, 1962-63 (PARD, Comilla, Oct. 1963), p. 3. *The Second Five Year Plan* (1960-65)

The responsibilities and tasks entrusted to the V-AID Workers were difficult and needed much intelligence and wisdom on their part. But the calibre of the V-AID Workers, who were either matriculate or middle pass, was not very good and thus, many of them could not exercise their functions efficiently. It was also reported that though they were supposed to be "friend, philosopher and guide to the villagers", in many places they displayed bureaucratic and authoritarian attitudes.

The Report of the Food and Agricultural Commission, published in 1961, recommended that the V-AID authority should be relieved of its responsibility in the field of agriculture because the V-AID personnel having no sound technical knowledge and background were not in a position to contribute to the agricultural extension programme. This recommendation was accepted by the government.[1]

One of the most serious defects of the V-AID programme especially in East Bengal was that there was no close contact between the V-AID organisation and the main executive and administrative arm of the government although the D.O. (or the S.D.O.) was made the Chairman of the V-AID Advisory Committee. The D.O.s and the S.D.O.s, who were already overburdened and many of whom were cynical about the programme, considered the V-AID function as an addition to their burden and tried to keep themselves aloof from the programme. It was generally felt that no pressure was also brought to bear on them by the government in order to compel them to take genuine interest in the V-AID programme. Of course, it was the V-AID personnel themselves who mainly stood in the way of the development of close relationship between the V-AID organisation and the executive arm of the government. The V-AID personnel tried to perform their duties as independently as possible and to avoid

---

(Karachi, 1960) also held that the relationship between the V-AID Organisation and the nation building departments had not been satisfactory. Of course, relatively speaking, such relationship had been better in East Bengal than in West Pakistan (p. 393).

[1] Mezirow, *Dynamics*, pp. 120-121.

the control and supervision of the local executive authority. Such behaviour of the V-AID personnel was, in fact, the result of the fact that the planners (most of whom were US ICA advisors) of the programme were cynical about the executive authority in the district and preferred to keep the V-AID organisation independent of its influence. The Comilla Academy observed that

> "The early designers of the programme had a basic misconception that law and order administration would by nature be an obstruction rather than a help to the programme because of the inherent unpleasantness of tax collection and police functions. The planners did not realise that all local development effort would have to be related closely with the civil administration because it has many constructive functions aside from tax collection and maintenance of peace."[1]

The following comment made by Aktar Hameed Khan, the then Director, Comilla Academy, during a speech delivered at the Michigan State University is pertinent:

> "The community development people seem to have an allergy or a special antipathy to public administration and economic planning. They think that there is a law and order mentality which vitiates the administrative machinery of colonial countries and they think, a new spirit is needed in development programmes, a spirit which is to be supplied by community development workers and officers."[2]

Because of such attitude towards the executive arm of the government the V-AID organisation made no effort to make proper use of the position, status and enormous influence of the D.O. and the S.D.O. which could have been of immense value to the V-AID programme. Thus the programme lacked the vigour and drive which it needed very badly.

Moreover, the local bodies were kept separate from the V-AID organisation with the result that two parallel institutions, intended for virtually the same purpose, were operating side by side. This situation often led to rivalry, jealousy and unnecessary competi tions between the two parallel institutions.

1 *The Comilla Rural Administration: History and Report*, p.4.

2 "On Principles of Rural Development" (June 11, 1964) in *Rural Development in East Pakistan: Speeches of Aktar Hameed Khan* (Asian Studies Center, Michigan State University, n.d.), p. 11.

Though the V-AID system had all these drawbacks it made at least some contributions to rural development. There is no doubt that it played a fairly important role in demonstrating new methods and techniques and in disseminating useful information. Many village teachers, students, midwives, adult literacy teachers and youth club members were given training for a short period. A number of adult literacy centers were built. It "introduced a new method of learning by doing, to help rural children grow up to be better farmers and citizens".[1] Though the village organisations set up by it were not very effective or successful their necessity was impressed upon the villagers. It also demonstrated the importance of self-help projects and the participation of rural people themselves in rural development works. Though the V-AID programme did not prove to be as great a success as had been expected, it was the beginning of a new era in former Pakistan.

Two US ICA advisors to former Pakistan observed that the V-AID programme was the second largest community development enterprise in the world.[2] An amount, well over $35 millions was invested.[3] By March 1955 the population covered by the "development areas" was 18.7% of the total population (according to 1951 census).[4] During the period between February 1954 and October 1959, 134 "development areas" were opened: 1954—6, 1955—15, 1956—23, 1957—28, 1958—17 and 1959—45.[5] At the time of termination of the V-AID programme (i.e. in early 1961) there were 176 "development areas."[6]

1 *The Comilla Rural Administration: History and Report*, pp. 2-3.

2 Mezirow and Santopolo, *Community Development*, p. 115.

3 Mezirow, *Dynamics*, p. 69. This amount does not include contributions by Asia Foundation, UNESCO, Colombo Plan, and Church World Service in tools, books and agricultural supplies and equipment. (*Ibid.*, p. 69.)

4 *Ibid.*, p. 74. 5 *Ibid.*, p. 68.

6 *The Second Five Year Plan*, p. 393. More than 4,500 V-AID Workers were trained in eleven V-AID institutes and were deployed under 390 Supervisors in more than 35,000 villages over an area of 100,000 square miles with a population of 22 million (Mezirow, *Dynamics*, p. 68.) So far as the material improvements were concerned, 3,000 miles of unmetalled roads were constructed, 4,000 miles of old roads were put in serviceable condition, and 1,000 miles of canals were dug. Moreover, some 150,000 agricultural

East Bengal did not receive an equal share of V-AID resources. "Approximately two thirds of the benefits were directed to the western wing up to 1959."[1] But the people of East Bengal were "much more successful" in creating Village Councils. In East Bengal there were 9,884 village councils compared to 5,817 in West Pakistan. Douglas E. Ashford observed that there were, "of course, geographical and other features affecting this performance, but the Bengali experience in village government appeared to have some lasting effects".[2]

With the termination of the V-AID programme the first phase of the community development in former Pakistan came to an end and the second phase began. At the beginning of the second phase an important departure was made from the former programme: The local bodies and the local executive arm (i.e. the D.O. and the S.D.O.) of the government were made closely associated with the whole gamut of community development. Under the second phase the new local bodies system was "essentially the formal institutionalisation of rural development. It sought to combine the style of persuasion which was the hallmark of Village-AID with the sanctional power of a formal bureaucracy."[3] Of course, as we shall see below, to a considerable extent such a step was the result of the political motive and interest of the Ayub Government.

Second Phase of Community Development in the post-47 period : Works Programme.

Background of the Second Phase. The Works Programme had its origin in the "Expanded PL-480 Agreement" signed by the

demonstration Plots were laid out. (*The Second Five Year Plan*, p. 393.)

1 Douglas, E. Ashford, *National Development and Local Reform: Political Participation in Morocco, Tunisia, and Pakistan* (Princeton, 1967), p. 112.

2 *Ibid.*, p. 112, fn. 35. We have already noted in chapter iii that the Simon Commission observed in 1930 that Bengal was one of the three provinces, others being Madras and the U.P., in which the local councils at the village level were relatively most successful. In this chapter we have already noted that under the V-AID programme the Village Council was the result of the desire of a group of village leaders to come together.

3 Braibanti, *Research*, p. 203.

governments of the USA and former Pakistan on October 14, 1961.[1] Dr. Gilbert of the University of Harvard, the then adviser to the Planning Commission of former Pakistan, who had worked in the 'New Deal' of President Roosevelt, said to Aktar Hameed Khan, the then Director of the Rural Development Academy in Comilla,[2]

> "Your villagers are in a state of depression. There is a lack of employment and there is a lack of capital works; there are no roads, no drainage system, no irrigation system. Why is it not possible to do the same thing here as was done under President Roosevelt when depression came to the States?...So...why can't East Pakistan also have a public works programme in the rural areas?"[3]

Dr. Gilbert also asked "Why is it not possible in the slack-work season [[4]] to put your idle people to work building roads,

1 *The Revised Estimates of the Second Five Year Plan* (Govt. of former Pakistan, Karachi, Nov. 1961), p. 3. (Hereafter cited as *Revised Second Five Year Plan.*) According to this agreement, former Pakistan received Rs. 160 crore (336 million) from the USA. (*Ibid.*, pp. 3, 25.)

2 A few words may be said about Aktar Hameed Khan whose drive and energy were largely responsible for whatever success the Works Programme achieved in the field of rural development. He was a member of the Indian Civil Service. He resigned from the service in 1943 when he was the Sub-Divisional Officer of Netrokona, British Bengal (now in Bangladesh). He came to East Bengal in 1950 as the Principal, Victoria College, Comilla. During the intervening period he had worked as labourer, cattle farmer, school teacher and as oriental scholar at Deoband. [Comilla US-AID Conference Report (cyclostyled) (Comilla, June 1963), p. 5.] Dr. Gilbert called him "a great teacher and organiser, combining with many saintly qualities, an illuminating intelligence and a tough pragmatism and objectivity. He assembled a faculty of great capability." [Richard V. Gilbert, The Works Programme in East Pakistan (cyclostyled) (A paper presented at the Conference on Labour Productivity, held in Geneva in Dec. 1963), p. 8.] Aktar Hameed Khan's role could be compared with that of F.L. Brayne of British India and S.K. Dey of India.

3 Quoted in a speech by Aktar Hameed Khan. See "Report of the Training Programme for Circle Officers in Rural Public Works Programme" (cyclostyled) (Comilla, 1962), appendix ii, pp. vii-viii. (Hereafter cited as Report on Training Programme for C.O.s.)

4 In Bangladesh immediately after *Amon* harvest the cultivators have little work to do. They remain idle.

drainage, canals, and an irrigation system—the very things the villagers need so badly?"[1] Aktar Hameed Khan agreed with Dr. Gilbert and felt that it would be possible to build up necessary rural capital or infra-structure.[2]

Dr. Gilbert's opinion had special relevance to East Bengal because the economy of West Pakistan was developing much faster than that of East Bengal. More money was being invested in West Pakistan with the result that industries and commerce were developing at a faster rate. So there was more work and progress was satisfactory. But in East Bengal there was stagnation. Though the policy makers in Karachi agreed with Dr. Gilbert that East Bengal needed a vast public works programme, they said

> "'It won't work in our country; public works require great engineering skill and we have very few engineers. Therefore, a programme on a vast scale cannot be undertaken'...they thought that without engineering supervision, the local people could not do it. 'Local people taking care of these *khals* canals], these *bunds*, these irrigation systems?—it's unimaginable. What do they know about hydraulics ? What do they know of water control? What do they know about the specifications of a road?' The second objection was that the Civil Administration has not the competence to organise so vast a project. 'In our country no work can be done without the engineer and the contractor. [So far as the construction work is concerned the]....civil officers are as incompetent as the local people.' [To them Aktar Hameed Khan's reply was that] Let us try. It is no use arguing whether the people are competent or incompetent, or whether the officers of the Civil Administration could mobilize them. Let us try and find out what happens."[3]

Aktar Hameed Khan decided that the programme would be based on the assumption that the local people had the knowledge, the competence and the integrity to undertake the work and that the civil administration would be able to organise the project without contractors and with some advice from engineers.[4]

[1] Quoted in *An Evaluation of the Rural Public Works Programme: East Pakistan* (PARD, Comilla, Oct. 1963), p.x. [Hereafter cited as *1st Evaluation Report* (*E. Beng.*).]

[2] *Ibid.*, p. 3.

[3] Report on Training Programme for C.O.s, pp. ix-x.

[4] *1st Evaluation Report* (*E. Beng.*), p. 5.

The decision was taken that the Comilla *Kotwali Thana* with an area of 100 square miles should be used as a testing ground. It was felt that the experience which would be gained here in the field of planning and implementation of projects would enable the Academy to explore the ability of both people and civil administration and to develop methods and techniques of planning and implementation which would be applicable throughout East Bengal.[1]

Aktar Hameed Khan managed to secure a modest sum from the Agricultural Department out of the funds available for minor irrigation schemes. And thus the Comilla *Kotwali Thana* programme, called the 'Pilot Programme', came into operation in the fall of 1961. The Comilla *Kotwali* Programme, carried out on an experimental basis, became very successful and the record of accomplishment was "outstanding".[2] Dr. Gilbert held that the "results were dramatic".[3] The "outstanding" and the "dramatic" success encouraged the government to allocate Rs. 10 crore for what was called the "province wide programme".[4]

It was recommended by the Comilla Academy that a programme of approximately the same size as that which had been "successfully" planned and implemented in Comilla *Kotwali Thana*, should be organised in all 54 *thanas*, which were located at 54 sub-divisional headquarters in East Bengal.[5] A massive training programme was undertaken by the Comilla Academy. The S.D.O.s and the C.O.s were brought to the Comilla Academy where they underwent a short training course. They were given an oppor-

[1] *Report on a Rural Public Works Programme in Comilla Kotwali Thana* (Comilla, June 1962), p. 1. (Hereafter cited as *Report on Comilla Kotwali Thana.*)

[2] *1st Evaluation Report* (*E. Beng.*), p.6.

[3] Gilbert, *op. cit.*, p. 14. Dr. Gilbert gave a fairly exhaustive analysis of the achievements of the *Kotwali* programme. (See *ibid.*, pp. 14-16.)

[4] *Pakistan Economic Survey, 1964-65* (Rawalpindi, 1965), p. 212. Of course, 50% of the amount was placed in the hands of the District Councils and the rest in those of other councils and committees.

[5] *Report on Comilla Kotwali Thana*, pp.15-17. *1st Evaluation Report*, (*E. Beng.*), p. 9.

tunity to see the work that had been successfully carried out and to discuss different aspects of the programme with the persons who had been responsible for the "success" of the programme so that on their return they could organise a similar programme in their respective areas. The D.O.s, who were made responsible for the successful working of the programme in their respective districts, were briefed at a conference in Dacca.[1] On the basis of the experience gained in Comilla *Kotwali Thana*, a manual[2] was prepared by the Academy in August 1962. This manual, which discussed various stages of planning and implementation of projects, was the key document and served as the basis of Rural Works Programme in East Bengal. The methods and techniques which were worked out from the experience gained in the Comilla *Kotwali Thana* came to be commonly known as 'Comilla Approach'.

During the year 1962-63 the "province-wide programme" on the basis of 'Comilla Approach' proved to be a "success". "The organisational and management talent in the villages, in the unions, in the *thanas*, has now been demonstrated on a province-wide basis."[3] The amount allotted for the Rural Works Programme in 1963-64 was doubled—Rs. 20 crore.[4] During the year 1964-65 the allocation was further increased to Rs. 25 crore "because it had become abundantly clear from the previous two years' performance" that the local councils "could very well absorb and fruitfully utilize much larger allocations".[5] Later the government decided to include Rural Works Programme as an integral part of the *Third Five Year Plan* (1965-60) and it was decided that the "Rural Works Programme will form a separate sector in the plan mainly

[1] Gilbert, *op. cit.*, p. 16.

[2] *A Manual for Rural Public Works* (Comilla, Aug. 1962).

[3] Gilbert, *op. cit.*, p. 19.

[4] "Now that the administrative capabilities of the local leadership have been fully established, the distribution of funds has been adjusted to place primary emphasis on the *Thana* and Union Councils, three quarters of the total allocation being placed at their disposal." (*Ibid.*, p. 19.)

[5] *Pakistan Economic Survey, 1964-65*, p. 215.

concerned with the growth and development of the rural economy."[1] In the *Third Five Year Plan* an allocation of Rs. 2,500 million was made for the Rural Works Programme in East Bengal and West Pakistan during the period between 1965 and 1970. Of course, the "success" of the Rural Works Programme was not the only factor involved. Later we shall see that political motives and self interest also encouraged the Ayub government to make an allocation of substantial resources.[2]

Thana and Union Council Plans. Each member prepared a plan for his ward, the population of which was roughly one thousand. While preparing the plan he was supposed to consult the villagers and to discuss it in a village meeting in which necessary modifications and adjustments would be made according to the suggestions put forward by the villagers.[3] This procedure was followed almost everywhere during the first year of the Works Programme (1962-63).[4] But in the second year (1963-64) in most places no village meetings were held and the villagers were not consulted.[5]

Each member submitted his plan to the Union Council. In the Council meeting these plans were discussed and then after having made necessary modifications and adjustments the plans were coordinated and a Union Council plan was prepared. The projects which were small in size and had "implications only within the union" were included in the union council plan. The plans for the projects which were big and had "implications beyond one union"[6] were sent to the *Thana* Council. These projects were discussed in the meeting of the *Thana* Council under the chairmanship of the S.D.O. or the C.O. The projects which were of *thana* importance were coordinated with necessary modifications and adjustments and a *thana* plan was prepared. Of course,

[1] *The Third Five Year Plan: 1965-70* (March 1965), p. 515.

[2] See above, chapter vii.

[3] *Manual for Rural Public Works*, p. 6.

[4] *1st Evaluation Report* (*E. Beng.*), p. 9.

[5] *An Evaluation of Rural Works Programme: East Pakistan, 1963-64* (Comilla, n.d.), p. 16. Hereafter cited as *2nd Evaluation Report* (*E. Beng.*).

[6] *2nd Evaluation Report* (*E. Beng.*), p. 25.

in preparing its plan the *Thana* Council was in no way restricted to the plans officially presented to it by the Union Councils.[1] If it was felt necessary the *Thana* Council could include new projects in its plan.

The Union Council as well as the *Thana* Council prepared a three-year plan.[2] The plan for the projects to be completed in the first year was worked out in great detail. And only a broad outline of the next two years' plan was prepared which was subject to necessary modifications depending on the following year's plan and on the first year's progress.

The Rural Works Manual suggested that in the plan, specifications—length, breadth, height, depth etc.—and estimates for each project should be correctly mentioned after having taken the accurate measurements of each project.[3] But, a survey revealed that in most cases the specifications and the estimates mentioned in the plans were not based on actual measurements but on guesswork. Incorrect specifications created problems at the time of the execution of projects. Moreover, some *Thana* Councils, instead of appoving a few projects supported by large allocations of money, approved a great many projects backed by small allocations. This was done only to please as many Union Councils as possible. But at the time of execution it was found that the estimates fell far below actual requirements.[4]

The Union Councils were responsible for the maintenance of projects built by the *Thana* Council in their respective jurisdictions. Thus, while submitting their plans to the *Thana* Council the Union Councils were required to indicate the provision made by them in order to maintain *Thana* Council projects in their respective jurisdictions.[5]

[1] Decentralisation and Development (cyclostyled) (BDLG Department, Govt. of the then East Pakistan, Dacca, n.d.), p. 2.

[2] *Works Programme Through Basic Democracies, 1963-64* (Dacca, 1963), (Popularly known as *Circular no.* 44), p. 10.

[3] *Manual for Rural Public Works*, p. 7.

[4] *2nd Evaluation Report* (*E. Beng.*), pp. 28-29.

[5] *Circular no.* 44, p. 9.

Each District Council built a large mileage of roads. And it was felt that the responsibility of maintaining these roads should be entrusted to the authorities closest to the projects. Thus, the maintenance work was mainly done by the *Thana* Councils. Of course, the schemes for the maintenance of District Council roads were initiated by the Union Councils in the same manner as *Thana* Council projects. On receipt of these projects from the Union Councils each *Thana* Council prepared a three-year plan for improving the District Council roads within its jurisdiction. And at the same time a list of bridges, the repair of which was beyond the technical skill available to the *Thana* Council, was prepared, so that this responsibility could be undertaken by the District Council itself. The three-year plans prepared by the *Thana* Councils were submitted to the S.D.O. who coordinated these plans and submitted them to the District Council for final approval and allocation of funds.[1]

The District Council Plan. The District Council projects were initiated and prepared by the Works Committee of the District Council[2] according to the provision of the allocations of funds in the District Council budget. While preparing the plan for the District Council projects the suggestions put forward by the *Thana* Councils and the non-official members of the District Council, many of whom were also the members of lower councils, i.e. *Thana* and the Union Councils, were taken into consideration and the plans of the *Thana* and Union Councils were kept in view. While preparing the plan the Works Committee was enormously helped and assisted by the Assistant Director of the Basic Democracies, who was usually a member of the then provincial civil service and also the Secretary to the District Council, and by the Engineering staff of the District Council. The opinion and view of the D.O. and the Additional D.O. (Development) played a very important role in the matter.

[1] *Ibid.*, p. 8.

[2] *East Pakistan Rural Works Programme: Report—1963-64* (Govt. of the then East Pakistan, Dacca, n.d.), p. 5. [Hereafter cited as *Report on Rural Works Programme* (*E. Beng.*).]

Like *Thana* and Union Councils, the District Council also prepared a three-year plan (and sometimes for a longer period). The District Council undertook those projects which were of district importance.[1] Attempts were made to prepare the District Council Plan in such a way as to make the similar projects of the *Thana* and the Union Councils more effective.[2]

The three-year plan of the District Council was placed before a special meeting of the District Council. The plan was discussed in the meeting and necessary modifications, alterations, additions etc. were made according to those suggestions of the members which were agreed upon by the majority.[3] The opinion of the D.O. or the Additional D.O. (Development) played a very vital role in the course of the discussion of the meeting.

A survey of the proposed projects was made and an estimate for each project was prepared by the Engineering staff of the District Council. If it was found that the estimates exceeded the allocation of funds, then the plan was revised. The revised plan was again placed before the District Council for approval.[4]

Approval by the Approving Authority. The approval of the plans of the District, *Thana* and Union Councils by the respective 'Approving Authorities' was the last stage in the process of planning. The 'Approving Authority' for the Union Council Plan was a committee of the *Thana* Council concerned composed of the S.D.O. as the Chairman of the Committee, the C.O. as the Secretary to the Committee and two official members of the *Thana* Council, chosen by the S.D.O., as members of the committee. The 'Approving Authority' for the *Thana* Council plan was a committee of the District Council concerned, composed of the D.O. as the chairman of the committee, the Assistant Director of "Basic Democracies" as the Secretary to the committee and two official members of the District Council respectively representing Works Department of the government and 'Water and Power

[1] Decentralisation and Development, p. 1.

[2] *Circular no.* 44, p. 7.

[3] *Report on Rural Works Programme* (*E. Beng.*), p. 5.

[4] *Circular no.* 44, p. 7.

Development Authority', as members of the committee. The 'Approving Authority' for the District Council was a committee set up by the then provincial government at the provincial headquarters which was headed by the Secretary, Department of "Basic Democracies", Government of East Bengal. Each "Approving Authority" had full power to approve or reject or amend any plan submitted to it for the approval. It could also make any suggestions which it deemed necessary for the improvement of the plan.[1]

Principles of Planning. One of the important principles which governed the policy regarding planning, especially the planning of roads, was that District, *Thana* and Union Councils should respectively build the roads of district, *thana* and union importance. The District Council usually built long metalled roads which were linked with the national highways or sometimes became part of the national highways. The *Thana* Council roads connected the rural places of economic importance such as rural markets, *bazaars*, agricultural producing centres etc. with the District Council roads. And the Union Council roads connected villages with the *Thana* Council roads.[2] Formerly (i.e. before 1959), in the absence of an intermediate body like the *Thana* Council between the District and the Union Boards, the District Board had been required to extend its road system down to the point where the Union Boards could build the final feeder roads. Thus the District Board had had to build huge mileage of roads which were relatively unimportant from the point of view of district importance and which were beyond the capacity of its engineering staff to supervise.[3]

The "development from below"or "planning from below" was another important principle which had special reference to Rural Works Programme. The idea was first put forward in the *First Five Year Plan* which held that

> "We consider that the Government should visualize an active process of decentralisation. Instead of being prepared and imposed from above, programmes, in particular in the sphere of rural development, should

---

[1] *Ibid.*, p. 6.

[2] Decentralisation and Development, pp. 2-3.

[3] *Ibid.*, p. 1.

originate in the villages and proceed upwards, so that their aggregate represents the needs, aspirations and thinking of the people...[It was thought that no plan would succeed unless the people] have a sense of participation and... extend their full support and cooperation in its fulfilment. Without the whole-hearted participation of the people, the development programme will not achieve its full proportions; progress will be slow; and its benefits will remain open to question. It should be one of the primary functions of district administration to promote the participation of villagers in the process of planning."[1]

During the subsequent years and especially towards the begining of the 1960s, the concept of "planning from below" became popular[2] and was gradually incorporated in the local planning system. The *Second Five Year Plan* which seconded the view of the *First Five Year Plan* held that the system of local bodies would "become meaningful only if a measure of local programme, planning and policy formulation rises upward to the points at which governmental decisions are taken".[3]

Execution of Projects : Thana and Union Council Projects. After receiving the approval of the respective "Approving Authorities" the execution of projects began. The use of contractors for the execution of *Thana* and Union Councils' projects was prohibited.[4] The projects were implemented by Project Committees. For each project usually one Project Committee was formed. Sometimes bigger projects were divided into smaller parts and the responsibility of executing each part was assigned to one Project Committee.[5]

---

[1] *First Five Year Plan*, p. 103.

[2] The following reports and papers strongly advocated the incorporation of the concept of the "planning from below" in the planning procedure: *The V-AID Plan*, p. 2. Syed Manzoor Hussain, "Role of Basic Democracies in Economic Planning and Development" in *Seminar on Planning and Development*, held at Lahore from March 26 to March 28, 1962 (Lahore, 1962), pp. 69-70. Hasan Habib, *op. cit.*, pp. 41-42, 51. S.R. Karim, "Planning from Below" in the *Proceeding of the Regional Seminar on Planning and Development* (Lahore, 1964), pp. esp. 25-27.

[3] *The Second Five Year Plan*, p. 112. It further held that the system of local bodies would assume "a crucial role in decentralised development planning". (*Ibid.*, p. 109.)

[4] *Report on Rural Works Programme*, (*E.Beng.*), p. 7.

[5] *Manual for Rural Public Works*, p. 15.

The role of the Project Committee was crucial to the success of the project.[1] Each Project Committee was headed by a member of the Union Council representing the project area. The size of the membership of most Project Committees varied from six to ten.[2] One of the members served as the secretary to the Project Committee. The Comilla Academy suggested that the leading and influential villagers should be included as far as possible in the Project Committee as members in order to ensure their active participation and cooperation and to make it "a truly representative body".[3] So it was further suggested that the members of each Project Committee should be elected in the village meeting at the project site. But later it was found that in most cases above procedures were not exactly followed. Only on rare occasions were the Project Committees formed at the project site. In most cases the selection of the members of the Project Committees was made by the Union Council Chairman either at the council meeting or in the informal sessions.[4] In 'one' case it was reported that a Project Committee was formed secretly by the Union Council Chairman along with his "own men" in order to misappropriate money.[5]

The Comilla Academy strongly criticised the officials and the members of the local bodies for not holding village meetings. According to the Academy the success or failure of a project largely depended on the method of selecting the members of the Project Committee. It held that "Selection of the Project Committee is not a mere formality—it is the main spring of the project."[6] It also pointed out that "Village meetings for the selection of schemes and the selection of project committees are fundamental to the programme and their use should be regularly insisted upon. Only by these meetings can public cooperation be secured."[7] It further added that

[1] *1st Evaluation Report* (*E. Beng.*), p. 33. [2] *Ibid.*, p. 33.

[3] *Manual for Rural Public Works*, p. 15. Also see *Comilla Kotwali Thana Report*, pp. 29-30.

[4] *2nd Evaluation Report* (*E. Beng.*), pp. 16, 30. [5] *Ibid.*, p. 30.

[6] *Ibid.*, p. 30. [7] *Ibid.*, p. 16.

"If this weakness persists, people will lose contact with and consequently faith in the programme...A good piece of work done by officers and union councillors alone cannot encompass the villagers' affection and aspirations. It can only be done by involving villagers through established procedures...in a village-centred programme the workers [Project Committee and staff] must not only be honest but they must appear to be honest. This can be ensured by following the procedures of accountability such as regular project meetings, displaying sign boards, distributing booklets, holding village meetings and so forth."[1]

Immediately before launching the "province-wide Rural Works Programme" for the year 1962-63, the Secretary to the local government Department in the Secretariat had also told the C.O.s at the Comilla Academy:

"The villagers and the Union Councillors should be taken into your confidence. What is required is that you should hold meetings with the villagers and the Union Councillors and discuss the problems with them... and if the villager is convinced that you are really taking an interest in his problems, he will show keen interest and will extend his full assistance and cooperation. Your task, then, will become very easy. It is important that we meet and understand each other. In short, we have to work as a team...But if you want to get things done by merely passing order, you will never succeed."[2]

The Comilla Academy also cited some examples of unsuccessful projects which failed because of the opposition from the villagers.[3]

[1] *Ibid.*, p. 19.

[2] Report on the Training Programme for C.O.s, appendix iii, p. iv.

[3] In Aminpur Union an old canal was choked up with silt and encroachments. A project was undertaken to re-excavate the canal. The Project Committee did not start the work in time and the villagers were not consulted and informed about the project. The farmers resisted the advance of the excavation work because the crops began to grow on the land required for the canal. The opposition from the villagers resulted in slow progress. At last the Project Committee had to stop the excavation work because the villagers gathered in a body and refused to allow further excavation. The committee excavated only two miles—about half of the length of the canal. [*2nd Evaluation Report* (*E. Beng.*), pp. 41-43.]

In Rasulghat a project was undertaken to construct a road. The unwillingness of the villagers to have their lands taken for the project resulted in the construction of a zigzagged and haphazard road. When the road was being constructed the C.O. was twice confronted by groups of

The principal functions of the Project Committee were (a) to organise local labour and volunteers, (b) to meet regularly for taking decisions regarding the project, (c) to take measurement of the earthwork, (d) to receive funds and to pay labourers, (e) to secure land and other contributions from the public, (f) to keep accounts and records, (g) to make all necessary arrangements for timely execution and proper maintenance of the project and (h) to publicise the purpose, the organisation, rates of payment to labourers etc. among the villagers in order to secure their cooperation.[1]

In most cases, the chairmen and members of Union Councils and Project Committees underwent a short training course which ranged from one to seven days and was held either at the *Thana* or at the Subdivisional headquarters. The training course was organised by the C.O. under the supervision of the S.D.O.Necessary instructions on technical matters were given by the officers of the technical departments. General instructions were given by the S.D.O. and C.O. The training course usually included instructions on such topics as measurement of earth works, preparation of plans, estimates, maintenance of master rolls, labour attendance register, keeping up accounts, canal and road measurement, payment procedures, labour recruitment, technical data and the aims and objectives of the programme.[2]

So far as the execution of the projects was concerned the role of the chairman of the Union Council was to act as the supervisor of the Project Committee and not as the "first line executor of the

---

about 200 villagers protesting against the project. The villagers threatened the Council Chairman and burnt the house of a council member who supported the project. One villager said "Our grandfathers, forefathers had led their lives well without such a road. We also can do without such a road. It is better to have our lands unaffected than to have a road. We don't require such a road. During rainy season we can go by boat, and during dry season we can walk on our lands." Another villager said "Being the public we cannot resist the will of the Government; otherwise we would resist it by fair means or foul." (Quoted in *ibid.*, pp. 43-45.)

1 *Manual for Rural Public Works*, p. 16.

2 *1st Evaluation Report* (*E. Beng.*), pp. 21-22. *2nd Evaluation Report* (*E. Beng.*), p. 31.

project".[1] A survey of the Comilla Academy found that in most cases the Chairmen of the Union Councils maintained this attitude. Such attitude helped them to avoid clashes with the Chairmen and the members of the Project Committees. The Chairman of a Union Council summarised his role with regard to Project Committees in the following words: "My duty is to direct the work according to the resolutions of the Union Council and to keep checking on whether the work is carried on rightly."[2] Another Chairman said "As Chairman of the Union Council I only supervise and inspect the works."[3] Another Chairman observed "My job is to form Project Committees and distribute work among them. I supervise this work. If there are any difficulties, I settle them."[4]

The lack of technical assistance was universally felt. The *Thana* and the Union Councils did not have qualified technical staff.[5] Only a few *Thana* Councils had appointed overseers or sub-overseers who were also not adequately qualified and did not have sound technical knowledge. Occasionally technical assistance was received from the engineering staff of the District Council and the staff of the technical departments of the government. But both the District Councils and the technical departments did not have sufficient staff. Moreover, they were mainly stationed at district and sub-divisional towns. And it was also not possible for them to render adequate technical assistance to *Thana* and Union Councils because they had got to give necessary attention to their departmental functions.

The quality of the work done by the *Thana* and the Union Councils would have been much better had they received necessary technical assistance. But in spite of this drawback their performance was fairly satisfactory.

Execution of District Council Projects. The administrative process of the execution of the district council projects was much simpler than that of the lower councils because the works of the

[1] *1st Evaluation Report* (*E. Beng.*), p. 41. [2] *Ibid.*, p. 42.
[3] *Ibid.*, p. 42. [4] *Ibid.*, p. 43.
[5] *1st Evaluation Report* (*E. Beng.*), pp. 90-91. *2nd Evaluation Report* (*E. Beng.*), pp. 32-33.

former were not usually done by Project Committees. The *pucca* (metal or concrete) works of the district council were done by the contractors.[1] As the district council undertook heavy and big *pucca* projects of highly technical nature such as long bridges over wide rivers, highways, network of drainage and irrigation system etc., which required fairly adequate technical skill, it was not possible to execute these projects through Project Committees.

After receiving the approval of the "Approving Authority" the tenders were called by the Tender Committee composed of both official and non-official members of the District Council. After receiving the tenders from the contractors, the Tender Committee selected contractors for different projects and submitted its decision to the meeting of the District Council for final approval. The approval of the District Council was very essential. The following example will further illustrate this point: At the ordinary meeting of the Pabna District Council, held on May 31, 1965, an unofficial member of the District Council held that the proceedings of a committee or a sub-committee should be subject to the confirmation of the District Council. While discussing the proceedings of the meeting of the Tender Committee held on March 19, 1965, he further pointed out that without the approval of the District Council, acceptance of tenders and issuing work-orders thereof were irregular and in no way binding upon the District Council. It was also pointed out by him that the rates of tenders were high. The S.D.O. of Serajganj also seconded the view that the tender rates were high. At this stage the D.O. asked the District Engineer in charge to explain the reasons for the high rates of the tenders. The District Engineer gave an explanation which was not accepted by the members. It was held that the proceedings of the meeting of the Tender Committee held on March 19, 1965 which was under discussion should not be approved and that fresh tenders should be called.[2]

1 *Report on Rural Works Programme* (*E. Beng.*), p. 7.

2 Proceedings of the Ordinary Meeting of the District Council, Pabna, held on May 31, 1965. (Proceedings of the Pabna District Council were preserved in bound volumes, which were partly hand written and partly cyclostyled.)

All earth works required in the District Council projects were entrusted without exception to *Thana* Councils. While entrusting this responsibility to *Thana* Councils the District Council provided them with plans and estimates and placed the estimated funds at the disposal of the S.D.O. These projects were executed by the *Thana* Councils through Project Committees in the same manner as their own projects and they submitted monthly progress reports to the District Council.[1]

Those projects of the District Councils which were executed by the Contractors were supervised by the Assistant Director of "Basic Democracies" and the engineering staff of the District Council and they kept the Council and the Works Committee of the Council informed about the progress or irregularities of the construction works. The D.O., the Additional D.O. (Development) and the S.D.O. also occasionally visited project sites and check the works of the contractors. The non-official members of the District Council also kept watch on the works of the contractors in their respective constituencies and if they found irregularities they brought them to the notice of the District Council. In the event of such complaints the District Council sometimes constituted enquiry committee to inquire into the matter. The enquiry committee was an effective instrument for supervising not only the works of the contractors but also those of the supervising staff of the District Council. The following example will further illustrate the point: An unofficial member moved the following proposal in the ordinary meeting of the District Council, Pabna, held on March 26, 1965:

> "Whereas the development work of old Ataikula road from near the 'new Ichamati bridge' to Sibrampur primary school has greatly deteriorated, it is resolved that a sub-committee be formed to enquire into the matter and to take suitable action against the contractor and the supervising agency."[2]

The proposal was seconded by another non-official member

---

1 *Circular No.* 44, p. 7.

2 The Proceedings of the Ordinary Meeting of the Pabna District Council, held on March 26, 1965.

and the District Council unanimously resolved that a sub-committee be formed to enquire into the matter and that the sub-committee would submit its findings before the District Council for a decision.[1] The Committee submitted the following report:

> "The road in question was inspected by the members of the sub-committee today, i.e. 14.7.65, from one end to the other. It was found that there was poor workmanship in the entire construction. There are patches here and there throughout the road and the joints of slabs are lying all broken and open. The age of the road is only about two years. It appeared that the brick chips are all disproportionate—somewhere they were very big ranging from 1″—2″ in diameter. On the other hand, at some places the chips are very small far below size having very low resisting power with the result that the level has gone down at places exposing the M/C rod...Both the contractor and the supervising staff of the District Council should be held responsible for such bad work under the nose of District Council executives. The contractor should be asked to review the work according to specification, failing which his pending bill, if any, may be held up and he shall be kept under suspension till the work is rectified. The supervising staff should be asked to explain as to why they should not be penalised for negligence of duty."[2]

Role of the Bureaucracy

In most developing countries, though the rural people play a fairly important role in the process of community development the programme is almost entirely government inspired and directed effort and the officials play the key role in it and, in fact, maintain almost full control over it. The necessity and importance of official initiative and control cannot be denied. Although with the spread of the concept of community development it has become rather fashionable among a section of the people, some of whom are in favour of rapid debureaucratisation of local administration, to denounce or minimise the importance of the active bureaucratic participation in the process of community development, such participation is indispensable and without it no community development programme can succeed. In under-developed countries

[1] *Ibid.*

[2] Proceedings of the Meeting of the sub-committee, set up to enquire into the condition of Ataikula Road, held on July 14, 1965.

systematic efforts to eradicate illiteracy, to remove ancient social barriers and orthodox outlook, to revitalize rural life, and to improve the socio-economic conditions are "unthinkable without the participation of government".[1] In fact, without such participation "very few plans for basic changes in the economic or social structure are meaningful or possible".[2]

The conference out of which the book: *Bureaucracy and Political Development* (Princeton University Press, 1963) emanated had made "an effort to direct attention to the vital role that bureaucracies can and do play in the various kinds of transformations that the developing countries are expecting".[3]

Of course, with the passage of time when the members of the local councils of under-developed countries will gradually mature and gain more experience, they will be in a position to act much more independently and to take more and more initiative. But in early and middle stages

> "the intervention of field officers, in fact, the supervision by them of local government affairs...is a necessity to ensure effectiveness and economy in operation. These are of vital importance when the new or reorganised authorities are on trial both in the eyes of the local people and of those who, for various reasons, seek to centralise rather than decentralise. Nor can one ignore the need to get the utmost value from money spent, when the country's resources are so overstrained by the multitude of demands upon them."[4]

Role of the Circle Officer (C.O.). The C.O. was usually described as the "leader of the *thana* and the people" and the "man on the spot".[5] The Circle Officer was specially entrusted with the task of supervising and guiding the activities of the *Thana* and Union Councils. By virtue of his authority to control *Thana*

[1] LaPalombara, "An Overview of Bureaucracy and Political Development" in LaPalombara (ed.), *Bureaucracy and Political Development* (Princeton, 1963), p. 5.

[2] *Ibid.*, p. 5.

[3] *Ibid.*, p. 5.

[4] Henry Maddick, *Democracy, Decentralisation and Development* (Bombay, 1963), p. 226. Also see Henry Maddick, "The Present and Future Role of the Collector" in the *Journal of Local Administration Overseas*, vol. ii, no. 2, April 1963, pp. 81-84.

[5] Report on the Training Programme for C.O.s, appendix iii, p. iv.

and Union Councils' activities on behalf of the S.D.O. and also by virtue of his position as the Vice-Chairman of the *Thana* Council, the C.O. held a key position in the matter of development works done by *Thana* and Union Councils. "He can do and undo many things. If he desires that some good should be done to the people he can do many things. But if he neglects his duty the position becomes quite different."[1] By influencing the 'planning bodies' and ultimately by changing the plans to conform with what he thought as general interest, he acted as the guardian of rural development projects.

The role which the C.O.s played in preparing development plans varied from *thana* to *thana* depending on their respective interests in the development works and the support that they received from their S.D.O.s Usually they had greater opportunity and more time to supervise the planning of the *Thana* Council projects than to supervise that of Union Council projects. A survey conducted throughout East Bengal by the Comilla Academy revealed that in the year 1963-64 while in most cases the C.O.s directly supervised the planning of the *Thana* Councils' projects, only in some cases they directly influenced that of Union Councils' projects.[2] In 47% of the cases the process of the selection of the Union Council projects was directly dominated by the C.O.s in their capacity as advisor. In the above mentioned 47% of the cases, each C.O. "gave general instructions to the councillors, stressed the overall importance of the union, attended the meetings in which the plans were discussed and consolidated and managed to have Union Councils follow his advice."[3] In the remaining cases the C.O.s could not attend the Union Councils' meetings in which plans were discussed and coordinated. These plans instead of reflecting the overall interest of the union as a whole usually reflected the ward interests of influential members. Most C.O.s claimed that when those plans were received by them they scrutinised them and

[1] S. Rahman, "The Working of Basic Democracies in East Pakistan" (cyclostyled), NIPA (Dacca) Staff Study no. 30 (Dacca, Jan. 1965), p. 38. (Hereafter cited as NIPA Staff Study no. 30.)

[2] *2nd Evaluation Report* (*E. Beng.*), p. 26.

[3] *Ibid.*, p. 26.

with minor modifications sent them to the 'Approving Authority'. Of course, some C.O.s claimed that they did not interfere with the process of the planning of Union Council projects.

If any Union Council insisted on selecting projects entirely according to its own wish and without paying any attention to C.O.'s advice, it was not very difficult for him to get the plan altered because he acted as the Secretary to the 'Approving Authority' for Union Council plans. Usually it did not become necessary for the C.O. to go to the extent of approaching the 'Approving Authority' for altering a Union Council plan because a threat of such step was enough to make the Union Council concerned to introduce changes wanted by the C.O.

With regard to the *Thana* Council plan the role of the C.O. was slightly difficult because he had less control over it though he was its Vice-Chairman. In most cases while the C.O. took the general interest of the *thana*[1] into consideration, the Chairmen of the Union Councils, who were ex-officio non-official members of the *Thana* Council, often took the interests of their respective unions or even of their respective wards into consideration.[2] The influential Chairmen pressed for inclusion of their projects in the *Thana* Council plan. One C.O. observed that "illiterate members were influenced and sometimes overpowered by one or two semi-literate but shrewd members who out of their jealousy proposed plans which are not at all of *thana* importance".[3] It was generally felt that if a C.O. thought that the *Thana* Council plan would seriously jeopardize the general interest of the *thana* he usually brought the matter to the notice of the S.D.O. If he gained the support of the S.D.O. the Chairmen usually gave in unless they had good contact with persons higher in the political hierarchy. Usually they did not want to antagonise the S.D.O. because, as

1 The general interest of the *thana* may be defined here. It was the responsibility of the C.O. to see that the *Thana* Council plan might not serve the interest of any faction or area. Moreover, all the unions or wards in a *thana* were not equally developed and it was his responsibility to see that the less developed areas received more attention and more allocation of funds.

2 *2nd Evaluation Report* (*E. Beng.*), p. 27.

3 *Ibid.*, p. 28.

noted above, the S.D.O. in his capacity as the administrative and executive head of the sub-division not only enjoyed enormous power, position and prestige but had a great deal of patronage in his hands. Moreover, they knew that even if they insisted on the inclusion of their plans in the *Thana* Council plan against the wish of the S.D.O. they were not going to succeed in the long run because if he requested the D.O., the latter in his capacity as the Chairman of the 'Approving Authority' for the *Thana* Council plans would almost definitely reject or alter the plan.

A survey by the Comilla Academy revealed that in 1963-64 in two-thirds of the cases C.O.s had conflicts with Union Council Chairmen in considering *Thana* Council plans.[1] In 60% of the cases the C.O.s could amicably resolve the conflicts in the *Thana* Council meetings. They exerted their influence and persuaded the members to take the general interest of the *thana* into consideration. In 23% of the cases they altered the plans in order to make them conform to what they considered the general interest of the *thana*. In 17% of the cases they yielded because the Union Council Chairmen supported their proposals with majority votes.[2]

The C.O. had the task of supervising and inspecting the execution of the work of the *Thana* and the Union Councils' projects. He supervised and inspected development works with or without notice. Inspection without notice enabled him to obtain information which was usually kept hidden during pre-arranged inspection.[3]

The role of the C.O. was quite difficult. He had got to deal with the chairmen and members of Union Councils and Project Committees who were not government servants and hence they were not his subordinates. "It depends on tactfulness of the Circle Officer

1 *2nd Evaluation Report* (*E. Beng.*), p. 27.

2 When the present writer mentioned the above mentioned example of 23% and 17% of the cases to both officials and non-officials, most of them held that in former cases, in which the C.O.s, altered the plans, they most probably received the strong support of the S.D.O. and in the latter cases in which they yielded, most probably full support was not extended by the S.D.O.s concerned.

3 *2nd Evaluation Report* (*E. Beng.*), p. 35.

to catch the Chairmen and put them to work...his tactful dealing with the Chairmen and Basic Democrats will account for the development of the area concerned."[1]

As the 'man on the spot' the C.O. was "better acquainted with the problems of the *thana* than the Sub-Divisional Officer who was burdened with heavy schedule".[2] To a considerable extent the S.D.O. and the D.O. were dependent on him for information and data concerning the *Thana* and the Union Councils' development projects. He was required to submit to the S.D.O. and also to the Assistant Director of 'Basic Democracies' on the first day of every month a financial statement of expenditure on development works showing the following particulars: (a) total allocation, (b) total advance in hand at the beginning of the month, (c) advance drawn during the month, (d) total advance in hand during the month, (e) total advance made to the Project Committees, (f) total of actual expenditure adjusted against advance to Project Committees, (g) other expenditures, and (h) balance in hand.[3]

Moreover, the tour diary of the C.O., as noted in chapter iii, was sent to the S.D.O. His tour diary provided the latter with a great deal of information about the *Thana* and the Union Councils' development programmes.[4]

[1] NIPA Staff Study no. 30, p. 38.

[2] Anisuzzaman, *The Circle Officer*, p. 43.

[3] *Circular no.* 44, p. 12.

[4] The following few passages from the diaries of some C.O.s will further illustrate the point:

"Attended the *Thana* Council meeting held in local (Joyapara) high school and discussed various topics. The assessment of development works like minor irrigation scheme, construction of free primary schools and charitable dispensaries was made. Officers and basic democrats responsible for each scheme were asked to complete all projects before financial year was out."

"...attended Tejgaon *Thana* Council meeting. Discussed with the members various subjects including principles of taxation, preparation of budget, maintenance of accounts...and afforestation. Training was also imparted to non-official members of the *Thana* Council in various fields including preparation of budget. The departmental officers spoke on their respective field of works and indicated to me the line of cooperation and

Role of the S.D.O. The S.D.O. played a vital role in the field of rural development though he was not so closely connected with it as the C.O. because he had to look after almost each and every aspect of the administration of the whole sub-division. The nature of his role in the field of community development was already indicated while discussing the role of the C.O. Most S.D.O.s acted as "coordinators, inspirers, advisors, clarifiers, guides, arbiters and prestige givers".[1] As the "Controlling Authority" of Union Councils[2] and as the Chairman of *Thana*

---

coordination required between various departments and basic democrats."

"I went out for inspection of development works done by the Panchupur Union Council—five tube-wells were found sunk and 5 miles of roads repaired...I met the local gentlemen and heard their problems. They apprised me of the pressing need of a maternity welfare centre at Atrai, and some gentlemen were found very anxious to have it and contribute to the best of their mite for this welfare centre."

"...went straight to Potakata to see the progress of excavation of the five mile long canal conducted by the Hasaigari Union Council. Talked to the people who were working voluntarily for the excavation of the canal expected to do immense benefit to the standing *Boro* crops over a large tract of area. This work of the Hasaigari union and in particular, people's enthusiasm displayed in it, is simply laudable."

"Accompanied the S.D.O. to the site of the proposed maternity welfare centre there, where $2\frac{1}{2}$ *bighas* of land was made over to the S.D.O. by way of gift by a local gentleman named Mr. Haji Shafiuddin."

"I accompanied the S.D.O. to Enayatpur in Kasimpur union to see the progress of construction of the model primary school there, and about 50 per cent work was found done."

"Development works in the Union Councils, I have visited so far, are going on in full swing, of course, by community labour on voluntary basis. Collection of taxes etc. by the Union Councils is, however, much less than satisfactory and I advised the Chairmen of the Union Councils and their councillors to start a vigorous collection campaign so as to get at their collection target by the end of the financial year."

(These passages have been quoted in Anisuzzaman, *The Circle Officer*, pp. 27-29, 35-36.)

1 *1st Evaluation Report* (*E. Beng.*), p. 15.

2 In chapter iii we have already noted the extent of enormous powers that the "Controlling Authority" enjoyed. For example, he could quash the proceedings of the Council, prevent the execution of any resolution passed by the Council etc. The Budget of the Council was also subject to his approval.

Councils and of the "Approving Authority" for Union Councils' plans he was in a position to exercise enormous control and influence over the development activities of *Thana* and Union Councils. As he enjoyed enormous powers, position and status, his backing and publicity enormously added to the vigour of the development activities.

We have already noted that the extent of effectiveness of the C.O. depended to a considerable extent on the backing that he received from the S.D.O. But while it was the responsibility of the S.D.O. to extend his support to the C.O., it was also his responsibility, if necessary, to keep him under restraint. It was generally felt that in some places where the members of local councils were not very influential or assertive the C.O.s often tried to impose their decisions on the members in an arbitrary way. It was the responsibility of the S.D.O. to prevent the C.O.s from doing so and to see whether they were properly discharging their duties.

One C.O. told the members of the Evaluation Team of the Comilla Academy "I could not do justice to some projects because of interference from the above...and non-cooperative attitude of Chairmen who get free access to the S.D.O. and even to some higher authorities and exploit the opportunity to defy the C.O."[1] We may draw one of two following conclusions from the above version of the C.O. Firstly, the S.D.O. prevented the C.O. from taking the right steps with regards to some projects. Secondly, the measures which the C.O. wanted to take were not just or suitable and the S.D.O. after having been informed by the members did not allow him to take such measures.[2] Thus, it is obvious that the S.D.O. was required to handle a very delicate situation. He held two different threads in his hands. Firstly, he had to see

[1] *2nd Evaluation Report* (*E. Beng.*), p. 26.

[2] The present writer mentioned the above comment of the C.O. to some officials and non-officials. These two conclusions are based on the impression gathered by him from their views and opinions. It was most likely that the second conclusion was correct because the S.D.O. usually did not turn down the wishes of the C.O. who was his 'own man' in the field of rural development, unless he was sure that the C.O. was doing something wrong.

whether the wishes and desires of the members were in conformity with the general interest and secondly, he had to review the actions of the C.O. Thus, it was generally felt that it was on his correct judgement or decision that the sound progress of rural development depended. In short, he was supposed to watch the activities of both officials and non-officials and to make sure that they took the right steps. A survey of the Comilla Academy found that most S.D.O.s "step in and exercise their authority publicly rather than see a project fail because of poor administration...or local discord".[1]

Role of the D.O. Lastly, we may now discuss the role of the D.O. who as the head of the district had a very vital and important role to play in organising and encouraging the development works. The interests which he showed in development activities and the support and help which he extended to them went a very long way to further the cause of the rural development. In the field of development he was required to provide leadership not only to the officials but also to the people and local representatives. In 1960 the Provincial Administration Commission explained in the following passage the role of the D.O. in the field of development:

> "The District Officer as the strategic link between the people and the government has to fill an important leadership role in the planning and execution of development programmes. He is at once the exponent of government's policies to the people and the interpreter of their needs and requirements to higher authorities. In this particular role, he will now be assisted by the District Council of which he will now be the ex-officio Chairman. It will be the District Officer's initiative, leadership and advice which will impart vigour to all the development plans of the district. The success which he achieves will depend in large measure on the active participation of the people that he is able to secure for this task."[2]

---

1 *1st Evaluation Report* (*E. Beng.*), p. 15.

2 *Pro. Adm. Com. Report*, p. 183. One author held that "In the district the degree of a person's access to the Deputy Commissioner...bears on his social and political influence." Thus the "Deputy Commissioner can provide psychological incentive for social and development activities by making himself more easily accessible to those who have made a significant contribution towards the development of the district." [Mahmood Iqbal, "Deputy Commissioner and Development" (cyclostyled) (A paper presented at the

He was supposed to see that all development programmes in his district were properly planned, coordinated and executed.[1] As the Chairman of the District Council he had a great say in the selection of the District Council projects. One of his main concerns was to see that the District Council plan should not serve the interest of any faction. He tried to bring his pressure to bear on the members so that the District Council plan could reflect the general interest of the district as a whole. But it was not a very easy task because some of the non-official members of the District Council were usually influential and politically oriented. Thus, he had to handle a very delicate situation tactfully and intelligently. As the head of the district and by virtue of his membership of the then Civil Service of Pakistan—the elite of bureaucracy—he was in a more advantageous position than any other official in the district to resist any undue political pressure. The D.O.s who were able to make use of their advantageous position contributed considerably to the cause of the development. In short, on one hand, he was supposed to save the development programmes from undue political interference by making his position strongly felt and on the other hand, he had to keep the politically oriented members in good humour. To a considerable extent his success lied in his ability to maintain a balance between the two.

He did not usually become directly involved in *Thana* and Union Council projects. In regard to these matters it was "his second line officers—the Sub-Divisional Officers—who take charge of the situation being nearest to the scene of action. The role of the D.C. [i.e. D.O.] is generally to guide and supervise the S.D.O.s."[2]

Seminar on Development Administration held at the Administrative Staff College, Lahore, n.d.), p. 4. (The author was a Deputy Commissioner.)]

1 Ghulam Sarwar Khan, "Commissioner and Deputy Commissioner" (cyclostyled) (A paper presented at the Seminar on Development Administration, held at the Pakistan Administrative Staff College, Lahore, n.d.), p. 8. (The author was a high ranking Government official.)

2 A. Rashid, "The Deputy Commissioner in Pakistan—Justification and Role in a Welfare State" (cyclostyled) (A paper presented at the Seminar on Development Administration, held at the Pakistan Administrative Staff College, Lahore, n.d.), p. 11. (The author was a Deputy Commissioner.)

The D.O. is one of the busiest persons in the district and, as noted above, has got to look after different aspects of administration in the district. So it was not possible for him to go into the details of the development administration. In the field of development he was assisted by the Additional D.O. (Development) and the Assistant Director of "Basic Democracies".

One of the important responsibilities of the D.O., the S.D.O. and the C.O. was to see that the local councils receive necessary assistance and guidance from the staff of the technical and other departments.

The Rural Works Programme in West Pakistan: A Comparative Study of the East Bengal Approach and the West Pakistan Approach

The success of the first "province-wide rural works programme" (1962-63) in East Bengal encouraged the Government of West Pakistan to draw up a similar programme for West Pakistan which was put into operation in 1963-64.[1] For this purpose an allocation of rupees 10 crore was made by the government. A conference of the D.O.s was held at Lahore in July 1963 to discuss the 'Comilla Approach.' The Government of West Pakistan decided to launch the programme straightway throughout West Pakistan instead of first carrying out a 'pilot project' on an experimental basis in any particular area.[2] Thus, no 'pilot project' similar to the Comilla 'pilot project' was organised in West Pakistan.

Efforts were made to follow the organisational and functional approach of Comilla as far as possible. But in practice there were many wide differences between the "Comilla Approach", i.e. the "East Bengal Approach" and the "West Pakistan Approach." Moreover, unlike East Bengal no uniform pattern emerged in West Pakistan. Before going into the details of the working of Rural Works Programme in West Pakistan a brief account of the factors which were responsible for such differences between the "East Bengal Approach" and the "West Pakistan Approach" will give us a better insight into the latter Approach.

1 *Pakistan Economic Survey, 1964-65*, p. 218.

2 *Rural Works Programme Evaluation Report, 1963-64* (Lahore, n. d.), p.14. (Hereafter cited as *W. Pak. Evaluation Report.*)

The topographical and the climatic conditions in East Bengal were not similar to those prevailing in West Pakistan. The topographical, the climatic and the cultural conditions were almost uniform throughout East Bengal and most areas, as noted above, had a very high density of population. As a result, the agricultural practices, the rural problems and the nature of development works were also more or less same in all the districts (with some exceptions in Chittagong Hill Tracts district) of East Bengal. Because of such uniformity it was much easier for the Comilla Academy to work out uniform techniques and methods for Rural Works Programme for East Bengal. But, in West Pakistan the topographical and the climatic conditions and the density of population, as noted above, varied widely from region to region. As a result, the agricultural practices and rural problems also varied from region to region. Such a situation in West Pakistan made it indispensable for Rural Works Programme to include a variety of projects ranging, for example, from "sophisticated" buildings and metalled roads in the Punjab to irrigation pumps and "river bed spurs" for reclaiming land for agricultural use in the stony and mountainous Kurram Agency of N.W.F.P. and *Karezes* (underground water channels) and "shingled roads" in the deserts of Baluchistan.[1] The diversity of conditions needed diversity of skills. The methods and practices followed in one region were not suitable for another region. Moreover, some regions especially tribal areas in the N.W.F.P. and Baluchistan were very backward and sparsely populated where the people were not capable of handling such projects.

It was, therefore, decided by the Government of West Pakistan that some departure should be made from the way the projects were planned and implemented in East Bengal. It was thought that one 'pilot project' similar to the Comilla 'pilot project' could serve as a model for whole of West Pakistan only to a very limited extent.[2] It was decided that allowance should be made in varying

[1] *Rural Works Programme for West Pakistan: First Report* (Lahore, 1964), p. 2.

[2] *W. Pak. Evaluation Report*, p. 12.

degrees for the local conditions and circumstances, that no rigid and uniform system for administering the Rural Works Programme should be introduced and that the system which would be introduced must be flexible enough to permit changes and adjustments according to local conditions and circumstances. Only a broad outline was prepared by the government and each district was given a considerable degree of autonomy to work out its own techniques and methods for administering the Rural Works Programme. Enormous discretionary powers were given to the D.O.s, who made the maximum use of them.[1] The *Pakistan Economic Survey* observed that the "Chairman of the District Council, that is, the Deputy Commissioner, is given extensive power over the compilation of the District Programme, for the sanctioning and execution of schemes and for the coordination of the resources of the Basic Democracies' Councils and the technical departments within the district."[2] The D.O. was made the Project Director of the Rural Works Programme in the district.[3]

As no uniform pattern of administering the Rural Works Programme in West Pakistan emerged, the discussion which follows can only be on the broad general pattern of the Programme. In West Pakistan no specific powers were granted to the *Tehsil* Councils which, as noted above, were the counterparts of the *Thana* Councils in East Bengal. But in some districts, (e.g. in Multan district) substantial powers were delegated to the *Tehsil* Councils by the District Councils.[4] In almost every district some powers were also delegated to the Union Councils. The basic idea of the 'Comilla Approach' that the projects of the Union Councils should be executed by the Project Committees was accepted in West Pakistan. In some districts (e.g. Cambelpur district) there was one Project Committee per Union Council which was responsible for the execution of all the projects of the Union Council

1 *Ibid.*, p. 14.

2 *Pakistan Economic Survey: 1964-65*, p. 219.

3 *Ibid.* Also see *Rural Works Programme: Loralai District, 1963-64* (Quetta, n. d.), p. 7.

4 *Third Five Year Plan*, pp. 513-514.

concerned. In these districts the Project Committee was headed by the Chairman of the Union Council concerned. In some other districts (e.g. in Sheikpura district), as in East Bengal, for each project one Project Committee was formed. Again in some other districts both the systems were in operation at the same time.[1] The degree of responsibility assigned to *Tehsil* and Union Councils and Project Committees varied from place to place. A survey of the Rural Works Programme in 1963-64 revealed that "even where the lower councils were granted wide authority their control and the task of supervising the work done by them remained in the hands of the Deputy Commissioner".[2]

Thus, we find that in West Pakistan the D.O. was entrusted with more responsibilities and given more discretionary powers than his counterpart in East Bengal and that while in the latter the government directly gave the *Thana* and the Union Councils fairly substantial powers with regard to planning and execution of projects, in the former the D.O. and the District Council determined the extent to which such powers should be delegated to *Tehsil* and Union Councils.[3] In West Pakistan the district was made the "basic unit of administration in Rural Works Programme".[4]

> "This decision is in contrast with the experience in East Pakistan where the *thana* has become the focal point of the Works Programme. This divergence has its validity in the size of a *thana* in East Pakistan and a District in West Pakistan measured in terms of population.[5]...In the West, physical factors have enabled the Deputy Commissioner to have close contact with Union Councils. In the East, the *thana* is a small compact administrative

[1] *Rural Works Programme for West Pakistan: First Report*, p. 7.

[2] *W. Pak. Evaluation Report*, p. 27.

[3] So far as the Rural Works Programme was concerned the administrative arrangements in West Pakistan were still in a fluid state. In some places more powers were being delegated to lower councils while in other places the powers that were already delegated were being withdrawn because the district authority was not satisfied with the work of the lower councils.

[4] *Third Five Year Plan*, p. 513.

[5] In chapter iii we have already noted that in West Pakistan there were 51 (now 55) districts for a population of 3.6 crores as against 17 (now 19) in East Bengal for a population of nearly 4 crores (1961 census).

unit and its effectiveness is heightened by the remoteness of the district from the Union Councils."[1]

There were several factors which made the *thana* the basic unit of the Rural Works Programme in East Bengal. We already noted that the rural people in East Bengal were relatively more advanced than their counterparts in West Pakistan[2] and that the rural leaders in the former had long experience in administering the affairs of the local councils at the union level.[3] Moreover, the *thana* was large enough to be an administrative unit at which the government could provide trained officers of various nation building departments[4] and at the same time it was small enough to enable the villagers to reach the *thana* headquarters and return to their villages before nightfall[5] and to enable the *thana* level officers to frequently visit the remotest parts of the rural areas. Thus, the *thana* was a level which was sufficiently close to the rural people.[6]

So, in the 1960s the Government of East Bengal decided that the administrative machinery of different nation building departments would be extended up to the *thana* level.[7] And according to this decision the officers of these departments were gradually posted at the *thana* level. The government also took the decision to build a *Thana* Training and Development Centre in each *thana*. And by the middle of 1964, 244 centres were constructed. These centres were designed to gradually accommodate *Thana* Councils, the C. O. and the officers of other departments such as Agriculture,

1 *Pakistan Economic Survey: 1964-65*, p. 219.

2 See above, chap. ii.

3 See above, chaps. i, iii.

4 Decentralisation and Development, p. 3.

5 Gilbert, *op. cit.*, p. 21.

6 In East Bengal there were 411 *thanas* each with an area of about 130 square miles and with an average population of 125000. [*Report on Rural Works Programme* (*E. Beng.*), p. 10].

7 Formerly, as noted in chapter iii, below the sub-divisional level no government departments except police, revenue and registration departments had appointed their officers unless some special circumstance of any particular area warranted such appointment. In each *thana* (which means police station) a police officer was posted with a small police force. The jurisdictions of registration and revenue officers below the sub-divisional level had not always coincided with the *thana* jurisdiction. Before 1962 the jurisdiction of a circle officer had covered 3 or 4 *thanas*.

Animal Husbandry, Fisheries, Education, Public Health, Cooperatives, etc. The purpose of these centres were "to serve as base of extension operations and centres of training for local people. The Government officers will act both as extension workers and teachers here. In addition, these centres will house all kinds of service institutions such as a veterinary clinic, a soil testing laboratory, perhaps a tractor station, a bank and so on."[1] These centres were intended to provide adequate opportunities for demonstration of new methods, new tools, new cropping patterns and the use of better seeds, fertilizers, pesticides etc.[2] Aktar Hameed Khan observed that

> "It affords a means to create in each *thana* of the province a living symbol of needed modernization process. This center can and should dominate the *thana* headquarters in the same way as it has been dominated in the past century by the police station. The new center in no way lessens the importance of law and order but rather it emphasizes the transcendent importance of local development activities in the years ahead."[3]

This new development at the *thana* level made the *thana* town a "community centre" to the surrounding villages.

From the foregoing discussion we find that the *thana*, which was "unique to East Pakistan but does not figure in the West Pakistan programme"[4] was "an effective unit of economic development in rural East Pakistan".[5] In short, we may conclude

[1] *Report on Rural Works Programme* (*E. Beng.*), p. 11.

[2] Gilbert, *op. cit.*, p. 21.

[3] Comilla—US AID Conference Report, p. 23. The first *Thana* Training and Development Center was built in Comilla. Other centers in East Bengal were modelled on it.

[4] Decentralisation and Development, p. 3.

[5] *Report on Rural Works Programme* (*E. Beng.*), p. 11. Some people in West Pakistan also thought that relatively densely populated and advanced areas (i.e. most parts of the Punjab) in West Pakistan the *tehsil* (or the sub-division) should be made the unit of rural development. In 1962 almost similar view was expressed by some authors in West Pakistan. [See Aslam A. Khan, "Role of Basic Democracies in Economic Planning and Development" in *Seminar on Planning and Development*, held at Lahore (Lahore, 1962), p. 57. Malik K.D. Khan, same topic in *ibid.*, p. 65. Hasan Habib, "Preliminary Notes on Decentralised Socialist Economic Planning in Yugoslavia and its relevance to Decentralised Planning under Basic

that while in East Bengal rural development was more decentralised, in West Pakistan it was more centralised at the district headquarters.

Works Programme in Bangladesh

In chapter iii we have noted that the post-1958 system of local bodies (i.e. "Basic Democracies") was abolished in January 1972 by the Government of Bangladesh, that since then appointed official administrators have been performing the functions of these dissolved local bodies as a temporary measure and that in the near future elected local bodies will be established.[1]

As the elected local bodies are not in existence, the following temporary measures[2] are now (mid-1973) followed in respect of Works Programme:

The Circle Officer (Dev.) prepares the union development plan and the *thana* development plan in consultation with the Union Relief and Rehabilitation Committee and the *Thana* Relief and Rehabilitation Committee respectively. These two committees consist of appointed official and non-official members. The union and the *thana* development plans are examined and approved as usual with or without modifications by the *Thana* "Approving Authority" and the District "Approving Authority" respectively. The composition of these "Approving Authorities" i.e. Committees are not different from that of the *Thana* and the District "Approving Authorities" in the 1960s. We have discussed above the various aspects of those Authorities.[3]

While all the plans for *pucca* (metal or concrete) works are executed through the contractors selected on the basis of competitive tenders, those for *katcha* (non-metal or concrete) i.e. earth works are executed through Village Relief and Rehabilitation

Democracies in Pakistan" in *Journal of Rural Development and Administration*, vol. iv, no. 1, Sept. 1964 (PARD, Peshawar), p. 50.]

1 See above, pp. 175-176

2 Circular No. S-XII/IF-6/72/370(145), July 25, 1972, Ministry of Local Govt., Rural Development and Co-operatives, Govt. of Bangladesh.

3 See above, pp. 290-300

Committee as a temporary measure and as substitute for the usual Project Committee. In those areas where no Village Relief and Rehabilitation Committee has yet been formed, the Union Relief and Rehabilitation Committee performs the functions of a Project Committee. Where the total number of the membership of the latter is too large, Sub-Committees are formed for different projects. The Chairman of the main Committee acts as the ex-officio Chairman of all Sub-Committees.

The respective Administrators prepare development plans for *Zilla* Board (i.e. formerly District Council) and *Pourashava* (i.e. formerly Municipal Committee) and submit them to the "Approving Authority" in the Ministry of local Government, Rural Development and Cooperatives.

It is generally felt that when the local bodies will be elected in the near future, they will undertake the responsibility of planning and executing the rural development plans. The Project Committees will be formed by them. Of course, the officials will be required to guide, help and supervise thep lanning and the execution of development projects. The Government of Bangladesh is also encouraging the establishment of cooperatives throughout the country for the purpose of rural development. It is felt that in the future when the local bodies will be elected, necessary arrangements will be made for establishing close and intimate relationship between these bodies and cooperative institutions.

In Pakistan the pattern of Works Programme administration has not undergone any significant change. The system is more or less same as that in former Pakistan.

Development Works of the Nation Building Departments

In Bangladesh and (former and present) Pakistan a considerable volume of development works are also executed solely through the nation building departments. The officers of these departments prepare plans for their respective departments. These plans are executed either by the contractors under the supervision of the departmental officers or by the departmental officers themselves depending on the nature of the works.[1] The volume of development works executed by the nation building departments is much more than that of the development works executed by the local bodies. The most important administrative aspect of the development works of the nation building departments in the district is the coordination of the plans and programmes of various departments by the D.O. which is discussed in the next chapter (vi).

[1] For example, all the works of the Roads and the Building Departments are executed by the contractors under the supervision of and according to the plan prepared by the engineers of these departments, whereas a considerable part of the plans and programmes of the Agricultural Department is executed by the staff of the department.

CHAPTER VI

PROBLEMS OF COORDINATION

Introduction

One of the most important aspects of district administration in Bangladesh and Pakistan is the organisational and functional relationship between the D.O. and other heads of the departments in the district. In chapter iii we have already noted the nature of such relationship.[1] In this chapter an attempt will be made to discuss the problems that are involved in such relationship and their causes.

It has been recognized by the government that besides "a vertical distribution of authority in a straight line of command running from the...[Chief Executive] through the directorates to the divisional and district Officers" (i.e. the divisional and district heads of other departments i.e. directorates), there should be "a horizontal coordination of governmental activities at the appropriate levels".[2] As the district is the focal unit of administration, it has also been recognized that coordination at this level should be very effective.

In view of the fact that the overall development of the district is considered as the product or result of the combined activities of the various nation building departments (as well as other organisations or groups which are also responsible or indirectly connected with development) rather than the sole province of one of them[3], it is essential that the functions of the heads of these departments, who generally work under the control and supervision of their respective central/provincial and divisional heads of the Directorates, should be effectively coordinated.[4] Moreover, without such coordination overlapping and

[1] See above, 119-120. [2] *Pro. Adm. Com. Report*, p. 89. *Cabinet Decisions*, p. 8.

[3] *Speeches of Aktar Hameed Khan in Michigan State University*, p. 10.

[4] In recent years an increase in importance and volume of development works has heightened to an enormous extent the importance of coordination.

duplication cannot be avoided. General administration also requires that the functions of all government departments as well as semi-government agencies should be effectively coordinated.

As the D.O. is the head of the district, he has been recognized as the agency most suitable for undertaking the overall responsibility for coordinating the functions of all government and semi-government agencies operating within his jurisdiction. But if he is to play an effective role as the coordinator it is essential that he should have adequate authority and control over these agencies. No doubt, on paper he has been given, as we shall see below, fairly considerable powers and authority in this respect; but in practice he finds it very difficult to exercise these powers and to play his role as an effective coordinator because there is tension between him on the one hand and other district level departmental heads, strongly backed by their respective central/provincial and divisional heads of Directorates on the other. As a result, instead of an intimate and cordial relationship there exists a very strained relationship between them. Of course, this is not a new problem in the administration of the district. It is, in fact, an old problem, though in recent years the situation, as we shall see below, has deteriorated to an extraordinary degree. A brief study of the problem in the past will perhaps put this aspect of the administration in a better perspective.

British India

During the second half of the last century, it was felt that the D.O. should be relieved of those functions which were of a highly specialised nature and that they should be entrusted to new officers having technical or specialised knowledge. Moreover, the scope of the functions of the government was gradually expanding. As a result, the government began to establish new departments in the district mainly from the third quarter of the last century. Most of the new officers at the district level had their respective heads of directorates at the provincial level. But the D.O., being the head of the district, was also required to "keep in close touch with the activities of these...services in his district and his advice and influence were sought and valued."[1] Although the D.O. exercised general control and supervision over other district level officers, his position in relation to that of the provincial heads of the Directorates was not very clear. There was some vagueness or confusion with regard to the nature of control that he and the provincial heads of Directorates were expected to exercise over these local officers. The confusion was cleared up in 1872 by G. Cambell, the then Lieutenant Governor of Bengal. He was of the opinion that "the local officers of districts have for some purposes had too many masters".[2] He was "anxious" to see that these officers "should not have too many masters and that the head of the district should control the local departments".[3] He made it emphatically clear that it was his "wish to render the heads of districts no longer the drudges of many departments and masters of none but in fact the general controlling authority over all departments in each district".[4] Thus he wanted to "make the Magistrate-Collector...the real executive chief and administrator of the tract of country committed to him and supreme over everyone and everything except the proceedings of the courts of justice".[5] He declared that the provincial heads of Directorates, whom he considered to be "very bad masters",[6] would only "aid, counsel and guide" their respective local officers "without exercising absolute authority over them."[7] Thus the authority and the supremacy of the D.O. was established without any ambiguity.

But with the passage of time local officers gradually became eager to gain independence as far as possible from the direct control of the D.O. and at the same time the provincial heads of Directorates also gradually began to try to exercise more and more direct control and supervision over their respective local officers.

[1] *Memorandum submitted by the government of Bihar and Orissa to the Indian Statutory Commission* (London, 1930), para. 448. (Hereafter cited as *Bihar and Orissa Govt. Memorandum.*) This comment was made while discussing the administrative history of the province.

[2] *Report on the Administration of Bengal: 1871-72* (Calcutta, 1872), p. 64.

[3] *Ibid.*, p. 65. [4] *Ibid.*, p. 66. [5] *Ibid.*, p. 67.

[6] *Ibid.*, p. 67. [7] *Ibid.*, p. 65.

Thus, there was a growing tendency on the part of these departments, which were also gradually expanding, to assert their independence. Thus the "growth and fissiparous tendencies"[1] of these departments gradually began to affect and change the pattern of administration. In 1909 the Royal Commission upon Decentralisation in India noted the gradual weakening of the position of the D.O.[2] and was "emphatically of the opinion that the position of the Collector as administrative head of the district should be recognized by the officers of all special departments".[3] The Commission felt the "necessity for a unifying influence over the various branches of government work in...individual districts".[4] But the special departments continued their efforts to bypass the D.O. as far as possible. It was observed that

> "Although government clung to the principle that the authority of the District Officer must be maintained in all departments, it was obvious that as the departments grew in strength and appointed their own local officers, his advice and control were less needed and the tendency was to transfer the control to local departmental officers...[Of course, these officers] were instructed to keep in touch with and consult the District Officer, and sought his help when they required it".[5]

But in spite of the fact that his contact with and his hold over other departments were less than before, his pre-eminence within his district and his position in relation to district departmental heads were not seriously affected by the changing administrative situation. He could still exercise effective control over them. In "varying degrees the District Officer influences the policy in all matters, and he is always there in the background to lend his support, or if need be, to mediate between a specialised service and the people".[6] But towards the beginning of the 1920s the political and constitutional reforms, resulting from the *Montagu-Chelmsford*

1 *Report of the Royal Commission upon Decentralisation*, para. 487.

2 *Ibid.*, para. 536. 3 *Ibid.*, para. 539. 4 *Ibid.*, para. 539.

5 *Memorandum submitted by the Government of Bengal to the Indian Statutory Commission*, part i (London, 1930), para. 272. (Hereafter cited as *Bengal Govt.'s Memorandum.*) This comment was made while discussing the "Tendency to Departmental Control before the Reform". (*Ibid.*, para. 272.)

6 *Montagu-Chelmsford Report*, para. 123.

Report, "affected district administration in various ways".[1] Many important departments (mainly nation building departments), called "transferred departments", were placed in the charge of Ministers responsible to the Legislative Council in which the majority of the members were elected.[2] The Ministers were inclined to rely more on their respective departmental officers over whom they had direct control rather than on the D.O. over whom they had no direct control. As a result, the importance of the officers of other departments increased. Moreover, political pressures also affected the position of the D.O. The influence of the new Legislative Council "accentuated the tendency to make departmental activities independent of the Commissioner and District Officer, especially in the transferred departments".[3] Thus the transfer of the control of these departments to the Ministers "reduced the scope of his [D.O.'s] initiative".[4] As a result, "On the transferred side of the administration, the District Officer has much less opportunity of influencing policy than before."[5]

But it will be wrong to conclude that these changes materially reduced his position in relation to district departmental heads.

1 *Bengal Govt.'s Memorandum*, para. 275.

2 According to the 1919 Act, the executive authority in the province was divided into two halves: reserved side and transferred side. Thus, all the departments under the provincial government were grouped into "reserved departments" and "transferred departments". The reserved departments were placed in the charge of the Governor in Council (consisting of not more than four members) responsible to the Viceroy of India and to the Secretary of State for India and not to the provincial legislature. The transferred departments were administered by the Governor acting with the Ministers who, as we have already noted, were responsible to the provincial legislature. The Ministers were appointed by the Governor. On the transferred side of the administration he was supposed to act on the advice of the Ministers "unless he sees sufficient cause to dissent from their opinion". (*Simon Report*, vol. i, para. 160.) Thus, on the transferred side of the administration he was a titular head. Of course, under special circumstances he could dismiss the Ministers or dissolve the legislature.

3 *Bengal Govt.'s Memorandum*, para. 276.

4 *Bihar and Orissa Govt.'s Memorandum*, para. 449.

5 *Simon Report*, vol. i, para. 321.

He still remained the most powerful officer and the central figure around whom the whole administrative machinery of the district revolved. It was not possible to ignore him. He wielded enormous power, prestige and patronage[1] which not only enabled him to bring pressure to bear upon other officials but also encouraged or required these officers to seek his help and support in order to promote and accelerate their departmental activities.[2] It was observed that he

> "is still the principal executive agent of government, the one man who can get things done whether it be the repression of an outbreak of disorder, the encouragement of recruiting or even—and this is particularly interesting as it refers to the transferred side—the initiation of a child welfare movement."[3]

But the Government of India Act 1935, which abolished the system of dyarchy and introduced that of provincial autonomy under which there were no "reserved" departments, affected the position of the D.O. to a fairly considerable extent. Previously during the dyarchy period, as noted above, he had not been under direct control of the Ministers. He had been mainly responsible to the reserved side of the administration i.e. to the Governor in Council. But from April 1937, when the provinces became "self-governing", he came under the control of the Minister who held

[1] *Ibid.*, para. 320.

[2] The D.O.'s support for any particular programme or plan could not only easily enlist the support and cooperation of the people but also those of local leaders or elites who in one way or another were dependent on him because he had a great deal of patronage in his hands and was responsible for the maintenance of law and order and the collection of land revenue, two very important aspects of administration in the sub-continent which greatly affected both the people and the local elites. Moreover, his support or help was essential when the cooperation of the officers of another department was necessary. It was also much easier for him to obtain the approval of a higher authority for a project or plan. For example, if the approval of the Ministry of Finance was necessary the recommendation of the D.O. would carry much more weight than that of a departmental head.

[3] *Memorandum submitted by the Government of the United Provinces to the Indian Statutory Commission* (London, 1930), para. 53. (Hereafter cited as *U.P. Govt.'s Memorandum.*) Also see *Simon Report*, vol. i, para. 322, quoted below, chap. vii.

the newly created office of the Home Minister. Usually the Chief Minister himself held this office.

Provincial autonomy also reduced the authority of the Chief Secretary and the Governor whose support and backing had been a very important source of the D.O.'s authority and influence.[1] Of course, the Governor had some discretionary powers.[2]

"In the districts, the change of government was viewed by the former Guardians with feeling resigned and wary."[3] No doubt, the D.O. continued to occupy a very pre-eminent position in the district, to enjoy enormous influence and prestige and to wield large powers of patronage; but they were definitely much less than before. Though the local leaders or elites in one way or another were still dependent on him, their dependence was much less than what it had been before because they were now in a position to bring some political pressure in varying degrees to bear upon him.[4] Thus, the constitutional changes further weakened his overall authority and influence which in turn correspondingly weakened his position in relation to other departmental heads because, as we have already noted, his overall influence and importance and the pre-eminent position within the district not only enabled him to bring pressure to bear upon them but also encouraged them to seek his help or support. His lessening influence over the heads of departments in turn further added to his weakness in this respect, because, as noted above, sometimes a departmental head had had to seek his favour in order to obtain the active cooperation of another departmental head.

It is also generally believed that the hostile attitude of the political leaders towards the ICS who, as noted in chapter iii, held most posts of D.O. further affected the position of the D.O. in relation to other departmental heads. Though the ICSs were now required to work under the supervision of the Ministers they were "not however completely amendable to the discipline and control of the Ministers"[5] because they enjoyed some immunity from the

1 Woodruff, *op. cit.*, p. 274.

2 See below, chap. vii.

3 Woodruff, *op. cit.*, p. 273.

4 See below, chap. vii.

5 N.C. Roy, *The Constitutional System of India* (Calcutta, 1937), p. 240.

direct political control and could seek protection from the Governor against undue political interference.[1] Such special privileges, enjoyed by the ICS, were resented by the political leaders.[2] The impression given by some officers who worked in the pre-partition days, is that in failing to exercise full control over the ICS officers, many political leaders developed a sense of rivalry with them. Moreover, from the earliest period of the nationalist movement the political leaders had disliked or hated the Indian Civil Service because they were of the opinion that it was serving and consolidating the British interest in the sub-continent.[3] Such beliefs considerably influenced and hardened their attitude towards the

[1] See below, chap. vii.

[2] At that time the widely held view was that "Their [ICS] extra-Indian recruitment and the peculiar conditions of their services hardly fit the principle of provincial autonomy." The general view was that "although in theory the provinces enjoy, under the Government of India Act, 1935, autonomy over a large sphere of public administration, it is considerably undermined in practice by the exercise of special responsibility on the part of the Governor and by the enjoyment of special privileges...They are not consistent with the principle of provincial autonomy." (*Ibid.*, p. 240.)

[3] Many national and political leaders strongly criticised the role of the ICS. For example, Jawaharlal Nehru wrote in his autobiography, "if this ability and efficiency are to be measured from the point of view of strengthening the British Empire in India and helping it to exploit the country, the ICS may certainly claim to have done well". He was of the opinion that "There were many earnest members, many with a conception of service, but it was service of the Empire, and India came only as a bad second." He continued to say that "It was not surprising that they had recourse to violence to meet a growing and aggressive nationalist movement. That was inevitable for Empires rest on that and they had been taught no other way of meeting opposition...The ICS were intellectually and emotionally not prepared for what happened...They did not realise that the order they represented was out of date under modern conditions, and that they were approaching as a group more and more the type which T.S. Elliot describes in 'The Hollow Man'." He further added that "so long as the present system prevails, their excellence will be devoted to objects which are not beneficial to the Indian people". He also said that Gokhale had already pointed out many defects and drawbacks of the Indian Civil Service. [*Jawaharlal Nehru: An Autobiography* (London, 1936), pp. 441-444.] In 1957 a member of the National Assembly of former Pakistan expressed almost similar views while commenting on the ICS. (See below.)

ICS. Under the changed constitution the latter continued to be regarded as an instrument of the colonial power. The "new Government [i.e. the Government which was formed in 1937] began with a feeling of distrust; they suspected that the District Officer was more concerned about maintaining his own prestige than about the welfare of his subjects".[1] It is generally believed that their resentment against the ICS made them inclined to be more sympathetic towards the officials of other departments or services. Moreover, the officers of other departments were much more susceptible to political pressures than the ICS—the elite of bureaucracy and the most powerful administrative institution. As a result, the former were liked more than the ICS. Thus, the greater susceptibility of the officers of other departments to political pressures strengthened their position in relation to the D.O. It is generally believed that the Minister's sympathy for the officers of other departments also indirectly encouraged their tendency or desire to make themselves free as far as possible from the control of the D.O. We have already noted such a trend in the dyarchy period. But during the autonomy period, when the Ministers enjoyed much greater authority, their support for or sympathy towards the officers of other departments carried more weight and had greater impact on administration than before.

Moreover, the gradual growth and expansion of the nation building departments which began to add to the importance and strength of the officers of these departments, the increasing volume of works of the D.O. which began to make it difficult for him to take adequate interest in the activities of other departments and the gradual changes in social attitudes and behaviour began further to complicate the problems of coordination.[2]

The D.O., who had exercised at one time his role as the coordinator quite effectively, began to lose effective control over departmental heads in the district. By the mid-1940s the situation had deteriorated to a fairly marked extent. Every department began

[1] Woodruff, *op. cit.*, p. 274.

[2] These factors have had much greater impact since partition. The nature of their impact on this problem is discussed in detail later.

to think "in terms of 'provincialised service' " and made "little attempt to disguise"[1] its determined efforts to go ahead with its own plan and programmes without making any reference to any other departments or to the D.O. All the departments were determined to "hoe their own row".[2] They pursued "their own whim" which resulted in "a test of strength"[3] between the D.O. on the one hand and the officers of other departments backed by their respective Directorates on the other. Both from the point of view of the District Officer himself as well as from the point of view of the efficiency of the administrative machinery as a whole and the welfare of the people, the situation became "thoroughly unsatisfactory".[4] Two years before partition (1947) the *Rowlands Report* observed that

> "The lot of the District Officer, like that of the comic opera policeman, is not a happy one. He is expected to see that nothing goes wrong in his district...He is supposed, to quote from an official publication, 'to compose differences between other officers'...He is regarded as responsible for stimulating the activities of the officers of other departments, but he has no real control over them, and although they are under an obligation to keep him informed of their activities, the extent to which this obligation is discharged depends in most cases on the personal factor."[5]

The Rowlands Committee was "forcibly struck" with the situation and felt that the independent and disconnected activities of different departments reached such "a point of confusion" that some effective steps "must" be taken to "counter the unfortunate results of such uncoordinated action".[6] The Committee became "satisfied that the time has come in Bengal and we do not doubt in other provinces as well, to coordinate all District Development activities under a single administrative head".[7] It held that the D.O. should "build up a combined operations' team" from the officials of all departments and that he should be in "command" of this team.[8] The officers of other departments would remain

[1] *Rowlands Report*, para. 66. [2] *Ibid.*, para. 66. [3] *Ibid.*, para. 77.
[4] *Ibid.*, para. 65. [5] *Ibid.*, para. 65. [6] *Ibid.*, para. 66.
[7] *Ibid.*, para. 67. [8] *Ibid.*, para. 79.

"directly responsible to the District Officers"[1] who would be the "undisputed Head of all Government agencies in his district except as regards the internal administration and technical methods of those agencies".[2] The technical officers would decide "how any particular project is to be carried out ; for instance, how teaching should be given, how a dispensary should be arranged, how tanks should be cleaned, how potato seeds should be stored, and so on. Technical Departments will lay down standards for such activities which the District Officer will be expected to accept."[3] But the District Officer would in fact decide "*what* is to be done, *where* it is to be done and *when* it is to be done. He will also set the time in which it is to be done."[4] A "target will be set for the District as a whole" and the District Officer, "in consultation with the technical heads and local advisors, will work out the manner in which the target is to be attained. He will be at the beginning, instead of only when something goes wrong."[5] Thus we find that the role of the technical officer would be to "suggest ways in which the plan should be shaped from their point of view" and that of the District Officer would be to "modify them in such a way as to ensure that the development of the District as a whole proceed as a really combined operation".[6] The technical officers would "thus be the direct subordinates of the District Officers for what they are to do and for actually getting it done".[7] The report also warned that "specialisation is itself a disruptive force"[8] and thus it should be kept under control. The measures suggested by the *Rowlands Report* were considered by the government to be very useful and they became the accepted principles of the organisational and functional relationship between the D.O. and the district departmental heads. But no effective steps

[1] *Ibid.*, para. 78. [2] *Ibid.*, para. 77. [3] *Ibid.*, para. 76. [4] *Ibid.*, para. 73.
[5] *Ibid.*, para. 77. [6] *Ibid.*, para. 73. [7] *Ibid.*, para. 77.
[8] *Ibid.*, para. 67. The Report quoted two passages from David Lilienthal's book on the "Tennessee Valley Authority" and from Luther Gulick's paper on the Theory of Organisation respectively in support of this view. (*Ibid.*, para. 67.)

could be taken to fully translate these principles into practice because the period between the publication of the report and partition and the period that followed partition were periods of unusual strain and the government faced a vast magnitude of diverse and multifarious problems. Thus, the administrative reorganisation and other similar tasks had to give way to more urgent and important tasks.[1] Later we shall see that in 1960 the Provincial Administration Commission repeated and reemphasised most of these recommendations.

Causes of Further Deterioration of the Problems of Coordination Since Partition

Expansion of Nation Building Departments. The increasing importance of development caused and warranted mushroom growth and expansion of nation building departments.[2] They gradually proliferated and gained both importance and confidence. As a result, the officers of different nation building departments became "more and more independent and conscious of their own

[1] In chapter iii we have already discussed these problems in some greater detail in order to explain why most recommendations of the *Rowlands Report* could not be implemented though they were considered very useful and indeed essential.

[2] For example, formerly the Directorate of Communications and Buildings was in the charge of one Chief Engineer. With the increase in the volume of development works, the Government in East Bengal gradually began to bifurcate this Directorate and in the early 1960s it was finally split up into two Directorates under two separate Chief Engineers: Chief Engineer (Roads) and Chief Engineer (Buildings). The number of Superintendent Engineers had been also gradually increased and two Superintendent Engineers—one for roads and one for buildings—had been appointed in each division. In the early 1950s only one Executive Engineer had been in charge of Chittagong division consisting of five districts. Later two Executive Engineers—one for roads and one for buildings—had been gradually posted in each important district in East Bengal. In those districts (e.g. Dacca, Chittagong, Lahore, Karachi, etc.) where enormous development works had been executed, several Executive Engineers had been appointed. Formerly, Overseers had usually been in charge of the construction works in a sub-division; an Assistant Engineer had been appointed only in a very important sub-division. But later, Assistant Engineers had been gradually appointed in most sub-divisions. This Directorate is being further expanded in both Bangladesh and Pakistan.

importance...The effectiveness of district officers and the unity of district administration have been impaired by the growing size and importance of individual departments, each anxious to emphasise its own entity."[1]

The problem became further aggravated by their conviction and belief that the D.O., being a generalist administrator, did not have the necessary specialised or technical knowledge to perform his role as the coordinator of the nation building departments. In consequence they fail to appreciate the fact that if one of the heads of these departments were given the responsibility of coordinating the activities of all the departments, other departments would not want to accord him that higher status which was essential for exercising some control over various departments, that he had specialised or technical knowledge only concerning his own department and not about other departments and that the D.O., who was concerned with the administrative, economic, social and political aspects of planning, would not usually interfere in the technical or specialised aspects of their work.[2] Of course, sometimes the high handedness of some generalist administrators also added to the hostility of the officers of other departments.

In the face of determined opposition on the part of the officers of nation building departments, some District Officers also became reluctant to assert their authority over the recalcitrant officers of these departments in order to avoid a strained relationship. Moreover, such reluctance of some D.O.s was reinforced by the fact that they were not directly responsible for the activities of other departments and that they were overworked.[3]

1 This comment was made in the mid-1950s. (*The First Five Year Plan*, p. 102.) Later, as we have already noted, these departments further expanded. Thus, the above mentioned tendency became more accentuated.

2 According to government instructions the District Officer was not supposed to interfere in the technical aspects of the functions of the Nation Building departments. (See below.) We have already noted that the *Rowlands Report* also made this point clear.

3 See above, chapter iii.

Lessening Influence and Prestige. We have noted that though his legal position remained unchanged, his overall influence and prestige began to wane long before partition. Since partition this process became further accelerated. His authority and influence were being eroded by the social and political transformation.[1]

Political Hostility. Although after partition the political leaders ceased to regard the central Civil Service as the instrument of the British,[2] many of them still maintained their hostility towards it as the lineal descendant of the Indian Civil Service.[3] Another

[1] See below.

[2] We have already noted that politicians usually used to regard the ICS as the instrument of the colonial power. (See above.)

[3] The following biased over-statement about both the ICS and the CSP by a member of the National Assembly of former Pakistan, who had also been a central Minister in former Pakistan for some time, will illustrate the nature of the attitude of at least a section of the political leaders towards the CSP: "The old Civil Service of India was supposed to be the steel frame of the British Empire...though it was neither Indian nor civil nor service in any sense...the Indian Civil Service was necessary from the point of view of the British...who wanted to rule this country...Nobody can deny that it was the basic principle which operated in the minds of the members of the Indian Civil Service. Even though recruitments were made from this country at [sic] a progressive basis in order to take the people of this sub-continent into confidence but [sic] scrupulous care was taken to see that the members of the ICS did not get mixed up with a native [sic] and they were made to feel, even though they were natives, that they were superior to natives. They belonged to the soil, yet they were taught to revolt against everything that belonged to the soil. That was the tradition of this service. Therefore, Sir, the question which now arises is whether after the creation of Pakistan, such a background of mentality should be allowed to continue and flourish in this country. Certainly, the old ICS believed in isolation, in working in their ivory tower detached from the people so that just on the mountain they could deliver a sermon as to what was wrong regarding the trivial affairs of the native people. Now, it was accepted that this mentality, this outlook, would change in a free country because the requirements of a free country are definitely of a different nature from the requirements of a ruling power... I was referring to the Civil Service that we have continued in the old tradition of the Indian Civil Service. Our Service has been formed and drawn up by the best talent in the country, yet what is the training that is imparted?. . . They are being taught, in the same tradition of the British days, to live in the D.C.'s [i.e.D.O.'s] bungalow in the Punjab and the D.M.'s [i.e. D.O.'s] bungalow on the hill top in East Pakistan. They are inaccessible people...

very important cause of such hostility was that though the position of the CSP in relation to political leaders was not as strong as that of the ICS and although, unlike the latter, the former did not enjoy protection against undue political interference, yet it was still the most powerful service in former and present Pakistan (the members of which, as we have already noted in chapter iii, occupied most key administrative and executive posts), which in comparison with other services was in a better position to offer some resistance to political pressure and interference.[1] The Vice Principal of the Pakistan Administrative Staff College, Lahore, wrote that the political leaders

> "were all busy pulling down the deputy commissioner and rendering him into a man of no consequence. This was mainly because in the freely corrupt exercise of patronage over public funds and other resources of the country, the deputy commissioner was virtually an obstruction rather than an aid to the political bosses. On the other hand the techni-

---

Is that it you are going to train your own people to hate your own civilization and culture? Are you going to give to the country out of this manufacturing laboratory of the Civil Service Academy at Lahore some more anglicised officers? If you are really keen that a person should be taught to become an adapt [sic] in what dresses should be worn on what particular occasions, and if you want to convert the youth of our country into connoisseurs of drinks and cocktails, then what the training would lead to? [sic]...So, if you really want to bring up a band of old ICS people stiff necked with a bow-tie and know how to bow and say 'How do you do?', then bring some from England. They will be better people with better integrity. Why not do that?" N.A.P.Deb., Feb. 15, 1957, vol. I, no. 2, pp. 433-435.

[1] Some authors even went to the extent of believing that the political leaders had been almost completely unable to exercise adequate control over the Civil Service of Pakistan. [See Goodnow, *op. cit.*, pp. esp. 131-133; Khalid Bin Sayeed, *Formative Phase of Pakistan* (Karachi, 1960), pp. 401-3; Khalid Bin Sayeed, "The Political Role of Pakistan's Civil Service" in *Pacific Affairs*, vol. 31, no. 2 (June, 1958); Albert Gorvine, "The Civil Service under the Revolutionary Government in Pakistan" in the *Middle East Journal*, vol. 19, no. 3 (Summer, 1965); Hamza A. Alavi, "Constitutional Changes and the Dynamics of Political Development in Pakistan (cyclostyled) (A paper read in the postgraduate seminar on Political Institutions at the Institute of Commonwealth Studies, University of London), p. esp., 4, para. 12.]

cal departments in the districts were less resistant and therefore better liked".[1]

The Report of the Provincial Administration Commission also held that from the Ministers the "separatist tendencies of these departments received encouragement".[2]

Deteriorating calibre. The general belief that the calibre and the academic standard of most D.O.s of post-partition period were much less than those of most D.O.s of pre-partition days, lowered the prestige of the former since partition. We have already noted in chapter iii that the percentage of Muslims in the Indian Civil Service was very low (only 9 %) with the result that an insignificant percentage of ICS officers opted for former Pakistan. After partition most of these ICS officers were mainly posted in the Secretariats. Thus, many posts of D.O. were filled by the members of the Provincial Civil Service many of whom, it was believed, perhaps could not have become D.O. if there had not been a sudden shortage of ICS officers. So, they were not held in great esteem either by the officials or by the non-officials. Of course, many of them were gradually replaced by the newly recruited CSP officers. But, as we have already noted in chapter iii, the calibre and the academic standard of the CSP (and also of the PCS) seriously deteriorated since partition. Both officials and non-officials widely believed that most persons who became CSP could not have become ICS in pre-partition days. The intellectual superiority of the ICS had been hardly doubted in pre-partition days. In those days the belief that most ICS officers had been exceptionally brilliant, had been one of the most important factors responsible for the great esteem in which they had been usually held. But the CSP did not enjoy that advantage because they were not considered as an intellectually superior class. On the contrary, the members of some other services especially those of Engineering Services sometimes

1 A. Qayyum, "The Role of the Deputy Commissioner in Basic Democracies" in M. Rafiq Inayat (ed.), *op. cit.*, p. 134.

2 *Pro. Adm. Com. Report*, p. 3.

claimed that they were more brilliant than the members of the Civil Service of Pakistan. This belief mainly resulted from the fact that since the war an increasing number of students took up courses in science or technology after having passed the school final examination. Most CSP officers came from the Faculty of Arts. But this argument did not justify their claim because they overlooked the fact that only brighter students (with a few exceptions, of course) of the Faculty of Arts could get into the Civil Service of Pakistan. Of course, for our present study it is not important to examine whether or not the members of the technical services were more brilliant than the CSPs. But it is important to note that this belief of the members of the technical services influenced their attitudes towards the CSPs, making them feel that they were being dominated or bossed by a class which lacked intellectual superiority to them. Especially in status oriented society[1] in which people usually had a false sense of pride and attached undue importance to social or professional or family status, degrees, the class or division obtained in examinations and so on, such impressions bred serious contempt and hostility.

Departure of the British. Moreover, the departure of the British also had an indirect impact on this problem. "It is, in many ways, easier to respect authority exercised by a complete alien than when it is in the hands of someone from a neighbouring region or a different caste."[2] One might argue that in British India all D.O.s were not British. But it should be noted that in pre-partition days those D.O.s who had not been British had also enjoyed considerable prestige and influence, though less than those enjoyed by their British colleagues. One of the most important reasons why they had enjoyed considerable prestige and influence had been that most of them had belonged to the Indian Civil Service—a service which had usually been identified with the British. This had been one of the most important factors which had contributed to the great importance and influence of this service. Of course, some PCS D.O.s had definitely enjoyed

[1] See above, chap. ii.

[2] Morris-Jones, *Parliament*, p. 36.

less influence and prestige than those enjoyed by ICS D.O.s. But as the very office of the D.O. itself had carried great prestige and influence (one of the important reasons for which had been that it had usually been manned by the ICS), the PCS D.O.s of pre-partition days also could exercise greater influence than that exercised by the PCS D.O.s in post-partition period.

Possible Impact of Social Tension on Administrative or Intra-Bureaucratic Relationships. In the following few sentences we may summarise what we have said in chapter ii about various aspects of social tension:[1] This part of the world, which was a traditional society, has been undergoing transformation especially since the end of World War II. Old and orthodox values are being increasingly resented by the younger generations. The older generations in turn resent such resentment. The society is horizontally and vertically stratified into a number of social classes, the values of each of which are usually widely different from those of many other classes. The members of the same class or somewhat similar classes dogmatically believe that their values are the right guides to right practices and behaviour in society and are unable to understand or appreciate the values of other social classes. The privileged position of the "upper" classes is being increasingly resented by other classes. Such resentment is in turn again resented by the "upper" classes. The class consciousness or loyalty considerably influences social interactions. There is an increasing feeling of frustration among most people who are not satisfied with the position or rank that they hold or the influence and prestige that they enjoy or the income that they earn. And there is a desire among most people to show off, to flout or disregard or undermine in one way or another the authority of those above and to make their position felt by others. Thus, as we have also mentioned in chapter ii, it is perhaps to be expected that the prevailing social conditions undermine the respect for and the influence of authority and discipline in society, encourage irresponsibility and create an environment which is conducive to the growth of parochialism,

[1] See above, chap. ii, pp. 69-76.

particularism and anomy with the result that the people become self-centred, contemptuous and abusive, lack tolerance, patience and mutual respect and understanding, show arrogance and indulge in irresponsible utterances and criticisms.

It is to be expected that such behaviour and attitudes in society at large not only indirectly influence bureaucratic behaviour and attitudes towards the people but also indirectly influence intra-bureaucratic behaviour and attitudes. Thus it was not unlikely that increasingly deteriorating administrative or intra-bureaucratic tension in post-partition period was partially the result or rather an extension of social tension. The prevailing social environment was probably one of the factors which played a role in undermining the respect for and the influence of discipline within the bureaucracy and the pre-eminence and authority which the D.O. and the central civil service traditionally enjoyed from the time of the introduction of the present system of administration in the sub-continent. Class or group consciousness or loyalty, which, as just noted above, influenced social interactions, was perhaps also reflected in service or department consciousness or loyalty which, in fact, influenced or determined the nature of intra-bureaucratic relationships and attitudes. The members of other services or departments were very conscious of the differences that existed between their official status and that of the D.O. and the CSPs. The relatively higher and privileged position that the latter (D.O. and CSPs) occupied in the administrative set up and the enormous prestige and influence that they, being the top administrative and executive officers, enjoyed in the status oriented society was being strongly and bitterly resented by the former. Such resentment was in turn strongly resented by the latter. Such a complicated situation became further aggravated by the desire of most officers (both CSPs and other officers) to show off and to make their position and authority felt. Moreover, the impression of the officers in some nation building departments that their contribution to national development was "much more" than that of the latter, further added fuel to the fire of their hostility towards the latter and resulted in frustration.[1]

Professor Morris-Jones' following comment on the Indian situation was equally pertinent to the situation in former Pakistan:

> "The inability to 'get on' with the other man, the reluctance to accept authority...the preference among politicians for splits rather than compromises, the tendencies among the educated class to indulge in unconstructive and unreasonable criticism--all these are closely connected, and they play an important part in influencing, for example, the relations between governments and oppositions".[2]

Professor Morris-Jones made this comment while discussing the impact of social behaviour on Indian politics. In applying this comment to our present study the words "politicians" and

[1] One might argue that service or department consciousness should also result in serious clashes between other services. But in practice service or department consciousness did not usually result in such clashes mainly because official status of most of the higher services were more or less same, none of them had any general or supervisory control over other higher services and they performed their functions more or less separately. Moreover, their hostility towards the D.O. or CSPs, who were regarded by them as "common enemy" brought them close to one another. But such service or department consciousness encouraged them to go ahead with their respective programmes or plans without making any reference to other departments. Such separatist tendencies also make it indispensable that there should be some one above them—preferably a generalist administrator who could coordinate their functions.

The clash at the local level between the D.O. and the departmental heads was, in fact, only a part of the bigger clash between the Civil Service of Pakistan and other services. Such a clash subjected the whole administration of (former and present) Pakistan—central, provincial and local to a serious strain and reduced its efficiency to a considerable extent. Broadly speaking, the officials in (former and present) Pakistan were divided into two groups—the Civil Service of Pakistan on the one hand and other services on the other hand. They were in a head on collision with each other. Of course, the Provincial Civil Service (PCS) was definitely different from and subordinate to the Civil Service of Pakistan. The members of other services admitted that all PCS officers did not hold higher or privileged position. But they argued that those PCS officers who were promoted to the rank of the Sub-divisional Officer or the D.O. or Deputy Secretary or Joint Secretary or Secretary or some other 'cadre' or 'listed' posts were, in fact, upgraded to a higher or a privileged position.

[2] Morris-Jones, *Parliament*, p. 36.

"governments and oppositions" could be replaced by the words "officials" and "District Officers and departmental heads" or "the Civil Service of Pakistan and other services" respectively.

No doubt, in British India the social factors also had influenced in varying degrees, administrative interactions or relationships. But in British India their impact had not been considerable for reasons given below: Though social transformation had began long before World War II, it became accelerated to a considerable extent since the war. In consequence, its enormous impact was increasingly felt since then. Moreover, several other factors—the impression that the Indian Civil Service consisted of brilliant persons, the presence of the British, less importance and less expansion of other departments, comparatively less political pressure or interference etc. (discussed above)—which had added to an enormous extent to the importance and influence of the D.O., had indirectly acted as counter forces against the impact of social factors and thus had minimised the extent of such impact.

Nature of the Problems of Coordination in Post-Partition Period.

We have already noted that (pp. 328-338) from the second half of the last century the changing situation had gradually begun to affect the position of the D.O. vis-a vis district heads of departments and that by the mid-1940s it had weakened his position as the coordinator of their functions to an appreciable extent. After partition, this process became further accelerated as a result of the factors discussed in the preceding section (pp. 338-347). By the second half of the 1950s it became absolutely clear that there was a "disinclination on the part of the development representatives in the field to accept District Officer's supervision"[1]. It was felt that

> "District Officers, speaking generally, have played but a minor role in the development programmes thus far...there has been a noticeable lack of coordination and unified planning at the district level among the various elements of the programme. This is not to say that district officers and their staff have not been cooperative; on the contrary they almost invariably lend every assistance to the development departments on call".[2]

---

1 Gladieux Report, p. 82.

2 *Ibid.*, p. 81.

A tendency was "growing to bring the district officer less and less into development planning".[1] The "independent and disconnected activities of government...led to a situation"[2] in which the departments were operating "along parallel and uncoordinated lines"[3] and each of them was "going its own way without considering its work as a part of the overall scheme of government".[4] It was felt that

> "There was virtually no coordination of governmental activities, except in the Cabinet, which was at too high a level to be of much use in the problems of day to day administration. The tendency to "compartmentalisation was particularly noticeable in field operations in the... District. While the ...District Officers were supposed to be responsible for coordinating the work of other departments, their authority suffered continuous erosion and they ceased to exercise any effective control over them".[5]

Thus we find that the situation became worse by the end of the 1950s. In July 1959 the Chief Secretary to the Government of East Bengal wrote a circular letter[6] to all the officers concerned in which he strongly emphasised the necessity and importance of firmly reestablishing the authority of the D.O. as the coordinator of the functions of other departments. He directed that all departments except the judiciary must extend the "maximum amount of cooperation" and "all assistance" to the D.O. who was "responsible for the work of all departments" and that his instructions must be carried out by the department concerned. He also pointed out that all the departments should "work as a team" under his guidance and supervision. Finally, he directed that the D.O. must submit to the government[7] quarterly reports

[1] *First Five Year Plan*, p. 102. [2] *Pro. Adm. Com. Report*, p. 98.

[3] *Ibid.*, p. 183. [4] *Ibid.*, p. 3. [5] *Ibid.*, p. 3.

[6] Home (G.A. and Apptt.) Department's Memorandum No. 4239-G.A., July 29, 1959. The present writer was told that in November 1959, a similar letter had been written by the Chief Secretary to the Govt. of West Pakistan.

[7] i. e. to the Home Department (G.A. & Apptt. branch) in the Secretariat. In the early 1960s this branch became, as noted in chapter iii, a separate department called Services and General Administration (S. & G.A.) Department.

regarding the working of other departments and that in his fortnightly report he would also mention their activities. He ended his letter with the following words: "The purpose of these instructions is to promote team spirit and to make a coordinated drive to accelerate the development of the country in every sphere with a view to achieve the well being of the people".[1]

The Provincial Administration Commission, which made a survey of the situation towards the end of the 1950s, took a very serious view of the problem and held that there was "urgent need of coordinating governmental activities at district...level".[2] For this purpose it made the following recommendations which (even the style of expression) were, in fact, almost entirely based on the Rowlands Committee's recommendations:

> "To discharge the essential role of coordinator, the District Officer... should become the captain of a combined operation team of...officials of various departments. [It also pointed out that he should not]...meddle in technical aspects of a programme or the internal administration of other departments. Nothing should be done to destroy departmental responsibility in the various sectors...The District Officer will not, therefore, be concerned as to how a particular project should be carried out; for instance, how teachers are to be trained, how a dispensary should be run, how potato seeds should be stored, and so on. All this will be the concern and responsibility of the staff in the technical departments. On the other hand, it will be for the Head of the District [i.e. D.O.] to decide how many schools or dispensaries should be provided and where, or what seeds are needed and where they are to be distributed."[3]

It further held that it was the responsibility of the district departmental heads to consult the D.O. "in all important matters affecting the welfare of the people"[4] and to provide him with necessary reports, files and papers wanted by him. For this purpose it was essential that the fact that the D.O. was the head of the

[1] Home Department's Memo No. 4239-G.A., July 29, 1959.

[2] *Pro. Adm. Com. Report*, p. 98.

[3] *Ibid.*, pp. 98-99. Thus we find that there are striking similarities between the ideas and the style of expression of the *Report of the Provincial Administration Commission's* and those of the *Rowlands Report*. (See above, p. 337.) It indicates that the authors of the former were profoundly influenced by the ideas and views of the latter.

[4] *Ibid.*, p. 99.

district should be made known and clear "unambiguously" again to them.[1]

The report also held that in the confidential reports to the government the D.O. should record his remarks on the activities of the officers of other departments under the following four headings: (a) integrity, (b) cooperation with other departments, (c) relations with the public, and (d) interest shown in development.[2] The report recommended that these remarks should form part of the permanent service records of respective officers.

On June 23, 1960, the central cabinet accepted the view and recommendations of the Provincial Administration Commission almost in toto.[3] At the Governors' conference[4] held in March 1961 the government decided that henceforth the D.O. would write an annual confidential report on the activities of each district departmental head, that he should record his remarks under the following three headings: (a) "the general behaviour of the officer concerned", (b) "his cooperation with other departments, and his relation with the public", and (c) "the interest shown in development work", that he would send the report to the divisional head of the officer concerned with a copy of the report to the Divisional Commissioner. They would forward the report to the government for inclusion in the permanent service record called "character roll" of the officer concerned, with their "own remarks if any".[5] But in August 1961 (i.e. after less than one and a half years only), the central government was reported to have changed its mind and decided to divest the D.O. of the power to write annual confidential reports (to be included in "character roll") on the

1 *Ibid.*, p. 99. 2 *Ibid.*, p. 100. 3 *Cabinet Decisions*, pp. 8-9.

4 We have already noted in chapter iii that the Governors' conferences were usually held in the central capital, and that the President of former Pakistan, the Governors of the provinces and the members of the central Cabinet attended these conferences.

5 Govt. of East Bengal, Home (G.A. & Apptt.) Department's Memorandum No. GAVIII/Con. 158 (40), dated Dacca, May 1, 1961. This memorandum was sent to officers concerned in order to inform them of the decisions taken in the Governors' conference and to direct them to take the necessary steps in pursuance of this decision.

activities of the officers of other departments.[1] It was decided that such annual confidential reports would be written by the respective divisional level officers of the Directorates. At the same time the central government declared that the D.O. would continue as the head of all governmental agencies operating within his jurisdiction, that he in that capacity would direct and coordinate their functions that he would have the right to report to the Divisional Commissioner any failure or inefficiency on the part of any officer to carry out his duties or obligations to him, that he would send his comments on their activities at least once a year to the Divisional Commissioner and that "in the event of an officer being adversely reported upon"[2] by the D.O., the Divisional Commissioner in conjuction with the divisional head of the department concerned, would enquire into the matter and then would take necessary remedial measures.

In early 1962 the Provincial Re-organisation Committee submitted its report. In its report the former repeated all the recommendations of the Provincial Administration Commission except one—i.e. the writing of the annual confidential report—and also recommended a few more measures:[3] It should be made clear to other departments that the District Officer had the authority to inspect all works and projects of every department, to suggest measures for acceleration of their progress, to inspect any office in the district and to call officers into conference for the purpose

1 The Central Govt. to the Provincial Govt., letter no. 27/CF-2/59-IV, August 1, 1962. It was not clear as to why the central government had suddenly decided to divest the D.O. of the power to write annual confidential reports on the activities of the officers of other departments. It might be that the pressures of other departments which had very strongly resented the power of the D.O. to write such confidential reports, or some political reasons or both, had led the central government to take such a sudden decision.

2 *Ibid.*

3 *Report of the Provincial Re-organisation Committee*, part ii, p. 6. This report remained silent as to whether the D.O. should be given the right to record his remarks on the activities of district departmental heads in confidential reports, probably because the central government, as we have noted above, had already taken negative decision in this respect.

of coordination and review of all the branches of administration. "The attendance of such a conference should be made compulsory."[1] It further held that if a D.O. felt that the continuation of a particular officer in his district was not desirable on grounds of inefficiency of the officer concerned or for other reasons, then his request for the transfer of that officer should be disregarded only with the approval of the Divisional Commissioner.[2] The government accepted these recommendations in toto and sent the necessary instructions to officers concerned.[3]

All these notifications and circulars failed to change the situation for the better. A few passages may be quoted below to illustrate the point. In October 1964, it was stated in a circular letter issued by the S. & G.A. Department, Government of East Bengal that

> "the quarterly reports[4] are not being submitted to Government regularly by all the Deputy Commissioners, mainly due to the default of some Departments in the Districts in furnishing in time the requisite material about their activities...the needed amount of cooperation is not forthcoming so much so that in one district other departments were even reluctant to place their transports at the disposal of the Deputy Commissioner during the visits of Heads of States.[5] It appears that the Govern-

---

1 *Ibid.*, p. 6. 2 *Ibid.*, p. 7.

3 Additional Chief Secretary's letter No. IC-20/62, May 18, 1962, S. & G.A. Department, Govt. of East Bengal. The present writer was told that almost exactly similar letter was sent by the Government of West Pakistan to officers concerned. We have already noted that since 1959, the administration became more and more centralised (chapter iii). As a result, many steps taken by the governments of former East and West Pakistan were similar. The measures recommended by the Provincial Reorganisation Committee and later accepted by the government were not novel. In British India the District Officer had enjoyed these powers and privileges and could exercise them effectively especially before the introduction of the Government of India Act of 1935.

4 We have already noted that in 1959 the Chief Secretary directed the District Officers to submit quarterly reports on the development works done by different departments. (see pp. 348-349.)

5 We have already noted in chapter iv that during emergencies—flood, cyclone, famine, earthquake, etc.—or during the visits of national or foreign dignitaries, or for some other administrative purposes (e.g. election) the District Officer has the full authority to requisition not only of the transport or

ment instructions for collective and coordinated work to accelerate development of the country are not being fully observed."[1]

In the following passage, a Member of the Board of Revenue mentioned some instances that he had come across when he had been Divisional Commissioner:

"One D.C. [i.e. D.O.] wanted a report from the Executive Engineer of the district. He added one more item to the usual proforma. The Executive Engineer refused to supply that information on the grounds that his Superintendent Engineer [i.e. the divisional head of the department] had asked him not to supply the information beyond the prescribed proforma. There was some hitch. I [i.e. Divisional Commissioner] myself had to intervene and I was surprised to find that a senior officer of the C & B [i.e. Communications & Buildings] Department was creating a hitch over a very small matter. Somehow or other they were under the impression that this was unwanted interference by the D.C. in their autonomy. I had to tell them that the Executive Engineer was bound by the Govt. circulars to comply with the D.C.'s order. Ultimately they had to comply but certainly not with an open mind. Then again one D.C. wanted to know the progress of construction of a sugar mill from the Manager who refused to supply the information on the grounds that he would require the order of the Chairman of the EPIDC [i.e. the then East Pakistan Industrial Development Corporation] to comply with the request. The D.C. had to write to the Secretary to the Provincial Govt. [i.e. Secretary to the Ministry of Commerce and Industries] who asked the EPIDC to supply the information wanted by the D.C. One D.C. wanted to know the progress of construction of an embankment in a flood affected area. This was refused. After a good deal of trouble the Executive Engineer had to supply the information."[2]

In the meeting of the Secretaries' Committee, held on June 23, 1965, it was again observed that

"the Deputy Commissioners are not receiving the amount of cooperation, originally envisaged in the government instructions. Without adequate

---

other possessions of other departments, but also the services of the officers of these departments. In British India District Officers could exercise these powers more effectively.

[1] Memorandum no. GAVI-O-11/61/64, Dacca, 9 Oct., 1964. (S. & G. A. Department, Govt. of East Bengal). At the end of the memorandum the Government again instructed the officers concerned to cooperate with the D.O.s.

[2] A member of the Board of Revenue to the Govt. of the then E. Pakistan, letter no. 4-CSR/65, March 9, 1965.

cooperation from the local officers, it is not possible for the Deputy Commissioner to discharge his functions as chief coordinator of governmental activities at the district level...There are instances where officers of the Directorates have flouted the authority of the Deputy Commissioner and deliberately non-cooperated with them. [The problem was] ...how to make the Deputy Commissioner more effective in his role as chief coordinator in his district."[1]

It was held that necessary instructions should be again sent to the officers concerned. On July 27, 1965, the Additional Chief Secretary wrote a circular letter to the officers concerned in which he held that the government "would like to re-emphasise that Deputy Commissioners shall be generally responsible for the work of all Departments...functioning within their jurisdiction."[2] In this letter and in another letter[3] written on the next day, i.e. on July 28, 1965, he discussed the matter in detail and emphasised the fact that for better administration it was indispensable that the D.O. should be an effective coordinator. He also repeated almost all the previous instructions which we have already noted. He also directed that henceforth the D.O. instead of sending a quarterly report, would send a half-yearly report to the government. In spite of the fact that from time to time government sent repeated instructions to the officers concerned, the situation did not improve.[4] It was widely felt that the then situation was in no way better than what it had been a few years back.[5] Some even thought that it had further deteriorated.

[1] Minutes of the meeting of the Secretaries' Committee (E. Beng.) on June 23, 1965 (cyclostyled), pp. 2-3.

[2] Additional Chief Secretary's letter no. GAVI-148/64-889(38), Dacca, July 27, 1965 (S. & G. A. Department, Govt. of East Bengal).

[3] Govt. of East Bengal, Services and General Administration Department, Additional Chief Secretary's letter no. GAVI-148/64-890, Dacca, July 28, 1965.

[4] The same was the situation in West Pakistan. So far as the problems of coordination was concerned, there was no significant difference between district administration in East Bengal and that in West Pakistan.

[5] The present writer had some contact with some persons who were familiar with this problem. He formed this impression from the views expressed by them.

It was generally believed that the central Cabinet's decision to divest the District Officer of the power to write annual confidential reports on the activities of district departmental heads had a very adverse effect on this problem.[1] The very fact that favourable or unfavourable comments of the D.O. in the annual confidential report on the activities of an officer would become part of his "character roll", upon which his future in the government service depended, would have made him realise that any irresponsible behaviour or uncooperative attitude could affect his career to a considerable extent. Moreover, it would have created a sense of accountability to the D.O. High ranking administrative officers felt that the D.O. should be again given the power to write annual confidential reports on the activities of the officers of other departments.

Of course, as we have already noted (p. 351), he could report against an officer of another department to the Divisional Commissioner; and in the event of such a complaint, the latter conducted an enquiry into the matter in conjuction with the divisional head of the department concerned. But such complaints and the resulting enquires, did not carry the same weight as his comments in the annual confidential report would have carried because such comments, as we have just noted, would have formed part of the "character roll" of the officer concerned. Moreover, the instances of non-cooperation were so numerous that "very few D.C.s will go on reporting to the Divisional Commissioner against officers of other departments...Some D.C.s reported but departmental officers got the full support of their organisations [i.e. Directorates] at all levels."[2] The major reason for such support

[1] When commenting on the fact that the District Officer had been divested of the power to write confidential reports on other officers, the Secretaries' Committee also argued that "while the Deputy Commissioners are still left with the responsibility of supervising and coordinating the functions of the officers of other departments, they have been divested of the necessary power to ensure their cooperation". (Minutes of the meeting of the Secretaries' Committee, p. 6.)

[2] The letter (no. 4-CSR/65, March 9, 1965) of a Member of the Board of Revenue in East Bengal.

was that the officers of Directorates (ranging from the Heads to junior officers) wanted to maintain "what they describe as complete autonomy or prestige of their departments".[1] The Directorates always considered the District Officer's supervisory authority over their officers as "an unwarranted interference with their functions".[2] The Directorates and the associations of various services[3] not only resented the authority of the District Officer but also that of the Secretariat which was mostly manned by the generalist administrators. Thus when the whole bureaucracy was divided into two hostile camps—the generalist administrators on the one hand and the officers of Directorates on the other hand—it was very difficult to ease administrative tension and to maintain administrative discipline.

The D.O. found it extremely difficult to get an officer of another department transferred from his district though according to the government circular he was supposed to enjoy this privilege.[4] In British India, especially before the introduction of the provincial autonomy (1937), the D.O. could have any officer easily transferred from his district. Even during the period of provincial

[1] *Ibid.* [2] Minutes of the Secretaries' Committee's meeting, p.3.

[3] Every service had its own association—e.g. Agricultural Service Association, Doctors' Association, Engineers' Association, etc. The last two associations included both officials and non-officials. In the event of serious clashes between generalist administrators and other officers, sometimes these associations also came forward in support of their respective members. The Civil Service Association was in a rather disadvantageous position in that respect because not only these associations but other professional groups (e.g. lawyers) and politicians were also hostile to the Civil Service because CSP people, as we have noted, were regarded as a privileged class. No doubt, they occupied an advantageous position in the whole administrative machinery and could offer, relatively speaking, stronger resistance to any pressure. If these advantages were viewed from another angle they could be also regarded as disadvantages in some respects because they aroused jealousies and hostilities of other departments and professional groups. Such jealousies and hostilities enabled the officers of other departments, the members of different associations and professional groups to develop a "we" feeling. Thus an association or department usually enjoyed the sympathy or support of other associations or departments. On the other hand, the CSP officers, though most powerful officers, played a lone hand.

[4] See above, pp. 353-354.

autonomy, it had not been so difficult for him as it was in the 1950s and 60s.

Here it may be pointed out that in British India when the head of a Directorate went to a district on tour he was under the obligation according to government instruction, to pay a courtesy visit to the D.O., and to discuss matters of mutual interest.[1] This visit used to remind the district head of the department that the position of the D.O. was much higher than his. In the course of their discussions, sometimes the D.O. and the head of the Directorate discussed the ability or efficiency of the district head of the department concerned. Usually the head of the Directorate found it necessary to take the comments of the D.O.into consideration because in the interest of his own department, as noted above, the support and cooperation of the D.O., who enjoyed enormous influence and prestige in his district, were essential. The same reason, in fact, reinforced the desire of the head of the Directorate to pay such courtesy visit. The instruction (issued in British India) that the head of the Directorate should pay courtesy visits to the D.O. was (and is) still officially valid, but in practice the central or provincial or divisional head of a Directorate usually did (and does) not bother to take note of that.[2]

Some Concluding Comments

It was generally felt that the problem of coordination would not be solved only by sending repeated instructions to the officers concerned unless strong disciplinary actions were taken against district departmental heads for violation of these instructions or for maintaining an uncooperative attitude. But at the same time it was also felt that it was very difficult to take such strong disciplinary actions because, as already noted, the whole

[1] A well-known British ICS officer Sir Percival Griffiths (*op. cit.*) with whom the present writer discussed this problem held that the utility of such visits had been enormous.

[2] In order to reemphasise the necessity of such visits, the Secretaries' Committee observed in 1965 that the "Heads of Directorates while visiting the divisional, district and sub-divisional headquarters should make it a point to meet the Commissioner, the D.O. and the S.D.O., as the case may be." (Minutes of the meeting of the Secretaries' Committee, p. 8.)

bureaucracy was divided into two hostile camps and such actions would be bitterly resented by the Directorates and the associations of various services.[1] Moreover, administrative sluggishness and mismanagement coupled with political factors also made it difficult to take prompt and strong actions.[2]

Both Bangladesh and Pakistan have inherited all the problems of coordination at the district level. The nature of these problems and their causes are same as those in former Pakistan. What has been said in the preceding pages is applicable without any modifications to Bangladesh and (present) Pakistan. Of course, in Bangladesh, as noted above[3], the structure and classification of public service system will, perhaps, undergo fairly considerable change in the near future. Most probably the number of public services will, perhaps, be reduced drastically and an integrated and much simpler system of public service will be introduced. But it will not, perhaps, solve the basic problem even to a limited degree in view of the fact that the tension between the generalist administrators on the one hand and the specialists (i.e. engineers, doctors, agricultural scientists, etc.) and the officers of particular departments (e.g. police) on the other hand, will continue. Moreover, other causes of the problems of coordination, which we have discussed in preceding pages, will also continue simultaneously. Therefore, no appreciable change is possible unless some positive and effective measures, as mentioned above, are taken.

We, therefore, find that as a result of administrative tension district administration in Bangladesh and Pakistan is subjected to a considerable strain and its efficiency is thereby

[1] The present writer did not come across or was not told of any instance of strong disciplinary action against any officer of another department for violation of the above mentioned instructions or for maintaining an uncooperative attitude.

[2] It is widely felt that since partition the efficiency of administration has been seriously deteriorating. We have already noted the impact of political factors on the relationship between the D.O. and the officers of other departments.

[3] See above, p. 189.

reduced and that the District Officer, whose authority remained almost unchallenged during the early part of this century, is now facing a serious challenge to his authority even from within the administration. In fact, his position vis-a-vis district departmental heads is materially reduced. In the next chapter (vii) we shall find that he is now facing equally serious challenge to his authority from outside the administration, i.e. from the political sector.

CHAPTER VII

DISTRICT ADMINISTRATION AND POLITICS

Nature of Politics At Central/Provincial Level : Some General Reflections[1]

1947-58. Though the parliamentary form of government was in operation during the first decade of the post-partition period, a responsible government, in the strict sense of the term, did not emerge in former Pakistan.[2] The extent of popular participation in the government was insignificant. Of course, it may be rightly argued that

> "government by the people is everywhere a myth and [that] large scale popular participation in government may in no case be the thing that matters...But some degree of responsibility to the people and some amount of genuine discussion of proposed policies...are inescapable features of a democratic regime. And Pakistan...displayed little of either."[3]

Several factors, discussed below, were responsible for this situation : Pakistan politics was characterised by "splintering and

[1] At the beginning of this section of the chapter it may be mentioned that no attempt will be made to discuss in detail the nature of politics at higher levels. Only a very brief account will be given in this section which is, in fact, intended to serve as a background to our main discussion (i.e. the discussion of district administration vis-a-vis politics) in this chapter.

[2] The term 'responsible government' is commonly used in various ways, but they may be reduced to "three main kinds of uses". Firstly, it is "responsive to public demands and movements of public opinion". Secondly, "it involves the concept of duty and moral responsibility". Thirdly, "it is accountable to a body of elected representatives for what it does". [A.H. Birch, *The Idea of Responsible Government* (An inaugural lecture delivered at the University of Hull on May 2, 1962), pp. 4-6. Also see A.H. Birch, *Representative and Responsible Government* (London, 1964), pp. 17-21.] In former Pakistan the institutional devices that were essential for creating a responsible government were no doubt present; yet the political system, as we shall see below, seriously lacked the above-mentioned characteristics or qualities. In fact, a spirit of responsibility did not develop among the politicians.

[3] Morris-Jones, *Political Quarterly*, p. 236.

multiplication of political parties"[1] which were again fractured into factions and sub-factions. The multiplicity of parties and factions was mainly the outcome of the fact that political interactions were profoundly and overtly influenced by personal, factional, communal and regional (including district) interests[2] of the politicians and that one of the most important elements in Pakistan's politics was "the little knots of politicians each held together by one leading person's influence".[3] There was a tiny collection of these leading persons who were the key figures in the arena of power struggles in Pakistan.[4] They "played for position, employed slogans almost at random and without scruple and... swung their followers behind the adopted course. They sometimes created organisations called parties. . .But the formation of parties and their disintegration...ceased to have meaning in terms of politics."[5] As a result, most politicians lacked party loyalty or discipline, did not develop any corporate spirit and were divided among themselves[6] and frequently crossed the floor of the House. They did not have a mass following and were reluctant to address themselves to the electorate and to face election. During this period the only elections to assemblies were those in the Punjab, Sind and East Bengal in 1951, 1953 and 1954 respectively.[7] They grew "thoroughly accustomed to the bargaining behind closed doors",[8] started a "ruthless scramble for power"[9] and "engaged themselves in political strife".[10] They violated the principles and

[1] Goodnow, *op. cit.*, p. 207.

[2] Exploitation of one region by another region caused and accentuated regionalism in many places.

[3] Morris-Jones, *Political Quarterly*, p. 235.

[4] The present writer owes the concept of arena to F.G. Bailey, *Politics and Social Change: Orissa in 1959* (Berkeley, 1963), chapter 10 (conclusion).

[5] Morris-Jones, *Political Quarterly*, p. 236.

[6] Goodnow, *op. cit.*, p. 79.

[7] G.W. Choudhury, *Democracy*, pp. 62 (Punjab), 64 (Sind), 57 (East Bengal).

[8] Morris-Jones, *Political Quarterly*, p. 237.

[9] G.W. Choudhury, *Democracy*, p. 115; also see chapters ii, iv, v.

[10] Omar, *op. cit.*, p. 51.

conventions of parliamentary democracy with impunity. Undue interference and active participation in the game of politics by the Head of the State, who enjoyed enormous powers but, according to conventions, was supposed to be politically neutral and a titular head in the parliamentary form of government, further aggravated the situation and seriously disturbed whatever balance that existed between political forces. He, in fact, became the real arbiter of Pakistan's politics.[1] Moreover, some politicians with bureaucratic background (as well as some high-ranking officials), who formed powerful knots and who were usually in close alliance with the Head of State,[2] further complicated the game of politics.[3] Another important characteristic of Pakistan politics was that the centre exercised enormous control over and frequently interfered in the provincial affairs and politics.[4] Such control and

[1] The summary dismissal in 1953 of Nazimuddin, the Prime Minister, who had the support of the great majority of the members of the Parliament, the dissolution of the Constituent Assembly and the appointment of so-called 'Cabinet of Talents' in 1954, the forced resignation of Shurawardy, the Prime Minister, in 1957 (He demanded that Parliament should be summoned, in order to see whether he commanded the support of the majority, but his demand was rejected.) and finally the abrogation of the 1956 constitution and the proclamation of Martial Law in 1958 by the Head of the State, are some of the examples which demonstrate the nature and extent of the powerful role that the Head of the State played in the politics of Pakistan. (For various aspects of his role, see Callard, *op. cit.*, chapter iv; Sayeed, *Formative*, chapters viii and xv.)

[2] Since 1951, the office of the Head of the State was held either by a former civil servant or by a former army officer.

[3] The following comment of Professor Braibanti on several new countries (including former Pakistan) in Asia is pertinent: The "competition for power between the new nationalist leaders, who were typically politicians or lawyers, and career administrators, who appeared to remain neutral during independence movements, was a problem...this problem resolved itself, sometimes by domination of one elite, sometimes by absorption of parts of one elite into the power structure of another. The whole administrative [as well as political] apparatus creaked under the strain, which was worsened in Pakistan, Burma and Ceylon by unstable political conditions." (Braibanti, *Modernisation*, p. 173. Various aspects of the problem of such competition in Pakistan are discussed in Sayeed, *Formative*, chapter xiv, Sayeed, *Pacific Affairs*, pp. 131-145; Goodnow, *op. cit.*, pp. 67-103.)

[4] Sayeed, *Formative*, chapters ix, xii, xiii.

interference, which often caused change in or of the provincial government and accentuated the tension between various parties or factions, became an added source of political complication especially in the province and impeded the natural flow of the political processes. Moreover, in West Pakistan, as noted above in chapter ii, the *Zamindar* feudal class, who, in fact, held the key to politics, and the *Ulema* (religious leaders), who were militant religious fanatics and who raised a ceaseless clamour for making Pakistan a theocratic state, were seriously disturbing elements in the political process of West Pakistan.

The interactions of all these factors created a situation or environment which was conducive to and, in fact, resulted in political chaos, confusion and instability of the worst nature. The Cabinets, which were uneasy coalitions of representatives of a number of factions, were short-lived. The Assembly met infrequently and was "in a position only slightly more privileged than the public".[1] The members of the Assembly as well as of the Cabinet, who were either too eager to remain in office or too ignorant fully to realise the gravity of their responsibility or too cynical to devote much time to deciding important policy matters, exercised very inadequate control and supervision over the administrative hierarchy unless their own interests required them to do so.[2]

For the first time a general election throughout Pakistan was due to be held towards the end of the 1950s. It was generally believed that the election would, at least partially, break the pattern and let in a cleansing breath of change in the politics of the country. But in October 1958, the army *coup d'etat* halted all political processes. The 1956 constitution was abrogated, the National and the Provincial Assemblies were dissolved, the central and the provincial Cabinets were dismissed, the political parties and activities were banned and Martial Law was declared.

Post 1958 Period. From late-1958 to early-1962 the country was governed by an autocratic system under Martial Law Regulations and all political activities remained almost completely

1 Morris-Jones, *Political Quarterly*, p. 236.

2 Goodnow, *op. cit.*, p. 205. Also see Omar, *op. cit.*, p. 51.

suspended. The political system under the second constitution, promulgated in March 1962, may be described as a "constitutional autocracy".[1] The President and the members of both the National and the Provincial Assemblies were indirectly elected by an electoral college ("Basic Democracies"), the members of which could "be bribed and intimidated...the popular vote has no relevance to the elections".[2] Under the 1962 constitution "the legislative arm of the government is a rubber stamp, the executive virtually untramelled".[3] The President and the provincial Governors enjoyed enormous powers and authority. The Ayub regime, which had "distaste for the politicians and the political processes",[4] in fact, controlled and guided the flow of the political processes in former Pakistan.

Even when the 1962 constitution was promulgated, article 173 continued the ban on the formation of political parties. But in view of a strong popular demand that such ban should be waived, it was later withdrawn in July 1962.[5] But the "political parties have remained weak and divided in Pakistan"[6] and the Ayub regime's "'polity without politics' is designed to keep them so."[7] Moreover, as was the case in the pre-1958 period, the predominance of a few leading political figures and the personal, factional and

[1] "Pakistan: A Special Report" in *The Times* (London), April 6, 1968. (Hereafter cited as *The Times' Special Report*.) Also see Sayeed, *Political*, chap. v.

[2] *The Guardian* (London), Nov. 14, 1968. In these sentences, the correspondent of *The Guardian* was referring to the general views in the country against the Ayub regime. For the editorial comment in *The Guardian*, see below, p. 365.

[3] Neville Maxwell in *The Times* (London), Nov. 14, 1968. Also in *The Times* (London), March 26, 1968, it was similarly observed that the Assembly in Pakistan was "no more than a rubber-stamp legislature".

[4] *The Times' Special Report*.

[5] Saleem M. Qureshi, "Party Politics in the Second Republic of Pakistan" in *The Middle East Journal*, Autumn 1966, vol. 20, no. 4, p. 459.

[6] *The Times* (London), March 26, 1968. Also in *The Times* (London) of November 14, 1968, it was similarly stated by Neville Maxwell that the "political parties have remained generally small, sterile and divided".

[7] *The Times* (London), March 26, 1968. Within the "rump party" (*The Times' Special Report*), which supported the Ayub regime, there were also many factions.

regional interests of the politicians also caused splits in the parties and profoundly influenced the political interactions. The following comments on political parties were pertinent:

> "Politics in Pakistan has never been based upon philosophy or programme; it has been almost always confined to and a prisoner of personalities. Ever since partition, there has been no other motive of alliances than personal gain and soon after the political game could be played again [i.e. when Martial Law was lifted], partisan politics reverted to its normal centers of gravity."[1]

The political parties "for the most part [were] not much more than cabals around particular—and now usually aged—leaders or regional groupings".[2]

The army *coup d'etat*, the Martial Law administration and finally the constitutional autocracy did not remedied the political maladies. They rather worsened these maladies. The control that was exercised on the political processes caused serious frustration which in turn often resulted in political irresponsibilities of a much more serious nature. "For Pakistan, the answer lies in the replacement of 'basic democracy' by something more representative and freer from corruption."[3]

Post-1971 Period. In the post-1971 period a clear pattern of politics has not yet emerged in Bangladesh and Pakistan. In the former, the party in power won a landslide victory in the last general election, held in March 1973. Almost all the members of the Parliament belong to the party in power with the result that it is in a very firm and comfortable position. Of course, it is generally believed that there are two powerful rival groups or factions within the party. Opposition parties are very weak and divided. In Pakistan the ruling party in the centre also commands the support of the majority of the members in two provincial legislatures (Punjab and Sind). Already a fairly good number of members have defected from it. Sharp differences of opinion within the party are quite pronounced. In two other pro-

[1] Saleem M. Qureshi, *op. cit.*, p. 472.

[2] Maxwell in *The Times*, Nov. 14, 1968.

[3] The editorial comment in *The Guardian* (London), Nov. 14, 1968.

vinces (N.W.F.P. and Baluchistan) no party has clear majority in provincial legislatures. There are considerable differences of opinion between the party which has single majority in these provinces and the ruling party in the centre. Interferences in the affairs of these provinces by the central government is strongly resented. In these provinces there are considerable chaos and confusion and political agitation is taking a serious turn. Opposition parties throughout Pakistan are becoming more and more powerful. It is often reported that force and violence are used to crush oppositions. It is also generally belived that from behind the scene the army is also playing a dominant role in the political game in Pakistan.

District Administration and Political Life

Before 1947. In a review of *Asian Bureaucratic System Emergent From the British Imperial Tradition*, it was observed that five Asian countries, including former Pakistan, "have had to make the change from a bureaucracy which was responsible only to itself, to one which retains its initiative but is answerable to democratic [perhaps more appropriately speaking, political] processes"[1] In this chapter it is primarily intended to examine the nature and extent of this change in Bangladesh and Pakistan. But the enquiry should also take into account "the extent to which the process had begun before" partition.[2]

Generally speaking, in British India upto 1921 "government had been, in its essential, at one with the civil service. The I.C.S. had been a great ruling corporation...He [the I.C.S. officer] had been the system of government, and, in the ultimate analysis, the government itself."[3] But the Government of India Act 1919, which, as noted above, had a far-reaching constitutional and political impact of considerable importance, substantially changed the pre-eminent and unique position of the ICS, which was now required to perform its functions in an altered, now political

1 Philip Mason's review of the above-mentioned book in *Pacific Affairs*, vol. XL, nos. 3 and 4, fall and winter, 1967-68, p. 347.

2 *Ibid.*, p. 347.

3 Rai, *op. cit.*, p. 124.

environment. The style of working of the administration both at the higher and the local levels underwent certain changes.

> "The effect of the constitutional changes of 1921 on district administration may be described as the effect of the creation of a new power, the power of a Legislative Council [[1]]...it has brought political influences to bear on district administration and has thereby...changed the position of the old district and divisional authorities, modified the attitude of local self-governing bodies and started a process of change in the attitude of the people towards Government."[2]

Before 1921, the D.O. and his subordinates had enjoyed, generally speaking, the advantage of being the only channel of communication from the district to the provincial headquarters. But now, especially on the transferred side of administration, they were no longer the only, though still the main channel of communication. In the changed situation, the politically oriented local leaders were in a position to "influence the government directly or indirectly through the Legislative Council, instead of through the District Officer".[3] Moreover, in comparison with the past, the D.O. and his subordinates could now exercise less control and influence over the affairs of the local bodies because of the fact that with "the exception of union boards, these bodies are now more subject to political influence than before".[4]

In short, we may say that during the diarchy period, which witnessed "a contraction of the influence of the local officers both in relation to Government and in local affairs",[5] the position of the D.O. "altered in several respects; and he has now neither so large a sphere of control nor has he quite so much freedom within the sphere that is left to him".[6] The questions asked in the legislature also "made even the remotest district officer conscious of the limitations on his power".[7] But in spite of such limitations,

[1] We have already noted in chapter vi that the majority of the members of the Legislative Council were elected.

[2] *Bengal Govt. Memorandum*, para. 275.

[3] *Ibid.*, para. 275.

[4] *Ibid.*, para. 279.

[5] *Ibid.*, para. 276.

[6] *U. P. Govt.'s Memorandum*, para. 48.

[7] Mason, *op. cit.*, p. 347. In his review article, Mr. Mason has not drawn any distinction between the situation in the diarchy period and that in the

he still remained the most powerful and influential person in the district. The Simon Commission observed in 1930 that "no changes or adjustments are likely to alter the central fact that the District Officer must remain a very important person, the embodiment of effective authority and the recourse to whom the country turns in time of difficulty and crisis".[1] (Though in comparison with the past the position and the authority of the D.O. in Bangladesh and Pakistan have weakened to a considerable extent, this comment of the Simon Commission is still valid in some degree.)

During the provincial autonomy period, as noted in chapter vi, the political authority was not only given more powers but also fairly adequate control over the whole administration of the province with the result that political pressure and influence on district administration correspondingly increased.

In pre-partition days, though political pressure was brought to bear on the bureaucracy, it could usually resist serious political interference in administration because when interference threatened to damage administration, the local officer could approach the Governor of the province, who was British and non-partisan, and solicit his help. "The Governors were always ready to protect the services under their discretionary powers from improper conduct of Ministries, which any way impinged against the principles of the Covenants the officers had signed or the Government Servants' Conduct Rules."[2]

Later we shall see that in Bangladesh and Pakistan undue political interferences in district administration have become rampant.

1947-58. In the post-47 period the D.O. and other local officers became more susceptible to political pressures[3] and the politically

provincial autonomy period. His comment, in fact, applies to both the periods in varying degrees.

1 *Simon Report*, vol. i, para. 322.

2 *Report of the Sargodha District Board Election, 1952-53* (*Leghari Report*) (Lahore, 1954), para. 68.

3 Braibanti, *Civil Service*, p. 274.

oriented local leaders, who had access to the leading members of the party or parties in power or to the Ministers, gained considerable influence and importance.[1] After partition, some increase in political pressure on district administration was quite natural and inevitable. But on many occasions, political pressures often amounted to undue political interference in normal and day to day administration.[2]

Men contesting an election would consider the money spent and effort put in as "an investment from which they expected to draw dividends in the shape of benefits by putting pressure on the party in power".[3] At the same time, Ministers and party bosses, anxious to consolidate their position and to strengthen their hold on their followers, often went out of their way to compel the bureaucracy to grant special favours to their henchmen.[4] It was observed that "political interference in the public services in

[1] Here it may be mentioned that in Bangladesh and Pakistan, as in India, the "man in the district who has access to a minister, is a man of power. The man who can 'get things done'—who can get permits, licences, and loans, who can obtain house allotments, admission of students to schools, who can influence appointments to district institutions—becomes powerful in the district...[such a man has] considerable influence over administration." [Paul R. Brass, *Factional Politics in an Indian State* (London, Berkeley, 1965), p. 219.] In the mid-50s, a West Pakistan author observed that "more weight seems to be given to the reports of the representatives of political parties than the Deputy Commissioner's opinion. (Aslam, *op. cit.*, p. 48.)

[2] Here the term 'undue political interference' may be briefly defined. Those political actions and pressures which prevent the members of the bureaucracy from acting impartially and require them to further the party or factional or individual interests of the politicians by means of their official powers and influence, may be regarded as undue political interference in administration.

[3] *Report of the Constitution Commission, Pakistan, 1961* (Karachi, 1962), para. 24.

[4] The following examples will further illustrate this point. In West Pakistan the district authority on one occasion was ordered by the Ministry to issue gun licences without any enquiry to a considerable number of persons "who would otherwise not have been permitted to bear arms". This unusual step was taken "mainly to please some of the members of the Legislative Assembly". (*Ibid.*, para. 22.) Here it may be mentioned that according to law the gun licences are supposed to be issued with great caution by the

[former] Pakistan [especially in West Pakistan] attained a pitch".[1] The officials were "victimised or favoured in the personal interests, or on the recommendation, of the Ministry's supporters, leading to complete demoralisation of the services".[2] The officers who tried to resist undue political pressures had to face such difficulties as "transfer to a remote district, passing over promotion and general disfavour".[3] As a result, although in the early post-partition period the bureaucracy strongly endeavoured to resist, and sometimes was successful in resisting, undue political pressures and although it increasingly resented such pressure, with the passage of time the strength of such resistance began to weaken. Some began to yield to such pressures in despair and with feelings of resignation and weariness; some remained defiant although they had to face many difficulties; some took advantage of the situation and became opportunist. Thus the *Leghari Report* observed that while the "officers with principles go down suffering... the unprincipled, who are ready to pander to the wishes of their political masters and prostitute themselves, receive positions of vantage, promotion, loaves and fishes".[4] Of course, it is also true that from the early post-partition period a fairly considerable section of the higher bureaucracy for their part tried to defy or flout the wishes of the politicians whom they considered as men of less

---

D.O. after having made due enquiries about the conduct and character of the persons concerned.

In East Bengal one of the Ministers, not even in charge of the Home Ministry, called the D.O. and the S.P. of Dacca to the Secretariat and requested them to release on bail an accused person who had been arrested on the charge of theft and rioting. Bail was ultimately granted. It created strong resentment among the administrative and executive officers. (*East Bengal Police Committee's Report, 1953*, para. 20.) Of course, in the first decade of the post-partition period, such interference was very rare in East Bengal.

Also see below the examples of undue political interference in the administration of Sargodha district in West Pakistan. (pp. 371-375.)

1 Tinker, *Ballot Box and Bayonet*, p. 90.

2 *Report of the Constitution Commission*, para. 24.

3 Tinker, *Ballot Box and Bayonet*, p. 90.

4 *Leghari Report*, para. 68.

calibre and mere amateurs.[1] As a result of all these factors, a tension developed between the higher bureaucracy and the politicians resulting in irresponsible behaviour and attitudes on the part of both.

The following brief account of undue political interference in the administration of the Sargodha district in the Punjab will give us some idea as to the nature and extent of such interference especially in West Pakistan and will further illustrate some of the points just made: From 1951 onward the administration in that district came very much under political influence because the powers and influence of Mia Md. Daultana, who became the Chief Minister of the Punjab in 1951, began to grow rapidly under the patronage of the late Liaquat Ali Khan, the then Prime Minister of former Pakistan, with the result that some of the friends and the relatives of the former, especially the Qureshis of Sabwal "came gradually to wield immense power in Sargodha district".[2] The Qureshis were led by Md. Saeed Qureshi who was married to Daultana's sister. In the *Report of the Sargodha District Board Election, 1952-53* (*Leghari Report*) it was observed that

> "evidence brought on the record has proved conclusively that the administration in Sargodha district was virtually under the thumb of Mr. Muhammad Saeed Qureshi...It could almost be said that he came to occupy the position of a virtual super governor of Sargodha district through his intimate connection with Mr. Daultana and through his real brother, Mr. Zakir Qureshi, P.C.S., being private secretary to Mr. Daultana...Close affiliations with Sh. Fazal Piracha, Minister of Resettlement and Colonies, of Bhera...also added to his influence... no officer could possibly remain for long in the district if he became a *persona non grata* to Mr. Said Qureshi. In fact, short exit was made of those incurring his displeasure, as a phone call had only to be put through to Mr. Zakir Qureshi, who found little difficulty in 'settling' [i.e. transferring] the officer."[3]

---

[1] Omar, *op. cit.*, p. 51. *PARD* (*Peshawar*) *Report No.* 9, p. 10.

[2] *Leghari Report*, p. xix.

[3] *Ibid.*, para. 9. The following are some examples of 'political transfer' of officials: On the eve of the provincial assembly election in the Punjab in 1951, Mr. Niaz Ahmed, CSP (formerly an ICS officer), who was the D.O. of Sargodha and who was the most senior D.O. in the province, was trans-

While conducting and supervising elections, the D.O. and his subordinates were supposed to be completely impartial and fair. But in West Pakistan they usually failed to play a neutral

---

ferred out of the province because the Qureshi group found him too difficult to tackle according to their wishes. He was transferred only a week after he had delivered a speech at a public meeting attended by important officers, *Zamindars* and politicians. "In this speech he gave out the warning that not only would he be absolutely impartial in the elections, but he would deal promptly with any officer taking part in politics, and would at least suspend him, whatever the eventual outcome may [sic] be." (*Ibid.*, p. xix.)

A person was murdered in Sargodha district and it was alleged that some Nawaz Khan Lahri, a prominent *Zamindar* and a supporter of Saeed Qureshi, was behind the murder. The Superintendent of the Police (S.P.) was approached by Saeed Qureshi with the request that the name of Nawaz Khan Lahri should be removed from the police record and that no action should be taken against him. The S. P. refused to interfere. Saeed Qureshi contacted Daultana government over telephone. Next day the S.P. received transfer order. He was directed to hand over the charge to his immediate subordinate at once without waiting for the arrival of his successor. (*Ibid.*, pp. xix-xx.) "Saeed Qureshi bragged about having 'settled him'...Nothing is more demoralising for the Services than for transfer orders to follow quickly in the wake of their refusal to comply with improper expectations or illegal requests of local politicians." (*Ibid.*, para. 68.)

Ataur Rahman Khan (*op. cit.*) has given in his book a revealing account (pp. 167-187) of the fact that his political followers often unreasonably requested him, when he was the Chief Minister of East Bengal to transfer those officers, whom they did not like, out of their areas. If they could get an officer transferred or prevent the transfer of an officer they felt that their prestige was enhanced in the eyes of the people. They argued that as the officers were transferred in the public interest (it is an official procedure to write in every transfer order that the officer concerned is transferred in the public interest) and as they were the "protector" or "guardian" of public interest, it was their "duty" to speak on the question of the transfer of an officer. (*Ibid.*, p. 177.) Once a very powerful political leader, who was in fact one of the king-makers of the party and who was very well-known in East Bengal and West Pakistan wrote to Ataur Rahman Khan "on receipt of this letter, transfer that District Magistrate immediately. Otherwise, I shall resign" from the party. (*Ibid.*, p. 173.) Once Ataur Rahman Khan transferred an officer from a district to a Secretariat department. But the Minister, who was in charge of that department, did not want that officer to join his department. He told Ataur Rahman Khan that the officer concerned had been the S.D.O. of his home subdivision and that he in his capacity as the S.D.O. had ill-treated him. Later, on the request of Ataur Rahman he allowed the officer to join his department. (*Ibid.*,

role during various elections mainly because of undue pressure that was brought to bear on them by the party in power.[1] For example, the D.O. and other officers in the Sargodha district were compelled to indulge in malpractices and to overlook gross irregularities so that Daultana's henchmen (who were mainly headed by Saeed Qureshi) could win the District Board election in 1953.[2] The Sargodha District Board Elections "turned out to be

---

p. 177.) Ataur Rahman's book is not an one-sided study. He has also bitterly criticised typical bureaucratic and authoritarian attitudes and behaviour of the officials. (*Ibid.*, pp. 123-167. Also see above, chapter ii.) Here it may be mentioned that, as we shall see below, the number of political transfers and political interferences in administration in East Bengal were much less than those in West Pakistan.

1 Also see below (p. 377, fn. 5) the comment of Khalid B. Sayeed.

2 For example, "under the influence of Mr. Fazal Ilahi Piracha", the Minister for Resettlement and Colonies, the Additional D.O., Sargodha, rejected the nomination papers of the candidates opposing the Qureshi group "on frivolous grounds". [*Leghari Report*, para. 25(2).] The S.P. "openly" helped the candidates of "Qureshi's party" and "persuaded the people to vote for the said party". [*Ibid.*, para. 25(1).] At the polling centre laws were violated and there were gross irregularities in the management of the polling centre. (*Ibid.*, paras. 39-57.) The *Leghari Report* observed that the "Court of Inquiry into the contemporaneous Punjab Disturbances of March, 1953 [see *Munir-Kayani Report*], found little evidence of effective steps being taken to deal with law breakers owing to interference at the political level. In the present enquiry, I have found not only that no effective steps were being taken, but open breeches of rules and foul play at elections were connived at by the two District Officers [i.e. the D.O. and the S.P.] at the helm, whose duty it was to come out and assert the authority of the law. Evidence on the record...as well as failure on the part of the Deputy Commissioner to organise surprise visits to the Polling Stations, notorious for flagrant abuses, and the absence of even one bold action to show that he or the Superintendent of Police realised their responsibilities, tends to show that they had both allied themselves with the big bosses [i.e. the bosses of the party in power]. They appear to have chosen the easy downhill road, instead of trudging the difficult 'uphill road'." (*Ibid.*, para. 62.) In another place the *Leghari Report* further observed that these two officers (i.e. the D.O. and the S.P.) "were considered fairly good officers in pre-partition days...[But they] have not been able to live up to their past reputation owing to the difficult circumstances obtaining under Mr. Daultana's regime which was determined to ensure successes of its henchmen at all costs in Sargodha District Board Elections...Ch. Abdul Hamid [i.e. D.O.] has brought to my

a standing disgrace in the whole history of District Board elections".[1] Here it may also be mentioned that the Daultana government, which "had drawn up a plan of winning the local election by hook or by crook"[2] had even amended the District Board Election Rules, 1936, in the early 1950s in such a way as to make it easier for the Daultana regime to win these elections. By virtue of this amendment the powers of delimitation of constituencies, which hitherto had throughout the history of local self-government been vested in the D.O.s, were suddenly withdrawn from them and placed in the hands of certain petty officials of the Ministry of Health and Local Self-Government, who were stationed at the provincial headquarters. "The reason for this change appears obvious. It would be difficult to get constituencies formulated in accordance with the wishes of the political party in power, if Heads of Districts, controlled by Commissioners of Divisions were to be tackled while petty officials... would be too willing to oblige. This would be more so when sops were thrown in their way."[3] For example, one of the above mentioned petty officials was granted the "unique privilege" of charging 8 annas a mile as travelling allowance (T.A.) for every journey performed by him, with the result that sometimes his monthly T.A.s came to one thousand rupees as against his monthly salary of six hundred rupees. It was pointed out by the *Leghari Report* that even such top-ranking officials as Financial Commissioners (now called Members of the Board of Revenue) did not enjoy such unique privilege and could only charge two annas per mile for journeys in between stations connected by rail,

---

notice numerous cases in which he withstood behests such as the false implication of Mr. Saeed Qureshi's inveterate enemy Mian Sultan Ali Nanghiana in foodgrain cases. In so far as the District Board Sargodha elections were concerned, he has assured me that nobody could have done better and remained in the district and he did whatever was feasible. Had he tried to put his foot down, some unprincipled officers would have been installed in the *gaddi* [i.e. chair or throne] and the results instead of being 60 per cent unopposed, might have been cent percent unopposed." (*Ibid.*, para. 68.)

[1] *Ibid.*, para. 8. [2] *Ibid.*, para. 7. [3] *Ibid.*, para. 8. Also see para. 11.

unless it was certified that travelling by car was in the public interest.[1]

As the powers concerning the maintenance of law and order were often misused by haughty administrators and most police officers in former Pakistan,[2] it would not be unjustified to expect the political authority to exercise strict and impartial control and supervision over the way the officers concerned exercised these powers. But in practice the political motives and interests of the party in power determined the nature and extent of such control and supervision. For this reason on certain occasions the officers concerned were required to take very harsh measures against political demonstrations and activities of political opponents, even if such harsh measures were not necessary. On other occasions, they were required to ignore serious disturbances or riots such as anti-*Ahmadi* riots in the Punjab in 1953 which were the outcome of the actions of fanatical religious leaders—the *Ulema*.[3] Formerly, in the event of a breach of peace or a threat to peace, the administrator on the spot had had the courage to take the necessary decisions and to act at once. But undue political interference in the field of law and order undermined the confidence and self-reliance of the officers concerned. If the interests of the party in power were directly or indirectly connected with the issue which had resulted in a breach of peace or a threat to peace, the officers tended to delay action and instead of taking the

[1] *Ibid.*, para. 8.

[2] For example, one outspoken administrator wrote "as magistrates and police officers, we occasionally take recourse to actions leading to manslaughter...a friend of mine was bragging that he had ordered firing upon people at least ten times" during his short official career. [Serajuddin Ahmed, "Impact of Traditional Culture on Public Administration in Pakistan" (cyclostyled and in pamphlet form) (NIPA, Dacca, April 1963), p. 8.]

[3] We have already noted in chapter ii that the *Ulema* have a very profound influence over the general masses of Pakistan. Therefore, during and prior to anti-*Ahmadi* riots the Daultana Ministry did not want that the officers concerned should take firm actions against the *Ulema* which were certain to be unpopular measures. (Also see above, chapter iv, p. 190, fn. 1. For detailed discussion, see *Munir-Kayani Report*, esp. part v. For further comments see below.)

responsibility for decisions and actions on their own, they looked up to the political authority for decisions and instructions. During the anti-*Ahmadi* riots in the Punjab, the situation in many places became worse because of the delay and hesitation in taking right and strong actions by the D.O. and the Superintendent of the Police.[1] Mr. Justice Munir and the late Mr. Justice Kayani, who made a thorough enquiry into the various aspects of the anti-*Ahmadi* riots, observed in their report, which "is one of the most revealing and terrifying documents on Pakistan politics"[2] that "At one time it seemed as if law and order were defunct—except in his [the S.P.'s] own body and in that of the District Magistrate—and the picture he has given shows both of them jogging along like helpless orphans. We pity them. We pity the administration that has produced them".[3] In another place of the report they commented that "it shows that the foundation of administration itself is creaky. Make your district officers self-reliant. If it is not in their character, give them some other job and replace them by men who have broad shoulders for responsibility".[4] They concluded their report by saying that

> "it is our deep conviction that if the *Ahrar* [the group responsible for the anti-*Ahmadi* riots] had been treated as a pure question of law and order, without any political considerations, one District Magistrate and one Superintendent of Police could have dealt with them. Consequently, we are prompted by something that they call a human conscience to enquire whether administrative problems of law and order cannot be divorced from a democratic bed-fellow called Ministerial Government, which is so remorselessly haunted by political nightmares. But if democracy means the subordination of law and order to political ends—then Allah knoweth best and we end the report."[5]

Before we end our discussion in this sub-section of the chapter, it may be stated that in comparison with its counterpart in East Bengal, the bureaucracy in West Pakistan was much more susceptible to undue political pressures. With some exceptions, the officers in East Bengal could usually resist such pressures. After having

[1] *Ibid.*, part v. [2] Morris-Jones, *Political Quarterly*, p. 237, fn. 7.
[3] *Munir-Kayani Report*, pp. 311-312.
[4] *Ibid.*, p. 307. [5] *Ibid.*, p. 387.

cited a rare incident in which the D.O. and the S.P. of a district in East Bengal yielded to an undue political pressure of a serious nature exerted by a Minister,[1] the report of a committee which was headed by a Judge (later the Chief Justice) of the Dacca High Court, stated that "We have been told that M.L.A.s [Members of the Legislative Assembly], do approach District Officers but that the latter are able to withstand the influence; but such interference is also fraught with danger, for subordinate officers may not be able to stand up to an M.L.A. . . if interference from Ministers and M.L.A.s goes unchecked, the possibility of this virus infecting the officers cannot reasonably be excluded".[2]

After having failed to win a by-election in 1948, the Muslim League party, which remained in power in East Bengal until the beginning of 1954, did not hold any other by-election although there were as many as 34 vacancies; their apprehensions were clear.[3] In the Assembly election, held in East Bengal in 1954, the Muslim League, which had control not only over the central government but also over all the provincial governments in former Pakistan, was almost completely wiped out in East Bengal.[4] These instances further demonstrate the fact that in East Bengal it was not possible for the party in power to compel the district bureaucracy to yield to its undue pressure in order to manipulate election results. On the other hand, in West Pakistan, as noted above, the party in power did not find it very difficult to compel the bureaucracy to yield to its pressure during elections.[5] Of course, unlike their counterparts in West Pakistan, the politicians in East Bengal

[1] The example has already been cited in para. 2, footnote 4, p. 369. (above).

[2] *East Bengal Police Committee's Report*, para. 20.

[3] *Report of the Constitution Commission*, para. 19.

[4] Out of 237 seats, the Muslim League won only (9) 10 seats. (Callard, *op. cit.*, p. 57.)

[5] We have already noted the example of Sargodha district Board Elections. One author observed that it "is common knowledge that general elections to various provincial legislatures in West Pakistan have never been free and honest". (Khalid B. Sayeed, "Pakistan's Basic Democracies" in *The Middle East Journal*, vol. xv, summer, 1961, p. 255.) This comment was intended to apply to the elections held in both pre-1958 and post-1958 periods.

usually did not attempt to bring such strong pressure to bear on the bureaucracy to yield to their pressure. The Higher political and social consciousness of the Bengali people,[1] perhaps helps to account for this difference. Moreover, the fact that the central government, which never fully trusted the government of East Bengal and which often (especially after 1954) clashed with the latter, required the top-ranking officials in East Bengal to provide it with information about political activities and to keep watch on the Ministers, further added to the strength of the bureaucracy.[2]

[1] See above, chap. ii.

[2] In 1950, during the PRODA [Public and Representative Offices (Disqualification) Act] proceedings against the then Finance Minister of East Bengal, the Chief Secretary to the Government of East Bengal revealed that the export of steel drums to India, which had been ordered by the Finance and Commerce Minister, had been effectively stopped by him under the instructions of the central government. (*Dawn*, Sep. 20, 1950, cited in Sayeed, *Pacific Affairs*, pp. 132-133.) It was also frequently claimed by the politicians both in the East Bengal Assembly and in the Constituent Assembly that fortnightly reports on the activities of the provincial ministers were sent to the central government by the provincial Chief Secretary. (*Ibid.*, p. 133.) A Minister from East Bengal complained in the Constituent Assembly that "officers who were under the direct control of the central government but working in that province [i.e. East Bengal] refused to carry out or obey the orders of the Ministers of the provincial cabinet or the provincial legislature". In reply, a central Minister had to say that "I must admit that there were instances where the civil servants of the country tried to stand against the wish of the local [i.e. provincial governments] government." (*C. A. P. Deb.*, Feb. 9, 1956, vol i, no. 68, p. 277.)

As most of the top-ranking officials in the East Bengal Secretariat were West Pakistanis [In 1954 Professor Mahmud Husain, the then central Minister, stated in the Constituent Assembly "If one went to the East Bengal Secretariat, one was surprised not to find a single Bengali Secretary in the whole of the Bengali Secretariat." (*C. A. P. Deb.*, vol. i, no. 26, July 17, 1954, quoted in Sayeed, *Pacific Affairs*, p. 132.)], close alliance developed between them and the central government, which as noted in chapter ii, was always in one way or another dominated by West Pakistani politicians. We have already noted in chapter vi that an increase or decrease in the influence and strength of the top-ranking officials such as the Chief Secretary correspondingly resulted in an increase or decrease of the influence and strength of the D.O. and his subordinates. Of course, most officials in the districts were Bengalis. But in the event of the undue political pressures they usually resorted to the support of the Chief Secretary, the Divisional Commissioner and the Secretaries. In short, we may say that the alliance

Of course, this was not an important factor. For example, the ruling party which was in power both at the centre and in the province suffered, as noted above, a crushing defeat in the Assembly election in 1954.

Comparison between the Pre and the post-1958 Periods.

In comparison with the past, the bureaucracy in both East Bengal and West Pakistan became much more susceptible to political pressures although the extent of such susceptibility was still much less in the former than in the latter. In East Bengal a fairly considerable number of high-ranking officials continued to be able to resist political pressures in varying degrees. It was mainly such petty officials as "Circle Officers [who] seem to have foresaken their traditional neutrality and were alleged to have been quite active in promoting the candidatures of some favoured nominees"[1] at the time of the "Basic Democracies" elections in 1964/65.[2] But in West Pakistan many high-ranking officials including D.O.s were reported to have yielded in varying degrees to pressures during these elections.

---

between the top-ranking officials in East Bengal and the central government strengthened to some extent the position of the bureaucracy vis-a-vis the politicians.

1 Rehman Sobhan, *Basic Democracies, Works Programme and Rural Development in East Pakistan* (Bureau of Economic Research, University of Dacca, 1968) (Hereafter cited as Sobhan, *BD,WP and Dev.*), p. 251.

2 Of course, during these elections such high-ranking officials as S.D.O.s, were reported to have indirectly supported the government candidates (see below). But it should be noted that before these elections there had been a wholesale replacement of CSP S.D.O.s by PCS S.D.O.s. At that time out of 37 outlying sub-divisions in East Bengal only two sub-divisions were in the charge of CSP S.D.O.s. [*Actual Distribution list of Officers* (Corrected up to Dec. 1964). We have already noted in chapter iii that the majority of the outlying sub-divisions, which are much more important than *Sadar* sub-divisions, usually remained in charge of CSP S.D.O.s and that the CSPs were never appointed as the S.D.O.s of the *Sadar* sub-divisions.] It was widely believed that such wholesale replacements were made in view of the fact that it would be much easier to compel the PCS S.D.O.s to yield to pressures. [We have already noted that the CSPs, who were the elite of the bureaucracy, were in a much stronger and more advantageous position than any other officers (chapter vi) and that most CSP

Several factors accounted for the increased susceptibility of the bureaucracy in both East Bengal and West Pakistan to such pressures in the post-1958 period. Formerly, as noted above, the government had not been stable and strong and had undergone frequent changes,[1] so that the officials could afford to incur the displeasure of the party or faction in power because it had been almost certain that soon it would be replaced by another party or faction. But in the Ayubian decade it was widely felt that under the system of constitutional autocracy the ruling party would enjoy unduly prolonged life, enormous authoritarian powers, with the result that the bureaucracy had now much less courage and determination to stand against the wishes of the members of the ruling group and their henchmen. Moreover, the officials did not feel secure because immediately after the proclamation of Martial Law, many high-ranking as well as junior officers were screened out of the services on the grounds of inefficiency or corruption or for having the reputation of being corrupt.

S.D.O.s belonged to the 25-30 age groups (chapter iii). So a few years ago as university students, they had participated in or remained associated with or at least aware of political movements especially against the Ayub regime. The memory of student life was still fresh in their minds (chapter ii.) with the result that they were still relatively radical, defiant and to some extent idealist. All these considerations, perhaps, prompted the government to cause such wholesale replacements. Moreover, it also took into consideration the fact that the PCS officers who, with the exception of some very bright officers, usually did not get the opportunity to become S.D.O.s of the outlying sub-divisions, would feel obliged to the government for appointing them as the S.D.O.s of these sub-divisions.] An example may be cited below: In 1965, the Election Tribunal in East Bengal found that under the pressure of one Kazi Kader, who was a Minister and who had suppported his henchman Rustam Ali in a by-election in Rangpur district, the S.D.O. had exerted undue influence in favour of Rustam Ali before the election. The Tribunal also found the said Minister guilty of corrupt practices before that election. It declared the election to be "vitiated and thus liable to be set aside". (*The Morning News*, Dacca, May 1, 1965.) The appeal against the judgement of the tribunal was rejected by the Dacca High Court. (*Ibid.*, Nov. 27, 1965.)

[1] On many occasions though the same party continued in the office, one of its factions replaced another faction.

Post 1958 Period : "Basic Democracies"

Identification of the Ruling Party, Local Bodies and District Administration. The introduction of "Basic Democracies" strengthened the position of the ruling party (i.e. Pakistan Muslim League) in rural areas and contributed enormously to the process of identification of three elements namely the ruling party, local bodies and the local bureaucracy. Under this system the "identification of [these] three elements" became "more and more perfect".[1] To be associated with the ruling party had "meant that one had some access to the ears of the local administration. But now the perfected identification means that to be associated with...[it] is to

[1] The above comment of the present writer is based on Professor W.H. Morris-Jones' comment on the introduction of the *Panchayati Raj* in India that it would add to the strength of the Congress Party in rural areas and that under this system "identification of three elements—Congress Party, local bodies and Government—will become more and more perfect." (W.H. Morris-Jones, "Democratic Decentralisation: Some Political Consequences" in *The Economic Weekly*, vol. xiv, nos. 28, 29, 30, July 1962, p. 1105. Hereafter cited as Morris-Jones, *Economic Weekly*.) Later this comment was seconded by C.N. Bhalerao. (C.N. Bhalerao, "Some Social, Political and Administrative Consequences of Panchayati Raj" in *Asian Survey*, vol. iv, no. 41, April 1964, p. 808.) Of course, it would be rather unjustified to compare the Indian situation with former Pakistan situation in view of the fact that while in India a representative system was in operation with considerable degree of success, in former Pakistan there was an authoritarian system. Moreover, the *Panchayati Raj* was a representative system of local bodies and was free, to a considerable extent, from the control of the bureaucracy, whereas most part of the system of "Basic Democracies" was non-representative and it was under the thumb of the bureaucracy. It should also be pointed out that the latter was introduced, as we shall see below, to serve the particularistic political interest of the Ayub regime and to ensure its perpetual continuance in the power. While the *Panchayati Raj* contributed to the process of democratic decentralisation, the "Basic Democracies" contributed to centralisation and to authoritarian process. Thus the influence of *Panchayati Raj* and that of "Basic Democracies" on local political and administrative systems were different in many respects. But, in some other respects, as local government institutions they naturally had some similar influences. Of course, such influences did not have, in most cases, same impact. For example, they contributed to the identification of the above mentioned three elements, but such identification did not have same impact on political and administrative processes. While in India it did not endanger the democratic system, in former Pakistan it strengthened authoritarian forces.

be part and parcel of the local administration. As the bureaucrats come down a step or two the party moves up."[1]

Several factors were responsible for such identification of the three elements in former Pakistan. The most important factor was that the "Basic Democracies", as noted above, also served as the Electoral College. We have already noted in chapter iii that in a nation of more than 100 million people, only 80,000 persons[2] (called "Basic Democrats"), who were the members of Union Councils and Union/Town Committees and who were elected on the basis of adult franchise, enjoyed the right to elect the President of the country and the members of both the National and the Provincial Assemblies, with the result that they were, in fact, the arbiters of the nation's political destiny, and that the relationship between local politics and higher level politics became institutionalised. This system was introduced by the Ayub regime "to keep the vote in the hands of a privileged few".[3] It is interesting to note that the Constitution Commission, which had been appointed by the Ayub regime, was in favour of direct election[4] and strongly opposed the idea that the "Basic Democracies" should also act as an Electoral College. The Commission also put forward quite logical and convincing arguments in favour of its recommendation.[5] Yet the Martial Law

[1] Morris-Jones, *Economic Weekly*, p. 1105. Also see present writer's comments in *ibid.*

[2] In the next election, as noted in chapter iii, this number would have been raised to 120,000.

[3] *Time* (Asia edition), Sept. 17, 1965, p. 25.

[4] Although it recommended that the franchise should be restricted on the basis of educational qualifications and property ownership. (*Report of the Constitution Commission*, para. 108.)

[5] In the next two sentences the Constitution Commission refers to the argument of the Martial Law regime; then it puts forward its own arguments: "The principle on which the average adult is excluded, under this scheme [i.e. "Basic Democracies" scheme], from electing directly the President and the legislatures, is that he is incapable of discriminating amongst the various candidates, who live outside his neighbourhood, which according to the scheme has been circumscribed both in territorial limits as well as in the number of inhabitants. The reason given for this view is that

regime did not accept the recommendation most probably because they felt that during elections it would be much easier to manipulate and to exert pressure on 80,000 people than the entire adult population of the country.

As the "Basic Democrats" elected the President and the Legislatures the political parties were bent on winning the support of as many "Basic Democrats" as possible. But, as noted in chapter ii, political parties in former Pakistan, including the party in power, either did not have any roots at all in rural society or in some places had only poor or ill-organised establishments below the district or sub-divisional level. Thus they found it difficult to communicate regularly and systematically with the "Basic Democrats". But the ruling group or party could and, in fact, did make use of the executive arm of the government in its attempt to win the support of the "Basic Democrats". Especially before elections, the leading members of the ruling party (including influential and powerful pro-government "Basic Democrats") rather compelled the bureaucracy through the Governor or the Ministers to exert pressure and influence on the pro-opposition or "neutral" "Basic Democrats" in order to compel them to support the ruling party. The bureaucratic pressure and the fact that the bureaucracy could and did dispense great favours and a great deal of patronage, played a very important role in influenc-

---

an average adult is capable of making a selection only from amongst those in whose neighbourhood he lives because he can reasonably be presumed to know them personally or have the means of acquainting himself with regard to their fitness to represent him. There are, however, no restrictions, by way of any educational or other qualifications, imposed on the candidates standing for election for "Basic Democracies". Therefore, any adult in these small constituencies, who can command the confidence of the majority of the inhabitants of that constituency will be elected. In these circumstances, we are unable to see how a person, who may not be better qualified than the average adult in the area concerned, merely because he commands the confidence of the majority of the people of that area, can become capable of judging as between the various candidates who stand for Presidency and Vice-Presidency and for membership of the legislatures. A person, though illiterate, may as regards the local needs be effective, but for the election of the President and the members of the Parliament, he may be as incapable as his electors." (*Ibid.*, para. 110)

ing many "Basic Democrats" to support the ruling party. In fact, the bureaucracy found itself in a rather awkward situation—on the one hand, it came under strong pressure from those influential and powerful "Basic Democrats" who allied themselves with the ruling party, and on the other hand, it was compelled to exert pressure on other "Basic Democrats".

But the most important factor which encouraged the "Basic Democrats" to support and ally themselves with the party in power was that "as a class" they found that the Ayub regime and the system of election through the electoral college "considerably enhanced their power".[1] Although the membership of local bodies offered them some status and privileges, it was mainly because they constituted the electoral college that they had an unique position in society and enjoyed many privileges and patronage extended to them by the party in power and local administration. So the popular as well as the opposition parties' demand that the system of direct election on the basis of adult franchise should be introduced, constituted a major threat or danger to their privileged position. This was the main reason why a great majority of the "Basic Democrats" voted in favour of the party in power during the presidential and assembly elections held in 1964-65. They realised that "no successor regime could ever be relied upon to serve their interests so completely".[2] The elections, in fact, "fully justified the faith put into the constitution and its bulwarks, the Basic Democrats"[3] by the Ayub regime, which had felt that "it could rely on the awareness of the Basic Democrat as to where his best interests lay".[4] In fact, it was this awareness which enabled the Ayub regime to build up "an eventually satisfactory alliance with the B.D.s [Basic Democrats]".[5] Therefore, it was

[1] Sobhan, *BD, WP and Dev.*, p. 259. [2] *Ibid.*, p. 259. [3] *Ibid.*, p. 258.

[4] Rehman Sobhan, "Basic Democracies and National Politics in East Pakistan" (cyclostyled) (A paper presented on October 30, 1968, at the postgraduate seminar on "Comparative Politics: Autonomy and dependence in 'Parochial' Politics", held at the Institute of Commonwealth Studies, University of London), p. 5.

[5] Sobhan, *BD,WP and Dev.*, p. 259.

felt that "as long as the constitution ensures that this same class remains the arbiter of the country's politics, the regime can be assured of a long life".[1] (Of course, as a result of the mass uprising in the late-1968 and the early-1969 Ayub Khan was "on his knees and frightened Muslim Leaguers" went "underground".[2] Ultimately Ayub had to step down and the system of election underwent change.)

As the "Basic Democrats" held the key to the political survival of the Ayub regime "political logic demands that they be kept in good humour".[3] On the other hand, the "Basic Democrats", who were also conscious of the fact that they held this key, also expected the Ayub regime to enable them to exert some influence on local administration. Of course, such privilege was naturally enjoyed by a few influential and powerful "Basic Democrats", who had hold over other "Basic Democrats" (i.e. rank and file) and who supported or were likely to support the Ayub regime.

The fact that the "Basic Democracies" also served as the electoral college, accelerated the process of identification of three elements—the then ruling party, local bodies and local bureaucracy.

Works Programme: Its Contribution to the Identification of Three Elements and to the Influence of the Rural Elite. At the local level of politics "tangible material benefits are an even larger part of the purpose of political activity than at higher, ideologically more susceptible levels".[4] The candidates of the government party might not always be successful, but the successful candidate might become the member of the government party "since the

[1] *Ibid.*, p. 260.

[2] *The Sunday Times*, London, February 9, 1969. Yahya succeeded Ayub and a General Election on the basis of adult franchise was held. But the election result was ignored by the Yahya regime which tried to ruthlessly crush the Bengalees with the result that the liberation struggle began in East Bengal and ultimately it emerged as a separate independent state of Bangladesh.

[3] Rehman Sobhan, "Two-Way Stretch in Basic Democracies" in *The Times*, Special Report on Pakistan (London), April 6, 1968.

[4] Morris-Jones, *Economic Weekly*, p. 1105. Also see present writer's comments in fn. 1, p. 381 (above).

source of assistance is the government".[1] So the material benefits that the ruling party could offer, sometimes contributed to the identification of the three elements.

We have already noted in chapter v that from the early 1960s an increasing allocation of resources was made from time to time for the purpose of the Rural Development Programme termed Works Programme, which was executed through the "Basic Democracies". By having control over hard cash, the "Basic Democrats" were in an advantageous position to derive direct financial benefits from the programme. In 1963-64, when the Rural Development Academy at Comilla conducted a survey, most people held that the entire amount was not properly utilised and that the programme was "not...free of political strings".[2] They bitterly complained that "political activity at the local level snatches money from the allotments...Most complaints blamed politics for the misuse of funds. They view politics in its coarsest meaning—as a mechanism by which individuals secure for themselves funds intended for the community. They see conspiracies among those entrusted with the funds." They also added that these people "changed their lots (conditions) overnight".[3]

Even if the "Basic Democracies" were not made the electoral college, the Works Programme would have been executed through them and in comparison with the past, more resources would have been allocated for this purpose. But in that case, as it is widely believed, the amounts of allocations would not have been so large. Moreover, no strict administrative arrangements were made in order to keep a careful watch on the various stages of disbursement of the funds. Moreover, the accounts of the Union Councils were not properly audited.[4] It was widely felt that the

[1] *Ibid.*, p. 1105. [2] *2nd Evaluation Report* (*E. Beng.*), p. 85.

[3] *Ibid.*, p. 85.

[4] The *Second Evaluation Report* of the Comilla Academy observed that "Many of the respondents harbour suspicions about the use of funds...One wrote: 'The most striking thing is that there is no system of spot audit. It is unprecedented that a large amount of national money is spent by persons without any check and balance.' Another said 'the money is being lavishly allotted and spent. No strict account is kept and verified.' Yet another wrote

absence of such arrangements was deliberate, so that the "Basic Democrats" could derive direct financial benefits from the programme and could feel obliged to the regime. In fact, there was "little disagreement" that the programme was of "singular benefit to the Basic Democrats" and gave them a "significant material stake in the regime".[1]

A considerable number of the "Basic Democrats" came from the influential or dominant sections or classes of rural society, many of whom were also the money lenders and land leasers. The Works Programme further added greatly to their influence and importance. So far as the *Thana* and the Union Councils' projects were concerned, they selected the persons (i.e. labourers) who would get work on these projects, also those who would serve on the Project Committees to supervise the execution of these projects and the rural traders or businessmen from whom the necessary materials should be bought.[2] So, now not only were they the money-lenders and land leasers in the villages but also "the dispensers of jobs and fringe benefits".[3] The Works Programme, therefore, gave them "a unique source of patronage in the villages"[4] and "scope for power and wealth beyond their most extravagant expectations".[5]

This combination of enhanced economic and political powers

---

that the works "under the projects are not verified properly; the audit is more on paper than actual; work in 1963-64 is done only to 70% on average at the estimated cost'." (*Ibid.*, pp. 85-86.)

[1] Sobhan, Basic Democracies and National Politics, p. 4.

[2] We have already noted in chapter v that while the *Thana* and the Union Councils' projects were executed by the councils themselves, in the case of the District Councils, most projects were executed by the contractors. The non-official members (including "Basic Democrats") of the District Council were directly or indirectly interested in the selection of the contractors. This accounted for the fact that a section of the non-official members of the District Council came from the business class.

[3] Sobhan, *BD, WP and Dev.*, p. 243.

[4] Sobhan in *The Times' Special Report*, April 6, 1968.

[5] Rehman Sobhan, "Social Forces in the Basic Democracies" in *South Asian Review*, vol. i, no. 3, April 1968, p. 171.

along with the scope for direct financial gains, made "the government in general and the Works Programme in particular, irresistable to the Basic Democrats".[1] The programme, in fact, "bound the B.D.s [Basic Democrats] more closely to the government both in general and more specifically in the machinery of local government".[2] This was mutually beneficial for both the government and the "Basic Democrats".

Increasing Competitiveness of Rural Life . Usually it is found that one of the characteristics of the new states is that in the newly introduced local bodies the increasing competitiveness of rural life finds a new political outlet and that the said competition for power is partly between social groups, partly between rivals for leadership within these groups and partly between individuals seeking personal advancement.[3] In former Pakistan also, the "Basic Democracies" provided an outlet for increasing competitiveness in rural society. During "Basic Democracies" elections in 1959 and especially in those in 1964, various social classes—(i) traditionally "aristocratic" classes of rural society (i.e. *Mia Bari*, *Talukder Bari*, *Khan Bari*, *Choudhury Bari*, etc.) from which previously most members of local bodies had come, (ii) such classes as *Kulu* (oil grinder), *Zola* (weaver) etc., which were regarded socially "inferior" or "lower" classes and (iii) the emerging rural business class—fought vigorously especially in East Bengal for the membership and the chairmanship of the Union Councils.[4] "Even as recently as ten years ago, it would have been almost unthinkable that a *Kulu* should be so bold as to contest an election for the Union Board."[5] In East Bengal, one of the

1 Sobhan, *BD, WP and Dev.*, p. 243.

2 *Ibid.*, p. 243.

3 Morris-Jones, *Economic Weekly*, p. 1105. Also see present writer's comments in fn. 1, p. 381 (above).

4 M. Rashiduzzaman, "Election Politics in Pakistan" in *The Journal of Commonwealth Political Studies*, vol. iv, no. 3, Nov. 1966. (Here it may be mentioned that in many places some members of the socially "inferior" classes were financially better off than the members of the traditionally "aristocratic" classes. Especially those members of the former who had taken up business as their profession had become fairly rich by the standards of the then Pakistani rural life.)

5 *Ibid.*, p. 194.

striking features of "rural leadership since 1960 is the emergence of a new group of people other than the traditional families"[1] (i.e. traditionally "aristocratic" families in rural society). (Social and economic changes and increasing political modernisation and consciousness also equally account for such trend in local politics.) A sample survey carried out in East Bengal in 1965-66, revealed that of the 129 Union Councils surveyed, 112 (86.82%) had members who came not only from traditionally rural "aristocratic" families but also from other than "aristocratic" families. The percentage of all members of such councils belonging to the latter category was 37.[2] So there were now a variety of members drawn from several social groups. Thus, we may say that increasing competitiveness meant "neither the protection of the established leadership nor its wholesale overthrow and replacement, but rather a shifting of its ranks and the political education of members who prove by their ability to be the fittest for the new political world".[3]

The accentuation of the competitiveness in rural society of East Bengal could be further illustrated by the fact that while in the 1959 elections the average number of contestants per seat was 2.12, in the 1964 elections it rose to 2.90, that in 1959 the percentage of candidates who were returned unopposed was 17.70, whereas in 1964 it was only 6.88, and that while in 1959 there were no contestants in 14 "Basic Democracies" electoral units, there was no such instance in 1964.[4]

[1] M. Rashiduzzaman, *Pakistan: A Study of Government and Politics* (Dacca, 1967), p. 253.

[2] *Ibid.*, p. 253. On the social background of "Basic Democrats" in former Pakistan, it was observed by another author that the "elected members did not come entirely from the wealthy land owning class [i.e. landed "aristocracy"], as was often true in the past. Nor were they representatives of a 'peasant uprising'. The voting was not a sweep by the illiterate, poverty-stricken masses. It included elevation to office of some wealthy, some educated, some middle class, some poor, some politically shrewed and some politically naive individuals." Harry J. Friedman, "Pakistan's Experiment in Basic Democracies" in *Pacific Affairs*, vol. xxxiii, no. 2, June 1960, p. 119.

[3] Morris-Jones, *Economic Weekly*, p. 1105. Also see above, fn. 1, p. 381.

[4] "Report on the Members Elected to the Basic Democracies during

Institutionalised Local Leadership. Combining of the representatives of several villages into a single administrative cum political structure or unit, namely Union Council, the similar combining of Union Councils into the *Thana/Tehsil* Council, and of *Thana/Tehsil* Councils into the District Council, and bestowing on them considerable administrative and executive responsibilities for the management of the welfare aspects of their respective areas not only provided the local leaders of varying influence and importance or grades with the opportunity to organise themselves and to play active political roles at various levels in the district but also with a series of forums where they could and, in fact, did discuss the local development problems and voiced their demands. Thus the system, in fact, resulted in the emergence of a new force (in the sense of both power or energy and organised collectivity or groups)—the local elite—in local politics as well as in local administration of the country. Of course, this force, no doubt, had informally existed in a loose form before the introduction of the system. But now the chain of local bodies institutionalised this force and enormously added to its strength and vigour, with the result that an institutionalised and graded leadership was rapidly emerging. This development was proving to be a potent and formidable element of change in the nature of district administration and in the local political culture. The relationship between the local leaders and the bureaucracy was undergoing gradual change. On the one hand, there was a decrease in the dependence of the former on the latter and on the other hand, there was also an increase in the pressure of the former on the latter.[1] Change in the mentality of both officials and non-officials were also becoming evident.[2] The latter were not so overawed by the officials as before. The bureaucracy was also increasingly aware of this attitudinal

1964" (cyclostyled) (Department of Local Government, Govt. of East Bengal, Dacca, n.d.), p. 1.

[1] *PARD (Peshawar) Report No.* 9, pp. 73, 143, 285.

[2] Lawrence Ziring, "The Administration of Basic Democracies" (cyclostyled) (Administrative Staff College, Lahore, n.d.), p. 11.

change and of the consequent necessity of some readjustments in their own paternal attitudes towards the local leaders in particular and towards the people in general. In fact, some such changes had already taken place.[1]

The institutionalised local leadership was gradually making its existence felt. The following example will further illustrate the point: In Nowshera *tehsil* in West Pakistan, one Union Council wrote 37 letters and another (nearby) Union Council wrote 29 letters to various government departments over a period. The latter received replies to 21 of its 29 letters and the suggestions and the recommendations contained in 19 of these were accepted and actions were initiated accordingly by the departments concerned. But the Union Council which had written 37 letters received no replies. When this council came to know about this differential treatment, all its members resigned in a body, with the result that the matter came to the notice of the higher authorities in the district. After having received assurances from the Assistant Commissioner, who made an inquiry into the matter, that such treatment would not be repeated, the councillors withdrew their resignations.[2] This example also illustrates the fact that the institutionalised leadership was now in a convenient position to bring the irregularities of the lower bureaucracy effectively to the notice of the higher bureaucracy. Of course, there was no doubt that such an incident was very rare. In most places, the council would have made a strong representation to the higher bureaucracy (e.g. D.O. or S.D.O.) or raised the matter in a meeting of the higher council. In any case, this example demonstrates the fact that the local leaders were becoming aware of the strength and effectiveness of their institutionalised position or of their collectivity. Thus, while formerly in local areas the officials had confronted local leaders individually, they now encountered them collectively. This was a situation which enabled the local leaders to exercise some influence, even pressure, on the

1 *PARD (Peshawar) Report No.* 9, pp. 27, 99, 138.

2 *Study of Union Councils in Nowshera Tehsil* (A report prepared by Inayatullah on the basis of a case study) (*PARD*, Peshawar, 1961), pp. 39-40.

bureaucracy. One author suggested that with the passage of time non-official members of local bodies "might like to attempt a revision of boundaries of bureaucratic power and seek to obtain a much larger say in administration at the district level than they ever had before".[1] The proceedings of the District Councils in East Bengal indicated that the non-official members had already made some efforts to attempt a revision of bureaucratic authority and to have much greater voice in development administration. They were no longer timid or passive but were becoming fairly assertive. The following discussion (pp. 392-397) of such proceedings will illustrate these points, will give us some idea of the role played by the non-official members in the meetings and the working of the District Council in East Bengal, and will indicate that the discussions and criticisms in the meetings could be so directed as to exert pressure on the bureaucracy.[2]

One non-official member of the Sylhet District Council in East Bengal suggested that while making an allotment of funds to deserving and needy Union Councils out of the resources placed at their disposal by the District Council, the S.D.O.s should consult those members of the Council who came from the unions concerned. The suggestion was "appreciated" by the District Council and it was decided unanimously that while making such allotments, the S.D.O.s should consult the local members of the District Council.[3]

At the budget meeting of the Pabna District Council in East Bengal, held in June 1961, the S.D.O., who in this case was the convenor of the Finance Committee, gave a brief explanatory

[1] Masihuzzaman, "Basic Democracies and District Administration" in Inayatullah (ed.), *D.A. in W.Pak.*, p. 190. (Hereafter cited as Masihuzzaman, *B.D. and D.A.*)

[2] For assertive attitude of the Chairmen of the Union Councils and for the tussle between them and the Circle Officers, see chapter v.

[3] Proceedings of the Sylhet District Council, East Bengal (special meeting), March 9, 1961. (Proceedings were preserved in bound volumes which were partly hand written and partly cyclostyled.)

account of the items of receipts and expenditures.[1] He pointed out that owing to the paucity of funds larger allotments could not be made for roads, buildings and communications. He observed that a greater amount of money was alloted towards health, sanitation and education and that a large sum of money had to be provided towards the revision of the scale of pay of the employees of the District Council. He added that in the absence of specific instructions from the government, the expected grant from the government towards the Works Programme could not be shown in the budget estimates, that such a receipt would be included in the revised budget estimates later and that the entire grant from the government would be spent for the improvement of the communication system—roads, bridges, culverts, etc. Lastly, he stated that keeping in view the above-mentioned points, the expenditure had to be strictly limited to the estimated income.

After his speech, the council took up the discussion on the budget with the permission of the Chairman (i.e. the D.O.). A non-official member called the budget a "welfare budget for the employees as it appears that a large amount of money has been provided in the budget towards the salaries of the employees." The S.D.O. pointed out that the District Council itself had sanctioned the revised pay scale for the employees of the council and that the fund was provided as per requirement. Thus, the amount provided in the budget could not be reduced. Members then said that they did not "grumble" about the extra amount required for the scale; rather, they thought that there might be some superfluous staff who might be retrenched. It was proposed that a Re-organisation Committee should be appointed to go into the details of the matter and to submit a report to the council for its consideration. So a Re-organisation Committee was set up with the following members: (i) S.D.O., *Sadar* sub-division, (ii) S.D.O., Serajganj outlying sub-division, and (iii) the Vice-Chairman of the District Council who happened to be a member of the then Provincial Assembly.

[1] Later we shall see the comments of the non-official members on the budget speech of the S.D.O.

One non-official member, who was also the Chairman of a Union Committee, held that the maintenance of many important roads had not been included in the budget. He also pointed out that no allotment had been made for "the projects under Works Programme". In reply, it was again explained that no such allotment could be made on account of lack of funds and that the amount required for the maintenance of roads, bridges etc. would be provided in the revised budget on receipt of grants from the government. But the member insisted that provision must be made for piling on the Pabna-Trimohin road, as the work was essential to save the road. The Vice-Chairman of the council also supported the proposal of the member. Finally a decision was taken to make a provision of Rs. 5000 in the budget for that purpose. Another non-official member argued that Rs. 200 as provided in the budget for removing water-hyacinth appeared to be a "very paltry amount" which should be increased. After some discussion, a decision was taken to provide Rs. 5000 over the existing allotment for the purpose.

After having taken some decisions in order to effect an economy in running the Council's administration and to increase its income, the District Council authorised the D.O. (i.e. the Chairman of the Council) to incur expenditure according to budget allotments.[1]

At the meeting of the Pabna District Council, held in February 1962, a resolution of the Finance Committee of the Council was discussed. In the resolution it was argued that it was not necessary for the Finance Committee to audit the accounts of the District Council monthly because the Accounts Committee was to audit the accounts quarterly and as such this matter was referred to the Council for its opinion and approval. The opinion of the Council was divided on this issue. Some members agreed with the Finance Committee's view, while some other members pointed out that the government had made it mandatory that the accounts were to be audited monthly and quarterly by the Finance and the

1 Proceedings of the Pabna District Council, East Bengal (special meeting), June 25, 1964.

Accounts Committees respectively. They argued that these Committees, therefore, must go on auditing the accounts accordingly. Lastly, the D.O. expressed his view that perhaps monthly audit would be rather impossible and therefore, it would be a good idea to require the Accounts Committee to audit the accounts quarterly and the Finance Committee to plan the expenditure. He further added that this step would help smooth working and also save duplication of labour. It is interesting to note that the suggestion of the D.O. was not accepted. It was finally resolved that the government should be asked to clarify the point.[1] Of course, it is almost certain that the D.O. did not insist on having his suggestion accepted. Had he insisted, the Council perhaps would have given way. But the very fact that the D.O.'s suggestion, although it might have been put forward in a casual way, was not accepted, indicated some change in the situation and in the attitudes of minds of the members.

The following questions were asked by a non-official member of the Pabna District Council :

Q. 1 "What action has the Government taken on the resolution of this House with regard to airport approach roads?"

A. "The matter is still under correspondence and nothing has yet materialised."

Q. 2 "The C & B [Communication & Buildings] Department has started earthwork on the Pabna Ishurdi road, but blocks of earth are just thrown over the *Kutcha* [non-metal] portion of the road without even breaking and levelling, with the result that when bullock carts pass, the wheels make deep lines making the road uneven. Is it the procedure of earthwork adopted by the C & B Department?"

A. "No reply could be given as the Executive Engineer (Roads) was absent. [It is very interesting to note that the Executive Engineer was the employee of the government and not of the District Council and that the activities of the C & B Department were not officially subject to the review of the District Council, but yet a non-official member pointed out the unsatisfactory nature of the work of the department. It indicates that the non-official members were gradually becoming inclined to extend their influence or pressure beyond the boundary or line between the authority of the nation building departments and that of the local bodies.]"

---

[1] *Ibid.* (ordinary meeting), Feb. 23, 1965.

Q. 3 "Why is the District Council Rest House still occupied by the Sub-Divisional Controller of Food [a government employee] against rules?"

A. "The Sub-Divisional Controller of Food was requested to vacate the Rest House several times but he could not vacate for want of accommodation. Again he was requested on 6-2-62 to vacate the room and clear up the dues but he prayed for one month's time..."

Q. 4 "How long is he actually in occupation?"

A. "19 months."

Q. 5 "What amount of rent has he paid to the District Council Fund?"

A. "Rs. 68."

Q. 6 "Is it a fact that he has been allowed concession rates?"

A. "He has prayed for concession rates. In this connection it was resolved that the Chairman [D.O.] would exercise his discretion in granting concession rates."

Q. 7 "What is the total difference of amount had he paid the rent on the usual rate?"

A. "Does not arise. [It is interesting to note that the questions concerning the Rest House were mainly intended to indirectly criticise and embarrass the D.O.]"

Q. 8 "What action has been taken for the extension of Rashid Hall to accommodate visitors?"

A. "There was no provision in the budget for 1961-62."

Q. 9 "Whether the proceedings of the House are immediately recorded in the Minute Book by any staff of District Council or are they later recorded from the brief notes taken during proceedings?"

A. "The procedure that is being followed in recording proceedings of the meeting is as follows: Resolutions as adopted in the House are being written very precisely against each item of the Agenda in the notice book by the Chairman, District Council; and the Secretary [a member of the D.O.'s high-ranking official staff] also takes down notes of important points of discussion on agenda so far practicable. The full proceedings of the meeting based on the above notes are then recorded within three days after the date of meeting."

Q. 10 "How many Union Multipurpose Cooperative Societies in this District got a loan during the current financial year?"

A. "45 Union Cooperative Multipurpose Societies have been provided with loans of Rs. 6 lacs during the current financial year."

Q. 11 "What financial assistance have the Fishermen's Cooperative Societies received in Pabna District?"

A. "No financial assistance has been given to the Fishermen's Cooperative Societies during the current year as none asked for it."[1]

---

[1] *Ibid.* (ordinary meeting), February 27, 1962.

In the same meeting of the Pabna District Council, another non-official member expressed the view that "the construction of the R.C.C. elevated tank was going to be a top-heavy structure as its foundation was reported to be only 5 feet deep. The Executive Engineer [The Divisional Head of the Public Health Engineering Department (Rajshahi Division) of the Government] informed the House that the foundation of the R.C.C. elevated tank would be 9½ feet and not 5 feet as reported by the Councillor."[1] The above-mentioned comment of the Councillor indicated that sometimes non-technical members even went to the extent of raising questions concerning purely technical matters.[2]

Of course, in West Pakistan, the non-official members were much less assertive than their counterparts in East Bengal. In the former, the extent of assertiveness also varied from region to region.

Two-Way Channel of Communication. In chapter iii we have already noted that the Chairmen of the Union Councils and the Union/Town Committees were ex-officio non-official members of the *Thana/Tehsil* Councils and that non-official members of the District Council, who usually came from both the rural elite class[3] and the urban elite class[4], were elected by

[1] *Ibid.* Almost all examples have been cited from the proceedings of the meetings of the Pabna District Council mainly because in Pabna the proceedings were recorded in greater detail, whereas in many other districts only the decisions of the District Council were usually recorded. Moreover, the present writer had easy access to the proceedings of the Pabna District Council.

Pabna was not a typical district in East Bengal. The generalisations which are based on the proceedings of the Pabna District Council fully applied to other districts (excepting Chittagong Hill Tracts District) in East Bengal.

[2] Also see above (p. 395) for the present writer's comment at the end of the answer to question no. 2, asked in the same meeting by another non-official member. That comment of the present writer is equally pertinent here.

[3] For example, *Zamindars*, big or surplus farmers, rural businessmen including contractors, the Chairmen and the Members of the Union Councils and other prominent persons.

[4] For example, lawyers, urban businessmen including contractors, those *Zamindars* who lived in urban areas, social and political leaders, the

an electoral college consisting of the chairmen of the Union Councils and the Union/Town Committees. Thus there was a chain of some non-official members who simultaneously became the members of two or three tiers of councils with the result that a non-official channel or line of communication opened up between various tiers alongside the bureaucratic channel or line—these two channels or lines were, in fact, closely related, or rather articulated with each other.

We have noted in chapter ii that a communication gap existed between the modernised urban elite and inarticulate tradition oriented rural masses. This gap could be filled at least to a very limited extent by a semi-educated and semi-modern class or by rural leaders who were partially capable of sharing the views and ideas of the modernised urban elite but were culturally much closer to inarticulate rural masses; they possessed the capacity to communicate with these two polarised groups.[1] No doubt, such a class existed in former Pakistan. But formerly this class had had very little opportunity to come into close contact with the urban elite. Now in the formal structure of the chain of local bodies (especially in the District Council) the urban elite and the semi-educated and semi-modern rural elite partially established such contacts. Moreover, the impression obtained by the present writer was that since the non-official members of the District Council were elected by the Chairmen of the lowest councils and committees, the urban elite who wanted to be members of the District Council found it essential to establish or maintain some contact with this section of the rural elite. The isolation of rural society, therefore, was in the process of partial elimination. Of course, it should be mentioned that such contact between the urban and the rural elites did not completely bridge this gap, though it was narrowed. But the most important point so far as the present chapter is concerned is that the increasing contact between

---

Chairmen and the Members of the Union/Town Committees and other prominent persons.

1 *PARD* (*Peshawar*) *Report No*. 9, p. 31.

the urban and rural elites enhanced the capacity of the rural elite to influence bureaucratic decisions concerning development administration.

The local councils were now gradually becoming an important structure of interest articulation. They were serving as "a vehicle for transmitting" needs and desires of rural society to higher bureaucratic authorities.[1] Of course, all the demands and interests of the rural leaders were not exactly the same as those of the general people of the rural areas with the result that those of the latter received only partial attention.

The local councils also provided the rural leaders with the opportunity to bring the irregularities in development administration and works to the notice of the higher bureaucracy and to exert pressure on it through the council in order to get things done. The following example may be cited: One non-official member of the Pabna District Council, who was also the Chairman of a Union Council

> "complained that contractors entrusted with earthwork for repairing roads constructed under Works Programme are doing earthwork by tempering old pits and no diagonal bars are also being kept in these pits which would make the measurement difficult of the actual earthwork done by the contractors in those pits.

---

[1] Friedman, *Pacific Affairs*, p. 123. Such needs ranged from those for roads, bridges, tubewells, primary schools, dispensaries, grants etc. to various types of miscellaneous needs. The following example illustrates the nature of the miscellaneous needs. In a meeting of the Pabna District Council a non-official member drew the attention of the D.O. to the difficulties in obtaining an Inter-District Route Permit and suggested that the government be moved through the council to authorise him (the D.O.) to issue the permit. The council welcomed the idea. At this stage, the D.O. told the members that a foreign expert who was attached to the Waterways and Road Transport department of the Government of East Bengal would visit Pabna soon and that he might be enlightened about the problem. The council unanimously resolved that a sub-committee be formed with the following members to draft and submit a memorandum to the foreign expert through the D.O.: (i) Vice-Chairman of the Pabna District Council (Convenor), (ii) S.D.O., *Sadar* sub-division, (iii) S.D.O., Serajganj outlying sub-division, (iv) the Chairman of a Municipal Committee, and (v) the Managing Director of Edruc Ltd. [Proceedings of the Pabna District Council (Ordinary Meeting), March 26, 1965.]

"The Chairman, District Council [i.e. D.O.] requested the Councillor to bring such matters to the notice of the Sub-Divisional Officer, Serajganj, for taking the necessary action.

"However, the House unanimously resolved that diagonal bars in all pits should be kept, without which no measurement should be recorded by the supervising staff and the District Engineer and other supervisory staff should keep an eye on that."[1]

The chain of local bodies was not simply a one-way channel of communication. The administrative agencies also found it convenient to communicate through it with the rural masses. This chain made it easier for them to have access to the innermost parts of rural society. Now many instructions, directives, information, etc. were channelled through the councils by the district and other subordinate authorities as well as by the provincial government. Thus, these bodies "proved [to be]. . .useful media for the expression of the view point of the public on the one hand and a useful channel for passing on the policies and directives of the government to the public through the members on the other".[2]

The nation building departments sometimes "seek and secure their [local council's] help in implementing their development projects in rural areas".[3] Such help facilitated the execution of these projects. In helping the execution of government projects, sometimes they added to the government's allocation of funds by raising local contributions, either in cash or through voluntary labour.[4] The seeking of help by departments also had the effect of adding to the influence of the rural leaders.

Many development plans or programmes of the nation building departments were explained to the members of the local councils[5]

1 *Ibid.* 2 *PARD* (*Peshawar*) *Report No.* 9, p. 264.

3 "Report from East Pakistan" by A.M.S. Ahmad in Aziz Beg (ed.), *Grass Roots Government* (Rawalpindi, 1962). p. 155.

4 *Ibid.*, p. 155.

5 For example, in a meeting of the Pabna District Council, the D.O. "requested the Executive Engineer P.H. [Public Health] Engineering [Department] to apprise the House about the comprehensive water supply scheme of Pabna town". The Executive Engineer "informed the House that Government had sanctioned a $9\frac{1}{2}$ lac rupee scheme for this town to be executed within a period of 4 years. The work had already begun. This year

either to achieve publicity or to coordinate plans with those of local councils or to seek, as noted above, the help of the non-official members. As a result, these members, and through them many others, came to know about various activities of the nation building departments. Such information enabled them to influence departmental decisions concerning the selection, planning and execution of the projects. Information is always a very important source of power.

Now the higher bureaucracy did not entirely depend on the lower bureaucracy for regular supervision of and for information about development works. The councillors were often asked by the higher bureaucracy to shoulder some responsibilities in these respects. For example, at a meeting of the Pabna District Council, the D.O. "requested the councillors to be vigilant about the development works going on in their areas and report to him about the defects of the works if found during their supervision of works".[1] For administrative convenience, the bureaucracy also asked for the cooperation of the councillors in respect of those matters which were not even directly connected with development administration or with the local councils. For example, at a meeting of the Pabna District Council, the D.O. "requested the councillors to exert their influence over local people in paying their rents, loans and other dues to the Government and he also requested the councillors to cooperate with the officials engaged in collecting loans, rents and other dues to the Government, in the interest of the people of the district".[2] The officials' readiness to seek cooperation from the non-official members in turn indicated

---

Rs. $2\frac{1}{2}$ lacs had been sanctioned. Contractors had come down to the spot and begun sinking an 8″ tube well. The construction work of the R.C.C. elevated tank was also in progress. This work would take 2 years for completion. He also informed the House that he had also been trying to get the services of one Engineer exclusively for this work and the authorities had been moved through the Deputy Commissioner [i.e. D.O.]." [Proceedings of the Pabna District Council (Ordinary Meeting), Feb. 27, 1962.]

[1] *Ibid.* (Ordinary Meeting), May 31, 1965.

[2] *Ibid.* (Ordinary Meeting), March 26, 1965.

that the former were now gradually becoming dependent, no doubt to a limited degree, on the local leaders in conducting various aspects of district administration.

Some Concluding Observations

From the foregoing discussion we find that while formerly the bureaucratic agencies had been the only regular link and the channel of the two-way communication between the top layer of the district bureaucracy and the rural people, now along with the bureaucratic channel a new non-official channel was established. Through this channel information moved backward and forward. This channel was "unfolding a process of diffusion of power in rural society".[1] Moreover, by opening a two-way non-official channel of communication and by providing common platforms for the officials and the non-officials, an effective fusion of official and non-official agencies were brought about at various levels of district administration. This was a situation which "brought the administration and the people closer together, [2] although bureaucratic influence is still very evident, especially in West Pakistan. Even so, a process of change has been initiated. The administration has become more responsive".[3]

From the foregoing discussion of the system of local bodies, it may now be observed that the members of the bureaucracy, who were officially and hierarchically responsible to the provincial government and who had all along exercised, generally speaking, unimpeded powers with ease and assigned to themselves the right of interpreting and protecting public interests,[4] were now required

1 Inayatullah, *Changing Character*, p. 40. Also see Masihuzzaman, "What is Basic Democracy" in Aziz Beg (ed.), *op. cit.*, pp. 27, 40.

2 The Constitution Commission also observed that "there is close association between the non-official members and the officers of government at various grades both in development and in non-development matters". (*Report of the Constitution Commission*, para. 111.)

3 B.G. Verghese, "Pakistan Visited: VII—Basic Democracies" in *The Times of India*, Dec. 8, 1964. Also see the comments in A.T.R. Rahman, "Rural Institutions in India and Pakistan" in *Asian Survey*, no. 9, vol. viii, Sept. 1968, pp. 795-796.

4 Of course, in the event of political pressure and interference, the powers and authority of the bureaucracy became circumscribed.

to perform their functions, mainly the development functions, in association and in consultation with the local leaders. These leaders were wielding increasing influence and power, speaking on behalf of the people, claiming to represent their interests and trying to be assertive, to have a sizeable share in the decision-making process of development administration at various levels of the district. The institutionalised local leadership was gradually making its existence felt. The bureaucracy was now facing a new challenge—a challenge of being responsive to the demands of the local leaders. In fact, an underlying tussle was gradually emerging between these leaders and the bureaucracy. In effect, it operated to the disadvantage or rather to the discomfort of the bureaucracy, and to the advantage of the local leaders. It seemed that from time to time the local leaders tried to widen the interpretation of the role and authority of the local bodies, in order to "enhance their power and control over the decision making machinery. The entrenched bureaucracy, on the other hand, would like to narrow and restrict it to ensure that the *status quo* is not disturbed."[1] Of course, it was "possible for a skilful official to exert great influence over lay representatives—but to speak in these terms is already to speak of a transformed situation".[2]

Before we end our discussion of the post-58 system of local bodies, the paradoxical effects of the system may be summarised below: The system of "Basic Democracies" was, in fact, a double-edged sword. On the one hand, as a four-tier system of local councils (as we have just noted), it became a structure for interest articulation, and a two-way channel of communication between the bureaucracy and rural society and also between the rural elite and the urban elite. It increased the competitiveness of rural political life, facilitated the planning and execution of the community development programmes, brought about a fusion of official and

[1] Masihuzzaman, *BD and DA*, p. 181.

[2] Morris-Jones, *India*, p. 147. Also see present writers' comments in fn. 1, p. 381 (above).

non-official agencies at the various layers of district administration, initiated a process of diffusion of power in rural society and institutionalised local leadership at the various levels with the result that the local leaders could influence in varying degrees the decisions of the bureaucracy, which was gradually becoming responsive to their demands.[1]

On the other hand, as the electoral college the system of "Basic Democracies" served the particularistic political interests and motives of an authoritarian regime and caused political ills, corruption and malpractices of serious nature. It had created a situation in which the ruling group or party could compel the bureaucracy, especially before the election, to exert undue pressure and influence on the pro-opposition or "neutral" "Basic Democrats", in order to force them to support the ruling party.[2] We have also noted above that this system, which disfranchised the people of former Pakistan and thus deprived them of their right to select their parliamentary representatives, was very unpopular especially in East Bengal. It was widely believed and felt that the Ayub regime which avoided direct election on the basis of adult franchise had deliberately introduced the system for giving itself an appearance of being a democratically elected government and for keeping itself in power for an indefinite period. As a result, there was a serious lack of confidence in and of public respect for these bodies especially in East Bengal. So the very fact that the "Basic Democrats" constituted the electoral college, seriously undermined and minimised the importance and effectiveness of the "Basic Democracies" as local government institutions.[3]

From our foregoing discussion in this chapter, we may say, in a nutshell, that the local administrative system increasingly became politicised and that the bureaucracy became responsive to the political process, rather than to the democratic process.[4]

[1] See above, pp. 388-404. [2] *Ibid.*, pp. 381-388. [3] *Ibid.*, chap. iii.

[4] Also see *Ibid.*, for Philip Mason's comment, p. 366.

Post-1971 Period. We have already noted that in Bangladesh the system of direct election on the basis of adult franchise has been introduced and that the "Basic Democracies" were abolished immediately after liberation. An outline of the new system of local bodies at the union, *thana*, and district levels and in urban areas has been given, though the details have not yet been spelt out. It is generally felt that the new bodies will consist of elected non-officials only and that most probably necessary arrangements will be made to ensure that certain percentage of the members of the higher local bodies are filled by the members of the lower local bodies so that a channel or line of communication may stretch from the highest to the lowest tier and bridge the gap between various grades of leadership. As it would not constitute electoral college, it will not be so unpopular. Thus we find that the new system has not inherited the worst defect of the former system. Moreover, the official influence and tutelage over local bodies will be less than before. So they will have more freedom of initiative and action. But it appears that in Pakistan the bureaucracy will continue to exercise considerable control and influence on local bodies in the foreseeable future.

In Pakistan also, the members of the local bodies will not be required to constitute electoral college. So, in both Bangladesh and Pakistan the nature of the relationship that existed between the local leaders and the national leaders under the former system of local bodies has undergone considerable change. Now the nature of the relationship is more or less similar to the relationship that existed in the pre-58 period. Of course, it is widely felt that nowadays the bureaucracy is much more susceptible to political pressure than the bureaucracy of the pre-58 period. One of the reasons is that in the period between 1947 and 1958, a considerable section of the bureaucracy inherited from British India the attitude and tradition of impartiality and neutrality. But in the course of the last twenty five years the situation has undergone enormous changes. Moreover, the secured position of the ruling parties in both the countries has also made the bureaucracy more submissive. It should also be noted that unlike its counterpart in the pre-1958 period, the present bureaucracy no longer enjoys security of service.

In the post-1971 period the relationship between the bureaucracy and the political sector is taking a new shape and after few years, when a clear pattern will perhaps emerge, it will be more appropriate to discuss about such relationship in clearer terms.

CHAPTER VIII

SUMMARY: CHANGING PATTERN

We may now repeat, in a nutshell, some of the main points, that we have discussed in preceding chapters, in order to have better idea of the changing pattern of district administration and that of its interactions with politics :

Modern district administration in Bangladesh and Pakistan had its origin in the first hundred years of British administration in South Asia. This period witnessed an ideological conflict between the Cornwallis or non-paternal school of district administration and the Munro or paternal school of district administration, which were profoundly influenced by the Whig philosophy (of John Locke) and the Utilitarian philosophy (of Bentham and James Mill) respectively. With the exception of some years, the Cornwallis system was in operation in the Bengal Presidency, while the Munro system was working in the rest of British India. Towards the end of the 1850s the paternal school emerged decisively victorious and thus the paternal system of district administration was introduced throughout British India[1] with the result that the Collector, in whose person the powers and functions of the District Magistrate were vested, became the all-powerful administrative and executive head of the district with full control over all the departments including the police but excluding the higher judiciary.[2] In fact, now the D.O. became the miniature governor of the district. The whole administration of the district revolved around him. His most important functions were the collection of revenue and the maintenance of law and order including the trial of

[1] See above, chap. i.

[2] Of course, in Non-Regulation Provinces he also held the po t of District and Sessions Judge for some time. M inly in the last quarter of the last century separate District and Sessions Judges, were gradually appointed in these provinces.

less important criminal cases.[1] Of course, there were considerable differences between Regulation and Non-Regulation Provinces. In the latter the D.O.s had much more discretionary and authoritarian powers than their counterparts in the former. With the passage of time, especially towards the end of the last century, steps were gradually taken to place the administration of the Non-Regulation Provinces on the same footing as that of the Regulation Provinces. But in practice, still there were some differences between them. At the time of partition in 1947 the areas which are now sovereign independent states of Bangladesh and Pakistan inherited administrative traditions of Regulation and Non-Regulation Provinces with the result that the D.O.s in Pakistan enjoy more discretionary and summary powers and authorities than their counterparts in Bangladesh.[2]

With the gradual increase in the number and importance of specialised departments and especially with the introduction of political and constitutional reforms under the 1919 and 1935 Acts, the influence and authority of the D.O. lessened in comparison with the past. But still he remained the most powerful and preeminent figure in the district, the embodiment of effective authority who could get things done (whether, for example, it was the question of handling the outbreak of violence or the initiation of a child welfare movement) and to whom the countryside turned in times of need and calamity.[3]

Since partition in 1947, although the formal structure of administration has changed very little, it has had to operate in a changed political, administrative and social environment. The D.O. and other officers have had to adjust their positions to the changed and changing environment. In comparison with the past, the local leaders as well as local people are much less overawed by the bureaucracy. The last three decades or so have witnessed increasing diffusion of official and non-official influence and a continuous process of redistribution of powers and authorities between them.

[1] See above, chap. i. [2] *Ibid.*, chaps. i, iv, v.

[3] *Ibid.*, chaps. vi, vii. Especially see Simon Commission's comment, quoted above in chapter vi, p. 332.

The line of division between official and non-official spheres of control and influence on the decision making process at the local level is being redefined. In comparison with the past, the local leaders have much greater say in the affairs of their areas. The officials have become increasingly responsive to their demands and wishes. The local leaders, who are gradually becoming influential and assertive, can influence the decisions of the bureaucracy, especially those concerning development. Local leaders, who have close contact with the leadership of the ruling party, bring to bear considerable pressure on administration. Political interference with administrative procedures has also increased to an extraordinary degree[1]. The D.O. and other officers find it essential to keep politically influential local leaders in good humour. (Also see above : "Some Concluding Observation", chap. vii, pp. 402-404.)

The D.O. is not only facing a challenge to his authority from outside the administration, i.e. from the political sector, but also from within the administration. The officers of other departments have become increasingly hostile to the preeminent position of the D.O. and try to bypass him or flout his authority. The result is that he finds it extremely difficult to perform effectively his role as the coordinator of the functions of the various departments. Such intra-bureaucratic tension impedes smooth running of administration and has seriously reduced its efficiency.[2]

Though the D.O. is still the most powerful and influential person in the district, in comparison with pre-partition days his authority has been materially reduced as a result of such challenge to his position from both outside and inside the administration. Nowadays in handling many administrative or extra-administrative affairs, he has often to cajole and persuade, whereas in the past he was rather assertive and forceful. He has to act tactfully or rather diplomatically in order to avoid head on collision or acute tension with the heads of other departments or the politically oriented local leaders. If he fails to act tactfully, he faces many difficulties and finds himself in a problematic situation. So, the

[1] *Ibid.*, chap. vii.

[2] *Ibid.*, chap. vi

style of administration has undergone considerable changes, although the formal structure of administration has remained almost completely unchanged.

With the increasing modernisation of administration and with an increase in the number and importance of other functions, and in the incomes from other and new sources, the land revenue function, which is the oldest and was one of the most important functions of district administration, has naturally become relatively unimportant and receives very little attention from the D.O. especially in Bangladesh[1] On the other hand, with the increaseing importance of community development,[2] the development function, which was once one of the miscellaneous functions of district administration, has become one of the two most important functions of district administration in both Bangladesh and Pakistan, the other being the law and order function.[3] It has now become incumbent on the D.O. to spend a good deal of time and energy in order to further the cause of development.[4] Thus, district administration which was formerly a revenue and law and order oriented administration is increasingly becoming a development oriented administration. The increasing importance of community development has also enormously added to the vigour and importance of local bodies and local leaders.[5]

The increasing volume of work in almost every branch of district administration has also gradually caused and warranted

[1] *Ibid.*, chap. iv. Of course, the importance of revenue function in Pakistan is much more than that of the revenue function in Bangladesh. But in Pakistan also its importance is much less than before.

[2] *Ibid.*, chap. v.

[3] The development and the law and order functions have some bearing on each other. The D.O. (and S.D.O.) makes use of the enormous influence and prestige, which he enjoys by virtue of being the head of the law and order branch of district administration, in order to further the cause of development in the district. So his law and order powers indirectly facilitate the process of development administration in the district. On the other hand, the development function brings him in close contact with rural elite who become an additional source of information sometimes concerning matters relating to law and order.

[4] See above, chaps. iii, v.

[5] *Ibid.*, chap. v.

some changes in it. Below the D.O., the number of both high-ranking as well as petty officials has considerably increased and some new functionaries have also been created with the result that the D.O., who once had very close contact with rural population, has gradually moved away from the people and now his contact with them is rather infrequent and impersonal. The early 1960s witnessed considerable delegation and decentralisation of authority from the higher levels to the district level and also from the district level to other lower levels. The D.O. was also relieved of many routine and unimportant functions, which were entrusted to his subordinate officers.[1]

Almost all the changes that we have noted in the post-partition period, in fact began long before partition although they have become accelerated since then.

There are considerable social, political, administrative and cultural differences between Bangladesh and Pakistan. Firstly, the politico-social environment in Bangladesh is much less authoritarian than that in Pakistan. Secondly, the people in the former are politically much more conscious than those in the latter. Thirdly, while most of the high-ranking officials in the former come from a variety of social classes, those in the latter mainly come from the "upper" classes, especially from the landed "aristocracy".[2] Fourthly, the administrative legacies of the former are different from those of the latter in view of the fact that at the time of partition the area which now constitutes Bangladesh inherited the tradition of the Regulation Province which was much less authoritarian than the tradition of the Non-Regulation Province, inherited by the area which now constitutes Pakistan. They also inherited different types of land tenure systems.[3] There are also other differences such as linguistic, cultural, racial, attitudinal etc. For such differences, district administration in Bangladesh is much less haughty and is closer to the people in mood and attitude than that in Pakistan.[4] So, the

[1] *Ibid.*, chap. iii.

[2] *Ibid.*, chap. ii.

[3] *Ibid.*, chap. i.

[4] *Ibid.*, chap. ii.

style of district administration in Bangladesh is also different from that of district administration in Pakistan.

Finale

In preceding chapters of this book we have discussed the changing pattern of various aspects of district administration and of its interactions with politics in Bangladesh and Pakistan. The two countries have been passing through a period of considerable socio-political transformation. The process of such environmental change has also caused and warranted considerable change in the actual working of district administration and in its relation with political forces because it is within this context that administration, as in any other country, operates. As a result, the style and the behavioural aspect of district administration have already undergone enormous change especially in the course of last twenty five years, though its formal structure has not changed in the course of last hundred years. We have also noted that for environmental and other differences between Bangladesh and Pakistan, the style of administration and space of change and development are not same in these two countries.

APPENDICES

APPENDIX A

DISTRICTS IN BANGLADESH:
AREA, POPULATION AND DENSITY OF POPULATION

		AREA IN SQUARE MILES	POPULATION IN THOUSANDS	DENSITY PER SQ. MILE	AREA PLACE	POPULATION PLACE	DENSITY PLACE
1	Mymensingh	6,361	7,019	1,103	1	1	5
2	Dacca	2,882	5,096	1,768	8	2	1
3	Comilla	2,594	4,389	1,639	12	3	2
4	Barisal	4,240	4,262	1,005	5	4	9
5	Rangpur	3,704	3,796	1,025	6	5	8
6	Sylhet	4,785	3,490	729	3	6	15
7	Faridpur	2,694	3,179	1,180	10	7	4
8	Chittagong	2,705	2,983	1,103	9	8	5
9	Rajshahi	3,654	2,811	769	7	9	12
10	Khulna	4,652	2,449	526	4	10	15
11	Noakhali	1,855	2,383	1,285	14	11	3
12	Jessore	2,547	2,196	860	15	12	10
13	Pabna	1,877	1,959	1,044	13	13	7
14	Dinajpur	2,609	1,710	655	11	14	14
15	Bogra	1,502	1,574	1,048	16	15	6
16	Kushtia	1,371	1,166	851	17	16	11
17	Chittagong Hill Tracts	5,093	385	76	2	17	16
		55,126	50,840	922	—	—	—

Sources: The Census of Pakistan, 1961, vol. 2, pp. ii—8, ii—11.

Note: The Districts that were created in 1969 are not shown in this table. As 1971 census was delayed, recent population figures are not yet available.

APPENDIX B

DISTRICTS IN PAKISTAN
AREA, POPULATION AND DENSITY OF POPULATION

		AREA IN SQUARE MILES	POPULATION IN THOUSANDS	DENSITY PER SQ. MILE	AREA PLACE	POPULATION PLACE	DENSITY PLACE
1	Multan	5,630	2,702	480	17	1	11
2	Lyalpur	3,516	2,684	762	28	2	4
3	Lahore	2,216	2,480	1,119	40	3	2
4	Montgomary	4,224	2,134	505	25	4	10
5	Karachi	1,357	2,044	1,506	46	5	1
6	Sialkot	2,067	1,596	772	41	6	3
7	Malakand Agency	12,344	1,537	124	6	7	32
8	Sargodha	4,775	1.468	307	23	8	15
9	Hazara	6,051	1,385	220	15	9	22
10	Gujrat	2,264	1,326	586	39	10	7
11	Gujranwala	2,312	1,292	559	38	11	9
12	Hydrabad	4,969	1,286	259	22	12	18
13	Peshawar	1,545	1,213	737	45	13	5
14	Rawalpindi	2,022	1,137	562	42	14	8
15	Sheikhpura	2,312	1,081	467	28	15	12
16	Jhang	3,401	1,079	317	31	16	14
17	Rahimyar Khan	4,493	1,016	226	24	17	21
18	Muzaffargarh	5,613	990	176	18	18	28
19	Sukkur	5,531	837	151	19	19	30
20	Bahawalnagar	3,428	823	240	30	20	19
21	Mardan	1,211	814	672	48	21	6
22	Dera Ghazi Khan	9,359	777	83	10	22	36
23	Cambellpur	4,148	767	185	26	23	25
24	Jhelum	2,772	749	270	35	24	17
25	Mianwali	5,403	747	138	20	25	31
26	Bahawalpur	9,587	736	77	9	26	39
27	Tharparkar	13,435	728	54	5	27	41
28	Nawabshah	2,896	692	239	33	28	20
29	Kohat	2,707	628	181	36	29	26
30	Larkana	2,866	604	211	34	30	23
31	Jacobabad	2,982	529	177	32	31	27
32	Dadu	7,342	485	66	12	32	40
33	Khairpur	6,018	472	78	16	33	38

(Contd.)

APPENDIX B (Contd.)

		AREA IN SQUARE MILES	POPULATION IN THOUSANDS	DENSITY PER SQ. MILE	AREA PLACE	POPULATION PLACE	DENSITY PLACE
34	Sanghar	4,142	430	104	27	34	33
35	Bannu	1,695	428	210	44	35	24
36	Dera Ismail Khan	3,476	383	81	29	36	37
37	Thatta	6,933	362	52	14	37	42
38	Kalat	30,931	341	11	1	38	47
39	Khyber Agency	995	301	303	49	39	16
40	Mohmand Agency	887	294	332	50	40	13
41	Quetta/Pishin	5,314	267	50	21	41	43
42	South Waziristan Agency	2,556	235	92	37	42	34
43	Kurram Agency	1,305	201	154	47	43	29
44	North Waziristan Agency	1,817	159	88	43	44	35
45	Mekran	23,460	147	6	2	45	49
46	Sibi	10,446	123	12	8	46	46
47	Loralai	7,364	111	15	11	47	44
48	Lasbela	7,048	91	13	13	48	45
49	Zhob	10,475	88	8	7	49	48
50	Kharan	18,553	42	2	4	50	50
51	Chagai	19,516	41	2	3	51	51
		310,403	42,880	138	—	—	—

Sources: All districts excluding Political Agencies—*The Census of Pakistan, 1961*, vol. 3, pp. I—35, II—13-14, II—19. Political Agencies—*Census Bulletin No.* 2 (Karachi, 1961), pp. 50-53.

Note: Districts that were created in 1969 are not shown in this table. As 1971 census was delayed, recent population figures are not yet available.

APPENDIX C

DISTRICT ADMINISTRATION AND RURAL PROBLEMS

[The nature of general administrative function is so diverse and varied that a general discussion, like the one in the text above, does not give a clear picture. The report, which is quoted below and which contains some examples, will give us a fairly clear impression. We shall also see that some general administrative activities are closely interrelated with development function as well as law and order and revenue functions. The report namely "Sulla is a Problem" was written in 1962 by an Assistant Commissioner (later became District Officer) who, at that time, was a CSP probationer in the Sylhet district in East Bengal. The typed report was obtained by the present writer from the author of the report.]

As desired by the Deputy Commissioner, Sylhet, I had a part of my circle-training at the Sulla Circle. Before I left for Sulla the Deputy Commissioner and the Sub-Divisional Officer of the Sunamganj, assigned these particular responsibilities to me, namely, (1) to select the site for a *Dak* Bungalow [Rest House or a place for night halts; especially meant for officers on tour] at Gungirgaon, the headquarters of Sulla *thana*, (2) to discuss and explore the possibility of merging the resources of Giridhar and Gungirgaon High Schools, (3) to select a site for Gungirgaon Township, and (4) to enquire into the peculiar problems and difficulties of the people of this area.

I reached Gungirgaon on the 19th September and stayed there up to the 23rd. I made an extensive tour by country boat and met the Basic Democrats and notary members of the public. I discussed with them their problems and difficulties and came to certain conclusions which are enumerated below:

As regards the selection of a site for the proposed *Dak* Bungalow I inspected the surrounding places including the local *Vaishnava Akhra*. The Circle Officer of Sulla circle and the Officer in Charge [i.e Sub-Inspector of Police] of Sulla Police Station were with me. Both of the officers agreed with me that the vacant water sub-merged space between the Inspection Bungalow and the *tehsil* office will be a suitable site. This is a *Khas* [government] land, and it is considerably higher than the surrounding lands. Still it has to be raised by about 8 feet. The earth work will cost about rupees 1000/-.

I talked to Mr. Mohendra Chandra Das (the doner and President of the Governing Body of Giridhar High School) and Mr. Ramesh Chandra Roy who was the doner of now dilapidated High School at Gungirgaon. I discussed with them if it was possible to pull out the resources of Gungirgaon High School and utilise those for smooth running of Giridhar High School. A few difficulties stand in the way of this proposition. I understand there is communal rivalry between the local *Das* and *Kaivartas*. The *Das* community is overwhelming in number and they are solidly behind the Giridhar High School. The *Kaivartas* (they usually use the title 'Roy') are a minority and they are in favour of a high school at Gungirgaon. As a matter of fact, a former Sub-Divisional

Officer of Sunamganj, Mr. B.R. Nizam, persuaded Mr. Ramesh Chandra Roy to construct now dilapidated tin shed at Gungirgaon. Mr. Roy is very conscious of the prestige of his family and community and he was in tears to listen to the idea of giving his resources for a school run by his rivals.

In the entire Sulla *thana* there is only one running High School that is, the Giridhar High School at Nayagaon which is at a distance of about two miles from Gungirgaon. This school cannot fully meet the need of the people of the western portion of the *thana* one reason being the absence of good communications, as students of Gungirgaon find it difficult and hence don't go to Nayagaon.

The plan of setting up a township at Gungirgaon as the Headquarters of Sulla *thana* warrants the necessity of establishing a High School at Gungirgaon. Moreover, I am inclined to believe that it is good to increase rather than decrease the number of schools in an area where there is only one graduate, three matriculates and no qualified doctor...

In view of these, I recommend that a plan to help run the High School at Gungirgaon may be taken up. Mr. Ramesh Chandra Roy is willing to donate more land to meet a part of the running expenditure of this school.

As passing reference, I have a few words about the primary school at the Gungirgaon village. This school was taken up by the Govt. as a Model Primary School and a sum of rupees 10,000 was spent for this school. But the school is left half constructed as private subscription could not be raised. I don't understand how the local officers and the Chairman of the Union Council could agree to select this school, as the people around are very poor and they have no capacity to donate for that school. Immediate action may be taken to save the Govt. money already spent and the whole matter may be enquired into.

The Circle Officer in charge of Sulla resides at the circle headquarters of Derai, as there is no office at Sulla. There is a proposal to select the site for a township at Gungirgaon to station the headquarters of Sulla. When asked by the Sub-Divisional Officer, Sunamganj the Circle Officer submitted a plan for the proposed township at Gungirgaon ..When he submitted the plan he did not see the tank belonging to the Police Station as it was completely under water and hence could not be distinguished from the adjoining fields. If this plan is approved boulder-works will be necessary to protect the southern side of the townshi pfrom the ferocious waves in rainy season. It will also be necessary to negotiate with the local *Vaishnava Akra*, the High School and the Police Station to acquire lands from these institutions.

I consulted the Circle Officer and the Officer in Charge of the Police Station of Sulla and both of them agreed with me that if a big tank is dug at the northern side of the Police Station a large township can be constructed without much difficulty. Moreover, this tank may be utilised by the fishery department for pisciculture which will bring revenue to the Government to the tune of rupees 2,000 per annum. The initial digging up the tank and raising of land will cost only about rupees 25,000. Considering all these I submit the enclosed plan no. 1 for favour of consideration. [This plan has not been incorporated in the appendix.]

During my stay at Sulla I found a number of peculiar problems and difficulties from which the people of this area suffer. The number one problem is the lack of communications. During the rainy season Sulla (and Derai too) is connected with Sunamganj and Ajmerganj by service launch and country boat. A journey from Sunamganj to Gungirgaon killed thirteen hours of mine. In winter the tale is more dreadful. A launch takes more time as Surma [name of a river] flows in a jig-jag way and there is no short cut. Within the area itself country boat is the only transport available in rainy season, and boat journey is risky enough. In winter one has to walk. There is no option.

A road was being constructed to connect Patharpur and Gungirgaon. I was told that this road has been abandoned after half construction. It has become necessary to complete this road within a short period of time.

I have already mentioned that during the rainy season it is highly dangerous. to undertake a journey by boat. There is every risk of straying away from the proper course. This is especially true in case of journey by night. I think if a light house is constructed at Gungirgaon the situation will improve greatly

Though Gungirgaon has been made the headquarters of Sulla *thana* there is no telegraph office there. The nearest telegraph office is at Marcoly at a distance of about six miles. The telegraph wire line for this area begins at Habiganj and ends at Derai. A telegram sent from Sunamganj to Derai reaches its destination via Sylhet, [i.e. district headquarters] and Habiganj after six to nine days. I think a direct telegraph line between Gungirgaon and Sunamganj is possible.

Any way, I was told that even the existing telegraph line is in a very dilapidated condition. Breakdown in telegraphic communication is frequent. A moderately strong wind or hail storm is sufficient to cause it. If the Gungirgaon township plan is approved the officials also will suffer greatly. A small wireless unit stationed at Gungirgaon will certainly speed up communications between Sulla and the outside world. Two transistor radio sets—one each at Sulla and Derai *Thana* Council offices will also prove useful, both for the public and the Government officers.

The nearest launch *ghat* [station] for the people of this area is at Patharpur though the Surma flows at a distance of three miles only. This causes great hardship for the people who want to go to Sunamganj or Sylhet. The local people want a launch *ghat* at Bherandahar. This, I was told, will remove a lot of botheration.

I learnt to my utter dismay that there is not a single private licentiate doctor within a radius of ten miles. There is a charitable dispensary at Sulla with one L.M.F. [i.e. not a medical graduate but has obtained a licence from a medical school—a licentiate doctor]. This dispensary is housed in a rented cottage. The Officer in Charge of the Police Station and the constables at Gungirgaon and the people around go unattended by a doctor—a horrible situation even to imagine. I think that this dispensary may be shifted immediately to Gungirgaon and housed in a portion of the Union Council office until land is raised and a dispensary building is constructed.

I was told by the local officers and some members of the public that this area is infested by dacoits, burglars and all criminals of this sort. The most funny aspect of this problem is that the criminals live in some well known villages. Throughout generations the profession of the inhabitants of these villages is burglary and dacoity. But both the police and the public are ineffective against them. The villages in which the criminals live are said to be (1) Ujangaon, (2) Chikadoobi, (3) Ballavpur and (4) Kamargaon. There is an outpost at Kamargaon to look after movements of the local criminals. When the police gives pressure upon them they go to the nearby areas of Mymensingh district. The criminal of these places allege that they have no land to fall back upon and hence they indulge in these activities. It is suggested that if govt. *khas* land can be distributed among these landless people they may stop their nefarious activities.

An outstanding problem of the people of this area is the absence of any *hat* or *bazaar*. I was told, the nearest market to the south is Ajmerganj at about a distance of ten miles, and to the north the nearest market is that of Derai, about nine miles away. The nearest market to the east is marcoly or Kaderganj. There is no market to the west until one crosses the district border and goes to Mymensingh district. As a result, with the local people suffer the local officials for whom the place has become almost a punishment centre of posting.

I talked to the local Basic Democrats about the matter and the Chairman of Bahara Union Council, Mr. Mohendra Chandra Sarkar assured me that he will manage to start a *hat* at Gungirgaon in no time. I hope he succeeds in his efforts.

During the last *Boro* [name of a kind of seasonal paddy] season hailstorms damaged the standing crops greatly. As a result, the people of this area are very much handicapped. Urgent reliefs, both in cash and in kind, may be sent to this area.

[signature]
Assistant Commissioner, Sylhet.

To
The Deputy Commissioner, Sylhet,
The Sub-divisional Officer, Sunamganj.

APPENDIX D

DISTRICT ADMINISTRATION AND EMERGENCY RELIEF OPERATION

[In early 1960s the coastal districts of East Bengal were thrice hit by very severe cyclone accompanied by very high tidal bore. So far as the districts of East Bengal were concerned many people regarded these cyclones as the worst storms of this century. Each of these cyclones resulted in death of thousands of persons and damaged property worth millions of rupees. The report, quoted below, will give a good picture of the emergency measures taken by the district authority of Chittagong district during the period which immediately followed one of these cyclones. Chittagong was one of the three worst affected districts in East Bengal. The report namely "The cyclone of 28th/29th May, 1963" was written by an Assistant Commissioner of Chittagong district who worked in the 'Control Room' housed in the office of the District Officer. The typed report was obtained by the present writer from that Assistant Commissioner. (later became District Officer).]

[The following six paragraphs are the account of the Additional District Officer (Revenue) incorporated in the report.] 'It was the 28th of May, 1963; I was in the midst of a conference of local revenue officers at the chamber of the Deputy Commissioner (i.e. District Officer) at about mid-day. The conference was due to discuss about the collection of revenue and find out ways and means to step up the progress of collection in the district speedily when the financial year was going to run out within about one month's time.

'The Deputy Commissioner who was presiding over the conference, however, instead of taking up the agenda of the meeting, asked all the officers present to go back to their headquarters as quickly as possible and warn the people about the coming cyclone. This was the first occasion when I came to realise the gravity of the situation regarding the apprehended danger about which the local Metrological Office had already made a forecast.

'...At about 11 P.M. the cyclone had already started...It was about 4.30 in the morning when the cyclone passed away, but the occasional gusty wind and the drizzling were still there...

'At about 6.30 A.M. I went out to contact the Deputy Commissioner. At the foot of the Deputy Commissioner's hill [Deputy Commissioner's residence is situated on a hill top] I found the Deputy Commissioner coming out in a Jeep along with the Officer Commanding [a Major] of the EPR [East Pakistan Rifles]. The Deputy Commissioner asked me to get into the jeep and we all went out for reconnoiterring the affected areas in the city and its outskirts...

'On our way back we stopped at the EPR Head Quarters where from the Deputy Commissioner sent his first report to Government about the cyclone through the EPR wireless.

'We then rode back to the Deputy Commissioner's office where other officers also joined in, and the Deputy Commissioner started planning the EMERGENCY RELIEF OPERATION.

[The following is the own account of the author of the report]....From the 29th onward reports poured into the Deputy Commissioner's office intimating the heavy damage sustained by the people. Within a few days we verified loss of 9,675 human lives and 82,501 cattle heads. Altogether 2,29,637 houses were damaged partially and 3,76,332 totally. In 5,27,758 acres of land crops were damaged. 6,170 boats were lost and 291 fishing nets were either lost or damaged beyond any use. No accurate account could be made of the total loss in terms of money; but a moderate guess would fix figure beyond 10 crores [of rupees].

Immediately after the cyclone it became imperative on the part of the administration to organise quick relief to the cyclone victims who turned paupers overnight...The Deputy Commissioner, Chittagong headed the operation...He was assisted by two Additional Deputy Commissioners, three Assistant Commissioners. At the sub-divisional level Relief Committees were formed with the S.D.O. at the top. In each *thana* a *Thana* Relief Committee was organised and a responsible officer was posted as the Relief Officer. Each *thana* was divided into blocks, preferably union-wise, and an officer was detailed as block officer....147 officers from the Provincial Secretariat and other districts joined the local officers. They were ably assisted by *Ansars* [auxiliary force] and officers and *Jawans* [soldiers] of the Armed Services.

In this connection we take note with gratitude of the services of private organisations like *Memo Khedmat* Committee, Lions Club, students organisations, etc.

The morning of 29th May presented to us a host of problems, viz. determining the extent of damage, restoring communications with the affected areas, burying the dead bodies and arranging food, shelter and medicine for the victims.

Since some of the affected areas were completely cut off from the rest of the world and the people were at the point of starvation, *Chira*, *muri*, biscuits, and other ready-to-eat food stuff were air dropped with the help of PAF [Pakistan Air Force] Freighters. In addition almost all schools, colleges, *Madrasahs* [religious schools] and godowns were converted into relief camps where food was supplied...

Reliefs distributed among the cyclone victims may be categorised as follows: cash grants and loans, foodstuff, clothes, house-building materials, medicine, sanitation and public health, relief to agriculturists and fishermen and test relief.

Food stuffs. Food stuffs were distributed to the cyclone victims under three heads: Air dropping, Gratuitous Relief and Modified Rationing. And items included ready-to-eat (viz. *chira*, *muri*, etc.) stuffs, rice, wheat, *atta* [flour] edible oil, dry milk and dry fish. Up to the end of the emergency 230 maunds of *chira*, *muri*, etc. and 25,00 lbs. of bread were airdropped. Distribution of gratutious relief stands as follows: Rice—102395 maunds; wheat and *atta*—47,9159 maunds; coconut oil—10 drums; soyabin oil—4½ tons; vegetable—2317 cartons; dry milk—900 bags, 41½ tons and 22948 cartons; and dry fish—36½ tons.

In addition to gratuitous relief modified rationing was introduced and rice, wheat and *atta* were made available to the victims at a nominal price. Under this system about 11,00,000 maunds of food grains were distributed through approved dealers.

House Building Materials. For sometime a great majority of the people of the affected areas did not have any roof to take shelter. As a temporary measure all the schools, colleges, *madrasahs* [religious schools] and godowns that were spared by the cyclone were converted into shelter camps. But the administration at the same time went on helping the destitutes with money and house building materials for reconstructing their houses. These materials were either sold at nominal prices from the 18 fairprice shops and 15 forest depots or distributed as outright relief...During the emergency 1946 tons of C.I. sheets were distributed free of cost. And 4,37,000 bamboos, 109 timber poles, 250 cubic feet of treated timber, 4 tons of iron hooks, 88 maunds of wire... [huge number of screws and bolts], 367 tins of kerosene oil, 3 dozens of hurricanes...were sold at nominal prices. Besides house building materials rupees 49,67,000/- and rupees 50,50,000/- were distributed as house building grant and house building loan respectively. From the House Building Finance Corporation also rupees 1,28,000 were sanctioned for the cyclone affected areas.

To protect the people of coastal areas against cyclone and tidal bore in future the Deputy Commissioner, Chittagong formulated a new house building plan. Under his initiative and guidance 'Shelter Houses' are being built, one in each union, to begin within the coastal areas.

Clothes. After the cyclone it became necessary to clothe the people as well. During the emergency 442 bales and 137 cases of *sarees*, *lungis* and plain clothes were distributed free of cost...

Agriculture. Out of 9,57,600 acres of land under cultivation in Chittagong district crops in 5,27,758 acres were damaged by the cyclone and tidal bore. A moderate assessment of damage caused to crops in terms of money will put the figure beyond rupees 3,50,00,00...almost all tanks were innundated by the flood water. To relieve the agriculturists from sufferings the Govt. placed a huge sum of rupees 76,27,064 at the disposal of the administration for distribution in the form of agricultural, cattle purchase and seed loan and grant. In addition to this the Agricultural Development Bank sanctioned rupees 4,71,872 and the Cooperative Bank sanctioned rupees 5,82,300 for the people of cyclonehit areas.

...saline water innundated almost all the reservoirs of sweet water and the cyclone and tidal bore damaged a majority of tube-wells in the affected areas. As a result problems of drinking and irrigation water became acute. The administration reacted quickly to this problem and within a few weeks 487 tanks were dewatered with power pumps and fresh water from 3,000 tube wells was made available to the people.

The Animal Husbandry Department treated 27,238 cattle and vaccinated 1,52,000. With the help of agriculture department *aus* [the name of a kind of seasonal paddy] plants were transplanted in 1,82,175 acres of land.

Public Health. The Department of Public Health did a good job during the emergency operation. With the help of Relief Officers and *Ansar Jawans* about 500 personnel from that department treated about 1,00,000 persons, and innoculated and vaccinated about 17,00,000 persons. The total of medicines distributed among the victims amounted to rupees 4,50,000 approximately.

*Relief to Fishermen...*As a relief to fishermen rupees 4,00,000 were distributed as grant and rupees 9,00,000 as loan.

Test Relief. To prevent further occurrence of tidal bore in coastal areas and to make cash money available to the victims a scheme was taken up for an embankment and rupees 10,00,000 were sanctioned as test relief...

[As grants to educational institutions and to poor students rupees 4,00,000 and rupees 50,000 were distributed respectively.]

In conclusion to this brief report we remember the great services rendered by the officers connected with the relief operation. They worked day and night under circumstances and living conditions to which they were not accustomed. Many of them fell sick and one of them died while he was working...We pay our glowing tribute to Mr. A.K. Das who died while performing his duties and others who worked so hard.

APPENDIX E

MAPS OF BANGLADESH AND PAKISTAN DISTRICTS, 1973

(SAME SCALE)

Pakistan

1. MOHMAND
2. MALAKAND
3. MARDAN
4. KHYBER
5. PESHAWAR
6. KURRAM
7. KOHAT
8. GUJRANWALA
9. SIALKOT
10. SHEKHUPURA
11. LAHORE
12. RAWALPINDI
13. CAMPBELLPORE
14. JHELUM
15. GUJRAT
16. SOUTH WAZIRISTAN
17. BANNU
18. DERA ISMAIL KHAN
19. NORTH WAZIRISTAN
20. JHANG MAGHIANA
21. MIANWALI
22. SARGODHA
23. LYALLPUR
24. QUETTA PISHIN
25. LORALAI
26. SIBI
27. ZHOB
28. CHAGAI
29. MUZAFFARGARH
30. DERA GHAZI KHAN
31. MULTAN
32. MONTGOMERY
33. RAHIMYAR KHAN
34. BHAWALPUR
35. BHAWALNAGAR
36. KHARAN
37. MAKRAN
38. KALAT
39. SUKKUR
40. LARKANA
41. KHAIRPUR
42. NAWABSHAH
43. JACOBABAD
44. LAS BELA
45. KARACHI
46. THAR PARKAR
47. HYDERABAD
48. TATTA
49. DADU
50. SANGHAR
51. HAZARA
52. CHITRAL
53. DIR
54. SWAT
55. AMB

Bangladesh

1. CHITTAGONG
2. CHITTAGONG HILL TRACTS
3. NOAKHALI
4. COMILLA
5. SYLHET
6. MYMENSINGH
7. FARIDPUR
8. DACCA
9. RANGPUR
10. PABNA
11. BOGRA
12. RAJSHAHI
13. DINAJPUR
14. BARISAL
15. KUSHTIA
16. JESSORE
17. KHULNA
18. TANGAIL
19. PATUAKHALI

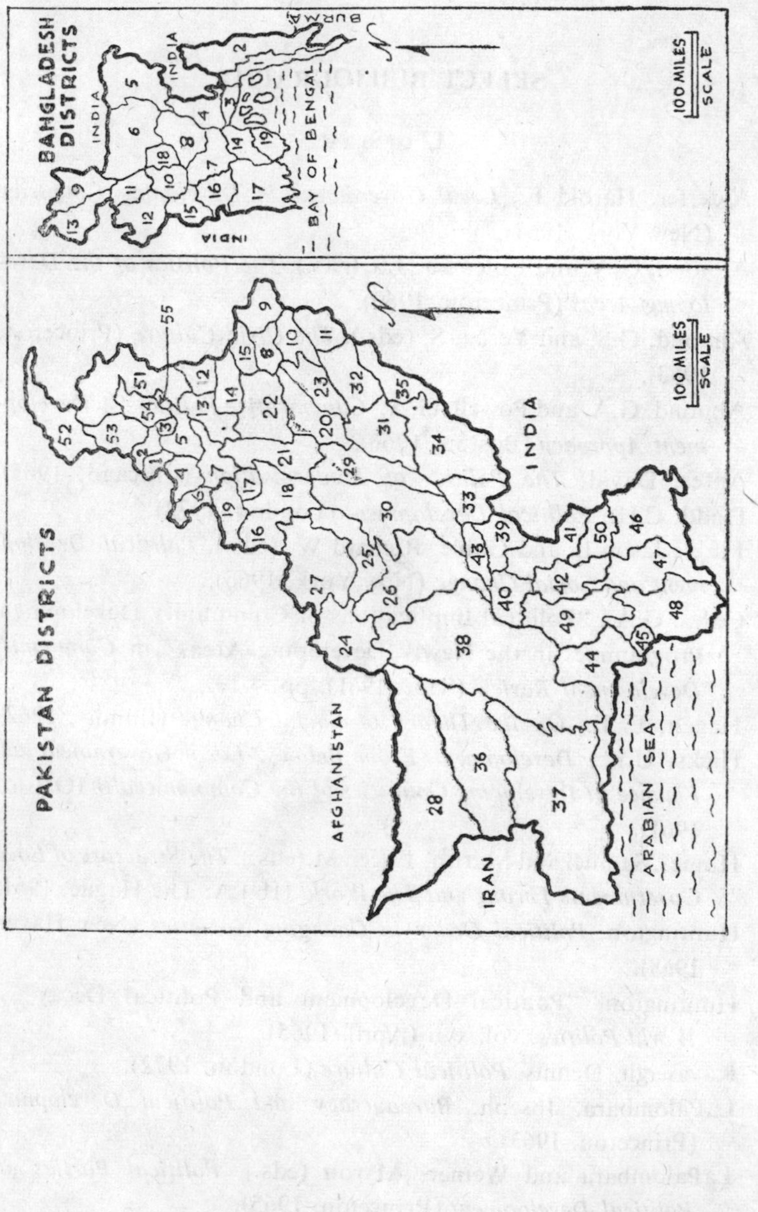
PAKISTAN DISTRICTS
AFGHANISTAN
IRAN
INDIA
ARABIAN SEA
100 MILES
SCALE
BANGLADESH DISTRICTS
INDIA
BAY OF BENGAL
BURMA
100 MILES
SCALE

SELECT BIBLIOGRAPHY

I. GENERAL

Alderfer, Harold F., *Local Government in Developing Countries* (New York, 1964).

Almond, G.A. and Coleman, J.S. (eds.), *The Politics of the Developing Areas* (Princeton, 1960).

Almond, G.S. and Verba, S. (eds.), *The Civic Culture* (Princeton, 1963).

Almond, G.A. and Powell, G.A., *Comparative Politics: A Development Approach* (Boston, 1966).

Apter, David, *The Politics of Modernisation* (Chicago, 1965).

Dodd, C.H., *Political Development* (London, 1972).

Finkle Jason L. and Gable, Richard W. (eds.), *Political Development and Social Change* (New York, 1966).

Gales, G.A., "Political Implications of Community Development Programmes in the Newly Developing Areas" in *Community Development Review* (Sept. 1961), pp. 4-13.

Hagen, E. E., *On the Theory of Social Change* (Illinois, 1962).

Hicks, U.K., *Development From Below : Local Government and Finance in Developing Countries of the Commonwealth* (Oxford, 1961).

Humes, Samuel and Martin, Eileen M.(eds.), *The Structure of Local Governments Throughout The World* (IULA, The Hague, 1961).

Huntington, *Political Order in Changing Societies* (New Haven, 1968).

Huntington, "Political Development and Political Decay" in *World Politics*, vol. xvii (April, 1965).

Kavanagh, Dennis, *Political Culture* (London, 1972).

LaPalombara, Joseph, *Bureaucracy and Political Development* (Princeton, 1963).

LaPalombara and Weiner, Myron (eds.), *Political Parties and Political Development* (Princeton, 1965).

Larner, Daniel, *Passing of the Traditional Society* (1968).

Local Government in the 20th Century (International Union of Local Authorities, Hague, 1963).

Maddick, Henry, *Democracy, Decentralisation and Development* (Bombay, 1963).

Montgomery, John D. and Siffin, William J. (eds.), *Approaches to Development : Politics, Administration and Change* (New York, 1966).

Pye, Lucian, "Community Development as a part of Political Development" in *Community Development Review* (March, 1958), pp. 1-31.

Pye, Lucian and Verba, Sidney (eds.), *Political Culture and Political Development* (Princeton, 1965).

Pye, Lucian (ed.), *Communications and Political Development* (Princeton, 1963).

Riggs, F. W., *Administration in Developing Countries: The Theory of Prismatic Society* (Boston, 1964).

Riggs, F.W., *The Ecology of Public Administration* (London, 1961).

Riggs, F.W., "Relearning an Old Lesson: The Political Context of Development Administration" in *Public Administration Review*, vol. xxv (1965), pp. 70-79.

Robson, William A., *The Governors and the Governed* (London, 1964).

Shils, Edward, *Political Development in the New States* (Hague, 1962).

Tinker, Hugh, *Ballot Box and Bayonet* (London, 1964).

Weiner, Myron (ed.), *Modernisation: The Dynamics of Growth* (New York, 1966).

Wriggins, H.H., *Ceylon : The Dilemmas of a New Nation* (Princeton, 1960).

Wit, Daniel, "A Comparative Study of Local Government and Administration" (cyclostyled) (Bangkok, 1965).

Zinkin, Maurice, *Development for Free Asia* (London, 1956).

Papers (cyclostyled) presented at the International Conference on Theoretical Problems of Administrative Reform in Developing States held at the Rockefeller Foundation Villa Serbelloni, Bellagio, Lake Como, Italy (July 16-22, 1967) under the auspices of the Duke University Commonwealth-Studies Center.

BEFORE 1947

II. OFFICIAL DOCUMENTS AND REPORTS

Parliamentary Papers, especially the following volumes: VII (1812) (The Fifth Report of the Select Committee on the Affairs of the East India Company), V (1810) (Cornwallis' Minutes, 11 Feb., 1793), IX (1831-32) (Bentinck's Minutes, Nov. 10, 1831.)

Report on the Administration of Bengal, 1871-72 (Calcutta, 1872).

Report of the Public Service Commission, 1886-87 (Calcutta, 1888).

Report of the Royal Commission upon Decentralisation in India (London, 1909).

Bengal District Administration Committee, 1913-14: Report (*Levinge Report*) (Calcutta, 1915).

Report of the Royal Commission on the Public Services in India (*Islington Report*) (London, 1917).

Report on Indian Constitutional Reforms (*Montagu-Chelmsford Report*) (Calcutta, 1918).

Report of the Government of India Secretariat Procedure Committee, 1920 (*Llewellyn-Smith Report*) (Reprinted by the NIPA, Karachi, 1963).

Report of the Royal Commission on Agriculture in India (London, 1928).

Memorandum submitted by the Government of Bengal to the Indian Statutory Commission (London, 1930).

Memorandum submitted by the Government of Bihar and Orissa to the Indian Statutory Commission (London, 1930).

Report of the Indian Statutory Commission (*Simon Commission*) (London, 1930).

Report of the Frontier Regulations Enquiry Committee, 1931 (*Niamatullah Report*) (Calcutta, 1931).

Report of the Government of India Secretariat Committee: 1935-36 (*Wheeler Report*) (Reprinted by the NIPA, Karachi, 1963).

Report of the Government of India Secretariat and Procedure, 1937

(*Maxwell Report*) (Reprinted by the NIPA, Karachi, 1963).
Report Regarding the Establishment of the Secretariat Departments (*Chapman Report*) (Govt. of Bengal, Calcutta, 1938) (Reprinted by the NIPA, Dacca, 1963).
Report of the Land Revenue Commission of Bengal (*Floud Commission*) (Calcutta, 1940).
Report of the Local Self-Government Committee, Sind, 1943, (Karachi, 1945).
Report of the Bengal Administration Enquiry Committee : 1944-45 (*Rowlands Report*) (Calcutta 1945) (Reprinted by the NIPA, Dacca, 1962).
Reports on the Re-Organisation of the Central Government : 1945-46 (*Tottenham Report*) (Delhi, 1946) (Reprinted in 1963 by the NIPA, Karachi).
"Outline of District Administration in Bengal" (cyclostyled) (Govt. of Bengal, Home Department, Calcutta, 1944. Reprinted by the NIPA, Dacca).
Civil Budget Estimates (Annually published by the Provincial Governments. From time to time the title varied.).

III. PUBLISHED PRIVATE PAPERS

Forrest, G.W., *Selections from the Minutes and other Official Writings of Honourable Mountstuart Elphinstone* (London, 1884).
Forrest, G., *Selections from the State Papers of the Governor General of India: Lord Cornwallis*, 2 vols. (Oxford, 1926).
Gleig, G.R., *Life of Sir Thomas Munro*, 3 vols. (London, 1830).
Kay, J.W., *Life and Correspondence of Sir John Malcolm*, 2 vols. (London, 1856).
Kay, J.W., *Selections from the Papers of Lord Metcalfe* (London, 1855).
Ross, C., *Correspondence of Charles, First Marquis Cornwallis*, 3 vols. (London, 1859).

IV. BOOKS

Ascoli, E.D., *The Early Revenue History of Bengal* (Oxford, 1917).
Aspinal, A., *Cornwallis in Bengal* (Manchester, 1931).

Bhargava, M.B.L., *Local Self-Government in India* (Lucknow, 1936).
Blunt, Edward, *The I.C.S.* (London, 1937).
Blunt, Edward (ed.), *Social Service in India* (London, 1938).
Bowring, J. (ed.), *The Works of Jeremy Bentham* (Edinburgh, 1837).
Brayne, F.L., *Village Uplift in India* (Gurgaon, 1927).
Brayne, F.L., *Better Village* (Madras, 1937).
Brayne, F.L., *The Socrates in an Indian Village* (London, 1929).
Buckland, C. E., *Bengal under the Lieutenant-Governors from 1884 to 1898* (Calcutta, 1901).
Dodwell, H.H. (ed.), *The Cambridge History of India*, Vols. V and VI (Cambridge, 1929).
Ghosal, A.K., *Civil Service in India (under the East India Company)* (Calcutta, 1944).
Griffiths, Percival, *The British Impact on India* (London, 1952).
Hart, S.G., *Introduction to Self-Government in Rural Bengal* (Calcutta, 1920).
Hunter, William, *The Indian Empire* (London, 1892).
Kabeer, Rokeya R., *Administrative Policy of the Government of Bengal (1870-1890)* (NIPA, Dacca, 1965).
Majumder, R.C., *et. al.*, *The Advanced History of India* (London, 1950).
Metcalf, T.R., *The Aftermath of Revolution: India, 1857-1870* (Princeton, 1964).
Mill, James, *The History of British India*, 6 vols. (London, 1820).
Misra, B.B., *The Central Administration of the East India Company from 1773-1834* (Manchester, 1959).
Moon, P., *Strangers in India* (London, 1944).
O'Malley, L.S.S., *The Indian Civil Service* (London, 1965 edn.).
Roy, N.C., *Village Self-Government in Bengal* (Calcutta, 1932).
Ramsbotham, R.B., *Studies in the Land Revenue History of Bengal* (Calcutta, 1926).
Ruthnaswamy, M., *Some Influences that Made the British Administrative System in India* (London, 1939).
Smith, V.A., *Akbar, The Great Mogul* (Oxford, 1917).
Spear, Percival, *India: A Modern History* (Michigan, 1961).
Spear, Percival, *The Oxford History of Modern India: 1740-1947* (Oxford, 1965).

Stokes, Eric, *The English Utilitarians and India* (Oxford, 1963 edn.).

Thompson, E. and Garratt, G.T., *Rise and Fulfilment of British Rule in India* (London, 1934).

Strachey, J., *India : Its Administration and Progress* (London, 1911).

Tinker, Hugh, *The Foundations of Local Self-Government in India, Pakistan and Burma* (London, 1954).

Woodruff, Philip (Mason, Philip), *The Men Who Ruled India*, 2 vols. (London, 1963 edn.).

SINCE 1947

V. ASSEMBLY AND DISTRICT COUNCIL PROCEEDINGS AND REPORTS OF COMMISSIONS, COMMITTEES AND INDIVIDUAL PERSONS APPOINTED BY THE GOVERNMENT

Constituent Assembly of Pakistan: Debates (1947-56).

National Assembly of Pakistan: Debates (1956-58) (1962-68).

Assembly Proceedings: East Bengal [later East Pakistan] Assembly (1947-58) (1962-68).

Constituent Assembly of Bangladesh: Debates (1972).

Proceedings of the Meetings of the District Councils (Dacca, Pabna and Sylhet districts in East Bengal) (1960-69).

Report of the Pakistan Pay Commission (Karachi, 1949).

Local Government Reforms Committee: First Interim Report (Govt. of Punjab, Lahore, 1951).

"The Report of the Enquiry into the Firing by the Police at Dacca on the 21st February, 1952 by Mr. Justice T. H. Ellis of the Dacca High Court" in *The Dacca Gazette*, Extraordinary, June 3, 1952.

The Improvement of Public Administration in Pakistan (A Report by Rowland Egger) (Karachi, 1952).

Report of the Administrative Enquiry Committee (Karachi, 1953)

The Pak-Punjab Panchayat Reorganisation Report (Lahore, 1954).

Report of the Court of Inquiry Constituted Under Punjab Act II of 1954 to Enquire into the Punjab Disturbances of 1953 (*Munir-Kayani Report*) (Lahore, 1954).

Report of the East Bengal Police Committee, 1953 (Dacca, 1954).

Report of the Local Self-Government Committee (Govt. of Sind, Karachi, 1954).

Report of the Sargodha District Board Elections, 1952-53 (*Leghari Report*) (Lahore, 1954).

"Reorganisation of Pakistan Government for National Development" (cyclostyled) (Gladieux Report) (Planning Board, Karachi, 1955).

Report of the Council for Administration of West Pakistan (Lahore, 1955).

Report by Sir Malcolm Darling, I.L.O. Expert, on Labour Conditions in Agriculture in Pakistan (Karachi, 1957).

Note on Re-organisation of Local Bodies in the Province (A report prepared by S.D. Khan) (Dacca, 1957).

"The Report of the Enquiry into the Firing by the Police at Sylhet on 5th December, 1957 by Mr. Justice A.J. Khan of the Dacca High Court" in *The Dacca Gazette*, Extraordinary, Dec. 3, 1958.

"Report of the Enquiry into the Incidents that took place on 20th and 23rd September, 1958 in the Chambers and Premises of East Pakistan Assembly by Mr. Justice Asir of the High Court of Judicature in East Pakistan at Dacca" in *The Dacca Gazette*, Extraordinary, May 9, 1959.

Report of the Land Revenue Commission, East Pakistan, 1959 (Dacca, 1959).

Report of the Land Reforms Commission for West Pakistan (Lahore, 1959).

Report of the Law Reform Commission, 1958-59 (Karachi, 1959).

Report of the Provincial Administration Commission (Lahore, Feb. 1960).

The following are the cyclostyled Reports/Minutes of the meetings of the Sub-Committee/Panel of officers constituted by the Govt. of East Bengal. (They were asked to work out schemes for implementing various recommendations of the Provincial Administration Commission, 1960. These Sub-Committees/ Panel of Officers put forward their recommendations in their respective reports/Minutes:) "Minutes of the Meeting of the Panel [of Officers] on Development" (July 6, 1960).

"Recommendations of the Panel [of Officers] on the Revenue Set Up" (July 6 and 7, 1960). "Minutes of the Meeting of the Panel [of Officers] on Basic Democracies" (July 7, 1960) "Minutes of the Meeting of the Panel [of Officers] on Law and Order" (July 7, 1960). "Report of the Panel [of Officers] on Reorganisation of Departments" (July 30, 1960). "Report of the Panel [of Officers] on Pattern of Administration" (n.d.). "Report of the Public Services Sub-Committee on the Implementation of the Cabinet Decisions on Chapter 7 of the [Provincial Administration] Commission Report" (n.d.).

Report of the Implementation Sub-Committee on the Re-organisation of District Offices (Dacca, 1960).

Report of the Implementation Sub-Committee on the Reorganisation of Provincial Administration (Dacca, 1960).

Report of the Constitution Commission, Pakistan, 1961 (Karachi, 1962).

Report of the Provincial Re-organisation Committee (Dacca, 1962).

Report of the Administrative Reorganisation Committee (Karachi, 1963).

Report of the Land Revenue Administrative Enquiry Committee, East Pakistan, 1962-63 (Dacca, 1963).

Review of the Office of Divisional Commissioners (S.&G.A. Department, Govt. of E. Bengal, Dacca, 1963).

Towns and Villages of Pakistan (A Study Report by Grenfell Rudduck) (Karachi, 1964).

A Study of District Councils and Municipal Committees made at the Request of the Secretary of Basic Democracies and Local Government by Richard O. Niehoff and George M. Platt (Report) (Dacca, n.d., 1965 ?)

Village Government in East Pakistan: A Study of Union Boards and Union Councils (typed) (A survey report prepared by M. Rashiduzzaman, Dacca).

VI. OTHER OFFICIAL REPORTS AND (IMPORTANT) DOCUMENTS.

Annual Reports of the Federal Public Service Commission, (Karachi).

Census of Pakistan, 1951 (Dacca, Karachi, Lahore, 1952).

Administration Report on the Working of District Boards in the North-West Frontier Province for the Year, 1951-52 (Peshawar, 1953).

Annual Report on the Working of the Municipalities and Notified Area Committees in the North-West Frontier Province for the Year 1951-52 (Peshawar, 1953).

Functions of Commissioners of Divisions (Govt. of East Bengal, Home Department, 1955).

The Constitution of the Islamic Republic of Pakistan, 1956 (Dacca).

The First Five Year Plan 1955-60 (Karachi, 1957).

Village AID Five Year Plan: 1955-56—1959-60 (Karachi, 1956).

Proceedings of the Local Government Seminar, 1956 (Lahore, 1957).

Village AID in West Pakistan (A collection of papers presented at various seminars on Village-AID) (Lahore, 1957).

Annual Report on Basic Democracies (1959-1960) (Karachi, n.d.).

Proceedings of the Seminar on Welfare Administration (Sept. 28-Oct. 1, 1959, Karachi) (Karachi, 1960).

Report on the All-Pakistan Seminar on Village Agricultural and Industrial Development Programme (held at Dacca from 18th to 23rd May, 1959) (Karachi, 1960).

Conference of Village-AID Directors and Deputy Directors (Sept. 3-5, 1960, Lahore) (Proceedings) (Lahore. n.d.).

The Second Five Year Plan: 1960-65 (n.p., June 1960).

Village AID: Some Articles and Report (Lahore, Dec. 1960).

The West Pakistan Basic Democracies Election Report, 1959-60 (Lahore, 1960).

"Delegation For Better Administration" (cyclostyled) (O. & M. Division, Cabinet Secretariat, 1961).

The Constitution of the Republic of Pakistan, 1962. (Dacca)

Census of Pakistan. 1961 (Dacca, Karachi, Lahore, 1962).

Census Report of Tribal Agencies, 1961 (Karachi, n.d.).

Decisions of the Cabinet on the Provincial Administration Commission (Karachi, 1962).

1960 Pakistan Census of Agriculture (n.p., 1962).

Seminar on Planning and Development, (held at Lahore from March 26 to 28, 1962) (Lahore, 1962).

Proceedings of the Regional Seminar on Planning and Development (held at Peshawar from November 25 to 27, 1963) (Lahore, 1964).

Rural Works Programme For West Pakistan: First Report (Lahore, 1964).

The Seminar on the Expanding Role of the Public Servant in Pakistan's Democratic Structure (Collection papers read at the seminar) (Lahore, 1964).

Statistical Abstract for East Pakistan (Dacca, 1964).

East Pakistan Rural Works Programme: Report, 1963-64 (Dacca, n.d.)

"Report on Election to the Basic Democracies in November 1964" (cyclostyled) (Department of Local Government, Govt. of E. Bengal, n.d.)

Rural Works Programme: Evaluation Report, 1963-64 (West Pakistan) (Lahore, n.d.).

Pakistan Economic Survey, 1964-65 (Karachi, 1965).

Works Programme through Basic Democracies, 1964-65 (Circular No. 44 of the Govt. of E. Beng.)

The Third Five Year Plan: 1965-70 (n.p. June, 1965).

Circular and Instructions Issued in connection with Works Programme From 25th September 1962 to 31st December, 1964.) (Dacca, 1965.)

Powers and Functions of Circle Officers (*Development*), *Assistant Directors and Deputy Directors of Basic Democracies Organisation* (Govt. of E. Beng., Memo. No. GAI-40/65-161 Feb.11, 1965).

"Report on the Election of Chairmen to the Union Councils, Union/Town Committees, held in August 1965 and the Background of the Persons Elected" (cyclostyled) (Department of Local Government, Govt. of E. Bengal, n.d., 1965?)

"Decentralisation and Development" (cyclostyled) (Department of Local Government, Govt. of E. Bengal, n.d.)

Gazetteer of Dacca District (Dacca, 1969).

Annual Reports on Basic Democracies in East Pakistan (Dacca).

Annual Reports on Basic Democracies in West Pakistan (Lahore).

Progress Report on the Activities of the Basic Democracies for the Month of.. (usually published every month by the Govt.)

Bangladesh Documents (New Delhi, n.d., 1971/72?).

Provisional Constitution of Bangladesh Order (1972).

The Constitution of the People's Republic of Bangladesh (1972).

VII. ACTS, MANUALS ETC.

The Code of Criminal Procedure 1898 (as modified from time to time).

Punjab Land Administration Manual by James M. Douie (First published in 1908. Reprinted in Lahore in 1960).

The Punjab Police Rules, 1934, 3 vols. (Lahore, 1934) (as modified from time to time).

Police Regulations of Bengal, 1943 (Calcutta, 1943. Reprinted in Dacca in 1958) (as modified from time to time).

"Civil Service of Pakistan (Composition and Cadre) Rules, 1950 and 1954" (cyclostyled) (Govt. of Pak.).

"The Code of Criminal Procedure (East Pakistan Amendment) Act, 1957", *The Dacca Gazette* (Extraordinary), Nov.11, 1957.

"The Code of Criminal Procedure (East Pakistan Amendment) Ordinance 1958", *The Dacca Gazette* (Extra-ordinary), March 1958.

The Government Estates Manual, 1958 (Dacca, 1958).

The Basic Democracies Order, 1959 (President's Order No. 18 of 1959) (Published as *A Hand Book of Basic Democracies*, Dacca.)

The Basic Democracies (conduct of Election) Rules, 1959.

The Municipal Administration Ordinance, 1960 (Ordinance No.X of 1960, Govt. of Pak.)

Municipal Manual (Govt. of E. Bengal, 1961).

East Pakistan Code, Vol. VII (Acts, Regulations and Ordinances from Aug. 15, 1947 to Dec. 31, 1959) (Dacca, 1962).

"The West Pakistan Criminal Law (Amendment) Act, 1963", first published in *Gazette of West Pakistan* (Extraordinary), April 19, 1963; later published by the Govt. printing press in pamphlet form under the following title: *The West Pakistan Criminal Law (Amendment) Act, 1963 (Act VII of 1963) and The West Pakistan Criminal Law (Amendment) Rules, 1963* (corrected up to 1st Oct. 1965) (Lahore, 1965).

The Establishment Manual, Vol. I (Rules, Regulations and administrative instructions on establishment matters issued during the years 1947-1962) (Compiled by the O. & M. Wing, Govt. of Pakistan, Karachi, 1963).

The Establishment Manual, Vol. 1 (corrected up to 30th June 1964) (O. & M. Unit, Govt. of West Pakistan, Lahore, 1964).

O. & M. Manual of Delegation of Powers Rules, 1958-1963 (O. & M. Unit, Govt. of West Pakistan, Lahore, 1964).

Reporting Manual for Works Programme (Govt. of E. Beng., 1965).

Rural Works Programme: Manual of Instruction (Govt. of W. Pak., Lahore, 1966).

VIII. MISCELLANEOUS OFFICIAL DOCUMENTS

Actual Distribution List of Officers (Published quarterly by the Government).

Basic Democracies: NDO-BD Integration and Training Programs (Karachi, n.d., late 1950s?)

Dawn of A New Era (Karachi, n.d.)

The East Pakistan Civil List (of Officers) (Usually published after every two years).

Gradation List of the Civil Service of Pakistan (Annually published by the Govt. of Pakistan).

A Guide to Basic Democracies (Government of Pakistan, Karachi, n.d.)

"Machinery for Revenue Administration in Former Sind Area" (cyclostyled) (A study note prepared by the Civil Service Academy, Lahore for the CSP probationers of 1964).

Pakistan: Basic Facts (Published annually by the Govt. of Pakistan).

The Scheme of Basic Democracies (Govt. of Pak., n.p., n.d., 1959 ?)

Scope and Functions of Basic Democracies and their contribution to Development (Rawalpindi, 1960).

The West Pakistan Civil List (of Officers) (Usually published after every two years).

West Pakistan Year Book (Lahore).

IX. BARD (COMILLA) AND PARD (PESHAWAR): REPORTS AND OTHER PUBLICATIONS (EXCLUDING BOOKS)

Annual Reports (Comilla,) (First three reports were cyclostyled).

Basic Democracies Manual (Comilla, 1959).

Village Dhanishwar—Three Generations of Man-Land Adjustment in an East Pakistan Village (Comilla, 1960).

An Analysis of Functioning of Seven Union Councils in Peshawar Tehsil (A case study by Inayatullah) (Peshawar, 1961).

An Analysis of the Working of Basic Democracy Institutions in East Pakistan (Comilla, 1961).

Assistant Directors of Basic Democracies: A Study of Values and Attitudes by M. A. Salam Ansari (1961).

An Experiment in Village Development; First Quarterly Report by Inayatullah (Peshawar, 1961).

Study of Union Councils in Nowshera Tehsil (A case study by Inayatullah) (Peshawar, 1961).

A Manual for Rural Public Works (Comilla, 1962).

Basic Democracies At The Grass Roots (A study of three Union Councils by A.T.R. Rahman) (Comilla, 1962).

Report on the Orientation Course of District Officers by M.A. Sabzwari (Peshawar, 1962).

Report on A Rural Public Works Programme in Comilla Kotwali Thana (Comilla, 1962).

"Report of the Training Programme for Circle Officers (Development) in Rural Public Works Programme" (Nov. 19--Dec. 11, 1962) (cyclostyled) (Comilla, n.d.).

Study of Selected Union Councils in Rawalpindi Division (A case study by Inayatullah) (1962).

The Academy at Comilla: An Introduction (Comilla, 1963).

An Evaluation of the Rural Works Programme, East Pakistan, 1962-63 (Comilla, 1963).

The Comilla Rural Administration Experiment: History and Annual Report, 1962-63 (PARD, Comilla, 1963).

Comilla—U.S. AID Conference Report (cyclostyled) (Comilla, June 1963).

Dynamics of Development In A Pakistan Village (Research Report No. 8 by Inayatullah and Q.M. Shafi) (Peshawar, 1963).

Rural Administration Pilot Project Experiment (Comilla, 1963). (Also issued as Circular No. 50 of the Govt. of East Bengal).

Basic Democracies, District Administration and Development. (PARD Report No. 9. A case study of two districts in West Pakistan by Inayatullah) (Peshawar, 1964).

The Comilla District Development Project (Comilla, 1964).

The Comilla Rural Administration Experiment (Annual Report for 1963-64) (1964).

An Evaluation of the Rural Works Programme, East Pakistan: 1963-64 (Comilla, n.d.).

Four Studies in Basic Democracies (Comilla, n.d.)

"The Path of Social Destiny" (cyclostyled) (A report on the story of the Antigonish Movement of Adult Education through Economic Co-operation by M. Sulayman, n.d.)

"Workshop Report on Basic Democracy as an Instrument for Rural Development" by M. Khalid Shams, M.R. Osmany and A.T.R. Rahman (Comilla, n.d., 1965 ?)

For other publications or papers of these Academies see Edgar A. Schules and Raghu Singh, *The Pakistan Academies For Rural Development, Comilla And Peshawar: A Bibliography, 1959-1964* (Asian Studies Center, Michigan State University, 1965).

X. DACCA AND PUNJAB (LAHORE) UNIVERSITIES: REPORTS

Human and Social Impact of Technological Change, 2 vols. (A report prepared by A.F.M. Husain) (Socio-economic Survey Board, Dacca, 1956).

Report on the Survey of Rural Credit and Rural Employment in East Pakistan, 1956 (Socio-economic Survey Board, Dacca, 1958).

Village Life in Lahore District: A Study of Selected Sociological Aspects (A report prepared by W.L. Slocum) (Social Science Research Centre, Lahore, 1959).

Village Life in Lahore District: A Study of Selected Economic Aspects (A report prepared by S.M. Aktar and A.R. Arshad) (Soc. Sc. Research Centre, Lahore, 1960).

Village Life in Lahore District: A Study of Selected Political Aspects (Soc. Sc. Research Centre, Lahore, 1960).

A Study on Knowledge and Attitudes towards Basic Democracies (Soc. Sc. Research Centre, Lahore, 1960).

Village in an Urban Orbit (A report prepared by A.S. Haider) (Soc. Sc. Research Centre, Lahore, 1960).

The Budhopur Report: A Study of the Forces of Tradition and Changes in a Punjabi Village in the Gujranwala District, West Pakistan by the members of the Cambridge University Asian Expedition) (Soc. Sc. Research Centre, Lahore, 1962).

Basic Democracy, Works Programme and Rural Development in East Pakistan (A Report prepared by Rehman Sobhan) (Bureau of Economic Research, Dacca, 1968).

XI. ADMINISTRATIVE STAFF COLLEGE, LAHORE: REPORTS, SEMINAR PAPERS, ETC.

Gorvine A. and Birkhead G.S., *Dacca Urban Division: A Proposal* (1963).

Hamid A.A., Faridi, A.R., and Ali, W., *Views of Administration in Pakistan* (1963).

"An Opinion Survey of Delegation of Authority in Building and Roads Department, Government of West Pakistan" by Zafar Hasan Mahmoud (cyclostyled) (1964).

"Contacts Between Villagers and Public Officials in Three Villages of Lyallpur Tehsil" (A Report prepared by Zuhra Waheed) (1964).

"The Comilla Project: An Experiment in Rural Administration" (A Report by the Members, Session 10) (cyclostyled) (1965).

The Pakistan Administrative Staff College, Lahore (1965-66).

Abbasi, M.W., *Civil Service in Pakistan* (n.d.)

Ziring, Lawrence, "The Administration of Basic Democracies" (cyclostyled) (n.d.)

The following are the papers (cyclostyled) (n.d.,1963 ?) presented at the Seminar on Development Administration, held at the Administrative Staff College, Lahore:

Beg. M.A.K., "Basic Democracies as a form of Local Government."

Hossain, K.N., "In Service Training".

Iqbal, M., "Deputy Commissioner and Development".

Khan, F.R., "In Service Training".

Khan, G.S., "Commissioner and Deputy Commissioner: Background and Short History".

Khan, M.J., "Integration of Services".

Rabbani, A., "Recruitment and Selection in Pakistan".

Rahman, A.M.F., "Deputy Commissioner and Development".

Rashid, A., "The Deputy Commissioner in Pakistan: Justification and Role in a Welfare State.

Vafa, Javed, "Local Government: The Need for and the Prerequisite".

XII. NIPA (DACCA AND LAHORE): MISCELLANEOUS PAPERS (CYCLOSTYLED)

Ahmad, Serajuddin, "Impact of Traditional Culture on Public Administration" (Staff Study No. 17) (Dacca, 1963).

Ahmed, N., "A Study of the Present Working of the Police in East Pakistan" (Participant Study No. 60) (Dacca, 1964).

Alam, A.F.M.N., "Qualifications of Top Administrators of the Government of Pakistan" (Reprint No. 162) (Dacca, 1963).

Alam, S., "Land Revenue Administration in Deputy Commissioner's Office in the Districts" (Participant Study No. 30) (Dacca, 1962).

Bari, M.F., "A Critique of East Pakistan Secretariat" (Participant Study No. 38) (Dacca, 1962).

Braibanti, Ralph, "Working Paper on Course of Study At The Civil Service Academy Of Pakistan" (Tentative Draft, March 21, 1961) (Reprint No. 17, Dacca, 1964).

Dass, S.B., "Organisation Study of Deputy Commissioner's Office, Dacca" (Participant Study No. 7) (Dacca, 1961).

Islam, A.K.M.N., "A Critical Survey of the Working of District Relief Committee, Comilla" (Participant Study No. 6) (Dacca, 1961).

Khan, A.A., "Pattern of Local Government in Pakistan" (A talk delivered at the NIPA, Lahore on Jan.17, 1963).

Majumdar, M.M., "A General Appraisal of Basic Democracies in East Pakistan with a Brief Report on Two Union Councils" (Participant Study No. 29) (Dacca, 1962).

Malik, G.Y., "District Administration" (A talk delivered at NIPA, Lahore on March 22, 1963).

Meerza, S.A.A., "Organisation Study in the Revenue Branch of Dacca District Office" (Participant Study No.10) (Dacca, 1961).

Muhite, A.M.A., "Analysis of the Organisation of the D.C.'s Office" (Participant Study No. 41) (Dacca, 1962).

Rabbi, A.B.M.F., "Criminal Administration: A Review of Certain Aspects" (Participant Study No. 1, Dacca, 1961).

Rahman, S., "The Working of Basic Democracies in East Pakistan" (Staff Study No. 30) (Dacca, 1965).

Rashid, Hossain and Mostafa, "Organisation Study of District Council Office, Dacca" (Participant Study No. 9) (Dacca, 1961).

XIII. BOOKS.

Ahmad, Muneer, *The Civil Servant in Pakistan* (Karachi, 1964).

Ahmad, Mustaq, *Government and Politics in Pakistan* (Karachi, 1959).

Ali, Choudhuri Mohammad, *The Emergence of Pakistan* (London, 1967).

Ali, M.I., *A Case Study of Land Acquisition by Government in West Pakistan* (Lahore, n.d.)

Anisuzzaman, Md., *The Circle Officer* (NIPA, Dacca, 1963).

Ansari, M.A.S. (ed.), *Social Research in National Development* (PARD, Peshawar, 1963).

Ashford, Douglas E., *National Development And Local Reform: Political Participation In Morocco, Tunisia, And Pakistan* (Princeton, 1967).

Ashraf, Khalid, *The Tribal People of West Pakistan* (Peshawar, 1962).

Aslam, A.H., *The Deputy Commissioner* (Lahore, 1957).

Aziz, M.A. (ed.), *Proceedings of the Third All Pakistan Political Science Conference* (Karachi, 1965).

Bailey, F.G., *Politics And Social Change: Orissa in 1959* (Berkeley, 1963).

Beg, Aziz, *Before And After Revolution* (Rawalpindi, 1962).

Beg, Aziz (ed.), *Grass Roots Government* (Rawalpindi, 1962).

Berry, Willard, *Aspects of the Frontier Crimes Regulations in Pakistan* (Duke University Commonwealth Studies Center, 1966).

Binder, Leonard, *Religion and Politics in Pakistan* (Berkeley, 1961).

Birkhead, G.S. (ed.), *Administrative Problems in Pakistan* (New York, 1966).

Braibanti, Ralph and Spengler, Joseph J. (eds.), *Administration and Economic Development in India* (London, 1963).

Braibanti, Ralph (ed.), *Asian Bureaucratic Systems Emergent from the British Imperial Tradition* (Durham, U.S.A., 1966).

Braibanti, Ralph, *Research on the Bureaucracy of Pakistan* (Durham, U.S.A., 1966).

Brass, Paul R., *Factional Politics in an Indian State* (London, 1965).

Callard, Keith, *Pakistan: A Political Study* (London, 1957).

Cambell, R.D., *Pakistan: Emerging Democracy* (Princeton, 1963).

Caroe, Olaf, *The Pathans: 550 B.C.—A.D.1957* (London, 1958).

Chanda, Ashok, *Indian Administration* (London, 1958).

Chaudhuri, M.A., *The Civil Service in Pakistan* (Dacca, 1963).
Chaudhuri, M.A., *An Examination of the Criticism Against Bureaucracy* (Dacca, 1965).
Choudhuri, M.A., *Local Government in Rural East Pakistan* (Dacca, 1970).
Choudhury, G.W., *Constitutional Development in Pakistan* (Dacca, 1959).
Choudhury, G.W., *Democracy in Pakistan* (Dacca, 1963).
Desai, K.S., *Problems of Administration in Two Indian Villages* (Baroda, 1961).
Desai, N.B., *Report on the Administrative Survey of the Surat District* (Bombay, 1958).
Dey, S.K., *Panchayati Raj* (London, 1961).
Dil, S., *Perspectives on Pakistan* (Abbottabad, 1965).
Dube, S.C., *India's Changing Villages* (London, 1958).
Feldman, H., *Revolution in Pakistan* (London, 1967).
Feldman, H., *Pakistan: From Crisis to Crisis* (Karachi, 1972).
Five Articles on Development Administration in Pakistan (Asian Studies Center, Michigan State University, 1966).
Gable, Richard W., "Introduction to District Administration" (cyclostyled) (University of Southern California, 1963).
Goodnow, H.F., *The Civil Service of Pakistan* (New Haven, 1964).
Hasan, Masudul, *Law and Principles of Municipal Administration* (Lahore, n.d.)
Hasan, Masudul, *Principles of Conciliation Courts* (Lahore, 1962).
Husain, S.S. (ed.), *Dacca University Seminar on Contemporary Writing in East Pakistan* (Dacca, 1958).
Husain, S.S. (ed.), *East Pakistan: A Profile* (Dacca, 1962).
Inayat, Md. (ed.), *Perspectives in Public Administration* (Civil Service Academy (Lahore, 1962).
Inayatullah, (ed.), *Bureaucracy and Development in Pakistan* (PARD, Peshawar, 1962).
Inayatullah (ed.), *District Administration in West Pakistan* (PARD, Peshawar, 1964).
Inayatullah, "Perspectives In the Rural Power Structure in West

Pakistan" (cyclostyled) (US AID Mission, Karachi, 1963).
Inayatullah, (no. 2) and Khan, A.T. (eds.), *Administrators and the Citizen* (NIPA, Lahore, 1964).
Inayatullah (no. 2) (ed.), *Basic Democracies, Development and Welfare* (Lahore, 1965).
Ishaque, H.S.M., *ABC of Rural Reconstruction* (Calcutta, 1945. Reprinted in Dacca, 1959).
Inside The East Pakistan Village—Six Articles (Asian Studies Papers, Asian Studies Center, Michigan State University, 1966).
Jafri, M. Haris, *et. al.*, *The Economy of Pakistan* (New Haven, 1956).
Jahan, Rounaq, *Pakistan: Failure in National Integration* (New York, 1972).
Kashyap, Subhash C. (ed.), *Bangladesh* (New Delhi, May 1971)
Khan, Ataur Rahman., *Ojaratir Dui Bachar* (*Two Years of Chief Ministership*) (Written in Bengali) (Dacca, n.d.).
Khan, Mohammad Ayub, *Friends Not Masters* (London, 1967).
Khan, Md. Hasan, "Duties and Functions of Tehsilder" (Unpublished Master's dissertation submitted to the Department of Political Science, University of Punjab, in partial fulfilment for the degree of Master of Arts, 1957).
Khera, S.S., *District Administration in India* (London, 1964).
Kothari, Rajni, *Politics in India* (New Delhi, 1970).
Larson, Don R. (ed.), *Selected Papers from the First Seminar on Public Administration* (Lahore, 1962).
Maron, Stanley, (ed.) *Pakistan: Society And Culture* (New Haven, 1957).
Mezirow, Jack D., *Dynamics of Community Development* (New York, 1963).
Morris-Jones W.H., *Parliament in India* (London, 1957).
Morris-Jones. W.H., *The Government and Politics of India* (London, 1964).
Muniruzzaman, Talukdar, *The Politics of Development: The Pakistan Case: 1947-1958* (Dacca, 1971).
The New India (Planning Commission, Govt. of India) (London, 1958).
Niehoff, Richard O., *Technical Assistance in the In-Service Training*

of Pakistani Civil Servants Since 1958 (Asian Studies Center Occasional Papers, Michigan State University, 1966).

Owen, John, E. (ed.), *Sociology in East Pakistan* (Dacca, 1962).

Philips, C.H. (ed.), *Politics and Society in India* (London, 1963).

Potter, David C., *Government in Rural India* (London, 1964).

Rashiduzzaman, M., *Pakistan: A Study of Government and Politics* (Dacca, Sept. 1967).

Rashiduzzaman, M., *Politics and Administration in the Local Councils* (Dacca, 1968).

Rashiduzzaman, M., *Central Legislature in British India* (Dacca, 1965).

Ray, Jayanta K., *Democracy and Nationalism on Trial: A Study of East Pakistan* (Simla, 1968).

Retzlaff, Ralph H., *Village Government in India* (London, 1962).

Rizvi, S.M.Z. (ed.), *A Reader in Basic Democracies* (Peshawar, 1961).

Roy, N.C., *The Constitutional System of India* (Calcutta, 1937).

Rural Development in East Pakistan: Speeches of Akter Hameed Khan (Michigan State University, n.d., 1964?).

Rural Works Programme: Loralai District, 1963-64 (Prepared by the Loralai District Council) (Quetta, n.d.).

Sastri, K.N.V., *Principles of District Administration in India* (Delhi, 1957).

Singh, B., *Next Step in Village India* (Bombay, 1961).

Sayeed, K.B., *Formative Phase of Pakistan* (Karachi, 1960).

Sayeed, K.B., *The Political System of Pakistan* (Boston, 1967).

Shils, Edward, *The Intellectual Between Tradition And Modernity: The Indian Situation* (Hague, 1961).

Speeches of Sheikh Mujib (Calcutta, n.d.)

Speeches and Statements by...Mohammad Ayub Khan (Vol. I—Oct. 1958—June 1959. Vol. II—July 1959—June 1960. Vol. III—July 1960—June 1961. Vol. IV—July 1961—June 1962. Vol. V—July 1962—June 1963) (Karachi, n.d.).

Spain, James, W., *The Pathan Borderland* (Hague, 1963).

Stephens, Ian, *Pakistan* (London, 1963).

Suleri, M.A., Union Councils in operation in District Sialkot

(Unpublished dissertation submitted to the Department of Public Administration, University of Punjab, in partial fulfilment of the requirement for the degree of M.P.A., 1964).

Tepper, Elliot, *Changing Patterns of Administration in Rural East Pakistan* (Asian Studies Center Occasional Paper No. 5, Michigan State University, 1966).

Weeks, R.V., *Pakistan* (Princeton, 1964).

Wilber, Donald N., *Pakistan: Yesterday and Today* (New York, 1964).

Wilber, Donald N., *Pakistan: Its People, Its Society, Its Culture*. (New Haven, 1964).

Wilcox, W.A., *Pakistan: The Consolidation of a Nation* (London, 1963).

Williams, L.F. Rushbrook, *The State of Pakistan* (London, 1966).

Vorys, Karl von, *Political Development in Pakistan* (Oxford, 1965).

XIV. ARTICLES

Alavi, H.A., "Constitutional Changes and the Dynamics of Political Development in Pakistan" (cyclostyled) (A paper presented at the post graduate seminar on Political Institutions, held on 15th Nov. 1967 at the Institute of Commonwealth Studies, University of London).

Ali, S.A., "8000 Rural Republics" in *Pakistan Quarterly*, Vol. XIII, Nos. 2 and 3, 1965, pp. 52-59, 120-124.

Ali, S. Murtaza, "Better Administration" in *The Pakistan Observer* (Dacca, Oct. 27, 1965).

Ahmad, A.M., "Cultural Renaissance of East Pakistan" in *The Concept of Pakistan*, February 1967, pp. 11-16, 53-55.

Ahmad, A.M., "Secularism versus Religion in Politics" in *The Concept of Pakistan* (Dacca, Nov. 1964), pp. 40-44.

Ahmed, G., "Changes in the Administrative Organisation of the Government of Pakistan Since 1953" in *Public Administration*, Vol. 39 (1961), pp. 353-360.

Ahmed, G., "Basic Democracies" *Morning News* (Karachi) Aug. 14, 1965.

"Basic Democracies", A Special Supplement in *The Morning News* (Dacca, Nov. 2, 1966).

Bertrand, A., "The Civil Service Academy of Lahore and the Training of Members of the Civil Service of Pakistan" in *International Social Science Bulletin*, No. 2, Vol. VII (1955).

Bhalerao, C.N., "Some Social, Political and Administrative Consequences of Panchayati Raj" in *Asian Survey*, No. 4, Vol. IV, 1964, pp. 804-811.

Braibanti, Ralph, "The Civil Service of Pakistan: A Theoretical Analysis" in *South Atlantic Quarterly*, No. 2, Vol. LVIII, 1959, pp. 258-304.

Burgess, G., "The Pakistan Civil Service" in *The Listener*, Vol. LVIII, Sept. 19, 1957, pp. 419-421.

Callard, Keith, "The Political Stability of Pakistan" in *Pacific Affairs*, Vol. XXIX (March 1956).

Chaudhuri, M.A., "The Organisation and Composition of the Central Civil Service in Pakistan" in *International Review of Administrative Sciences*, No. 3, Vol. XXVI (1960), pp. 279-292.

Chaudhuri, M.A., "The Ecology of Public Administration in Pakistan"—Series of Articles in *The Concept of Pakistan*, 1966.

Choudhury, G.W., "Constitution of Pakistan" in *Pacific Affairs*, Vol. XXIX (Sept. 1956).

Choudhury, G.W., "The East Pakistan Political scene: (1955-57" in *Pacific Affairs*, Vol. XXX (Dec. 1957).

Cornelius, A.R., "Restoration of Judicial Responsibility to People" in *The All-Pakistan Legal Decisions* (Journal Section), Vol. XV, 1963, pp. 1-13.

Edlefsen John D. and Aktar, Jamila, "Caste Differential Among the Muslims of West Pakistan" (cyclostyled) (Paper read at the Annual Meeting of the Pacific Sociological Society, San Francisco, April 1959).

Egger, Rowland A., "Ministerial and Departmental Organisation and Management in the Government of Pakistan" in *Public Administration*, Vol. 39, 1961, pp. 149-173.

Falcon, W.P. and Gotsch, C.H., "Two Approaches with the Same Result" in *Asian Review*, No. 4, Vol. I, 1968, pp. 239-255.

Friedman, Harry J., "Pakistan's Experiment in Basic Democracies" in *Pacific Affairs*, No. 2, Vol. XXXIII, 1960, pp. 107-125.

Friedman, Harry J., "Notes on Pakistan's Basic Democracies" in *Asian Survey*, No. 10, Vol. I, 1961, pp. 19-24.

Gorvine, Albert, "The Civil Service under the Revolutionary Government in Pakistan" in *The Middle East Journal*, No. 3, Vol. XIX, summer, 1965.

Hizbullah, S., "District Administration and Development" (cyclostyled) (A paper presented at the Seminar on Public Administration, held at PARD, Peshawar, in March 1962).

Husain, M., "Rural Unemployment and the Works Programme" in *The Morning News* (Karachi), Aug. 14, 1965.

Inayatullah, "Impact of Basic Democracies on Rural Power Structure" in *The Pakistan Times*, Lahore, Dec. 13, 1959.

Inayatullah, "Democracy In A Rural Community of West Pakistan" in *Sociologus*, No. 1, Vol. IX, 1959.

Inayatullah, "Caste, Patti and Faction in the Life of a Punjabi Village" in *Sociologus*, No. 2, Vol. VIII, 1958.

Jahan, Rounaq, "Bangladesh in 1972 : Nation Building in a New State" in *Asian Survey*, No. 2, Vol. XIII, February 1973.

Jahan, Rounaq, "Elite in Crisis : An Analysis of the Failure of Mujib—Yahya—Bhutto Negotiation" in *Orbis*, Summer, 1973.

Khan, A.Z.M. Obaidullah, "Rural Development and Administrative Reorganisation" in *Journal of the Pakistan Academy for Rural Development*, Comilla, No. 4, Vol. IV, April 1964, pp. 190-202.

Khan, S.D., "Local Government Administration Development in Pakistan with Particular Reference to East Pakistan" (typed) (A paper read at the W. German Cultural Centre, Dacca, n.d.)

Khera, S.S., "District Administration" in *The Indian Journal of Public Administration*, No. 3, Vol. IX, July-Sept. 1963, pp. 465-468.

Maddick, Henry, "Control, Supervision and Guidance of Panchayati Raj Institutions" in *The Indian Journal of Public Administration*, No. 4, Vol. VIII, 1962, pp. 500-511.

Maddick, Henry, "The Present and Future Role of the Collector in India" in *Journal of Local Administration Overseas*, No. 2, Vol. II, 1963, pp. 75-87.

Muniruzzaman, T., "Group Interests In Pakistan Politics, 1947-1958" in *Pacific Affairs*, Vol. XXXIV, Nos. 1 and 2, 1966.

Maron, Stanley, "The Problems of East Pakistan" in *Pacific Affairs*, Vol. XXVIII, 1955, pp. 132-144.

Marshall, C.B., "Reflections on a Revolution in Pakistan" in *Foreign Affairs*, No. 2, Vol. 37, 1959, pp. 246-256.

Masihuzzaman, "From Village-AID to Basic Democracies" in *Community Development Review*, No. 1, Vol. V, Sept. 1960, pp. 20-27.

Masihuzzaman, "How Pakistan is Governed" in *Pakistan Quarterly*, Vol. XIII, Nos. 2 and 3, 1965, pp. 90-95, 124-127.

Mellema, R.L., "Basic Democracies System in Pakistan" in *Asian Survey*, No. 6, Vol. 1, 1961, pp. 10-15.

Mezirow, J.D. and Santopolo, F.A., "Community Development in Pakistan: The First Five Years" in *Community Development Review*, No. 1, Vol. VI (March 1961), pp. 90-98.

Morris-Jones, W.H., "Experience of Independence—India and Pakistan" in *Political Quarterly*, Vol. 29, No. 3, July-Sept. 1958, pp. 224-237.

Morris-Jones, W.H., "Democratic Decentralisation: Some Political Consequences" in *The Economic Weekly*, Nos. 28, 29 and 30, Vol. XIV, 1962.

Morris-Jones, W.H., "Pakistan Post-Mortem and the Roots of Bangladesh" in *The Political Quarterly*, No. 2, Vol. 43, April-June 1972, pp. 187—200.

Muhith, A.M.A., "Political and Administrative Roles in East Pakistan's Districts" in *Pacific Affairs*, Vol. XL, Nos. 3 and 4, 1967-68, pp. 279-293.

Mukherji, Partha N., "Influx And Reflux: An Explanatory Study of the Evacuees from East Bengal" (cyclostyled) (J. N. University, New Delhi, 1972).

Pai, M.A., "The Emerging Role of the Collector" in *The Indian Journal of Public Administration*, Oct.-Dec. 1962, Vol. VIII, No. 4.

Pakistan Today (cyclostyled) (London), summer, 1960.

Park, R. and Wheeler, R. S., "East Bengal Under Governor's Rule" *Far Eastern Survey*, Vol. XXIII (1954), pp. 129-134.

Platt, George M., "District Council Government in East Pakistan" in *Journal of the Pakistan Academy For Rural Development*, Comilla, No. 4, Vol. IV, April 1964, pp. 143-167.

Qureshi, A.A., "The Pattern of Administration" in "October 27 Supplement" in *The Pakistan Observer* (Dacca, Oct. 27, 1965).

Rahbar, Rafic, "The Provincial Polls" in *The Concept of Pakistan*, June 1965, pp. 54-56.

Rahman, A.T.R., "Training Programme for Provincial Civil Servants" in *Journal of The Pakistan Academy for Village Development*, No. 5, Vol.II, April 1962.

Rahman, A.T.R., "Rural Institutions in India and Pakistan" in *Asian Survey*, No. 9, Vol. VIII, Sept. 1968, pp. 792-805.

Rahman, Habibur, "Basic Democracies as Institutions of Local Government in Pakistan" in *Journal of Local Administration Overseas*, No. 4, Vol. I, Oct. 1962, pp. 239-246.

Rai, Haridwar, "The Changing Role of the District Officer (1860-1960)" in *The Indian Journal of Public Administration*, No. 2, Vol. IX (1963), pp. 238-257.

Rai, Haridwar, "Local Government, Local Administration and Development: Role Adaptation of the District Officer in India" in *The Indian Journal of Public Administration*, No. 1, Vol. XIV, Jan.-March, 1968.

Rashiduzzaman, M., "Election Politics in Pakistan" in *Journal of Commonwealth Political Studies*, No. 3, Vol. IV, 1966.

Rashiduzzaman, M., "Union Boards and Union Councils" (A Series of Articles) in *The Morning News*, Nov. 3, 4, 5, 6, 1966.

Rashiduzzaman M., "Pakistan's Local Bodies and Social Change:

The Emerging Pattern of Local Leadership" in *Orient* (1968), pp. 125-128.

Rashiduzzaman, M., "The Awami League in the Political Development of Pakistan" in *Asian Survey*, X, 1970, pp. 574—587.

Rashiduzzaman, M., "The National Assembly of Pakistan under the 1962 Constitution" in *Pacific Affairs*, XLII, 1969-70, pp. 481-493.

Rural Works Programme Supplement, *The Pakistan Times* (Lahore, March 7, 1966).

Sankaranarayanan,M., "Role of the District Officer in Changing Administration" in *The Indian Journal of Public Administration*, No. 4, Vol. XII (1966), pp. 757-765.

Siddiq, M. M., "Local Government in Pakistan" (cyclostyled) (Sargodha, n.d.)

Sayeed, K.B., "The Political Role of Pakistan's Civil Service" in *Pacific Affairs*, No. 2, Vol. XXXI (June, 1958), pp. 131-146.

Sayeed, K.B., "Martial Law Administration in Pakistan" in *Far Eastern Survey*, Vol. XXVIII (1959).

Sayeed, K.B., "Pakistan's Basic Democracies" in *The Middle East Journal*, No. 3, Vol. XV, 1961, pp. 249-263.

Schuman, Howard, "The District as an Ethnic Unit in East Pakistan" (cyclostyled) (University of Michigan) (Paper presented at the annual meeting of the Association for Asian Studies, March 22, 1967, Chicago).

Seshadri, K., "Administration of Panchayati Raj Planning in India" in *Journal of Local Administration Overseas*, No. I, Vol. III (1964), pp. 20-26.

Smith, Mariana W., "The Misal: A Structural Village-Group of India and Pakistan" in *American Anthropologist*, No.1, Vol. 54 (1952), pp. 41-56.

Sobhan, Rehman, "Social Forces in Basic Democracies" in *Asian Review*, No. 3, Vol. I, April 1968, pp. 166-176.

Sobhan, Rehman, "Two-way Stretch in Basic Democracies" in "Pakistan: A Special Report" in *The Times* (London), April 6, 1968.

Sobhan, Rehman, "Basic Democracies and National Politics in East Pakistan" (cyclostyled) (A paper presented on 30th Oct., 1968 at the post graduate seminar on "Contemporary Politics: Autonomy and Dependence in 'Parochial' Politics'", held at the Institute of Commonwealth Studies, University of London).

Spain, James W., "Pakistan's North West Frontier" in *The Middle East Journal*, No. 1, Vol. VIII (1954), pp. 27-40.

Spear, Percival, "From Colonial to Sovereign Status: Some Problems of Transition with Special Reference to India" in *Journal of Asian Studies*, Vol. XVII (1958), pp. 572-575.

Thomas, Woodward, "Work for the Poor of East Pakistan" in *Asian Review*, No. 1, Vol. 2, Oct. 1968, pp. 45-52.

Tinker, Hugh, "Authority And Community in Village India" in *Pacific Affairs*, No. 4, Vol. XXXII (1959), pp. 354-375.

Vepa, Ram K., "New Pattern of District Administration in Andhra Pradesh" in *The Indian Journal of Public Administration*, No. 1, Vol. XIV, Jan.-March 1968, pp. 105-116.

Verghese, B.G., "Pakistan Visited: VII—Basic Democracies" in *The Times of India*, Dec. 8, 1964. From November 17, 1964 to January 1965, he wrote 13 articles on various aspects of former Pakistan in *The Times of India*.

Wheeler, R.S., "Changing Patterns of Local Government and Administration in Pakistan" in *South Atlantic Quarterly*, Vol. 62 (1963), pp. 67-77.

Wilcox, W., "Political Change in Pakistan: Structures, Functions, Constraints and Goals" in *Pacific Affairs*, No. 3, Vol. XLI, fall 1968.

Williams, L.F. Rushbrook, "Basic Democracies as Institutions of Local Government in Pakistan" in the *Journal of Local Administration Overseas*, No. 4, Vol. I, (1962),, pp. 247-256.

"The Works Programme in East Pakistan and its Progress" in Third Five Year Plan Supplement, *The Morning News* (Dacca, July 1, 1965).

INDEX

Names

Names

Reports, Plans etc. (Summarised Titles)

General subjects

General subjects

General subjects

Najmul Abedin, who obtained the B.A. (Honours) and the M.A. degrees from the University of Dacca and the Ph.D. degree from the University of Durham, is Associate Professor of Political Science, University of Chittagong. He previously taught at the University of Dacca.